Jar
2(
AH

How to Sell Technical Equipment and Services

PennWell®

How to Sell Technical Equipment and Services

James R. Hutton

Copyright© 2006 by
PennWell Corporation
1421 South Sheridan Road
Tulsa, Oklahoma 74112-6600 USA

800.752.9764
+1.918.831.9421
sales@pennwell.com
www.pennwellbooks.com
www.pennwell.com

Director: Mary McGee
Managing Editor: Marla Patterson
Production/Operations Manager: Traci Huntsman
Production Manager: Robin Remaley
Assistant Editor: Amethyst Hensley
Book Designer: Wes Rowell

Library of Congress Cataloging-in-Publication Data Available on Request

Hutton, James R.
How to Sell Technical Equipment and Services

ISBN 1-59370-066-0

All rights reserved. No part of this book may be reproduced, stored in a retrieval system, or transcribed in any form or by any means, electronic or mechanical, including photocopying and recording, without the prior written permission of the publisher.

Printed in the United States of America

1 2 3 4 5 10 09 08 07 06

To my gorgeous wife, Margaret, and to our customers
from whom I learned it all.

Contents

PREFACE

The leitmotif of this manuscript is honesty and integrity.

Selling is one of the most rewarding careers an individual can choose. It can be financially, intellectually, and socially rewarding to someone who likes to deal with people. It is always challenging, usually involves travel, and is never dull. It is a fulfilling profession, since choosing the best, most appropriate equipment is critical for businesses that purchase high technology merchandise. A well-trained, dedicated technical salesperson can dramatically influence these choices, giving invaluable assistance to customers in making the most cost-effective choices for their firms. Salespeople are profitable employees for their own companies as well.

Having a good sales force is vitally important to every business. Outstanding salespeople often make the difference in whether a company is extremely successful or only average—whether it succeeds or fails.

Success in selling is hard to predict. Education alone is not enough; mostly it is attitude, focus, and intensity. In these pages I have put down the cardinal rules and approaches to be used when selling to well-educated customers. This manual is written for a technical salesperson who will call on and sell to a limited number of customers on a continuing basis.

To many customers, the salesperson represents the equipment company because the majority of all their dealings with the firm is through sales. Many accounts have been dominated over a long period by the outstanding performance and loyal service of sales representatives who cared for their accounts so well that the competition could never get a foothold. Long after retirement many customers recall with incredible reverence that they always bought a certain brand of products because of the persistent work and service of one salesperson.

The objective of this book is to show how a salesperson can gain the enviable position of being the customer's sincere preference for doing business.

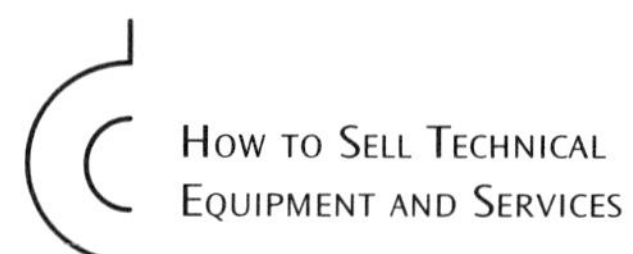

Quality is on everyone's mind these days and certainly improved industrial quality is essential if America is to survive, prosper, and maintain its current standard of living.

To most people quality implies the correctness of the products shipped to the outside customer, together with the overall service provided to these customers. Quality applies across the board, not just in the finished product, as a shortsighted view would identify. It applies to everything a salesperson does in the organization to turn out a reliable, efficient, high quality product. Since selling is so vital to a successful company's overall program, what better way to start a quality program than in the sales force? The proven techniques in this book will enable a salesperson to do a quality job and thereby generate enormous benefits to the company and customers, as well as reaping personal benefits.

In order to achieve outside customer quality, many things must also be done inside the company. This manual then addresses not only how a salesperson can service and sell to these customers, but also what must be done internally to optimize sales efforts and the company's general efforts toward the servicing of the customers who buy from him.

There is very little that is new in these pages. Many good salespeople know, and some practice already, these contents. This is a genuine attempt to assist technical salespeople scale the heights. If followed, the ideas contained herein will enable anyone to take a giant step toward success in selling high technology equipment.

These suggestions are not classroom approaches, but have been proven in the crucible of the selling trenches for more than 40 years to customers in virtually all countries of the world. The methods and procedures are a reflection of direct learning from smart, sophisticated, intelligent customers who buy millions of dollars worth of highly engineered equipment every year in socialist as well as capitalistic economies. Some ideas may appear redundant or unnecessary, but all are included after observing neglect on the part of not just junior salespeople but also senior representatives.

While this book is written primarily for those selling technical products, the methods can easily be adapted to other sales situations. It is also directed toward handling relationships with analytical individuals who, in my opinion, are the hardest to deal with. If a salesperson can successfully sell to analytical people using the ideas contained herein, I believe it is relatively easy to adjust techniques and deal successfully with other groups of individuals.

An outstanding salesperson must always take good care of the customers. Responding to all the customer's needs demonstrates clearly that his order is in the right hands. A truly outstanding salesperson will have customers going out of their way to do business with that person. There will always be obstacles to lashing down the sale and obtaining the order. Lesser salespeople will hide behind these excuses, lose the orders, and continue to rationalize away their failures.

But if a salesperson has really gained the customer's business confidence, the customer will help overcome these roadblocks, or at least advise of them so the salesperson can take the initiative to overcome them and secure the order. This is very important to remember because the race is almost always close, with only a small margin separating the winner from the competition. One who is aware of these small differences ahead of time can take steps to overcome them, but if they remain unknown, there is no chance to address them. A lesser representative will learn about them much too late. But if the customer had really and truly wanted to give that salesperson the order, he would have pointed the way or led him home to the order.

Selling is an inexact science. What works on one customer will not always work on the next—or even on the same customer again. Salespeople must always tailor pitches to the customer, the situation at hand, and the particular job.

There are no easy paths to doing an outstanding job in selling. If you are looking for shortcuts or easy solutions, don't bother to read this book. If, on the other hand, you are dedicated, desperately want to succeed, willing to work very hard, and sincerely and genuinely want to be good at selling, this book offers many valuable hints, tips, and suggestions. There are no shortcuts in these pages—no quick fixes and no band-aid approaches. Instead, outlined here is a recipe for success.

I want to give special thanks to my long-time Administrative Assistant Lee Sommers; my first employer and colleagues at Dresser Clark; my current employer and colleagues at Compressor Engineering Corporation; and all of our many fine, loyal customers who taught me so much and gave us so much business. My thanks also to the *Harvard Business Review* and to Max Depree, former CEO of Herman Miller Corporation, for permission to quote their materials in this book.

James R. Hutton
October, 2005

I

Fundamental Requirements

1

Know the Products

Superior product knowledge is one of the strongest weapons in a salesperson's arsenal. The technical competence of a salesperson rates first with customers—nothing opens a customer's doors more quickly or keeps them open longer. Since superior product knowledge is fundamental, it almost seems redundant to mention that a salesperson should know the products well. However, many salespeople actually enter customers' offices selling products they know very little about.

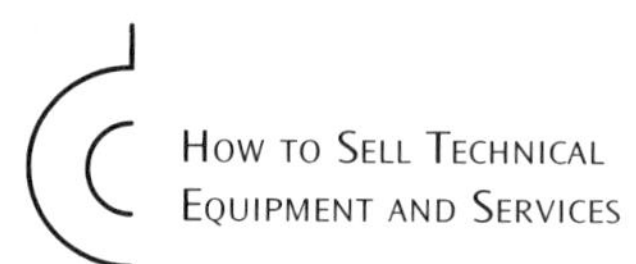

Knowing the products well will enhance a salesperson's reputation with the purchasers. It places the salesperson in the position of being beneficial to the customers as an expert in that field. Doors will more likely be open to a knowledgeable salesperson, and he will be called first when new estimates are required. The knowledgeable salesperson will be the first to learn about new expansion plans, and in additional meetings, he will stand out in the crowd of salespeople.

Through the years I have asked many buyers what impressed them the most in salespeople who have called on them. Time and time again, the answer was, "Product knowledge." Even when product knowledge was not mentioned as the most important attribute, it usually ranked second or third in importance.

A salesperson who knows his products well is able to more effectively overcome objections, since a rebuttal is best done on the spot as soon as the customer raises objections. Knowing products expertly will help a salesperson avoid misapplications and will enhance his prestige among peers and even among competitors. Such a person will be constantly sought out for technical knowledge, making his sales job easier and enabling him to cover more ground. The less a person knows about his work, the harder it is to do. Conversely, the more a person knows about his work, the easier it is to do.

Customers are impressed by a salesperson who is an expert on what he is selling. This is true with consumer products, but it is even more important with industrial products. To fulfill this expert role, a salesperson should know the products inside, outside, backward, and forward. A salesperson should:

- know from memory the model sizes, ratings, and capabilities
- have approximate prices and delivery dates readily available
- know the outstanding features of the products and why they are superior to the competitors' products
- know the performance and efficiencies, if important, together with any restrictions or limitations
- be familiar with the systems or processes in which the products are used and how they fit into the overall operation
- be conversant on the outside support required to make the products work
- know its compatibility with other products or systems already installed or available in the marketplace

- know the floor space required, if this is important
- know the number of operators required, if needed
- know the training required or the education requirements of the operators
- know its expandability capabilities
- know the auxiliary requirements
- know something about any controls required to make the products function optimally
- be aware of precautions to be observed in engineering, installing, commissioning, and operating the products

Since our world gets more complex every day, a successful salesperson must venture forth into battle armed with facts and knowledge. When a salesperson lacks such ammunition, he is vulnerable—and the customers as well as the competitors will find and exploit these chinks in his sales armor.

Customers usually are very intelligent, very busy, knowledgeable, dedicated individuals who are anxious to select for their company the very best products for a particular job. Customers are always searching for additional knowledge to support their choices. The fear of making a mistake by the wrong selection is uppermost in their minds, and this pervasive fear manifests itself in almost all their thinking. The customer's anxieties and expectations increase with increasing complexity of the products involved. A successful salesperson should keep in mind that customers buy expectations, not products. They purchase the expectations of benefits promised by the seller, and they also buy peace of mind.

A successful salesperson should keep in mind that customers buy expectations, not products.

A salesperson who knows his products well can satisfy the prospect's thirst for information and can greatly assist the customer in making certain the product is applied properly. The salesperson can aid the customer in reaching the correct decision and can allay any fears about making the wrong decision. The customer needs assurance at the outset that the salesperson knows his products and that the two parties can work harmoniously.

If a salesperson is an expert on his products, customers will think of him first when their needs initially arise. Buyers and plant engineers usually have someone they call first when they need quick, unofficial estimates or technical information on a given project or often when just making routine purchases. This person is someone they know is an expert in his field. It is someone they feel comfortable with, trust, and can talk to informally.

A successful salesperson should work to become the resource person who first comes to a customer's mind. This provides an opportunity for a salesperson to get in on the ground floor of a new project or large order and allows him to present his sales pitch early in the process. It also influences how the specifications are written so that they will tend to favor what the salesperson has to offer, often to the competitors' detriment.

All of us have observed salespeople who never knew anything about a large project until the formal inquiry arrived in the mail. However, it is likely that some salesperson did know, and this person probably gave early estimates or technical information, influencing the specifications. Someone else had already been making his sales pitch, and that salesperson was ahead of the competition. A successful salesperson works very hard to become an expert on all his products so that he is the person who is called first.

A well-developed knowledge of the products will enable a salesperson to concentrate on the differences between his products and those of the competitors. This, in turn, will prepare him to handle any comparisons with the competitors' products. The more a salesperson knows about his products as well as the competitors' products, the easier it will be for him to point out and accentuate important differences. As a consequence, the salesperson is better positioned to respond when a customer complains that the product is too expensive, because cost is a relative thing. The price of the product is high only if the identical product can be purchased elsewhere for less money. The more ways in which a salesperson can show that his product is unique, the less important price becomes. Product knowledge makes these distinctions possible.

It is not an easy task for a salesperson to know his products intimately. If a company offers a wide range of products, this can require constant study and effort to become and to remain familiar with everything offered. This is because a person usually does not work with every model regularly. Considerable time will often pass during which a salesperson is not involved with certain sizes of products or phases of business.

A salesperson should therefore study his products regularly to refresh his memory and, prior to making a sales call, he should always brush up on the specific items or categories likely to be discussed. This should not be left until the last minute. A salesperson may have to close his office door or review carefully the night before if no other time is available. This is better than being caught unprepared.

One way to facilitate this task is for a salesperson to always have product information in his briefcase or in his laptop, available to read every chance he has in a plane, in a taxi, or in waiting rooms. A person who takes the time to do this will keep current on all of his products and will avoid being caught off guard. It is not always possible for a salesperson to predict when he will be quizzed for information, as this could occur on virtually any sales call or at any time the office telephone rings.

Since a salesperson cannot possibly memorize all of these details, he should prepare current summary data sheets with this important information and keep them within easy reach. A salesperson should have sales kits on all of his various products, and these can even be manila folders in which a salesperson keeps all information encountered on each item. In these sales kits together with information on his laptop a person can keep:

- photographs
- specifications
- sales letters
- features and benefits
- product brochures
- letters from satisfied customers

A well-prepared salesperson will be alert for additional information to put in these files, as he cannot afford to treat product knowledge lightly.

One of the best ways for a salesperson to know his products well is to see them in operation. A salesperson should never let a month go by without observing either some of his models or his competitors' units in actual operation. Visiting where machinery is being used, discussing its performance with the operators, and watching it operate will remind the salesperson of the product's important features. It will enable him to learn about previously unknown advantages, especially if he visits regularly with installation and operating people. While products are usually well described in bulletins and manuals, nothing compares to seeing them operate and talking to the people who install, maintain, and monitor them. A salesperson should ask customers what they like or dislike about the product and how they feel it can be improved.

Another way for a salesperson to learn more about his products is to talk to customers who use them. Often a customer will discover a positive feature about which not even the engineers, designers, or product managers are aware. With constant usage, customers may discover features that are not ideal and thus need improvement. Plant visits will enable a salesperson to learn about these features and to work to get them changed, backed up by the customer's experience and opinion. A knowledge of a customer's inputs, experiences, and suggestions strengthens a salesperson's hand in dealing with his engineering and management people in order to initiate changes and improvements in the product.

A salesperson should consider customer plant visits to be mandatory on any new products introduced. Despite all of the thought, study, and engineering that goes into a new product, few are initially perfect and trouble-free. Therefore, when a new product is introduced in a salesperson's territory, he should go see it in operation more than once. In fact, the salesperson should be there when it starts up.

During visits to the customers' plants, a salesperson should not just ask the managers or superintendents what they think of the products. The salesperson should ask the people who are closest to the products, like the operators. The managers or superintendents may only know what they are being told. It may be helpful for the salesperson to ask the operator and the maintenance people what they would do to improve the parts or products so that they will perform better, be easier to work on, or be less expensive to install.

On trips to these various locations, a salesperson should make a lot of notes. If this is impossible or awkward to do inside the plant, then he should make these notes as soon as he leaves the premises. A salesperson who waits until he gets back to the office will likely forget vital information. It is important for a salesperson to report what he learns—especially any improvement suggestions—to his company's management and designers. Often these improvements can be reflected in future production at little or no cost.

Another way a salesperson can learn more about his products is for him to talk with his company's designers. A salesperson can ask them why the products were designed the way they were, especially in areas where their features differ substantially from the competitors' products. It also is important for a salesperson to weigh the designers' answers carefully. While some responses can be used to help sell products, others must be discarded, because few design engineers are sales oriented. If a designer told a salesperson that he designed a feature a certain way or furnished certain material because it was cheaper, the salesperson would not want to tell the customer this in these words. A persistent salesperson, however, will eventually come up with information that will help his sales pitch.

A salesperson also can visit with his service departments and ask them about performance and any potential improvements. Any suggestions or comments on operation or maintenance can be passed along to the customers or to the designers for improvement.

At every opportunity, a salesperson should take time to go out into his own manufacturing plants to observe components being machined and assembled and, if possible, watch complete units undergoing testing. He should ask someone in manufacturing to accompany him so his questions can be readily answered. A salesperson should be sure to observe critical procedures, especially work being done on components or in manufacturing sections unique to his company's products. This will not only refresh his memory in these areas but also will enable him to learn more details so he can better explain or relate them to prospective customers on the next job.

During these visits, a salesperson may uncover unique features that he can use in his selling efforts. If possible, he should make arrangements with the company photographer to take pictures of special parts and unique machining operations. These photos can be useful tools for salespeople to show their customers.

On a trip through our manufacturing plant, I observed a machining operation where a unique critical part was being machined from a solid forging. Realizing our competitors did not manufacture their comparable parts in this manner, I asked the company photographer to take pictures of this operation. When promoting products using this assembly, I showed these photographs to many customers over the years and thereby illustrated this unique, superior feature. These photographs helped us close a lot of orders.

A salesperson should talk regularly to his engineers about the products, making notes in order to remember what they say. A salesperson should not ask the same questions over and over—he should write down the answers and remember them.

There are other ways that a salesperson can find product information and learn more about the products. He can

- read magazine articles devoted to the products.
- read books about the products.
- ask his boss about the products.
- get information from other salespeople.

Sales Examples

The following examples will show how superior product knowledge enables a salesperson to close orders and beat the competition.

Example 1

While working on a very big order, I went one day with a colleague to call on the major decision maker. While in the waiting room, we learned that two vice presidents from our competitor's company had just left his office. Later, during our meeting with the decision maker, we reemphasized the technical superiority of our products. I then told him that I had learned in the lobby that senior executives from the competitor's factory had visited him. I went on to say that we also had vice presidents and that I could get them down if necessary. He replied that we did not require them and that my colleague and I knew our products so well that we did not need help from our factory. We received the order a few days later.

Example 2

Early in my career we were asked to bid on a new model of our products. This was a dramatic extension of this type of product and had not yet been built by us or our competitors. When the technical details of our machine arrived from our factory, I learned we were offering a model designed in a very conservative manner. Later, during the negotiations, I found out that some of our competitors were offering a different concept or a different style unit that was less conservative in design.

Since time was short and the job was moving fast, I called our designers at the factory to ask them why we proposed to design our unit the way we did. Their response was that we could accurately calculate the critical speed of the unit we were offering. However, with the other design as proposed by the competition, it was impossible to calculate accurately or to closely predict the critical speed. I quickly related this orally to the decision maker and confirmed it by letter. We received the order two days later for five of these units.

Later, our president told me this was the most profitable order we had ever put through this new division of our company. My conversation with our designers was decisive and enabled us to secure this very large and profitable order.

Example 3

While based in London, I was called unexpectedly to the office of an engineering contractor. When I arrived, I learned they wanted me to discuss product details with a project manager from the Soviet Union who was in the market for a packaged unit to use in testing on a pipeline project about to get underway in the Middle East.

The Soviet project manager quickly explained what he needed and asked, "Are you prepared to discuss technical details or commercial details?" I replied, "Both." He said, "Great," and spread out his drawings and specifications, amplifying in depth what he wanted. He asked about our delivery, price, and capacity. By satisfactorily answering all of his technical and commercial questions that day, we received the order a couple of days later without competition. No doubt detailed knowledge of our product was the deciding factor.

Example 4

The retired president of a large company told me on the golf course 5 years ago that because of one dedicated, knowledgeable salesperson, they used nothing but one brand of lubricating oil for more than 40 years. This salesperson was such a specialist on lubricating oil and its application, and gave all their personnel such good service, that no one else had a chance to get any oil business.

It is refreshing to encounter a salesperson who really is a specialist in his product area. A customer's confidence factor is very high when they buy products from him.

This becomes even more important when someone is buying for his company. If the salesperson, through lack of product knowledge, allows a buyer to purchase the wrong product, the buyer's reputation can be severely damaged. In extreme cases, it could even cause him to lose his job. The salesperson and his firm also lose face as well as future business.

A salesperson has an awesome responsibility to his customers and to his employer. In-depth product knowledge can help a salesperson take a giant step toward satisfactorily handling this responsibility.

There are other reasons why a salesperson needs to have superior product knowledge and why he needs to know the products extremely well:

- It builds enthusiasm. The more a salesperson knows about his products, the more he can believe in them and be enthusiastic about them when talking to prospects.
- It builds confidence. A fear that grips all beginning salespeople is the fear of the prospect asking them questions that they cannot answer. The only salesperson who should fear questions is the one who does not know his products.
- It makes a salesperson an expert and gives him personal satisfaction.
- It enables the salesperson to speak confidently with experts in the customer organization—buyers, engineers, and other professionals.
- It enables the salesperson to answer objections effectively. When buyers say the price is too high, a well-prepared salesperson can more easily illustrate quality and value and how his products are different. This removes them from direct comparison with the competitors' products.
- The more a salesperson knows about his products, the more advantages to users he will discover in them.
- It enables a salesperson to meet competition effectively. It is hard for a salesperson to convince a prospect that his product is better unless he can state the facts to prove it.
- It gives a salesperson self-assurance, which dictionaries define as *a state of mind free from doubts or misgivings.*
- It enables a salesperson to gain the confidence of his prospects.

With all the advantages of superior product knowledge, every salesperson should work every day at increasing his knowledge of his products.

Summary

1. Superior product knowledge is a salesperson's strongest weapon.
2. Nothing opens doors faster.
3. It sets a salesperson apart from most other salespeople and gives him a useful foothold with buyers and decision makers.
4. A well-prepared salesperson will be called first when new estimates are required.
5. Product knowledge enables a salesperson to effectively overcome objections.
6. Product knowledge enhances a salesperson's prestige among his customers and his peers.
7. It makes the salesperson's work easier to do.
8. A salesperson should know all the important details about his products.
9. A salesperson who knows his products well will be able to concentrate on the differences between his products and those of the competitors, thereby removing his products from direct comparison.
10. This is not an easy task, because a salesperson does not usually work with the same items every day. It requires constant study and memory refreshing.
11. A salesperson should always have product information available to read and study while traveling and in waiting rooms.
12. A salesperson should maintain sales kits with photographs, specifications, features and benefits, sales letters, and current brochures.
13. A salesperson should observe his products in operation.
14. It is important for a salesperson to talk to customers who use his products to determine their likes as well as their dislikes.

15. There are many reasons a salesperson needs to have superior product knowledge:

    - It builds enthusiasm.
    - It builds confidence.
    - It makes the salesperson an expert.
    - It enables the salesperson to speak confidently with the customer's experts.
    - It enables the salesperson to answer objections.
    - It enables the salesperson to point out more advantages over the competition.
    - It gives the salesperson self-assurance.
    - It helps the salesperson to gain the confidence of his customers.

Know the Competitors and Their Products

For a salesperson to be an expert on his own products requires that he be knowledgeable concerning what is available from competitive sources. Some salespeople go about selling their own products and extolling certain virtues and features without realizing that their competitors' products have characteristics equal to or better than their own. It is, therefore, very important that a salesperson know his competitors and their products almost as well as he knows his own products.

Chapter 1 mentions that a salesperson's product knowledge enables him to concentrate on the differences his product offers. The salesperson can use this knowledge to protect his product from unfair comparisons with the competition's product. The more a salesperson knows about the competitors' products, the easier it will be to identify and to concentrate on the differences. The more ways in which a salesperson can demonstrate that he is selling something unique, the less important price becomes. If a salesperson knows about his own products and those of his competitors, he increases his chances of successfully demonstrating his point.

The differences between a salesperson's products and what his competition offers can constitute a crucial area in sales. It is an area of great interest to buyers. By the nature of his job, the salesperson is centered on his own products. The buyers, the operating people, and the maintenance people hear pitches on and observe all the competing models. They are apt to conclude, and quite rightly so, that a salesperson who does not know his competitors' products does not really know his own.

One way for a salesperson to gather this vital knowledge about competitors is to visit stations or plants where the competitive item is used or is in operation. This is not always easy, but he should do this as often as possible. If permission is required, a salesperson should ask for it, so that his visit conforms to the rules. In the plant, he should ask the operator's opinions concerning the product, any outstanding features it has, and what its pluses and shortcomings are.

A salesperson should make notes, but in a plant that uses the competitor's products, he should be even more discreet than when reviewing his own products. The salesperson should memorize details, features, facts, and figures, and then write them down as soon as possible upon leaving the plant. A salesperson who waits to write down these notes until he is back at the office will forget many important details.

A salesperson can supplement what is learned during plant visits by studying available literature and bulletins published on competitive products. These bulletins can usually be obtained at trade shows. Additional facts can be gathered by reading trade journals and competitors' advertisements. It may be helpful for the salesperson to cut out and save each ad run by the competition, because these ads reveal what products they are pushing. These ads will also reveal what features and benefits they are promoting on their products. Having this information enables a salesperson to make counter pitches. A salesperson can also compare competitive ads and bulletins with his company's material and perhaps assist the advertising department in improving the company's brochures and advertising. He can also obtain information from the competitor's Web site.

A salesperson should organize and maintain files on each competitor's product. He should learn about competitive models by visiting displays at trade shows and not hesitate to visit the competitor's area. The competitors likely will do the same with any information they can get about the salesperson's company. It may be best for a salesperson to go at off hours when not many people, such as any customers they might have in common, are around. A salesperson should never barge right in but should observe from a respectable distance, using good judgment.

To assist in gathering competitive intelligence, a salesperson should always have a camera along at trade shows. Taking pictures of competitive displays or models will not always be easy, but a salesperson can sometimes accomplish this as the show is closing or when it first opens. With high-speed film, a salesperson can take pictures unobtrusively at almost any time, but this should always be done discreetly. He can sometimes take photographs in a customer's plant, but he should be sure to obey all their rules and obtain the necessary permissions. These photographs will be valuable additions to his sales kit.

If possible, a salesperson should buy shares of stock in his major competitors' companies. Annual reports and quarterly letters thereby received on a regular basis will provide photographs and other useful information. This information will also reveal what they are concentrating on and what they are de-emphasizing. It will also indicate earnings and future plans. Knowing the competitors' products as well as his own enables a salesperson to emphasize where his product excels and allows him to explain why he thinks his product's features are best. The salesperson leaves himself wide open to the competition if he stresses certain features of his product and the competition's product has the same features.

A salesperson can obtain further information on his competitors and competitive products by discussing them with his boss. The boss usually has had more experience and will know a lot about competitive models. A salesperson also may find it helpful to visit with other sales colleagues. They may be particularly helpful if they have recently been involved with or regularly work on orders or quotations involving competitive products that the salesperson does not encounter often. Usually sales colleagues will be flattered by the queries and will be responsive.

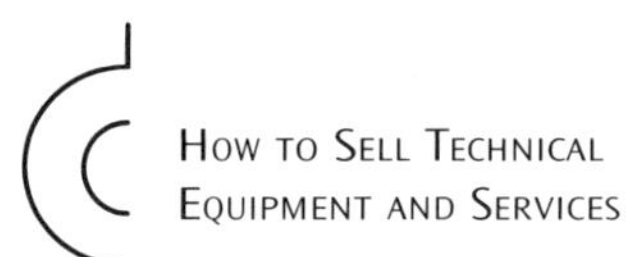

There are other good sources of information on the competitors' products. These include consultants, buyers, maintenance, or machinery specialists who work for end users or contracting firms who prepare specifications and recommend purchases. Information from these sources is best obtained when there is no active job underway. A salesperson should tap these sources between jobs and ask what features they like and dislike about competitive products.

If these people are buying mainly or exclusively from someone else, a salesperson should ask why they prefer that vendor or that brand of products. It is important that a salesperson not assume he knows the answer to this question. He should ask the buyer, the engineers, the maintenance people, and others involved in the buying decision. The salesperson should always make certain to ask several people within each company to improve the accuracy of the information obtained. He should write down what he is told so that he can strive to meet their requirements on the next quote or project. A salesperson then can slant his sales pitch toward what they like and are looking for. Unless he knows for sure why they are buying from his competitors, he will not know how to change specifications, tactics, or his sales pitch on the next quotation.

All of the information thus gained will be virtually useless unless the salesperson takes the time to see that it is properly recorded and appropriately filed. As he learns more about these likes and dislikes, he must take notes and make certain this information is conveniently and safely stored away for expeditious retrieval when needed.

During the gathering of this information is a good time for a salesperson to ask decision makers what they put first when they buy the products in question. This will often give the salesperson useful insight into their decision-making process—information he can use later to a good advantage.

The customer will always appreciate a salesperson's knowledge of what is available competitively, but he will not look favorably on the salesperson criticizing his competition. Criticism of competition should be avoided, since it can backfire and be counterproductive.

On the other hand, the competition cannot be ignored or brushed off lightly. It is a serious error for a salesperson to underrate his competitors or to pretend they do not exist. A salesperson should not be obsessed with the competition, or he may become preoccupied and neglect stressing his own product's features and benefits. He should, however, be aware of the competitor's products and always be ready to analyze with his prospect the advantages and disadvantages of buying from him or his competitor. Expert product knowledge of both his own products as well as those of the competitors will enable him to do this.

On one hand, silence about competition is an indication of weakness and defeatism. On the other hand, the worst thing a salesperson can do in this regard is to criticize his competitors. If this is done, the buyer will rise to the defense. Instead, a salesperson should give a soft-spoken, fair, and factual appraisal as he emphasizes how his products differ from what the competition offers and how his products excel. A salesperson has to be careful how this is said. If it is said kindly, it is advice. If it is said caustically, it is criticism.

Strong competition that might discourage or slow down a weak salesperson will inspire and stimulate a good salesperson into action. Properly armed with expert knowledge on his products as well those of his competitors, he will not only welcome the challenge but will also savor it.

Competitors should not usually be mentioned by name. It is sufficient for a salesperson to say, "Others do it this way, but we think our way is best, and here is why." The use of soft, careful language in all remarks or comments about the competition is important for any salesperson. He should avoid strident language and should not antagonize his competitor, who already has enough reasons to want to nudge him out of an order. It would not be wise to give the competitor incentive to work even harder.

Competitive vendors often say they do not knock competitors or their products, but they must know those products well so they can identify their weaknesses. They then say they are in a better position to accentuate those features in their own equipment that make their machines superior and thereby help the customer get more for his money by buying their products.

Competitors should not usually be mentioned by name. It is sufficient for a salesperson to say, "Others do it this way, but we think our way is best, and here is why."

Most companies have predictable policies and negotiating styles that rarely change. If a salesperson takes time to learn a lot about each major competitor, it will make his selling job a bit easier. He will then be able to predict to some extent the competitors' selling strategies and pricing policies. Knowing their basic methods, it will be easy for him to update his knowledge if they do change.

To do an outstanding job in this area, a salesperson must have a pretty good knowledge of all of his competitors. The reason for this is that he will not face the same major competitor on every job, but eventually he will run up against all of them. This is an ongoing exercise and not something a salesperson does once and then stops.

A salesperson should keep in mind that the contest for an order is almost always very close, and the margin of victory is narrow. He should always be searching for something that will give him an advantage. Sometimes it does not take much, and he should not disregard what may seem to be minor points. This same thing may strike a responsive cord with the customer and be decisive.

It is vital that a salesperson not try to be too clever and make judgments for the buyer. If there are advantages, he should point them all out. Furthermore, a salesperson should remember that he will not always have a long list of advantages. Sometimes he will be scratching to find any advantages to stress and to capitalize on, so he should not be too quick to reject any possibilities.

Sales Examples

Example 1

An example of how knowing the competitor's products can enable a salesperson to do a better job of selling was brought into sharp focus several years ago. A major competitor had introduced a new unit with great fanfare and success. One model was installed in a plant a few hours' drive from my base. I made an appointment and drove to the plant to have a look. For several hours I made careful mental note of the unit's size, physical arrangement, and overall installation. I also discussed the pluses and minuses with the plant personnel.

Before leaving, I stopped by to see the station manager to thank him for his hospitality and for allowing me to visit his plant. During our conversation, I asked him what he thought of this new unit and if it had given him satisfactory service.

He replied that, overall, the machine had performed fairly well without too many problems, but he added that it was very difficult to work on and to repair. When I asked what particularly he had in mind, his answer was astonishing. He revealed to me that the unit could not be maintained using conventional methods and procedures. This meant that to remove a major normal wearing part, the power piston, someone also had to simultaneously remove an additional major part, the power cylinder liner. This is a part one would not normally disturb, and it would require probably twice the amount of time as the normal job. This was so unusual and so unlikely that I found it hard to believe. Sensing my disbelief, he repeated the facts.

There was a smile on my face all the way home, because I realized that by going to this plant, I had struck gold. I knew that in the future all I had to do was to make sure prospective buyers, especially maintenance people, knew about this major shortcoming, and they would reject the product. Reject it the customers did, and the product line suffered an early demise in the marketplace. By going to this plant and learning about my competitor's product, I was able to greatly increase our sales against this competitor.

Only by knowing the features of the products that the competitors offer can a salesperson point out where his product excels and use this to his advantage.

Example 2

This is further illustrated by another sales example. We knew that one of our products had a higher efficiency than that of the competition, which meant it consumed less fuel for the same rating. We would exploit this only by knowing the efficiencies of competitive units, which we obtained from published data and brochures on their products. We knew also that one of our competitors was limited in the number of impellers that could be used in its compressor case. We could successfully operate many more, often enabling us to do in one unit what the competition required two to accomplish. Not only would our overall price be lower, but also the installation and maintenance would cost less.

Example 3

As a final example, when selling our products, we knew that our major competitor employed high-speed turbochargers designed and built by others. In contrast, we supplied medium-speed turbochargers designed by our own design engineer and built in our own facilities, giving the same longer life as the rest of our products. The high-speed devices used by the competition required more maintenance. Stressing this often gave us an edge with the customer. As mentioned earlier, since the contest for the order is usually very close, a salesperson must always look for any advantages his products have.

Knowing and keeping abreast of the competitors and their products is not easy but is mandatory for a successful salesperson. A salesperson should arrange manila folders for all major competitors and keep the accumulated information in these files. He should also keep copies of all applicable facts in the respective sales kits ready for instant use when competing on that product or against that competitor.

Summary

1. To be able to maximize sales, a salesperson must know his competitors and their products almost as well as he knows his own.
2. The differences in a salesperson's products and what the competition offers is of vital interest to buyers. If successfully presented, this will enable the salesperson to remove his product from direct comparison. He can gain this information in many ways, including the following:

    a. visiting plants where competitive products are in use
    b. asking users, especially buyers, maintenance people, and mechanical experts
    c. asking consultants
    d. studying competitive literature
    e. visiting his competitors' Web sites
    f. reading trade journal ads by the competitors
    g. visiting competitive booths at trade shows and taking pictures wherever possible
    h. reading annual reports and quarterly messages to stockholders
    i. asking customers why they are buying from the competitor

j. asking more than one person within the company

k. quizzing other salespeople in the firm

l. quizzing his boss

3. A salesperson should file this information in sales kits for fast, easy retrieval.
4. A salesperson should have a sales kit for each competitor but also should file the appropriate information in sales kits for specific products.
5. It is important that a salesperson avoid criticizing competitors by name, or his remarks will be counterproductive and will damage his relations with his customer. The salesperson should just say, "Others do it this way."
6. Strong competition should inspire, and not discourage, a successful salesperson.
7. A salesperson should learn the competitors' negotiating styles, which are usually predictable. This will help to counter their strategies.
8. A salesperson should not hesitate to use all the ammunition available. He should not hold something back because he thinks it will not influence the customer.
9. It is important for a salesperson to work hard at learning more about the competition and their products. The knowledge gained will enable him to sell much more intelligently and to close many more orders.

3

Know the Customers

Sometimes salespeople call for years on companies they know very little about. The better a salesperson understands and knows the prospective customers, the better he can provide what they need and close the maximum amount of business for his company. Some salespeople take their executives along to see a prospect without knowing what business he is in, what his requirements are, and what their own firm can provide to this customer.

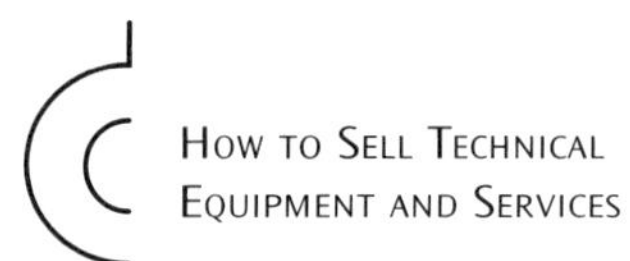

Years ago, a senior executive with a major customer of ours shared an interesting observation. He mentioned that several times each year, different salespeople would bring their executives to his office to help them sell. These executives and salespeople knew almost nothing about the company they were calling on. Many times this company had no need for what the salespeople were trying to sell.

A salesperson should never allow this to happen. This situation can be avoided by a salesperson who expends a bit of effort to learn about an organization before making a sales call. He should certainly do this before permitting his executives to make their first visit. Virtually all companies have someone a salesperson can reach by phone who will discuss the nature of their business and whether or not they have current or future requirements for the product. Intelligence gathered ahead of time will reveal whether or not a salesperson should spend time on this account.

A lot of free information is readily available about virtually all companies. Some sources of useful, accurate information are the following:

1. Annual reports
2. Corporate Web site
3. Other salespeople (not competitors)
4. The company itself, including:
    - The public relations department
    - The chief or assistant chief engineer
    - The maintenance division
    - The purchasing department
5. Other companies in a related or similar business
6. Trade journals in which the companies advertise
7. Trade journals in which news of the companies appears
8. Business sections of newspapers

In any case, it is always best for a salesperson to make the first sales call by himself. Even with careful preparation and investigation, a salesperson will want to make certain he has a good prospect before involving others from his company.

Once it is established that the firm is a potential customer, and a salesperson has made contact, he should then remain current concerning what the firm is doing. The salesperson should also determine what the company's needs are and how he can fill those needs.

This will usually take a lot of digging on the part of the salesperson. The annual report of public companies is a good source of general information. It may be possible for the salesperson to call and obtain a copy free from the company, but the best way is for him to buy stock in the company. This is especially true concerning companies with which a salesperson regularly works. If he buys shares, he will receive this information regularly; not only the annual reports, but quarterly reports, letters to stockholders, and proxy statements. This information then will be sent without further effort on the part of the salesperson, which proves helpful when things are busy. A stockholder will receive a steady flow of these important facts.

Trade journals relating to the customers' businesses are good sources of information on future plans and trends. These publications also will expose the salesperson to technical advertisements that will help with current information on the customer. A salesperson should tear out the pages and file them under the company's name. When a big job comes along with this firm, he can refresh his memory by quickly reading this information.

It is also important for a salesperson to understand how a customer goes about evaluating, purchasing, installing, and commissioning the products used. This requires in-depth study, because it will rarely be the same from customer to customer. The method by which purchasing decisions are reached will not necessarily be apparent from the organization chart or from what a salesperson may be told. Customer officials exert varying amounts of authority on decisions in purchasing products, and it is not always in exact proportion to their position within the company.

For a salesperson to sort this out requires a thorough analysis of each customer. The salesperson must be observant and should question many people, both inside and outside the customer organization. A salesperson should visit with the customer's counterparts in other companies in the same line of business. These sources can be informative, because they meet each other and develop friendly relations, often in trade associations.

In pursuing this information, a salesperson should not forget other noncompetitive salespeople who also call on these customers. The successful among them may know the customer well. It will help if the salesperson determines which other salespeople have been the most successful and ask them who exerts the most influence on purchasing decisions. The responses may be surprising. Ex-employees or retired employees are also good sources of information on who has influence in the company. Acquiring all of this information is not a waste of time. It will actually save the salesperson an enormous amount of time over the long run as he services these accounts.

The information-gathering process may extend over several months, allowing time to collect and sift facts and make more contacts. A salesperson should be inspired as he goes about this. There are many uninspired salespeople who get nowhere because they do not know their customers.

It may also be helpful for a salesperson to learn other details, such as the following:

- working hours
- restrictions on calls from salespeople
- whether or not appointments are necessary

Concerning the last point, I would never make a sales call without an appointment. I have read numerous call reports indicating that buyers would not see salespeople without an appointment. This should clearly have been established ahead of time.

Once a salesperson finds a good prospect, he should not stop there. The next step is to determine what products the customer makes and how the salesperson's products fit into the overall production picture.

Empathy is one of the two fundamental requirements of an outstanding salesperson. In chapter 5, I point out how important it is for a salesperson to be able to see events and situations as the customer sees them. The more a salesperson knows about the buyer and his company, the more successful he will be in practicing empathy.

For example, Allen Mebane, retired chairman of Unifi, Inc. (a textile giant), said he must know his customer's business and problems at least as well as he knows his own. "I have to show him how much I can help him—not vice versa." (*Wall Street Journal* August 29, 1983)

Customers value a knowledgeable salesperson. They will be more likely to buy from a salesperson if he does his homework so he can better understand the customer's problems, needs, and how the customer goes about satisfying those needs. Knowing the customer's business well may even help a salesperson avoid any misapplications. When near a customer's plant, it is always a good idea for a salesperson to ask if he can observe the equipment running or see his products in operation.

Customers value a knowledgeable salesperson.

While it is very important to know what the customer is now buying, a salesperson should work hard at expanding what can be sold to him. To accomplish this, the salesperson must look at the entire area in which the customer and his products are involved. He must make sure to promote all of the applicable parts or complementary products. A salesperson should look into this carefully and give it serious thought, because it can represent an area in which sales can be greatly expanded.

When a salesperson receives an inquiry, either verbal or written, he should not restrict his response to only what the inquiry covers. The salesperson should analyze the inquiry thoroughly and also offer subsidiary products for modernizing the operation, as well as offer particular items that will save the customer money. It is always a good idea for the salesperson to quote what the customer asks for, but he should not hesitate to then offer alternatives and additional parts or products. Customers like to save money.

A salesperson should not wait until he receives an inquiry to think about expanding his sales to a customer. This should be considered on an ongoing basis with all customers. The salesperson should explore the ways he can make the existing products more reliable or more efficient.

A key requisite often pointed out by others in the selling business is a genuine interest in a customer's operations, problems, and needs. Until a salesperson knows these things, he cannot sell effectively to the customer.

If a salesperson knows the customers well, he can help keep some of their young engineers out of trouble within their own company. For example, if a customer has strict rules on how communications must flow when prices are involved, the salesperson can avoid sending correspondence directly to an engineer. Even if the engineer requests it, the salesperson should diplomatically

remind him that from past practices, he knows that his reply should go directly to the purchasing department. At the very least, they should receive copies. These situations can be delicate, but a salesperson should do his best to keep everybody happy. The salesperson has the most to lose and will usually be faulted if rules are not followed.

Most customers have their own purchasing and negotiating styles. Some solicit bids and buy from the lowest evaluated bidder. Others seem to find a way to purchase what they really want, even if a higher initial price was submitted. A salesperson would do well to learn this. The negotiating style of a customer usually changes little. The salesperson must keep this in mind, because it can greatly influence not only how he bids but also how he handles and services the account.

Sales Examples

Example 1

Once while calling on a new customer who had a big need for my products, I asked the receptionist for a copy of their annual report. Inside was a small booklet giving the entire history of the company since its founding during the Depression, including the difficult struggle it had to maintain profitability in the early years. This greatly increased my knowledge of the company and enabled me to do a better job selling to them. They appreciated that I had taken time to read and learn more about their company.

I also learned from this annual report that someone I had dealt with years before but had lost track of was then a senior vice president in charge of the area that bought my products. Knowing these facts enabled us to increase our business with this company.

I mentioned earlier the importance of visiting customer plants and observing products in operation. The following is an example of how a visit to a jobsite greatly assisted us in obtaining a very large order.

Example 2

We were attempting to introduce a new product and had traveled to the customer's main offices for meetings. We knew they would make a decision that week on what to purchase. During the first day's meeting, we asked for permission to visit their jobsite 500 miles out in the outback of Australia the next day. We told the customer we wanted our engineers to see the exact conditions under which our products would operate if we were awarded the order. To make the trip, a plane had to be chartered. The customer not only granted us permission but made all the necessary arrangements, including booking the charter flight.

To commit to this time and expense prior to receiving the order took courage, but I felt it would show seriousness on our part. It would show that we sincerely appreciated their problems, and it would thereby enhance our chances. It did, and to the astonishment of our competitors, we received the order the day after the jobsite visit. While we were at this jobsite thoroughly inspecting and observing the conditions under which our machinery would operate, our overconfident competitors were waiting in their hotel rooms for a call that never came.

Summary

A successful salesperson must take time to learn about his customers and evaluate their need for the products he sells. He then must continue to learn all he can about his customers in order to be more successful selling to them. A salesperson must bear in mind that his company's most precious assets are its good relationships with the customers. He must work very hard to develop and maintain excellent relationships with all his customers by knowing them well and understanding their needs.

An Insatiable Desire to Obtain Orders

The *Harvard Business Review* published an article entitled, "What Makes a Good Salesman" (Mayer & Greenberg, 1964). The authors discussed the enormous amount of money spent every year by American industry due to the high rate of turnover among salespeople. They went on to discuss what accounts for this expensive inefficiency, explaining, "Companies have simply not known what makes one person able to sell and another not. A very high proportion of those engaged in selling cannot sell. If American sales efficiency is to be maximized and the appalling waste of money and manpower which exists is to be minimized, a constructive analysis must be made of what selling really is and how its effectiveness can be enhanced. We must look a great deal further into the mysteries of personality and psychology if we want real answers."

It was the obvious need for a better method of sales selection that led them to embark on seven years of field research in this area. This article was based on the insights gained as to the basic characteristics necessary for a salesperson to sell successfully.

The authors' conclusion was that an outstanding salesperson must have at least two basic qualities: empathy and ego-drive. Another way to describe ego-drive might be to call it *an insatiable desire to obtain orders.*

Webster defines insatiable as "incapable of being satisfied" (Merriam-Webster, 2005). This means that a salesperson with an insatiable desire to obtain orders would never have enough orders to be satisfied. That individual would be a great salesperson—he would never be satisfied, never have enough business, and never have enough orders!

A salesperson must keep in mind that obtaining orders keeps the plant running, the company making money, and people working. The salesperson, therefore, makes an extremely valuable contribution not only financially to the company, but also to society. His efforts enable people to keep their jobs and help keep companies in business. A salesperson should, therefore, do everything possible to develop an insatiable desire to obtain orders.

To enter the race in this category, a salesperson must be highly motivated and inspired. Motivation can be defined as an inner drive or need that results in action on the part of the individual. Most people are failures not because they are stupid, but because they are not sufficiently impassioned or motivated. There are many good books on motivation for those desiring to read more on the topic. When all is said and done, however, a salesperson should be self-motivated. The salesperson should not expect to be motivated by a boss or a spouse, although a person who receives this type of help from others is fortunate indeed. Motivation generally requires a continuing effort on the part of the salesperson and must be addressed daily.

Most people are failures not because they are stupid, but because they are not sufficiently impassioned or motivated.

There are a few tips for a salesperson to remain motivated:

1. A salesperson must not allow failure or adversity to be personally discouraging. Failure should act as a trigger to spur a person on even more vigorously the next time.
2. It is important for a salesperson to think positively and to sincerely believe that events will turn out favorably. Thoughts govern moods, not the other way around. Milton put it well in *Paradise Lost* when he wrote, "The mind is its own place and in itself can make a heaven of hell, a hell of heaven."
3. A salesperson must work hard to influence events favorably.
4. A salesperson must always think and feel that he can excel and should act as if it is impossible to fail.
5. It is important for a salesperson to learn from failure or temporary setbacks.
6. A salesperson must approach all problems with gusto and look upon them as opportunities for himself and his company. If sorted out expeditiously, problems can enhance the standing of both the company and the salesperson with the customer.
7. A salesperson should not expect bad or unfavorable things to happen. Instead, he should be optimistic and expect things to turn out well.
8. While expecting and truly believing events will turn out favorably, a salesperson should be prepared for adversity. Life is not a super highway but instead contains many roadblocks.
9. A salesperson should never treat lightly the loss of an order for whatever reason.
10. A salesperson should put his subconscious to work.
11. It is important for a salesperson to believe in himself. He must remember, however, that his self-assurance hangs by a thin thread and will be challenged by the winds of every crisis that confronts him. In selling there is a crisis almost daily, so a salesperson must have the confidence to remain self-assured.
12. A salesperson must believe that he can make a difference.

13. It is helpful for a salesperson to believe that people are basically good; otherwise paranoia and cynicism will slow him down. The walls cynics build around themselves to keep other people from getting in also prevent themselves from getting out. It is counterproductive.
14. A salesperson should eliminate from his thinking such words as *worry*, *doubt*, *self-doubt*, *fear*, and *despair*.
15. A salesperson should be enthusiastic. Henry Ford said, "Enthusiasm is at the bottom of all progress. . . . With it there is accomplishment. Without it there are only alibis."
16. Finally, a person who loves his work is highly motivated. There is an old proverb that says:
    - If you would be happy for one hour, take a nap.
    - If you would be happy for a day, go fishing.
    - If you would be happy for a week, kill your pig and eat it.
    - If you would be happy for a month, get married.
    - If you would be happy for a year, inherit a fortune.
    - If you would be happy for life, love your work.

When a salesperson loves his work, he crowds a lot of it into his 24-hour days. He has the zest to become increasingly efficient. He makes the time to get more things done. He eats better, sleeps better, and lives longer. Through the work he loves, he finds an outlet for the great capacities bottled up within. He takes frustrations and dejection in stride. Nothing develops his time sense so keenly as love of work. The salesperson who loves his work will always have a job and will seldom get fired, retire early, or be downsized out of employment.

As a salesperson approaches the customer when an order is at stake, his attitude must be that he has to make the sale and that the customer exists to help him fulfill his personal need. This means that to an outstanding salesperson, the conquest provides a powerful means of enhancing his ego. His self-image is improved dramatically with success and diminishes with failure. A salesperson loses more orders than he wins. For this reason, an outstanding salesperson must have an extremely strong desire for orders so that failure does not get him down.

Much of sales ability is fundamental, more so than the products being sold. Some authorities think that the qualities of outstanding salespeople are developed at an early age. They believe that long before an outstanding salesperson begins a career in selling, he is developing many of the qualities essential for successful selling. Many qualities however, can be learned and improved on. This is the message that the successful salesperson needs to understand.

A salesperson must at all times have an insatiable desire for the next order. The efforts to succeed must be indefatigable and must dominate the person's thinking throughout the course of each active job and even between projects. A salesperson who is truly obsessed will put his subconscious to work. When he is out of the office at an athletic or social event, while all others may be glued to what is going on, his thoughts will often be drawn to thinking about an impending order. He will then be amazed at what new thoughts, challenges, advantages, or points come leaping to mind. Some of his best ideas can come at a time like this, but they must be initiated by the overwhelming, insatiable desire for the order.

A salesperson should continually be asking himself the following:

- What else can I do to enhance my chances on this order?
- Who else can I call on?
- What other points can I stress?

Sales Example

I was once working on a job that involved introducing a new product. This is never easy, but in this case my company was having a difficult time. We had an inquiry from a customer overseas and I was leaving on Monday for the final negotiations. Selling our first new unit so far away was going to be very difficult, but we had to obtain our first order or the program faced collapse. I was determined that we would get this order and had spent the previous few days thinking almost desperately for new things to do to improve our chances.

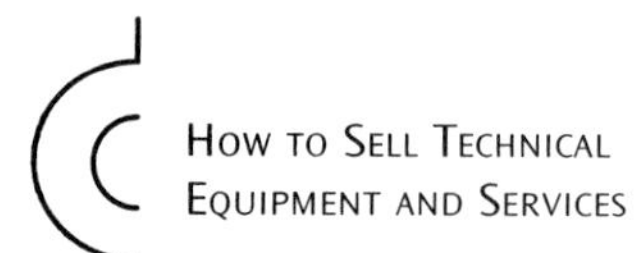

The Saturday before I was to depart, I took my family and some extra children to the rodeo. After I got everyone settled, I sat down to watch the show, but my thoughts immediately fell on the impending order. I kept asking myself what else we could do to make sure we got the order. What else could we offer the customer as an inducement?

All of a sudden, it occurred to me that I should obtain letters from our president and from the president of our major partner stating their personal commitment to the success of this new unit. I composed the letter later that day, and our president signed it Monday morning. I called the West Coast home office of our partner and requested a similar letter from their president. They agreed it was a super idea. I dictated my draft letter over the phone, and when I arrived on the West Coast that night, I was handed the letter signed by the president of our major partner.

Two days later I presented these two letters to our customer overseas. We ultimately received the order to the astonishment of our competitors, and even to the astonishment of our home office. These two letters were decisive and tipped the scales in our favor. Without my insatiable desire to obtain this order, I never would have thought of taking these vital letters with me.

As pointed out earlier, studies have shown that salespeople with strong personal drives, together with empathy, outperform all others by a wide margin. These traits are mandatory if a salesperson is to be consistently outstanding in his achievements. However, a salesperson should never allow his tireless efforts and this intense desire to blind him to reality. He should never step on people, upset his customers and colleagues, or stray from the truth in achieving his goal. The salesperson should want the order for personal satisfaction and to enhance his image with his contemporaries, not just because it will earn additional money for himself or his company.

A salesperson should keep in mind that it is too late after the order is gone to do anything to salvage it. Fretting and wringing hands will not help at this stage. The salesperson must be extremely conscientious and alert as he works on each order. He must decide what can be done then, not later, to obtain the order. A successful salesperson will do everything he can, consistent with good judgment and within his company's guidelines, to get the customer to buy from him.

To further succeed in this category requires performing in an inspired manner. Everyone has seen what deeply inspired athletes can accomplish against teams far superior in innate athletic ability. A salesperson may have a superior or someone else to inspire him, but he should not count on it—he should be prepared to inspire himself. A salesperson can help by practicing the following:

1. He can imagine what receiving orders will do for his image and prestige among his peers.
2. When he is working on a large order, he can determine how many man-days of work are involved in the design, the engineering, the manufacturing, and the commissioning of the units. Then he can relate that to how many people he provides with employment by selling the product.
3. He can visualize the satisfaction he will feel when he learns that he has been chosen the successful vendor.
4. He can keep in mind the feeling he experiences in a job done well.
5. He can consider the financial security he is providing for himself and his family.
6. He can imagine how he will feel if he is the leading salesperson in his organization, and he can contemplate the recognition resulting from this distinction.
7. He can consider the service he is providing his customer by selling him the best and most reliable product for the project. By doing his selling job well and obtaining the order, the salesperson will make sure his customer does not make a mistake and buy inferior products.

In order to be an outstanding salesperson, be highly motivated, and work in an inspired manner, an individual must have an insatiable desire for orders. To do this requires eternal vigilance and deep dedication, but the rewards are tremendous. These characteristics will place the outstanding salesperson in a very select category.

Summary

1. It is very difficult to determine what makes one person able to sell and another not able to sell.
2. A very high proportion of those engaged in selling cannot sell.
3. A seven-year field research study determined that outstanding salespeople possess two basic qualities: empathy and ego-drive, or an insatiable desire to obtain orders.
4. A salesperson should remember that orders keep the plants running and enable people to stay employed.
5. In order to have this insatiable desire, a salesperson must be highly motivated and inspired.
6. Most people who fail in selling are not highly motivated.
7. A successful salesperson never depends on others to motivate him. He is self-motivated.
8. A successful salesperson does not let failure become personally discouraging.
9. A salesperson must always think positively.
10. A salesperson works hard to influence events favorably.
11. A salesperson must always think and feel that he can excel.
12. A salesperson must be able to learn from failure.
13. A salesperson must view all problems as opportunities.
14. A salesperson must expect good things to happen.
15. A salesperson must be prepared for adversity.
16. A salesperson must never treat the loss of an order lightly.
17. A salesperson puts his subconscious to work.
18. A salesperson believes in himself.
19. A salesperson believes that he can make a difference.
20. A salesperson should believe that people are basically good.
21. A salesperson should keep negative words out of his thinking.

22. A salesperson should be enthusiastic.
23. A salesperson should love his work.
24. A salesperson should always feel he must make the sale to enhance his ego.
25. Much of sales ability is fundamental.
26. A salesperson must always have an insatiable desire for the next order.
27. A salesperson's efforts must be indefatigable.
28. A salesperson must never allow his tireless efforts to blind him to reality and upset his customers or associates.
29. A salesperson must work in an inspired manner.
30. When working on an order, a salesperson should have a mental image of the successful outcome.
31. A salesperson should maintain constant vigilance and deep dedication.

5

Empathy

As mentioned previously, the Mayer & Greenburg *Harvard Business Review* article (1964) identifies the two fundamental traits of a good salesperson as ego-drive, or an insatiable desire to obtain orders, and empathy. Chapter 4 reviews the importance of the desire to obtain orders. The second trait, empathy, is also vital to a successful salesperson. Empathy can be defined as the imaginative projection of one's own consciousness into another being. In simpler terms, it is being able to slip inside someone else's skin and see, feel, hear, and examine things and events as he does. It comes from the Greek word for "feeling pain with."

Actually, these two fundamental traits go hand in hand, with one reinforcing the other. In a discussion of these two factors, however, they should be treated separately. Indeed, they are separate characteristics, since a salesperson can have a great deal of empathy and various levels of insatiable desire to obtain orders. Also, someone with poor empathy can also have a high level of desire to obtain orders. Yet, as determinants of sales ability, these two traits act on and, in fact, reinforce each other.

The salesperson with a strong desire to obtain orders has the maximum motivation to fully utilize whatever level of empathy he possesses. Hungering for the sale, he is not likely to allow his empathy to spill over and become sympathy. His desire for the sale is not likely to allow him to side with the customer. Instead, it spurs him on to fully use his understanding of the customer to make the sale.

Surprisingly, the person with little or no desire to obtain an order is hardly likely to use his empathy in a persuasive manner. He understands people and may know perfectly well what things he might say to close the sale effectively, but his understanding is apt to become sympathy. If this person does not need the conquest, his very knowledge and understanding of the real needs of the potential customer may tell him that the customer should in fact not buy from him. Since he does not desperately desire the sale, he may not persuade the customer to buy. Thus, there is a dynamic relationship between empathy and the insatiable desire to obtain the order. It takes a combination of the two, each working to reinforce the other, to make the successful salesperson.

Empathy, the important central ability to feel as the other person does in order to be able to sell him a product or service, must be possessed in a large amount if one wants to be an outstanding salesperson. Having empathy, as mentioned before, does not necessarily mean being sympathetic. A salesperson can know what the customer feels without agreeing with that feeling. A salesperson, however, cannot sell well without the invaluable and irreplaceable ability to get a powerful feedback from his customer through empathy.

A parallel can be drawn in this connection between the old antiaircraft weapons and the new heat-seeking missiles. With the old type, the gunner aimed at an enemy aircraft, corrected the best he could for windage and driftage, and then fired. If the projectile missed by just a few inches because of a slight error in calculation or because the enemy plane took evasive action, the miss might just as well have been by hundreds of yards for all the good it did. This is like a salesperson with poor empathy. He aims at the target as best he can and proceeds with his sales pitch, but if his target, the customer, fails to perform as assumed and predicted, the sale is missed.

On the other hand, the new heat-seeking missiles, if they are anywhere near the target, become attracted to the heat of the targeted plane's engine, and regardless of the evasive action taken, they finally home in and hit their mark. This is like a salesperson with good empathy. He senses the reactions of his customer and is able to adjust to these reactions. He is not bound by a prepared sales pitch, but he functions in terms of the real interaction between himself and the customer. Sensing what the customer is feeling, he is able to change tactics, double back on his track, and make whatever modifications are necessary to home in on the target and close the sale.

To be able to hit its mark, the heat-seeking missile relies on feedback from its target. A successful salesperson uses empathy and relies on feedback from his target—the customer. To obtain good feedback and to be able to see, hear, and feel things as the customer does will require knowledge on the part of the salesperson. The salesperson must know his customer, as well as his customer's background, needs, goals, objectives, and the demands of his job. The best way to learn all of this is to get the customer to talk about himself and his job. As related in a separate chapter, when an individual is talking, regardless of the subject, he is to some degree talking about himself.

A successful salesperson uses empathy and relies on feedback from his target—the customer.

An empathetic salesperson is an individual with keen sensibilities. He reacts well, and his common sense is enormous. When a salesperson develops empathy beyond the ordinary, he has acquired perhaps the choicest of all personality traits. Empathy is the basis of popularity. Without empathy, a salesperson cannot have discernment and compassion.

Experts say empathy tends to be strongest among those individuals who like people and want to be liked by them. However, a person cannot like others or want to be liked by them unless he respects and likes himself.

Can empathy be developed? Most experts think it can. Courtesy is a reflection of and a developer of empathy. A good salesperson practices courtesy to develop empathy. There are a few courteous suggestions a salesperson can follow if he is interested in becoming a more empathetic person:

1. Keep appointments promptly
2. Dress neatly
3. Use correct grammar
4. Use good posture
5. Have pleasant facial expressions
6. Listen well
7. Avoid nervous mannerisms
8. Avoid being loud
9. Address prospects in a friendly, but not overly familiar, way
10. Show deference or be thoughtful of the ego and comfort of others
11. Avoid rudely disputing a person's word
12. Be polite to secretaries and receptionists
13. Never smoke in a customer's office
14. Avoid drinking on the job
15. Avoid tasteless stories
16. Be a good conversationalist
17. Be at home in polite society
18. Watch his table manners
19. Have good telephone manners
20. Control his temper
21. Acknowledge communications promptly
22. Keep promises
23. Say *thank you*
24. Say *good-bye* when departing a customer's presence; do not leave abruptly

By following these suggestions, a salesperson can create a favorable impression on his prospect. This will encourage the prospect to feel better toward the salesperson and to be more willing to open up and to talk about himself. The more the prospect talks, the more the salesperson will learn about him, his problems, his likes, his dislikes, and his needs. As a result, the salesperson will be able to more accurately empathize with the prospect and be able to see, feel, hear, and evaluate things and events as the prospect does.

Too many salespeople are busy talking to their customers about their own agenda, their own products, and their own objectives. They fail to slow down and try to determine what the customer is thinking about and to discover his feelings and his needs.

Sometimes a salesperson makes a statement about his products, and then he makes another and another, without stopping to think, ask questions, and give the customer a chance to respond. Soon the customer just sits back and pretends to listen but does not really hear, because he long ago tuned out the salesperson's monologue. By allowing the salesperson to ramble on, the customer misleads him into thinking he agrees with and subscribes to everything the salesperson has said. After making a comment or two about his company or his products, the salesperson should pause and give the customer time to say something. If the customer does not respond, the salesperson should ask him if what he considers to be product advantages are indeed advantages to the customer on this project or order. Then he should listen to what the customer has to say.

Central then to a salesperson's success is the ability to project himself across the customer's desk, to sit in his chair, to walk in his shoes, and to observe the situation as his customer will. A salesperson who can do this will obtain an enormous amount of feedback, which is necessary if he is to obtain orders. In order to accomplish this, the salesperson should not sit in his chair and continue to think as a salesperson with his own firm. He must see things from the customer's viewpoint, not his own. He must imagine himself in the decision maker's shoes and ask himself questions that the decision maker must consider:

- How can I be certain I am buying the safest, most reliable products and, hence, be least likely to make a mistake?
- What benefits and features should I look for in the products about to be purchased?
- What should I expect from the successful vendor?
- What do my superiors and colleagues expect?

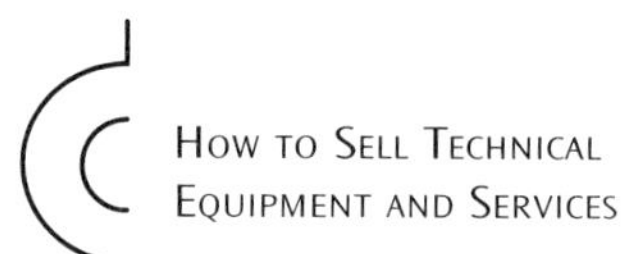

- What do I like and dislike about the various products being quoted to me?
- What do I like and dislike about the various vendors bidding this job?
- What experiences have I had with the various vendors and their products?

A salesperson with empathy will always be sensitive to the customer's reactions and will be able to adjust his efforts to accommodate these requirements. He will be less rigid and more receptive to the customer's wishes and desires. Factoring this feedback into his judgment and actions, he will be constantly readjusting his aim to make certain he is exactly tracking an ever-moving target. While this attribute is important at all stages of selling, it is mandatory as a salesperson works a specific job and follows it through the closing stages. The situation is usually changing daily, and sometimes hourly.

It is essential that a salesperson not lose sight of the objective—closing the order. With good feedback, he should lock in and make the necessary accommodations and take the required actions to obtain the order. He must listen very attentively and make sure he hears what the customer is saying at each stage. He must keep asking himself, "What would I do and expect if I were in his shoes, had his background and objectives, and faced his problems and pressures?"

A salesperson must be sure to listen to what the customer is saying, especially when he expresses reservations or misgivings about the offer. The salesperson must not assume he understands what the customer is saying. He should ask clarifying questions to make absolutely certain. The salesperson should try to evaluate how strongly the customer feels about the misgiving and if it is decisive. He must try to listen to what is not being said and must not treat the customer's comments lightly.

One way the salesperson can do this is to rephrase his questions to the customer and listen closely to the responses to make sure he understands the answers he is receiving. Once the objections are understood, the salesperson can respond to them by explaining again how and why his products will do the best job. He should repeat and accentuate its strong points and advantages. If additional concessions are still required, the salesperson should do his best to grant them.

For example, perhaps a salesperson included standard materials in his quotation. During later discussions, the customer mentions that his experts feel they should consider switching to special stainless steel. The salesperson should immediately determine if the customer is serious, and if so, must change his quote to reflect what the customer wants. In that manner he is accurately tracking a moving target.

A salesperson cannot allow his feeling of empathy to become sympathy. If he does, it can become counterproductive, and he will be known as a nice guy but will rarely obtain many orders.

In addition to empathy, the salesman must possess sufficient desire to obtain the order so that he can close the sale and enhance his image with himself, his family, and his peers. As mentioned earlier, one of the best ways to develop empathy is for a salesperson to ask questions and intently listen to the replies given by the customer. The more the salesperson learns about the customer, his problems, and his way of thinking, the easier it will be for the salesperson to empathize with the customer. A salesperson must remember that he cannot continue to think as a products salesperson in his own environment. Instead, the salesperson must try insofar as possible to mentally put himself into the customer's environment and consider his problems, his desires, and his background.

Historical Example

There is a good historical example of why a salesperson will fail if he sits at his customer's desk and continues to think as himself in his own surroundings. The German High Command committed this blunder when they tried to anticipate where the Allies would cross the English Channel in 1944. They placed themselves in the Allies' shoes but continued to think as Germans, theorizing that the landing would occur at an existing port, where the channel was narrow, and would be led by General Patton. They were wrong on all three points. The Allies landed in Normandy, not Calais. They went ashore where there was no port (they brought the port facilities with them), and General Patton was not the leader. In anticipating the situation, the Germans continued to think as Germans, not Allies. This is one of the biggest mistakes a salesperson can make—he continues to think as the seller, not the buyer.

A salesperson must work hard to be empathetic. It will pay big rewards, especially if coupled with an insatiable desire to obtain orders.

Summary

1. The two fundamental traits of a good salesperson are empathy and an insatiable desire to obtain orders.
2. Empathy is defined as the ability to mentally view things from another's vantage point.
3. These two fundamentals go hand in hand, and one reinforces the other.
4. The salesperson with a strong desire to obtain orders has the maximum motivation to utilize whatever level of empathy he possesses.
5. There is a dynamic relationship between empathy and an insatiable desire to obtain an order. It takes a combination of the two, each working to reinforce the other, to make an outstanding salesperson.
6. A parallel can be drawn between the old antiaircraft weapons that just fired and the heat-seeking missiles that are attracted to the heat from the targeted plane's engines and home in for the hit.
7. The heat-seeking missile relies on feedback from its target. An outstanding salesperson with empathy also will rely on feedback from his target, the buyer.
8. To obtain good feedback requires a salesperson to gain extensive knowledge of the customer.
9. The salesperson can best accomplish this by encouraging the customer to talk about himself.
10. When a salesperson develops empathy beyond an ordinary level, he has acquired perhaps the choicest of all personality traits.
11. Experts say empathy tends to be strongest among individuals who like people and want to be liked by them. A person cannot like others or want to be liked by them unless he respects and likes himself.
12. Empathy can be developed.
13. Courtesy is a reflection of and a developer of empathy.
14. When pushing his products and making his sales pitch, a salesperson should pause often and give the buyer a chance to respond or ask questions.

15. An outstanding salesperson will be able to project himself across the customer's desk and to observe the situation as his customer would.
16. A salesperson must then see things from the customer's viewpoint, not his own. From his customer's vantage point, the salesperson should ask himself detailed questions about the situation as seen through the customer's eyes.
17. Doing this will provide enormous feedback to the salesperson.
18. Factoring this feedback into his judgment, the salesperson will be constantly readjusting his aim to make certain he is accurately tracking an ever-moving target.
19. The salesperson must listen carefully at this stage to make sure he hears what the customer is saying so he can respond properly. He should listen and try to determine what is not being said but is on the customer's mind.
20. The salesperson should reflect into his own thinking, insofar as possible, the customer's environment, problems, desires, and background.
21. The salesperson should be alert to changing his offer to reflect the customer's desires.
22. The salesperson must work hard at being empathetic. Coupled with an insatiable desire to obtain orders, it will pay big rewards.

6

Avoid High-pressure Tactics

It is important for a successful salesperson to have empathy and an insatiable desire to obtain orders, and to be an unquestioned expert on his products and his competitors' products. Combined with knowledge of his customers, these will enable the salesperson to take a giant step toward becoming successful. However, these abilities are not sufficient by themselves. As far as possible, a salesperson must do the selling indirectly, without the customer feeling pressure of any kind. This is not easy to do, because a salesperson must have a strong desire to obtain the order, but this must be a controlled desire. He must think constantly about how to achieve his objective while always avoiding pressuring the customer. This requires a lot of thought and effort.

Pressure-type selling is prevalent and perhaps even effective in some areas of consumer selling, such as life insurance and other situations dealing directly with separate and unrelated individuals. This involves situations in which the salesperson calls on the potential purchaser just once or maybe twice and never again encounters him. In these instances the salesperson must make the sale, or the opportunity is forever lost. If by using high-pressure tactics the salesperson upsets the potential buyer, there is no long-lasting damage. They probably will never meet again, and the chances of one customer talking to another about high-pressure tactics is remote. The salesperson in this situation has an almost unlimited number of potential disassociated prospects to contact. He may figure that he can afford to upset some of them.

However, the situation involving the sales of industrial goods to a group of somewhat related customers and buyers is completely different for the following reasons:

1. Salespeople in this area sell to a limited number of people.
2. These prospects buy repetitively, so if a salesperson does not succeed in obtaining the current order, he will have many later opportunities.
3. These customers represent a relatively small community of people. The buyers and customers talk to each other inside their own companies as well as at meetings and in trade associations. They often exchange information and opinions about the various salespeople they encounter. Word of high-pressure tactics will spread fast, and the salesperson's selling task will become much more difficult.

The pressure a salesperson may place on his customer can assume any of several forms:

1. A salesperson may contend that he deserves the impending order because of past favors or deeds, or because he lost the last order. A salesperson should never say this or even hint at any of it to his customers. If the customer feels an obligation, he will realize this on his own, but he will not want to be reminded by the salesperson.
2. A salesperson may attempt to scare the customer into buying by suggesting that all other products or solutions will fail or give poor service.

3. A salesperson may maneuver the customer into a corner so that he has no face-saving way out except to buy from that salesperson.
4. A salesperson may relate to the customer how badly he or his firm needs the order.
5. A salesperson may threaten to go over the customer's head to higher authority.
6. A salesperson may stay too long in the customer's office.
7. A salesperson may make other threats of any kind, such as suggesting, as if from a position of command, that he may not bid next time if not given this order.
8. A salesperson may mention reciprocity. This tactic nearly always backfires. The customer may investigate and discover that the salesperson's firm already receives more than its share of business based on the amount the salesperson's company purchases from them.
9. A salesperson may threaten to not ship custom-made or critical parts unless certain terms are agreed to.

Most professional people, as well as virtually all those concerned with buying, resent even the slightest bit of pressure. Many decision makers place this first if asked to list what a salesperson does that offends them. While mild pressure is sometimes necessary to obtain the order, it must be very gentle and unobtrusive. A salesperson must, therefore, be able to influence the buyer in a subtle manner so that he is not aware of any pressure. Here are some of the ways a salesperson may accomplish this:

Most professional people, as well as virtually all those concerned with buying, resent even the slightest bit of pressure.

1. The salesperson can practice empathy and the Golden Rule. He should put himself in the customer's shoes and treat the customer as he would like to be treated under the same circumstances.
2. The salesperson can establish by his attitude and performance that the customer's orders are better off in his hands and that he will take better care of his orders than anyone else in the business.

3. The salesperson can identify, where possible, unique superior technical features of his products that are beneficial to the customer's company and that no competitor can match.
4. The salesperson can ask for the order. Some customers need a slight nudge during the early stages of reaching a decision on what to buy. One of the best ways a salesperson can gently push things along is to ask for the order, especially if he thinks things are in good shape. If the customer cannot or does not agree to the order yet, the question itself will almost always flush out product objections, shortcomings, or problems not otherwise known to the salesperson. It can also reveal that the customer is really not quite ready to buy.
5. A salesperson can demonstrate his expert product knowledge and help the customer. He can show that he is helping the customer get the best deal for his organization.
6. A salesperson can make sure all orders placed with his firm are engineered, manufactured, and shipped as promised and on schedule.
7. A salesperson can make certain that the products the customer buys from him perform extremely well and as represented. If minor trouble does occur, the salesperson's company should be responsive and sort it out without delay.
8. A salesperson always should negotiate in good faith and reach fair and equitable settlements on all warranty claims. He must not give up until the customer is satisfied.
9. A salesperson should keep the customer appraised of new trends and new developments in the industry.
10. The salesperson must respect all of the customer's company rules, especially with regard to calling on and entertaining the company's employees.
11. The salesperson should respond on time to all inquiries and requests for quotations.
12. The salesperson must make himself available without delay when the customer needs help. He must always stay involved himself and not delegate this to someone else.

13. The salesperson always should work through the proper channels and never go around people.
14. The salesperson should not play games.
15. The salesperson must always keep his promises.
16. It is important that a salesperson make an appointment before going to see the customer. When he enters the customer's office, he should promptly get down to business and always have something to say and something to show the customer, such as product photographs or drawings.
17. A salesperson must respect the customer's time schedule and not overstay his welcome on sales calls.
18. A salesperson must be sincere and avoid making rash statements or trying to bluff. If the salesperson does not know the correct answer to a question, he should admit it and then get the answer as soon as possible.
19. A salesperson should not change his attitude or posture or allow his factory people to change theirs after they have been awarded the order. He should be certain that extras are priced reasonably and should be responsive and sympathetic when order changes are requested.
20. A salesperson should never tell stories or say anything to others, either inside or outside the customer's organization, that make the customer look bad.
21. The salesperson should say only good things about his customers, ignoring their faults and shortcomings.
22. The salesperson must give the buyer the benefit of his convictions but should keep his doubts to himself. The customer has enough doubts of his own.

The first three are crucial. If a salesperson applies these three, as well as the others, consistently and over a long period of time, there will be no need to apply pressure to obtain business. It will come his way. He may not get an order from every potential customer immediately. However, if the salesperson has commercially and technically competitive products, he will eventually sell his share by following these guidelines.

Sales Examples

Example 1

A senior executive with a major company told me that the practice that most quickly offended him was to have a salesperson come into his office just after losing an order and say, "You owe me the next one." This executive went on to relate that his company did not owe any salesperson or any company anything, and that this habit caused these salespeople to lose the next orders also. This is a crude way of applying pressure.

Example 2

Another customer related that one salesperson, upon learning that he had just lost an order, exclaimed that he would be terminated by his company for losing this order. Until then, he had received virtually all of the orders this firm placed for products in this category. The customer continued by saying that the salesperson, in attempting to exert pressure, was destroying his relationship with his customer.

Example 3

During my selling career, I observed that one particular vendor exerted pressure on the buyers and other decision makers by going over their heads on virtually every project or big order. This sales technique was related to me so many times by so many people over so many years that it actually appeared to be an established corporate policy of this manufacturer. The supplier's salespeople eventually antagonized virtually every customer, and the supplier had a very poor image in the marketplace, even though it was a large business and built fairly good products. These high-pressure tactics cost them a lot of orders, and they suffered unusually high back charges on warranty problems.

Example 4

A salesperson who had under priced a contract told the customer that unless he obtained extra money, he would lose his job. This is another unfair high-pressure tactic that will severely damage a salesperson's reputation with his customers and will rarely be successful.

Example 5

I can also recall a situation in which others in my own firm threatened in writing to hold up shipment on critically needed products unless certain extra charges were agreed to. Up until that time, we had received more than 80% of this customer's business. Following this incident, we did not receive another order from this firm during the next 15 years.

Summary

A salesperson should demonstrate to the customer by his actions, and with complete product information and competitive pricing, that the customer will benefit most from buying from him. If he does this, he will not then need to use pressure. What this amounts to is that the salesperson must sell himself as a dependable, reliable person of unquestioned integrity. He must demonstrate that he will follow through to make absolutely certain the customer is completely satisfied with the machinery or products long after the sale.

7

Send Out the Right Signals

"If you send the right signals out, you will get the right signals back." These words were forever etched in my memory in December 1985 when I received a call from an overseas customer I had dealt with for several years. This gentleman called upon learning from our local office that I would be retiring at the end of the year. He exclaimed that he did not realize that I was leaving and, instead, thought I would be around for another 10 years. I expressed my appreciation for his compliment and went on to say how lucky I felt I was in choosing my profession and my company. I not only had superior colleagues and bosses to work with, but also fine, outstanding customers with which it had been a privilege to associate during my 33 years in sales. I had been treated superbly. His reply was, "If you send the right signals out, you get the right signals back."

These words did not come from another salesperson or from someone in public relations. Instead, they came from a brilliant German engineer who spent his entire career with his company in engineering.

Consciously and subconsciously, I was always aware of the importance of presenting a good image to people, especially customers, but I had never thought of this in these exact words. This demonstrates that customers are astute and very aware of the image projected by salespeople.

The more I thought about this, the more it occurred to me that some salespeople, by their proper conduct, reaction, and demeanor, send the right signals out. Others do not send the right messages out, or worse, send mixed signals. A salesperson can send out the right signals by being responsive to the customer's needs and requirements, by speaking softly, never stridently, and by expressing sympathy to hardships when things go wrong. This type of salesperson will get the right signals back.

How else does a salesperson send out the right signals? Here are a few suggestions:

1. A salesperson should never talk down to customers.
2. It is important that a salesperson practice humility and avoid appearing arrogant or cocky, regardless of how successful he is or how superior his products are.
3. A salesperson should always exhibit an outward manifestation of a sympathetic regard for the feelings of others. He should practice humility and not lose it after he becomes successful.
4. A salesperson should be empathetic and practice the Golden Rule.
5. A salesperson must exhibit integrity at all times.
6. At the very first meeting, a salesperson should show a genuine interest in others, asking them questions and getting them to talk about themselves.
7. A salesperson must strive to be fair in all his dealings. He should not try to take advantage of others and make one-sided settlements in disputes.
8. A salesperson must demonstrate a genuine willingness to help, not a reticent attitude.

9. A salesperson must always keep the customer's best interests in mind.

10. When a customer relates troubles to a salesperson or otherwise gives him information, the salesperson should indicate interest. He can let the customer know he is listening by asking a question or two before changing the subject or before relating his own similar experience. Everyone likes to be heard sympathetically. A salesperson should keep in mind that if something has gone wrong at home with the customer's family, it will be more important to him that day than business events under discussion.

Everyone likes to be heard sympathetically.

11. A salesperson should wear the same face all the time.

12. A salesperson should not play games.

13. It is important that a salesperson be consistent. He should not tell one version of an incident to one person and a different version to someone else. Also, when he repeats or relates an event, he should not distort, exaggerate, or embellish, but explain things accurately.

14. When confirming details of a meeting or an agreement, the salesperson should never take liberties and include something that was not specifically discussed. He should not even slightly change what was actually agreed to.

16. A salesperson should make the other person feel important but do it sincerely.

17. A salesperson should talk in terms of the other person's interests.

18. A salesperson should become genuinely interested in other people and their welfare.

19. A salesperson should smile.

20. A salesperson should remember that a person's name is to him the sweetest and most important sound in the English language.

21. A salesperson should be a good listener and should encourage other people to talk about themselves.

22. A salesperson should be a giver and not just a taker, and he should convey to his customer that he hopes to benefit him. A salesperson is not someone who only takes and never gives.
23. A salesperson should be empathetic. He should place himself in the customer's shoes and treat him like he would like to be treated.
24. A salesperson should always display a warm disposition.
25. A salesperson should be solidly sold on his company and should never degrade it.
26. A salesperson should have a strong conviction of the importance and value of the product he sells.
27. A salesperson should never relate his troubles to others. The customer likely has enough troubles of his own and may not be interested in hearing about the salesperson's problems. Besides, people do not react favorably to gloom peddlers. They prefer to be around and respond favorably to upbeat, optimistic people.
28. A salesperson should answer sympathetically, rather than in a short-tempered fashion, when customers do not make themselves clear.
29. A salesperson should avoid cute remarks and sharp comments.
30. Attempts at humor may backfire and offend someone.
31. A salesperson should avoid giving short or abrupt answers.
32. A salesperson should praise the customer genuinely in a sincere manner and recognize the customer's accomplishments, including his ability, his character, and his reputation.
33. A salesperson should have the self-discipline to submerge personal likes and dislikes.
34. A salesperson should have the fortitude to rise above discouragement.
35. A salesperson must have a sincere appreciation of the customer's problems.
36. A salesperson always should demonstrate a commitment to excellence. Customers will sense this immediately in a salesperson and will react favorably.

A salesperson must learn to send these right signals out from the beginning, from the first meeting or first contact with the customer, and must send them out continuously. By doing so, he will make a good initial impression. These signals must be absolutely sincere. They cannot be a put-on, because customers and colleagues will see through a false front immediately.

If a salesperson has vastly superior products and by far the lowest price, then these things admittedly may not matter as much. Unfortunately, very few salespeople and firms find themselves in such an enviable position. Even if they do, they will not be there very long if they have the wrong attitude.

In other chapters, I relate how I sorted out difficult delivery and product problems in first-time meetings with customers. In one case, a problem was made infinitely worse by an earlier bad-faith approach from my colleagues and their refusal to listen to the customer and take the problem seriously. When thoroughly analyzed and sincerely approached, the solution was obvious, simple, and inexpensive.

The overall aim of a successful salesperson is to develop good relations with all of his customers. This should be done not only to receive orders when the decisions are close, but also to enable him to sort out all product problems on an equitable basis.

It appears to me that outstanding salespeople always obtain the orders that are close. Other salespeople never seem to win unless they have an overwhelming advantage.

During my career I observed some salespeople who could always reach fair warranty settlements, even in difficult situations. Other salespeople always had problems reaching reasonable agreements, even when the responsibility was clearly the customer's. It all came down to the relationship between the salesperson and the customer. As the Japanese believe, whatever the problem is, the solution will be found based on the relationship with that person.

The bond of trust between a salesperson and his customers is built up hourly, daily, and yearly, over a long period of time. This bond is tenuous and can very easily and very quickly be severely damaged or destroyed. A salesperson who is loose with the truth, plays games, or demonstrates devious or deceitful behavior can place the customer on guard. It may cause the customer to be forever skeptical and hesitant afterwards to accept the salesperson's word at face value. The customer will then be looking for hidden meanings in what the salesperson says or does. The customers will be placed in a position of trying to determine what the salesperson left unsaid, what he really meant, or in what manner he was being less than forthright. This is a dangerous and losing position for the salesperson.

Several years ago a large sales organization did a study to try to determine the outstanding characteristic of its top performers. The results were astonishing and showed that among the one-quarter of the salespeople who brought in three-quarters of the business, no significant differences could be identified. The high performers were not better looking, better dressed, better educated, smarter, older, or younger than their counterparts. However, they did all have one overriding characteristic—customers repeatedly rated them as nice people. A nice person sends the right signals out and gets the right signals back.

Of course, a salesperson must do more than just be nice to sell technical products. He should bear in mind, however, that quite often the products from various vendors are very close to being equal. The service and product support offered by different companies may be evaluated as a stand off. In these cases, quite often the decision is actually based on which salesperson the customer likes the best and wants to give the order to.

Sales Examples

Example 1

On one occasion we received one of the largest orders in my company's history. We were not the low bidder initially, but we ended up the low bidder because the customer wanted to buy from us. Our salesperson and the others who worked the job sent the right signals out and received the order.

Many firms have lost orders in situations in which they had similar or even superior products technically and a competitive price initially. Somehow, however, they eventually lost the order because the customer just wanted to buy from someone else. In those situations the decisions were very close, but this is usually the case.

Example 2

Early in my career as I was working a job, we had reached the point just prior to the organization making its final decision. One of the most influential members of the customer's buying team said that on this project, the products were pretty much equal, the delivery was comparable, and the price was essentially the same. The decision, he said, boiled down to which salesperson they liked the best.

Buyers need assurance at the outset that the two parties can work well together during the periods in which the purchases get transformed into deliveries.

People buy expectations, not things. They buy expectations of benefits promised by the vendor. The better the impression they have of the salesperson, the more likely they are to rely on his promised benefits and to buy from him.

A salesperson's most precious asset is his relationship with his customers. What matters to customers is what they think of the salesperson and what impression he makes on them. Their impressions and perceptions are created by the signals they receive and by what the salesperson says and does throughout the entire sales relationship.

To sell successfully to customers over a long period of time, a salesperson must send out the right signals. If he sends the right signals out, he will convey the correct impressions from the beginning and will get the right signals back in the form of lots of orders.

What I have related so far pertains to a salesperson and his relations with his customers. Much of it also applies to his interactions and dealings with his colleagues and other people inside the company.

It always grieves me to observe people working together who do not get along. These people allow petty grievances to sap their strength and diminish the time and energy left to do their primary job of selling to their customers. I was often called in to adjudicate and settle extremely petty disputes—disputes that really never should have arisen.

A salesperson cannot wear his feelings on his sleeve. He must not be on the alert for someone else's misstep. If a copy of a letter, a memo, fax, or e-mail is directed to someone else when it should have come to the salesperson, he should not get upset. He should assume it was an honest mistake or a genuine oversight and should practice forgiveness.

Also, if a salesperson is walking by a group of colleagues and overhears his name mentioned, he should never assume anything negative. Instead, he should assume they were only saying how great he is, how smart he is, or how good-looking he is.

A salesperson's highest priority is to sell to his customers and beat his competition. A good salesperson should never hamstring or dilute his sales efforts by engaging in petty grievances inside his own company with his colleagues. Remember also that salespeople who treat one another well serve customers better and, therefore, sell more.

Amazing as it may seem, most people fail to be outstanding not because they do not perform their jobs well. They fail because of their inability to get along well with people. They send out the wrong signals.

Example 3

A few months ago, I was playing golf with a retired senior executive from a major oil company. While waiting between holes, I asked him a few questions about his career. He told me that during his last few years, he spent several hours each week on a committee whose only job was to evaluate the outstanding performers. They then would recommend which among this select group would be promoted and move up to even bigger and better jobs and to eventually run the company. He went on to say that invariably those not selected for promotion failed because of shortcomings in getting along with people. He said all were competent technically and all knew and did their jobs well. However, their failure to move still higher in the organization was due almost entirely to their inability to get along well with their colleagues, superiors, and subordinates. They failed in the *people* category.

The evidence is overwhelming that getting along with people is decisive to success. Salespeople should devote more time in this vital area and work harder to send out the right signals, both to the customers and to their colleagues. The rewards will be outstanding.

Summary

1. A salesperson must send the right signals out to his customers and associates starting with his initial encounters or dealings with them.
2. These signals must be sincere.
3. Customers as well as associates will quickly see through a false front.
4. Having good relations with customers will enable a salesperson not only to obtain more orders that are close, but also to more easily settle disputes or misunderstandings.
5. The bonds of trust are built up slowly but can be broken or destroyed quickly.
6. Salespeople who send out the right signals obtain a greater share of orders.
7. Very often when buying decisions are close, customers buy from the salesperson they have the best impression of and like the best.
8. Customers buy expectations, not things. The better impression buyers have of a salesperson, the more likely they are to believe his promises of these expectations.
9. A salesperson's most precious business asset is his good relations with his customers.
10. A salesperson must have good relations with his customers if he is to sell successfully over a long period of time.
11. A salesperson should not wear his feelings on his sleeve and should practice forgiveness.
12. A salesperson must not engage in petty grievances.
13. Employees in general fail to advance in their careers not because they are not technically competent, but because of their inability to get along with people. They fail to send the right signals out.
14. A salesperson who sends the right signals out will get the right signals back in the form of good relations with customers and colleagues and will receive more than his share of orders.

II

Preparing for the Sale

8

Game Plans for Large Projects

On all large projects or potential orders, a salesperson should prepare and execute a game plan to enhance his chances of success. Large jobs usually do not come up every week or even every month. In some industries only one or two huge projects present themselves each year, so that the success for the entire year hinges on the closing of very few large potential orders. For these reasons it is vital that a salesperson plan early and well in this crucial area. He should prepare his plan and review it with his superior to make certain it is thorough, attainable, and covers all aspects of the job.

As early as possible, the salesperson should identify the products he will be quoting so he can tailor the plan to the specific models he will be offering. This is usually necessary since a salesperson will be stronger in some areas than his competitors. On the other hand, the salesperson's products may be substantially weaker on some models than his competitors. He will usually need all the time available to execute his plan, so he should not delay in the preparation. Furthermore, some of his tasks will take a lot of time and effort.

A salesperson should never wait until the inquiry is out. By then it is usually too late. The customer's people will be too busy to spend much time on plant visits or other meetings. Also, by the time the inquiry is out, the competitors will have already made a lot of headway.

A salesperson should never wait until the inquiry is out. By then it is usually too late.

Here are guidelines for a salesperson to follow as he prepares his strategy:

1. The salesperson must determine which person or persons will evaluate the bids and make the decision. He should analyze these people and make a note of their likes and dislikes and should concentrate on these people individually, if possible. If the salesperson knows that one of these individuals likes a certain feature, he should do his best to accommodate that preference in the products that he bids. If one of the group favors the competition, then he knows he must do something to neutralize or overcome this. Sometimes there have been problems with the salesperson's products. If this is the case, then he must be sure to point out what design changes or corrective actions have been taken on what he will be quoting.
2. A salesperson should find out if there are any partners, and if so, to what extent they will be involved in the decision. This may require asking a lot of different people in order to obtain a complete picture. A salesperson should think carefully before approaching these other partners. He should ask for guidance from the people in charge of the project so as not to alienate the customers. The salesperson should keep in mind that many times more intelligence and feedback can be obtained from minority partners than from the primary contact.

3. A salesperson should make a list of all of his competitors. He should not assume he knows who will be bidding. He should determine this by asking the customer or others involved who will know.
4. The salesperson should tabulate the strengths and weaknesses of each competitor as specifically related to this project.
5. The salesperson should study each major competitor's strengths and weaknesses and decide how he will discreetly counter the strengths and exploit the weaknesses.
6. A salesperson should look very critically and objectively at his firm's strong points and weak points. He must decide how he will utilize his company's strengths to his best advantage on this project. More importantly, he must decide what he will do to overcome any weaknesses or shortcomings. This exercise should be thorough and objective. However, a salesperson should not rely too heavily on his company's strengths. The customer may not give the salesperson as much credit as he expects for these strengths. On the other hand, the salesperson should not become obsessed with his company's weak points. He should keep them in mind, however, so he can do everything possible to offset them or render them meaningless.

There are many factors for a salesperson to consider in arriving at his lists of pluses and minuses for his competitors as well as for his own company. He should make a list of factors he feels his customer will take into consideration while arriving at the purchase decision, such as the following:

- price
- delivery
- experience
- the salesperson's plant location
- product performance or quality
- labor relations in the salesperson's plant
- the customer's perception of the salesperson's firm
- the customer's perception of the competitors
- the financial strength of the various vendor organizations

A salesperson needs to consider these factors along with the strengths and weaknesses of his firm and those of his competitors. He should thus be able to prepare a game plan of what he will do to overcome any of his company's shortcomings. What he will do to implement his plan depends on his company's strengths and shortcomings compared to those of the competitors.

- If the salesperson thinks price will be a problem, he must make sure he selects and offers his most cost-effective product. Also, he should start early to work on his pricing people to convince them that he must quote his very best price so as to be competitive. If this customer buys strictly on price, the salesperson must make certain his pricing authorities know this.
- If delivery will be a problem, the salesperson must identify the bottleneck and/or pacing factors and then insist that his manufacturing people do something about them to enable a competitive delivery time to be quoted. The salesperson can offer to provide monthly charts and progress reports documenting that he is on schedule.
- If one of the salesperson's competitors has built more units, he cannot change that fact. What he can do is to demonstrate that although his reference list may be shorter, his company has been successful with what it has done. He should explain why his shorter list is adequate.
- If the salesperson's company has a more favorable plant location, he must be sure to point this out. On the other hand, if a competitor has the salesperson bested in this category, he should do what he can to overcome this. For example, he could offer to have all coordinating meetings at the customer's offices. If travel expense will be a problem, the salesperson could consider paying the travel expenses of the customer's people who must travel to the salesperson's facilities for meetings.
- If there has been a product problem in the past, especially with this customer, the salesperson must point out what his company has done on subsequent units to correct these shortcomings. He should provide a list of satisfied users together with individual names and telephone numbers.

- If the products have had a quality problem, the salesperson should get management to agree to do extra inspections on this order. The salesperson can provide up-to-date information on his company's current quality program and make sure the decision makers are aware of his company's quality assurance manual and guidelines.
- If the salesperson's company has a longer running union contract than his competitors, he should be sure to point this out. If the union contract with the salesperson's company will shortly expire, he should not announce this. Instead, he should become familiar with the status of the current union negotiations. Then if the question arises, the salesperson can reveal how good his company's labor relations are and that he expects no trouble signing a new contract.
- If the salesperson has a credibility problem with this customer, he should zero in on what caused it and what he has since done to correct the situation.

A salesperson must determine if formal presentations will be allowed. If they are, he must do his best to be scheduled last. Being last has the following advantages:

1. The customer's representatives will remember more of what was presented when they later meet to make a purchase decision.
2. Since the customer will have already heard other vendor pitches, he will be in better shape to evaluate the salesperson's presentation.
3. The customer will have more questions, because he will have been exposed to so much information about competitive products.
4. If others have mentioned a certain appealing feature, the customer is more likely to ask the salesperson if he can also provide it. This will reveal a particular customer interest on which the salesperson can capitalize. On the other hand, if the salesperson was the first presenter and he did not mention this feature, the customer would most likely not bring it up, and might assume his products do not have that feature.

If a salesperson gives a presentation, he must be extremely alert to the customer's reaction and respond in depth to any area of keen interest.

The salesperson should also write individual sales letters to all of the key people giving a thorough list of his product's features and benefits, explaining why they should buy his products. Even if this was covered in a formal presentation, he should confirm it in writing.

The salesperson must take care to implement his game plan and obtain regular and continuous feedback from his customer. The salesperson then can expand on any areas of keen interest or in areas where he learns that his competitor is making headway. This will also enable him to stay on top of the job and to quickly detect competitive moves. The salesperson will be able to give current and accurate reports to his superiors as the job unfolds.

A salesperson should not be afraid to repeat what he has related before. He should keep mentally going over his entire game plan as he implements it. This will help stimulate his thoughts towards discovering any additional information to cover.

As soon as the customer has had time to analyze the bids, the salesperson should ask for the order. This can flush out objections to his products before the buying decision has been made, and hopefully will give him time to do something about them.

As the salesperson executes his game plan, he should not be misled by favorable reactions he receives from the decision makers. It is very easy at this particular time for a person to hear what they want to hear. Instead, the salesperson should ask strategic questions, such as, "Will you recommend our products?" "Can we place this product on order?" "Do you have any misgivings or objections to our products or our firm?" and "Do you think we can meet our quoted delivery?"

Too often a salesperson gives presentations covering all of these items and assumes, since they voiced no objections, that the buyers are completely satisfied. A salesperson should ask questions to flush out any objections.

Summary

A salesperson's game plan is successful only if he receives the order. He should prepare a good plan and execute it well. To do this he must ask questions to uncover any objections, overcome those objections, and close the sale.

9

Handle Inquiries and Submit Quotations

How well a salesperson handles a large new inquiry can be decisive, and therefore it deserves very careful attention. There are a few suggestions a salesperson should follow. First, he should quickly pass the new inquiry on to his application group. This is especially important if he has a tight deadline to meet and if the application engineers are located in another city. The salesperson should then confirm that it has been received.

At the same time, the salesperson should take time to read and analyze thoroughly what the customer has requested. There may be an objectionable provision or a requirement that will cause the salesperson difficulty, whether technical, commercial, or even political. The difficulty might even make it impossible for the salesperson to respond quickly. If so, the salesperson should immediately contact a responsible person in the customer's or end user's organization. If the inquiry comes from an intermediary such as a contractor, then it will be prudent to visit first with the contractor's people. If the stumbling block is big or cannot be resolved with them, the salesperson must not stop there. He should point out that there is a problem, but hopefully it can be sorted out if he has the opportunity to speak directly to the ultimate customer—the end user.

The salesperson then should outline the problem to the end user. If the salesperson is unable to obtain relief, he should very carefully explain why he cannot respond. The salesperson should never send this kind of unfavorable information through a third party. He should present his problem factually and ask for guidance. The salesperson should give his end user a chance to argue with him and possibly change this decision. A face-to-face visit might permit the objection to be overcome so the salesperson's company can give a quote. If not, the salesperson's position is accurately known to his customer. The salesperson will also directly hear the customer's reasons for the unusual requirements. Usually, additional light will be shed on the problem. The salesperson often will be given a wider margin in which to quote or a sufficient modification of the requirement so that he can proceed with the quote.

All of this assumes that the salesperson does not sell to just contractors or intermediaries but that he sells and promotes his products to both end users and contractors. If a salesperson sells only to contractors or intermediaries, then he should visit with only them and forget the end user.

A salesperson should be alert to unusual opportunities in an inquiry. He should not hastily reject a provision that initially seems ominous. If the salesperson cannot accommodate a certain requirement within his organization, perhaps some reliable organization outside his company can. For example, a salesperson may be asked to quote on and to include a price for his service people to live in a foreign country for several months. The salesperson may not be able to predict the cost within his company and may be inclined to reject this provision. However, the salesperson could turn to a reliable party in that overseas country. He could hire them to calculate the costs involved so he can accommodate his customer. A salesperson who is flexible can use unusual requirements to enhance his chances if he does not give up easily. He should remember that the world is changing, and his methods of doing business may need to change also.

There is often more than one way a salesperson can satisfy a customer's product requirements. If so, the salesperson should visit with the appropriate engineers for additional input and guidance. He should determine from his customers precisely what they expect the products to do and what they are seeking.

There is often more than one way a salesperson can satisfy a customer's product requirements.

If possible, the salesperson should talk to the people who will actually operate the products. They will usually give the salesperson better insight on what is required. It will often reveal a unique requirement that he can use to his advantage and to the detriment of his competitors. Quite often the customer's requirements can be handled with one unit or multiple units. The salesperson should determine what the customer is thinking in this regard. He should satisfy the customer's initial requirements but should not hesitate to offer alternatives that will do the job either more efficiently or at a lower initial or installed cost.

If the inquiry specifies products that are out of date or less efficient, the salesperson should discreetly call this to the customer's attention. The salesperson should explain to them that he has a better way of accomplishing what they want to do. He should realize, however, that his new, up-to-date method might be rejected because of the following:

1. It might be too new and unproven.
2. It might not fit into their existing scheme, or it might duplicate existing facilities.
3. It might not allow adequate flexibility or expandability.

On the other hand, they may ask the salesperson to quote both ways. A salesperson should always point out methods or innovations that reduce initial, installed, or operating costs, because his competition certainly will.

A salesperson should carefully consider what kind of product the customer currently operates. If it is the salesperson's product, he should determine if some of the new offer might duplicate the customer's existing equipment. Perhaps he could select models to quote that could use at least some of the existing spare parts. Or the salesperson could plan so that some of the spare parts could serve both the existing machinery and the new machinery quoted. A salesperson should give this careful consideration, as it could have a big influence on the outcome.

Sometimes the inquiry specifies that the salesperson's product possess or be arranged to accommodate a new feature that the company's products do not have. Sometimes the salesperson has no experience with the new feature or arrangement. Still, he should not reject the request out of hand. He should insist that his engineering department investigate this requirement. Just because it is new does not mean it is bad and will not work. The salesperson must be innovative and receptive to change. That is how progress occurs. If this new requirement is reasonable, someone will embrace it. The salesperson should not lose an order because he refused to change.

A salesperson should not hesitate to offer a new or different way. He should be the expert and should know his business. On the other hand, the customer will make the decision, and for various reasons, he may not want the salesperson's new method. The salesperson must remain flexible. He should point out more efficient ways of doing the job without jeopardizing the order by dogmatically insisting on the latest up-to-date model or his way of doing the job.

Most application groups that put proposals together are busy, overworked, and often staffed by young, inexperienced engineers. A salesperson should find out who in his organization will handle his inquiry, particularly if it is a large job, and ascertain his method of approach and experience level. The more experienced the engineer, the less guidance he should require from the salesperson. If the salesperson does not think the engineer is capable of handling the job, he should insist upon a substitution.

It is the salesperson who must accept the ultimate responsibility, even if the order is lost because of poor application and a lousy proposal. Therefore, he should not be bashful in sorting this out to his satisfaction. Regardless of the engineer's experience level, the salesperson's input is vital. He knows, or certainly should know, his customer better than anyone else. He should never just hand over a large, detailed inquiry to his application engineering group. He should study it and visit about it with as many knowledgeable people at the customer's company as possible. He should determine where his best chances are and pass this information to the people who will prepare his proposal. He must make sure they understand what the customer wants.

The salesperson should establish contact early with the application engineer in his company and confer regularly with him as he prepares the proposal. The salesperson should respond quickly to any questions the engineer has. He should use his sales skills with the engineer to encourage him to do an excellent job on the proposal.

The salesperson should insist that a timely, attractive, complete, accurate, and competitive bid is put together. It must reflect what the customer asked for and take into account his specifications, including any changes that were made along the way. The salesperson must be sure it reflects the best efficiency and latest engineering input. It should be organized into logical sections that are clearly marked with tabs. If the customer requires a certain format, the salesperson should be sure it is followed religiously. Prices on everything requested must be included. However, if the inquiry specifies gold-plated trim, the salesperson should not hesitate to also quote a less-expensive alternative that will adequately do the job.

In addition, the salesperson should insist on the maximum use of originally printed pages in his bid. He should not allow copies of photographs, legal documents, or terms and conditions to dominate the first few pages. The salesperson must make sure the proposal is easy to read and clearly presents what the customer wants to buy. He should make sure that the customer's specifications are read by his application group and adhered to insofar as possible. Any exceptions to these specifications should be listed in the quotation in a way that is courteous, prominent, and clear, not abrupt or insulting. If a salesperson cannot adhere to certain aspects, he should explain this diplomatically and give good reasons. Most customers will respond reasonably.

The salesperson should rarely allow his people to just ignore and reject the customer's specifications and simply quote to his company's own specifications or terms and conditions. He should do this only after consultation with the customer. Customers spend a lot of time writing specifications and usually feel strongly about them. They cannot simply be rejected without good reasons.

A salesperson can include photographs or drawings of the products he is offering, together with lists of customers who use the products. He should highlight salient features and label all photographs, curves, charts, and drawings.

If the customer issues changes or additions to the initial inquiry, the salesperson should read and analyze these very closely. He should point out any big deviations in writing to the application engineer immediately. He must not treat these modifications routinely, because sometimes they include important information that cannot be ignored or overlooked.

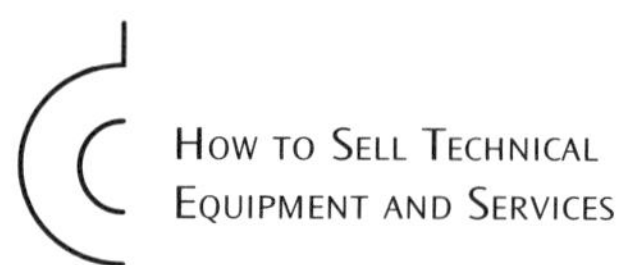

Sales Example

At one time we had received and were working on an inquiry involving several million dollars of products. A week or so after receiving the initial inquiry, the customer issued an addendum. The sales engineer who received this addendum forwarded it to the home office without reading it. The application engineer handling the inquiry failed to detect this major change in the requirements. Our sealed bid was submitted without taking into account this latest change, and we were almost disqualified. The salesperson should have read this new document and pointed out its significance when forwarding it along to the application group.

A salesperson must make certain he receives the proposal in time to read it thoroughly, make the necessary changes, and still meet the customer's deadline. If practical, he should deliver proposals on very large jobs in person. He should not take chances on being eliminated from the bidding because his bid is late. He should start early with his follow-ups and not allow the application group to be tardy. The salesperson should stay on top of this and insist on the best.

Whenever possible after a job is over, the salesperson should obtain a copy of competitors' quotations to see how they responded. This is often instructive.

Summary

How well a salesperson handles a large new inquiry can be decisive, so a salesperson should give this careful attention. He should quickly pass the new inquiry on to his application group and confirm that it has been received. At the same time, the salesperson should review the inquiry himself, identifying any problem areas and working them out with the customer. He can use these problems as opportunities and can quote more than one way on the project to offer different possibilities. The salesperson should work closely with his engineer to assure they meet the customer's needs. The salesperson will bear the ultimate responsibility for the quote, so he must make certain that it is timely, attractive, neat, accurate, complete, and competitive. The successful salesperson will use a competently and professionally prepared quote to meet the customer's needs and generate sales.

Early Meetings with Customers

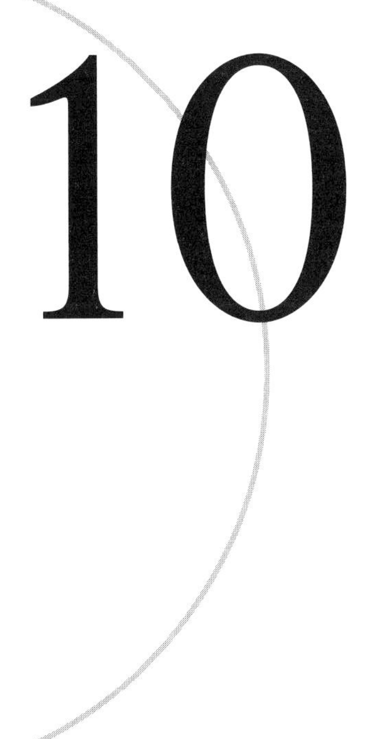

The very first impressions a salesperson makes on his customers count the most and can be decisive. Virtually every day he meets people who instantly judge him by the impression he makes. These are often snap judgments, but once made, they are difficult to change. It follows then that a salesperson absolutely must make a good first impression in his early meetings with a customer.

There is an old adage that initial impressions are lasting, and that is certainly true with customers. Early meetings provide the salesperson with excellent opportunities not only to make a good impression, but also to find out a lot about his prospect. Sometimes the chance does not present itself again.

I have known a lot of salespeople during my career who called on individuals for years and knew almost nothing about them except their names and job titles. When a salesperson knows a lot about his customer, it makes their relationship richer. It enables him to better understand the customer and his reasoning and reactions. Later, a salesperson might encounter a reprint or other information that would interest the customer because of his background or his interests. He could send it along or mention it during their next encounter.

When a salesperson knows a lot about his customer, it makes their relationship richer.

To get along with people, a salesperson must show a genuine interest in them. He should ask questions and listen to the answers. If the customer is down in the dumps, the salesperson should listen sympathetically to his problems and ask a few questions to demonstrate that he is listening. Another way he could show genuine interest in people is to ask them something about themselves. The salesperson should avoid questions of a personal nature that could be construed as prying. However, he could ask the customer such questions as the following:

1. How long have you worked for your company?
2. (If it hasn't been a long time) Where did you work before that?
3. What were your first job responsibilities with your current firm?
4. How long have you lived here?
5. Where did you live before that?
6. Were you born in this area? In which part of the country were you born?
7. Where is your wife from? Where did you meet her?
8. What college did you attend?

Any questions about college should, of course, be asked carefully. If the customer has likely attended college, this could be a good question to ask. However, the salesperson should be careful to not embarrass the customer if he did not attend college.

It also demonstrates interest if a salesperson asks how many children the customer has and their ages. If his children are grown, the salesperson can always ask where they live and what business they are in. The salesperson should not press if the customer is reluctant, and he should be careful to not overdo it. Usually people are quite happy to discuss their children and grandchildren.

These questions should not be asked in a machine-gun fashion. The salesperson should space them out so that he does not offend the customer. He should never ask questions that are too personal, especially with someone he has just met. Also, a salesperson should not slap backs or give hugs, unless perhaps it is a special occasion involving very old friends.

A salesperson's questions should always be discreet and should be tailored to the situation and the customer. He should bear in mind that people vary widely. These questions are best asked when a salesperson is alone with his customer, perhaps in his office after they have finished business discussions or while they are walking to lunch. If the customer seems ill at ease when asked a question or two, the salesperson should not persist. He can resume his questioning during their next meeting, if appropriate. On the other hand, most people are quite anxious to talk about themselves, their families, and their job experiences.

All of these same questions should not be asked of every new person a salesperson meets. If they are, word will get around that the salesperson asks everybody these questions, and their importance might be diluted. Variety can be gained by spreading them out over several meetings.

The salesperson should never write down the answers in the customer's presence. He should wait until he is out of the customer's office to make those notes. However, he should write them down when it is convenient, otherwise he will forget most of what he learned. These notes will be handy as he continues his association with the customer. It will help the salesperson to know the customer better and to do a better job of selling to him. The more a salesperson learns about his customer, the longer he will remember him. If the salesperson only knows the customer's name, there will not be much to recall. It will be harder for the salesperson to remember his customer's likes, dislikes, and idiosyncrasies.

The salesperson should never misuse the information learned during these early encounters. In other words, he should not mention that information every time he subsequently sees the individual, unless it is appropriate and comes up naturally in the conversation. Also, the salesperson should not broadcast everything he learns. He must be discreet. He should file the information away and use it sparingly, usually just as a reminder of how to better relate to, sell to, and respond to that individual.

Perhaps the customer has been involved in the salesperson's industry for quite some time. In this case, the salesperson should ask if he has installed or operated any of the salesperson's products, or has otherwise been associated with his company or products. If the customer answers affirmatively, the salesperson should find out if the product worked properly. He should also ask if the customer had any problems or if he received good service or reliable spare parts deliveries. It is surprising what a salesperson can learn if he asks questions along this line. This is a good way to find out about any latent complaints or resentments the customer has toward the salesperson's firm or products. The customer may tell the salesperson that he purchased some of his products five years before, and that he had trouble with short service life, bad deliveries, or high prices.

With these items in mind, the salesperson can demonstrate how his company has corrected these shortcomings. He can explain that if the customer buys his products or spare parts now, he would not have to contend with these problems. Later during negotiations and when the customer is placing orders, the salesperson can stress the fact that he will take specific steps to avoid a repetition of the customer's early experiences. The salesperson does not have to specifically mention the problems. The customer will understand what he is saying.

On the other hand, the salesperson may find that his client has always had good experiences with his products and, therefore, is a good friend already and is not antagonistic. Many times, however, the salesperson will find that the customer has had no experience with any of the salesperson's products. By asking these questions, the salesperson may find that he has always used and admired the competitor's products. In this case, the salesperson knows that he has a real selling job on his hands when a new project comes up. Alternately, by asking the right questions, the salesperson may learn that the customer has had bad experiences with his competitor's products.

The replies to these queries will give the salesperson valuable insight on how to best deal with this person. He will know more about the customer's personal and professional interests. This will give the salesperson clues as to minor gifts or presents that he could consider sending the customer. For example, if the salesperson learns that the customer has a certain technical interest, he could send him published articles or a book on the subject.

One unusual question to ask a senior person is, "What achievement in your career gave you the greatest satisfaction?" It is astonishing what a customer will tell a salesperson in response to this question. Many times he has never been asked that question before, and the response can be very interesting. It should not be a question that the salesperson asks every senior person he meets in the customer's company, as it would lose its originality and importance. Because people vary, the salesperson should judge when this is an appropriate question.

A few years ago, I asked a senior executive with a major U.S. engineering company what achievement or what activity in his career gave him the most satisfaction. He replied that shortly after the end of the Korean War, his company had a contract to assist in the rehabilitation of the South Korean industry. He headed the project, and every Monday morning met for several hours with the president of South Korea. My friend then talked for several minutes about some of the meetings that he obviously had enjoyed very much. I could tell that he enjoyed talking about this experience and had not had a chance to do so in a very long time.

The point is that people like to talk, and if a salesperson gives them the chance, they will enjoy doing so, and they will feel good about being with him. The salesperson will have created a favorable impression by sending out the right signals.

It is important, however, that a salesperson never ask overly familiar questions. This is especially easy to do in the early stages of a business relationship. Sometimes a person who knows the prospect very well will introduce the salesperson or refer the salesperson to the customer. The salesperson should be careful not to assume this warm and special relationship can immediately be transferred to him. It is not that easy. All too often a salesperson will place too much emphasis on this introduction. He should never attempt to trade on these long-standing relationships or take anything for granted. He must be prepared to earn his own spurs, build his own reputation, and establish his own rapport with this prospect. This will take time and effort on the salesperson's part.

If someone arranges an appointment for the salesperson, he must make sure to show up on time and otherwise make a good impression. He should remember to call and finalize the arrangements. The salesperson should also report the results of this meeting back to the person who arranged the introduction or the appointment.

I can think of several times when, upon request, I communicated with people I knew quite well to alert them that a colleague would be in touch for an appointment on a certain day. Not only did the colleague not get in touch with my friends, but also he did not bother to let me know this. Months later I would incidentally learn the colleague had run out of time and was unable to make contact. At the very least, he should have called and apologized to my friends. He also should have told me that he was unable to keep the appointment. Needless to say, incidents like these made me less anxious to try to set up other meetings for this individual.

If someone arranges a meeting or an introduction for a salesperson, he must make absolutely certain that he follows through. Otherwise, the initial impression this prospect receives of him will be unfavorable. If he does eventually meet the customer, he will start out at a distinct disadvantage because of his earlier failure to follow through.

During all these initial meetings, the salesperson should not be too anxious to volunteer information about himself, such as his school, religion, politics, or where else he has worked. A salesperson who does so may run the risk of discovering the customer's prejudices or preferences the hard way. He should wait until he knows the person better and use the available time in early meetings to learn as much as he can about the customer and his company. After the salesperson knows more about the prospect, he can then tell him more about himself. He should do so selectively, though, omitting anything that he suspects might be inflammatory or otherwise cause negative reactions.

For example, perhaps a salesperson attended a state university and went in loudly proclaiming that information in his first meeting with his customer. He then might learn to his sorrow that the customer's school is an arch rival. If asked, the salesperson should, of course, answer every question forthrightly. He merely wants to avoid blowing his own horn or volunteering too much about himself at these early meetings. This information can be revealed later in a low-key fashion. The salesperson should spend this initial time learning all he can about his customer. He can do this by asking questions about the customer, his operations, his areas of responsibility, and what his company makes or produces.

The salesperson should be on guard with people who, upon first meeting him, tell him that they know all about his company and products. These people may assure the salesperson that he does not have to sell his products to them, but the salesperson should be careful. These people may turn out to be his worst enemies. When the decision time arrives, they may not really know enough about his product or his company to discuss them intelligently and to justify purchases to their superiors. A salesperson should never challenge someone who says this. He should just be sure to discuss his sales points with these people as well and should send them sales letters to refresh their memories. He should concentrate on these people. They may not deliberately mislead the salesperson, but if not properly sold to, they may cost him orders.

Any time the salesperson is with a customer, he should be alert to the mention of anniversaries, birthdays, or other special events that are mentioned to him in the normal course of conversations. Specifically, if the customer has had a new addition to his family, he will be eager to tell the salesperson the child's name and the date of birth. After the salesperson leaves the customer's office, he should make a note of this information so that he can be reminded of the ages of the customer's children. A small gift with the child's name and birth date will be remembered for a long time.

Sales Example

When I first started making sales calls, I was always alert to information about the engineers and their families, especially any new additions to their families. One day I went to see an engineer with a major oil company. He related that he had had a new addition to his family the day before—a baby girl. I asked the baby's name, and when I got back to my office, ordered a small sterling silver juice cup engraved with her name and her birthday. Nineteen years later, I called on this same gentleman in Southeast Asia. At the end of our meeting, he invited me to his home after work. When I arrived, he introduced me to his 19-year-old daughter, Susan, and reminded me that I had sent her a juice cup when she was two weeks old!

A salesperson must build relations like this with his customers, starting with the earliest meetings. This will greatly improve his chances of obtaining new business and will set the salesperson apart. It also will help his cause when he has problems to sort out with his customer. It will enable the salesperson to convince the customer that he will make the difference and that the customer's orders will be better off if placed with him. It will enhance his overall sales efforts and enable him to sell much more.

Summary

1. Initial impressions are lasting and can be decisive.
2. Early meetings provide excellent opportunities for a salesperson to find out a lot about the customer.
3. One way the salesperson can do this is to show a genuine interest in the customer and get him to talk about himself.
4. The salesperson should ask questions and listen carefully to the answers.
5. Questions should always be discreet and tailored to the occasion. The salesperson should back off if the customer is not responsive.
6. If the customer is down in the dumps, the salesperson should listen sympathetically to his problems.
7. The salesperson should not ask the same questions to every person he meets.
8. The salesperson should not slap people's backs or give hugs.
9. The salesperson should never write down answers in the customer's presence, but he should take notes as soon as he leaves the customer's office.
10. The salesperson should ask the customer if he has had any prior experiences with the salesperson's company or products. If so, he should determine if they were good or bad.
11. The salesperson also should determine if the customer has had good or bad experiences with the competitors and their products.
12. The salesperson should avoid asking overly personal questions. This is especially important with customers he has just met.
13. The salesperson should never assume that an introduction from someone who knows the customer well will also guarantee him a special relationship with the customer. The salesperson must be prepared to earn his own spurs.
14. If a friend or colleague arranges an introduction or a meeting, the salesperson should be certain he shows up and that he makes a good impression. He should follow through and report back to the person who gave him the introduction.

15. The salesperson should be slow to volunteer information about himself early in his sales visits with a customer. He should do this later and do so selectively.
16. The salesperson should be on guard with people who say that he does not have to sell his product to them.
17. The salesperson should be alert at the mention of birthdays, anniversaries, or special events in the normal course of conversation with the customer.
18. The salesperson should ask questions and get his customers to talk about themselves. It will pay handsome dividends.

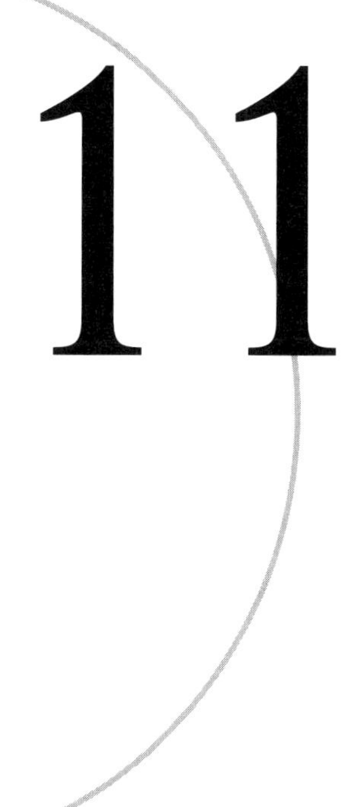

11 Maintain and Use Sales Kits

I hear and I forget. I see and I remember. I do and I understand.

—Confucious

As pointed out previously, it is very important for a salesperson to get right down to business when he goes to see a customer in his office. He must always have an objective or a goal and a specific message to leave with his customer. The salesperson's primary goal should be to familiarize the customer with his product. At the same time, he should encourage the customer to talk about his needs, fears, and preferences regarding products purchases.

The information in good sales kits not only will enable a salesperson to convey product information but also will encourage the customer to talk. Before each call, the salesperson will decide which of his products he wants to emphasize, and then he should have available the appropriate sales kits. A sales kit is a useful tool to help the salesperson quickly approach the topic, and it gives the customer something tangible to review. It will aid the salesperson in progressing toward his goal by giving him something to show the customer and providing something specific to talk about. Factual information in good sales kits provides this.

In chapter 1, I point out that product knowledge ranks first in what impresses customers. There is no faster or better way for a salesperson to achieve this than to have sales kits into which he has channeled all the information he has on his products, competitors, customers, and their industry.

If the salesperson's firm sells a wide variety of products or models, it may be difficult for him to stay current on all aspects of the products. One way he can make his task easier is to establish and maintain sales kits on each model or each category. These kits can consist of simple folders in which he keeps the key information available relative to each model or category. These kits should continually grow as more information is accumulated. The salesperson should always be alert for additional data that will help sell his products and increase his product knowledge.

Whenever something applicable comes across the salesperson's desk, he should file it immediately in the appropriate folder for future use. When he sees a trade journal ad or newspaper article, or hears something that applies to one of his products, he should clip it out or write a short memo for the appropriate folder. The salesperson can also include lists of users and satisfied customers, pricing history and feedback on lost orders, as well as new pricing information on orders received. He should be diligent to do this, so when he needs this information, he will not have to search for it.

This sales information should be steadily accumulated, and the salesperson should always be looking for items to include. He should add to his kit any testimonials or statements from satisfied users, even if they are only given verbally. He can put them in a memo and file them in his sales kit. Time is always short when preparing for sales calls, but if a salesperson maintains current information in these sales kits, they will provide an instant reservoir of valuable information. The salesperson should also add any photographs of his products being manufactured, assembled, installed in the field, or undergoing testing at his factory.

Some of the salesperson's products will be built and supplied for many years. In this case, he will find that his sales kit information will be especially valuable. It will have photographs or documents indicating how many years the salesperson's company has supplied that model.

Keeping these kits current and continuously supplied with data will not be easy for the salesperson to achieve. He must work at it, and there is a pitfall to be avoided. Sometimes when a salesperson is working to sell one of his products to a customer on a given project, he will keep his sales information in that file. However, when the job is finished, it is easy for him to leave all his accumulated information in that same file. The salesperson should not allow this to happen. He must make sure he makes copies for his own sales kit, so this general information can continue to be used as he sells this product in the future.

These kits are of little use to the salesperson if he is traveling and they remain behind in his office. Most of the sales kits should be kept with the salesperson. First, he cannot always predict which files he will need. Second, he can read them to refresh his memory while waiting to see his customers.

The salesperson should consider including the following items in these sales kits:

1. Photographs of:
   - units installed and operating in a customer's plant
   - units during assembly at the factory, which will reveal any details of features obscured in a completely assembled machine
   - units undergoing factory tests
   - major components
   - the company's facilities
2. Trade journal ads on his products
3. Drawings, sketches, or prints of the product
4. Testimonials and letters from satisfied users
5. Lists of product users, broken down by model numbers and also by Service category
6. Product specifications
7. Descriptions of outstanding or unique features
8. Performance data

9. Copies of sales letters previously written on a specific product
10. A list of improvements or upgrades that have been made on the products
11. Research or test-stand work that has been done to improve reliability, quality, or efficiency
12. Photographs and write-ups about the products that appear in the company magazine

Photographs of the salesperson's products are his best tools. At the beginning of the sales visit, he should show these pictures to his customer, always having them arranged in a logical order and giving an explanation of each. Everyone likes to look at pictures, and most people will make comments while doing so. Many times these photographs will cause the prospect to think about a future project in which he can use this product. The salesperson thus will flush out inquiry information ahead of the formal release and before his competition knows about it.

After making brief comments about each photograph, the salesperson should be quiet and allow his customer time to examine them and to respond. Not everyone will make an immediate comment, so time must be allowed for this. Most salespeople are too impatient and miss this important opportunity by not allowing enough time for customer response.

The salesperson should be sure to show photographs of his facilities, especially to customers who have not seen them and do not know much about his company. Often the customer will have no idea whether the salesperson's facilities are large or small, but viewing photographs will remove all doubt. It will also help create a favorable impression.

A salesperson will want to show photographs, drawings, and charts as he talks, because his prospect will remember much more if he sees something while he hears the explanation.

A salesperson will want to show photographs, drawings, and charts as he talks, because his prospect will remember much more if he sees something while he hears the explanation.

Various information retention tests show that what a listener remembers after three days is greatly influenced by how the information is presented. If the information is only conveyed verbally, less than 5% is recalled after 72 hours. If it is only conveyed visually, approximately 10% is retained after 72 hours. However, if the listener hears *and* sees the information, retention rises to more than 50%. When the listener is allowed to physically participate in the exercise, retention is much greater, reaching perhaps 90%. *Hear only and forget. See and remember. Do and understand.*

The point is that it's much more effective if a salesperson shows his customer photographs, charts, or drawings, and also gives verbal descriptions. In these cases, the customer will retain 25 times more information than if the salesperson merely talks to him. This should be a sobering reminder to a salesperson why he needs to present visual information to his customer and not just talk to him.

I have always suggested to salespeople that after relating sales points to a customer by phone or in his office, these points should be confirmed in a sales letter. These salespeople usually followed my instructions, but I never had the feeling they really believed it necessary. At that time, I lacked the facts to reinforce my instructions. Furthermore, many times I suggested to a salesperson that he should tell a customer about certain benefits of our product. His response would invariably be, "I told him that last week." If last week the salesperson only told the customer this information, as opposed to showing him as well, the customer would by now remember only 2% of that information!

It should be obvious why it is important for a salesperson to use photographs, samples, sales letters, and printed brochures in his presentations. It will help as well if he leaves material with his customer or sends it by mail to supplement his sales comments. All of this information should be available in well-maintained sales kits.

In face-to-face meetings, the salesperson should always have something for the customer to touch and to look at as he gives his presentation. When making sales pitches by telephone, the salesperson must then confirm his remarks in a sales letter. He should include such things as brochures, photographs, lists of product users, satisfied customer lists, or a list of features and benefits. A salesperson who gives his customer visual information as well as verbal information will more fully involve the customer in the presentation.

The salesperson also should organize similar folders for competitive products, with a general file on each competitor. In this he can keep general trade journal ads, financial information from newspapers, and general bulletins. He can include any information that he considers important, even if it is not related to a specific product.

If product size permits, the salesperson should carry samples of his products with him, something the customer can touch and examine as the salesperson gives his presentation. As he relates his pitch on a given product, he can point out the features on the sample. If a salesperson's products are too big for him to take representative samples along, he should make extensive use of models to achieve his goal. Models that are light enough to be carried make excellent sales tools. Digital media presentations can also be used to give the company's story or explain special products, and portable equipment makes this easily feasible. As with all presentations, the salesperson should make sure his comments are well organized. Before the meeting, he should prepare his comments, arrange them into a short presentation, and then memorize them.

The salesperson must be alert at trade shows to collect competitive bulletins. If possible, he should collect them before the show opens or after it closes. Usually they will be given to him directly. If not, the salesperson should ask a customer he knows well to obtain them for him. A camera is always useful at meetings like this to photograph displays and special products. Again, it is best for the salesperson to take photographs before the show opens or after it closes, always being discreet.

If a salesperson encounters competitive intelligence in any form, he should write a note and put it in the file on the competitor, otherwise he will not be able to recall it when needed. These competitive kits can be tremendously useful.

Sales Examples

Example 1

In 1971 one of our competitors issued an announcement that they were withdrawing from building one line of their products. In fact, for all practical purposes, they went out of the business altogether. Seven or eight years later, this same market was booming, and they began to try to scratch their way back in.

Every time they bid a job against us, we would break out this announcement from our competitive sales kit and show it to customers. We kept them out of many jobs that way.

The public announcement we showed was dated, and it revealed in their own words why they went out of that business. They admitted in print that their product line was inadequate, they had a very small market share, and they could not afford the research, development, and engineering expense necessary to keep up. The effects of our actions were so damaging to this competitor that its chairman appealed to our CEO for the practice to stop. Needless to say, we did not stop, because we were using factual data and quoting their own words.

Example 2

There is another example of how good sales kit information came in handy. I had a rather extensive competitive file on a foreign manufacturer. We learned that we had lost an order to them, and that a major U.S. company had purchased three machines from them to be installed in the Gulf of Mexico. Using information from my competitive sales kit, I was able to show this customer a map indicating where this competitor's plant was located. The plant was in a region with a socialist (i.e., communist-controlled) government, making visas for their service people difficult to obtain.

I told the customer that when the service person applied for a visa, the consular officer would probably request a background check, requiring at least 10 days. During this waiting period, the customer's products would be idle. This got the chief engineer's attention, and we were able to get them to reverse their decision and buy our machines. Without good documentary information on this competitor, we would not have been able to salvage this order.

From experience, I know that most salespeople do a poor job of keeping sales kits current. When I first became a salesperson, I started developing sales kits. After a few years, I had several very good ones. My boss observed me using them and later asked if he could borrow them to duplicate the contents for the rest of his sales force. I was flattered and, of course, obliged. About three years later, he again borrowed and duplicated my sales kits, because the other salespeople had failed to keep the original ones current.

I cannot overemphasize how important it is for a salesperson to build and use sales kits. This will not be easy for the salesperson to do, but it will pay off in sales orders.

Summary

1. When calling on a customer either in person or by telephone, a salesperson should always have a goal.
2. A salesperson should get right down to business by using information in his sales kits.
3. A salesperson should prepare and maintain sales kits on each model or category of product and for each competitor.
4. A salesperson must be alert for information to include.
5. A salesperson should keep information regularly flowing into his sales kits. He should not wait until he needs it to try to find it.
6. A salesperson should keep his sales kits with him when traveling.
7. Photographs are the best tools in his sales kits.
8. A salesperson should use photographs and encourage his customer to make comments and thus participate in the sales presentation.
9. When a salesperson gives a customer information both verbally and visually, he dramatically increases the amount of information the customer retains.
10. A salesperson should use physical product samples or models, if possible.
11. A salesperson should be alert at trade shows to collect competitive information.

12

Don't Play Games

This above all: to thine own self be true, and it must follow, as the night the day, Thou canst not then be false to any man.

—William Shakespeare, *Hamlet*

Selling technical goods and products is serious business and should be approached seriously. The number of people involved is small. A salesperson tends to see the same decision makers often and usually over a long period of time, and they talk to each other. The salesperson should be sincere with his customer to his face and never say unkind things about him elsewhere. He should be consistent in his approach and with what he tells his customer. If the customer asks a question that the salesperson cannot answer, he should admit this and volunteer to obtain the answer. He must then follow through and give the customer an answer. He should never try to bluff with his customer by pretending to know when he doesn't.

The salesperson should be sincere and should behave the same way at all times. This is so vital that it cannot be overemphasized. As a famous industrialist said, "No matter who you are dealing with, reveal your own true nature. Do not cover up who or what you really are." Customers are intelligent, sophisticated people. Virtually all can spot a phony a mile away, and they see many of them every day.

Customers are intelligent, sophisticated people. Virtually all can spot a phony a mile away, and they see many of them every day.

The salesperson should never disparage his company, competitors, or other people. If he talks unfavorably about a company or a person, it will eventually be discovered. Word gets around. Furthermore, most people conclude that if a salesperson is always saying unkind things about others, he will say unpleasant things about them when they are out of sight.

When a salesperson repeatedly disparages a company or an individual to others, it inhibits his ability to deal objectively with that person or that firm. This will create a residual resentment that will influence a salesperson's attitude or action when dealing with this customer or this individual, even though he may be unaware of it. I have cautioned salespeople about making unkind or unfavorable comments about a customer or a person. The reply is usually, "Oh, but I wouldn't let that influence my dealings with him." But it will.

A good salesperson will not get involved in his customer's internal politics. He should stay aloof and should not take sides and try to predict who will win. This does not mean that the salesperson should not stay alert as to who the bright, promising, and advancing people are. He should know this, but he should be objective.

Most big purchasing decisions are close races, decided sometimes on extremely minor points. In a close contest, the salesperson wants other customers to be able to tell the prospective customer good things about him. It could cost him the order if they say, "Watch him," "He is shifty," or "Make him put everything in writing." Being two-faced will destroy his reputation. He should not tell one company one thing and another company something else. He should always be honest and consistent.

Sales Example

Years ago while in my office, one of my colleagues asked if a certain individual ever bothered me. I replied negatively and said I rarely saw or encountered him. My colleague then said, "I wish he would leave me alone and stay out of my sight. He is always coming in my office and taking up my time. I can't stand him." I responded by saying I almost never saw this person and had no strong feeling about him. The conversation ended, and I thought no more about it.

The next day, just outside my office, I heard this same colleague profusely greeting someone like a long-lost friend. He was saying how much he had missed him and how glad he was to see this individual and asked why he did not come around more often. Since the greeting was so overwhelmingly pleasant, I could not resist moving toward my door so that I could identify who it was that my colleague was so glad to see. To my utter astonishment, it was the same individual he had said one day before that he detested and wished would leave him alone.

Needless to say, the perception I had of my colleague was shattered. From that moment forward, I had absolutely no respect for him. His image melted before my eyes as if made of wax. After that incident, I never was sure what he really thought of me or of anyone or anything else. His reputation, as far as I was concerned, was in shambles.

It goes without saying that a salesperson should always be honest with his customers on test results, inspection reports, deliveries, and in other areas. He should never bend the truth or try to cover up. He should not be enticed by his factory or headquarters people to take part in a cover-up. He must turn them down flat. Soon they will learn to not even consider asking him to deviate from the truth. Suggestions like this usually come from the lower level people, not from top management, but the salesperson's response should be the same regardless of where it originates. Honesty is not just the best policy, it is the only policy.

Don't Make Enemies

Be it true or false, what is said about men often has as much influence upon their lives, and especially upon their destinies, as what they do.

—Victor Hugo

The world is pretty small, and the business world is even smaller. In a given industry, various salespeople call on many of the same customers. Customers and salespeople attend the same technical meetings and conventions. Customers talk to each other, and so do salespeople. A salesperson will keep running into the same people for at least as long as he stays in his particular profession.

It should follow then that the salesperson should not make enemies, because doing so will come back to haunt him. Even if someone he has wronged leaves the company and goes to work somewhere else, either the salesperson or someone from his company will encounter him again. The salesperson may go to call on a different organization, and when he opens the door, there will be the person he offended.

It is almost impossible for a salesperson to have everyone supporting him. However, he should at least minimize the effects of those who are against him. He should not allow them to become enemies if he has in some way, intentionally or not, offended them. Salespeople most often cause enmity by not properly taking care of orders in progress or product problems. They may neglect to handle a customer's resultant back charges, or they may offend by failing to respect the chain of command. A large portion of a salesperson's difficulties with his customers is caused by product problems, either operational or with delivery. Usually he feels that his factory, superiors, the engineering department, or someone else is to blame when he has to relay an unpopular or unacceptable decision to his customer.

The salesperson should never let the impasse reach this stage. He should use all of his sales skills internally on his own colleagues and management to obtain a fair and equitable settlement on warranty claims, back charges, or products problems. He should then try sincerely to convince the customer that this settlement is fair and equitable. Most customers are reasonable if made aware of all the facts. Unfortunately, many decisions on back charge claims or warranties are made not only by customers but also by the supplier on the basis of insufficient or erroneous information.

Once a settlement position is established by the salesperson's management, it is virtually impossible to reverse or alter it. It is also difficult to change a position taken by a customer. Loss of face is involved. Sometimes after a salesperson makes the proper people in the customer's company aware of all the facts, they are still unhappy. In this case he should get their side of the story in more detail and find out exactly why they are not satisfied. He should ask them many questions in the process. Sometimes reasonable and penetrating questions from the salesperson will cause them to alter their position if it is indeed unreasonable.

If a salesperson fails to convince a dissatisfied customer to alter his position, he should relay all this information to his superiors. Often something new will come to light, something of which his people were not aware when they made their original decision or settlement offer. The salesperson should continue his efforts by asking both sides questions about the reasons for their respective positions and attitudes. Eventually this will bring them closer together, until sooner or later, they will be so close that perhaps the salesperson can split the difference and satisfy both sides.

To settle major back charges, warranty claims, and performance problems will demand serious involvement from the salesperson, the top sales management, and the top management beyond sales. In most cases, lower level plant service people and marketing people in a salesperson's organization have certain guidelines by which they abide. They do not have any authority to deviate from these guidelines, since that authority is necessarily retained by just a few management people. It is the salesperson's job to determine the facts and present them to the proper authorities in his company. If this is done, he will nearly always reach a fair and reasonable settlement that the customer will accept happily.

The salesperson should never cease his efforts until he has satisfied the customer. If the salesperson does his job well, his company will be satisfied also. The salesperson should use all of his persuasive ability and sales skills in a concentrated effort to succeed. In case of an impasse about which he feels strongly, he should remind his management in writing that their decision will cost him future business with that customer. He should quantify the annual business, if possible.

Quite apart from back charge problems, the salesperson should never let a customer down after he purchases the products. The salesperson must take care of his manufacturing, operating, or engineering problems. Otherwise, he can leave the customer exposed to criticism from his management because of delayed start-up, lost production, downtime, or increased costs. The customer may conclude that the products or parts are not reliable, and the salesperson will not receive any more business.

The salesperson should always keep in mind that there will be a tomorrow as far as business with his customer is concerned, and that the customer will

The salesperson should always keep in mind that there will be a tomorrow as far as business with his customer is concerned, and that the customer will not forget.

not forget. Sooner or later, he will again be in the market to buy. Someone will ask his opinion of the salesperson and his organization as product decisions are being made. A favorable response can tilt the order in the salesperson's favor. An unfavorable comment can cause him to lose the order.

There are other ways to make enemies. The following should be avoided:

- reneging on verbal promises
- making or repeating unfavorable comments about people
- getting involved in customer politics
- violating another person's confidence
- violating a customer's house rules
- going around them or over their heads

Writing offensive letters is another sure way of making enemies. A salesperson should be very careful and should never put unfavorable comments or statements in letters to customers. He must be objective and should never criticize his company's people, operating procedures, or management, especially in writing. Unfavorable comments will often get people in trouble or even fired. These letters will often be retained for years and reread repeatedly.

Sales Examples

Example 1

I once made an appointment and went to see a plant manager who was in the market for some of the products I sold. He greeted me in his office and listened to my sales pitch, but I could detect he had reservations. After I finished my remarks, he reached down, opened his lower right-hand drawer, and took out a letter. He handed it across his desk for me to read, saying, "Here is what your company thinks about my operations here at this plant."

I read the letter, which was several years old, and learned to my astonishment that our manager had in this letter made very critical comments about the maintenance in this plant. He had even attached a report by one of our service people, containing nasty and unnecessary comments about this plant's repair people.

This letter had been carefully saved and had apparently been reread occasionally by this plant manager. Naturally, we did not get this new order. Offensive letters will usually come back to haunt the salesperson. He should not put unfavorable comments about a customer in print.

In all of a salesperson's dealings with customers and others, he should keep in mind that when he says something harsh to a person or otherwise shortchanges him, others will know about it. When others learn of this indiscretion, the salesperson's reputation will suffer. Sometimes a salesperson has sold his products to an intermediary and treated him shabbily. He should rest assured that his bad conduct will be related and usually magnified to the ultimate user. His image will suffer just as much as if he had done these things directly to the customer.

Example 2

A foreign customer of my firm and a long-time friend was in my home city and called to visit socially because of our lengthy friendship. During the evening, he related to me that his company had purchased some of our products—not directly, but through a contractor who was putting together a package. He went on to say that my firm's home office was taking a very hard line with the contractor on all matters and sending nasty letters and wires. Evidently our main office and the salespeople involved did not realize that this contractor was passing on these messages exactly as written. The damage was just as serious as if my firm had sent these messages directly to the customer.

Summary

A person's reputation does not follow him—it precedes him. A salesperson should treat not only his customers with respect and consideration, but also everyone he meets. A salesperson needs all the help he can get. Therefore, he should not make enemies.

14

Make Appointments

When selling technical products, a salesperson must always maintain a professional attitude. It is, therefore, extremely important that he make appointments even when he is dealing with those customers he knows well and on whom he has been calling for a long time.

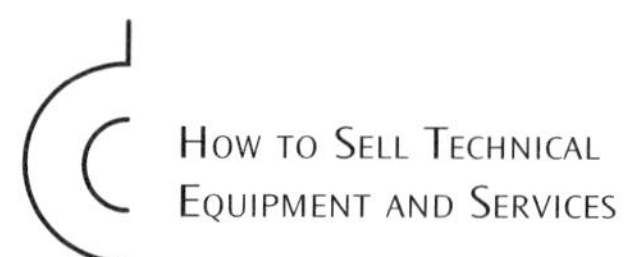

A salesperson has a limited amount of time, and he cannot afford to waste any of it in the waiting room by dropping in to make a surprise visit on someone. Many times, even though the customer is quite willing to see him, he has other commitments, plans, or meetings. The customer usually cannot break into his routine to see an unscheduled visitor. Customers are busy people whose time is valuable. When a salesperson makes an appointment, he shows consideration. Appointments help customers and salespeople plan their time wisely.

The salesperson should keep in mind that some customers, if they know the salesperson well, are uncomfortable if they are unable to see him when he drops by unannounced. Also, it lowers his standing in their eyes if he habitually strolls in and offers to wait an hour or so to see them. It gives customers the impression that he is not in great demand and is disorganized. Most customers prefer to do business with busy, well-organized salespeople. If the salesperson is busy and values his time, it assures customers that others also buy the salesperson's products.

When the salesperson is calling to arrange a meeting, he should have several potential times available. The customer will usually select a suitable hour when the salesperson can come without having to wait. If the salesperson is making an appointment very far in advance, he should confirm it in writing and call again the day before to make sure everything is in order. This is mandatory if a salesperson is bringing anyone with him.

The salesperson should plan his visits for a time that suits the customer best. In general, early in the day is a good time for a sales visit. The salesperson will be able to cover more ground and will promote better relations with the customer by respecting his obligations to his company.

If the salesperson is bringing people with him, he should tell the customer. He should also make sure when he arrives that the receptionist announces everyone's names to the host. The customer may have forgotten how many were coming, and it can be upsetting for him to expect one person and have three or four arrive. If his office is small, he may need to meet in a conference room.

When the salesperson makes the appointment, or at least before the meeting begins, he should give his customer a list of the titles and specialties of the other members of the sales group. The customer may choose to invite his own people with equal titles or with similar expertise. If the salesperson writes the titles down, they will be correct. If he gives them verbally, he might not give them accurately, and the customer's people likely will not remember them anyway. The salesperson can use this list to introduce the members of the sales group and then hand it to the customer for his use. The salesperson should obtain a list of all of the customer's people in the meeting, which he can accomplish by passing around a pad for everyone to fill out names and titles. The salesperson and his sales team members should also sign the list.

It is usually inappropriate for a salesperson to call an important, busy person for an appointment when that person knows little or nothing about the salesperson or his firm.

Often the salesperson is calling on strangers. An aggressive salesperson will do this regularly to enlarge his circle of acquaintances and to influence an increasing number of people. It is usually inappropriate for a salesperson to call an important, busy person for an appointment when that person knows little or nothing about the salesperson or his firm. A better idea is for the salesperson to write the prospective customer a note that explains briefly who the salesperson is, what his company does, what he would like to discuss, and that he will call for an appointment. This will make a surprising difference.

When the salesperson calls, he still may not get the meeting immediately. However, he will have a much better chance if he takes time to write a note on his personal or company stationery so that the prospective customer will know who he is and what he wants. The salesperson will not then be a complete stranger. If the salesperson is out of his office, a handwritten letter will suffice and will often work magic. Sometimes a handwritten note will be better even if the salesperson is in his office. If time is short, he could have it hand-delivered.

When the salesperson then calls for the appointment, the customer will know who he is and what he wants to discuss. He may refer the salesperson to someone else, but he will know more about the salesperson and his company and will be in a better position to talk to him on the phone. If the salesperson skips the note and instead calls the prospective customer's office for an appointment, he will likely have to explain to the office assistant who he is and what he wants. It would be much better for the customer to have a note from the salesperson requesting the meeting. This approach will get the salesperson more appointments with busy people than phone calls alone will accomplish. It will also create a much better impression for the salesperson and his company.

In making appointments, especially with busy customers, the salesperson should find out something about their work habits. Some busy people start to work very early. If the salesperson learns that the customer starts at 7:00 AM, he should ask for an appointment at 7:30 AM. Often these people will agree to see a salesperson early. This can enable the salesperson to see a person who would otherwise always be too busy. It will establish the salesperson as one who also starts early and will help to develop a good rapport with this individual.

Sales Examples

Example 1

One of my superiors was dealing with a customer whose executive vice president was the key decision maker and someone who commenced work at 7:00 AM. My superior always scheduled his appointments with this person shortly after 7:00 AM. My superior would fly into town the night before so he could be on time for these early meetings. Over several years, he obtained many very large orders from this individual, mostly due to these early-morning talks. The competition apparently never learned the secret and lost orders consistently.

Example 2

On another occasion, one of my colleagues always lost orders to a customer in New York City. He reported that he could never get in to see the most important person. This important person later traveled to my location, and I was able to visit with him socially. During our dinner, I learned that he, too, always started to work at 7:00 AM. No doubt if my New York City colleague had known this much earlier, he could have arranged to see this gentleman early in the morning. He might well have converted his lost orders into purchase orders.

Summary

1. A salesperson should always make appointments. He should make them as early in the day as possible, taking into consideration the customer's schedule.
2. Before the meeting, the salesperson should give his customer a list with the names and titles of his sales team. It shows professionalism. He should also obtain a list of all of the customer's people in the meeting.
3. Making appointments enables the salesperson to better utilize his time and accomplish more.

Always Keep Promises

What you are speaks so loud, I cannot hear what you say.

—Ralph Waldo Emerson

It may seem superfluous to encourage a salesperson to keep his promises, but customers report that few salespeople actually do this. The smaller the promise, the more important it is to keep. A salesperson who takes care of the small items and the small commitments he makes will certainly take care of the big and more important matters to which he agrees. A salesperson should keep notes on the promises he makes so that he does not forget them.

Because of their importance, a salesperson should be conservative in making commitments. If he always delivers more than he says he will, he will never be caught short. He should be on his guard about this, particularly when on unfamiliar ground. When he undertakes something, the other person will usually hear what he wants to hear and often will read something more into a salesperson's words than he intended. The salesperson must be sure to make himself clear in this regard. It is a good idea for him to repeat his commitment in different words to make sure it is clear and does not include more than he intends to deliver. This is vital when a salesperson is dealing with an unfamiliar subject or when he is commenting on a matter he did not know would come up in their discussions. He can also add, "I want to be careful not to mislead you, and here is what I am going to do."

When a salesperson keeps all of his commitments, he develops credibility with customers. They soon know they can count on him. Integrity is one of the strongest components of salesmanship. It is vital that a salesperson keep his word when he is working with the customers before an active job comes up, during the time the project is being worked on, and more importantly, after the purchase. The salesperson must do all of the things that he told the customer he would do prior to the sale. He should keep in mind that many salespeople will promise the moon before the order comes through. Once they have the order, however, they change their attitudes, back away, become careless and flaky, and do not follow through or deliver on what they promised. Customers look favorably on vendors who keep promises and who will keep supplying and standing behind what they sold.

When a salesperson keeps all of his commitments, he develops credibility with customers.

It is very important for a salesperson to treat the customer with the same degree of respect after he places the order as he did before. The customer feels that most of his leverage is gone once he has given the salesperson the order. He will be anxious, sensitive, and alert to the salesperson's reaction after the order is placed. If the salesperson reacts and treats the customer with the same enthusiasm after he receives the order as he did before, he will win his customer's confidence. This effort will make him a truly outstanding salesperson.

A salesperson's credibility is extremely important to customers. After a customer buys capital products, they can rarely be ripped out and replaced if they do not work. Once a customer selects and installs the salesperson's products and trains personnel to operate and maintain them, they usually are stuck with the salesperson's firm on that project. To a great extent they are at the salesperson's mercy in that particular plant or on that batch of products. Consequently, reliability and confidence are extremely important in the customer's mind as he makes his selection. Often, trustworthiness on the part of the salesperson is the difference in making the sale or losing the sale. It can be decisive. A salesperson's credibility is developed, maintained, and strengthened when he keeps his promises.

The salesperson should remember that his reputation precedes him, rather than follows him. The industry he is in is small, and word gets around. The salesperson's image is created by all that he says and does both inside and outside his company. To many people, a person's word transcends what is put in writing. It follows then that the salesperson should not keep his word just with his customers, but with everyone he deals with both inside and outside his company. The salesperson's reputation is also extremely important within his company. He must be believable and reliable so that he can get things done for his customers. His customers will soon find out what kind of standing he has inside his own company. He should make sure it is excellent and favorable.

When a salesperson keeps all of his promises, it helps him to develop trust and confidence among his customers, which is a crucial ingredient in his relationship with them. The salesperson does not always have access to the ultimate decision maker. However, that person will often ask his own people their opinions of the salesperson and his company. He will likely ask if the salesperson is believable, if he keeps his word, and if his firm can be trusted to make the promised delivery. Trust and confidence can make the difference for a salesperson, and so can keeping his promises.

Sales Examples

Example 1

At a technical meeting, I met for the first time an engineer working for one of our customers in another city. During the conversation, I learned he was interested in a particular subject. I told him I had a unique write-up on this topic and would mail it to him, which I did the next day. Three weeks later, I again encountered this same engineer at another technical meeting in another city. The first thing he said was, "I received the article you promised." Then he added, "I must tell you I never expected to receive it." Astonished, I asked why not, since I had promised it to him three weeks earlier. He said, "Yes, but salespeople come in to my office all the time promising things, and I never hear from them again." What was even more devastating was that another person standing in our group agreed. This individual added, "He is right. People almost never keep their promises." This incident shocked me, but it also revealed that in general, salespeople just do not keep their promises.

Example 2

Once when I was newly assigned to a customer and had just begun the process of resurrecting the account, I was having lunch with two of their junior engineers. One asked for additional engineering information on an item delivered quite some time before to his company by my firm. I made notes of what he wanted and said I would get back to him. I wired our factory for the information. When it arrived in my office two days later, I called this engineer to say I had the information and asked if he wanted to hear any of it before I posted it to him in writing.

The engineer seemed astonished and reacted as if he did not know what I was talking about. I reminded him that he had requested this information two days previously during our lunch. He replied, "I asked both of your predecessors for that information starting over a year ago, and neither ever responded!" I told him when I promised something, I delivered. He ended up suggesting that I put the information in a letter to him. I never learned if he actually needed the information, or if he was just testing my credibility.

Example 3

I arrived at a customer's office to attend a follow-up meeting to discuss a very delicate issue representing a very major problem—the most difficult of my career. We thought the senior person in the meeting would be the local manager. Instead, to our surprise, the general manager from overseas met us in the conference room. He greeted me warmly, and we sat down to begin the crucial meeting. On his side of the table were three or four of his people, each ready to pounce on our every word because of the difficult discussions about to resume.

The general manager opened the meeting by quietly saying that the two of us had had business dealings only once 10 years before, but that I had kept all my promises and sorted out all their problems to their complete satisfaction. This had an amazing effect on his people, who throughout the rest of the meeting treated us with renewed respect, not once again showing their fangs. We settled our problems very favorably to my firm at a later meeting, but the tone was clearly established that day.

The remarks by the general manager were astonishingly significant for the following reasons:

- His impression of me was gained in one encounter 10 years previously.
- We had seen each other only once in the meantime.

This proves that a salesperson does not need 10 chances to establish a solid reputation. Sometimes he will get only one opportunity, as I did in this case.

Summary

A salesperson must develop and protect his reputation for being trustworthy by keeping all of the promises he makes.

New Products or Customers

If a salesperson's company is new and trying to break into an industry or if it is offering a new, unproven product, he will have a lot of work to do. A salesperson working for an established company selling proven products will also have an uphill battle when trying to break in with a new customer. In order for a salesperson to convince customers to do business with him, he must make it extremely attractive to them to switch their orders. He should remember that the customer's greatest fear is making a mistake and buying something that will not work. The customer also is afraid of buying something that will be delivered late or buying capital goods from a firm that subsequently goes out of business. These customers have been purchasing their products elsewhere and they will be reluctant to change, especially if they are happy with their current suppliers.

There are some things that a salesperson can do to improve his chances of making a sale and being successful in these situations. These include the following:

In order for a salesperson to convince customers to do business with him, he must make it extremely attractive to them to switch their orders.

1. The salesperson can make sure his firm and its products or services have exposure. The salesperson's company can advertise in magazines and publications read by his prospective customers and can arrange for displays at trade shows that his prospects attend. In this way the salesperson's company will not be completely unknown when he approaches prospects. If funds are short, the salesperson's company should run small ads in these publications and should run them regularly over a long period of time.
2. The salesperson can attend trade shows that his prospective customers go to even if his company is unable to exhibit. He should attend all presentations for maximum exposure.
3. The salesperson should cultivate engineering contractors and consultants who provide advisory services to the companies with which he would like to do business. He should give these specialists technical details on his products and explain to them why and how they are better than what is now available.
4. The salesperson should join professional groups that his prospective customers attend. He could work to become an officer for maximum exposure.
5. The salesperson can bring customers to his company's plant for visits or product presentations by his experts, and to meet his executives.
6. The salesperson can get his executives involved in visits to see the customer in his office. If necessary to secure the first order, the salesperson should provide a letter from his president confirming his personal involvement and commitment to making reliable products and insuring the customer's complete satisfaction.

When launching a new product, the salesperson must carefully choose the best prospective customer for the product introduction. The criteria include the following:

1. The customer's firm should be receptive, one that he knows fairly well, or one that has a tie to someone in the salesperson's company or is familiar with it.
2. The customer's firm should be one that will be sympathetic to problems and will be patient while the salesperson sorts them out.
3. The customer's firm should be a reputable operator with qualified people and good maintenance procedures.
4. The customer's firm should have a high potential need for this new product.
5. The customer's firm should have a plant location that is logistically accessible so that the salesperson can provide good service, engineering assistance, spare parts, and follow-up.

The salesperson must make sure he fully understands the customer's operating parameters and specifications. Even with a substantial product advantage, the salesperson should be prepared to reduce his normal price considerably and to give extended warranties, including free service and spare parts. If possible, he should offer products that have advantages over and above that currently available from the competitors. The salesperson should identify which of the following his products possess and stress the advantages in sales letters and in his sales presentations:

- lower first cost
- lower maintenance
- higher efficiency
- greater durability
- greater safety factors and a longer life
- requirement of fewer people to operate
- safer to operate
- more closely meets or surpasses environmental requirements
- does the job faster or better
- more easily expandable
- more compatible with other similar products

The salesperson who is trying to sell well-proven products or services to a new customer will also need for his company to have exposure in well-read trade journals and at trade shows. He should send his product brochures to prospective new customers. They should be sent with a transmittal letter, which should be a sales letter pointing out real benefits. It should be an original letter signed by the salesperson and must be addressed to the key people. The salesperson should devote a lot of thought to this sales letter, because there is a lot at stake. He should demonstrate how the prospective customers will benefit if they buy his product.

The salesperson should determine the prospect's needs or requirements and what he purchases most. With this information, he can concentrate his sales efforts in the areas offering the best prospects of success. The salesperson should be alert for areas in which his company or product excels, because he will then be able to offer more compelling reasons why his product is best. He also should provide a long list of product users and ample references. The prospective customer will have less risk if he buys a product in which the salesperson's company surpasses the competitors. For example, if a salesperson is trying to sell a specific product, he will want to show his list of satisfied users of that item. If he is selling services, he should have available a list of customers for whom his company has provided these services.

Before proceeding too far, the salesperson should determine the prospective customer's buying habits. Does he buy strictly on price? Does he pay a premium for quality? Does he have specific likes and dislikes in the products he buys? Does he have detailed specifications? Does one person strongly influence or make the buying decisions? Do others get involved? How long has he been doing business with his current suppliers? The salesperson should determine who the key decision makers are in the customer's purchasing, maintenance, and engineering departments. If possible, he should find out something about the various individuals involved. The more he learns about them ahead of time, the more accurately he can focus his sales efforts and the better his chances are of getting along with the customers.

The salesperson should also find out if there is a special reason the customer has not been doing business with his company. He should keep in mind that the customer's needs are now being satisfied by his competitors, and dislodging them will not be easy. A lower price alone usually will not do it. Good service may help, but the salesperson must receive the opportunity to demonstrate how he can perform. Higher quality will also help, but he must get the customer to try his products in order to demonstrate this.

The salesperson should also try to find out why the customer is now buying from his competitor. In other words, he must determine what the competitor is doing to maintain the customer's loyalty. Knowing this should help the salesperson determine what he must do even better if he is to sell to this customer and replace the current supplier.

To know for sure why the customer is not now doing business with the salesperson, he should ask more than one person inside the customer's company. If possible, he also should ask several of these inside people why the customer is now buying from his competitor. The more people he asks, the more accurate his information will be. The salesperson should identify and ask individuals outside the customer's firm who might also know this information. For instance, other suppliers who are not the salesperson's competitors may be able to help. Since they are successful, they have found the solution, and might be willing to share with the salesperson what they did to become a successful vendor.

To proceed, the salesperson should make an appointment to see the prospect. Rather than calling, it is always best to write a letter requesting an appointment. This does not have to be a formal, typewritten letter. Sometimes a handwritten letter will do just as well. In the letter, the salesperson should say why he would like to meet with the customer, and he should close by saying he will call to arrange a convenient time. Shortly before going to the meeting, the salesperson should prepare himself mentally just as he might for a tough or unpleasant existing customer. He could do this in several ways:

- relaxing
- building up his self confidence through visualizing past successes, such as when he just finished a very good sales call or when he received a very large order
- thinking positively and believing that his meeting will go well and be successful
- imagining the meeting going well, and picturing himself tuned into his prospect, resolving all objections, and answering all questions satisfactorily

At the agreed time, the salesperson should give a presentation on his product or services. He should do this personally and not take a lot of people with him on this first visit. Depending on the number of people involved, this can be done in the customer's office or in a meeting room, using portable equipment.

The salesperson should discuss the products the customer uses most and those in which the salesperson's company excels. The salesperson should emphasize why his product is better for the customer. He should address the customer's interests, and not his own. He must show how the product will benefit the customer.

After the salesperson has made his presentation or during his first meeting, there are other steps he can take:

1. The salesperson could show a list of his firm's current customers.
2. The salesperson could show purchase orders from current customers without, of course, revealing the specific prices.
3. The salesperson could give him a list of satisfied customers to call at the appropriate time. He should give out these names only with his customers' permissions. If he feels they will be called by this prospect, he should alert them so they are not taken by surprise.
4. If the salesperson has letters from satisfied customers, he will, of course, show them at this time. The best letters are those that are written spontaneously by the customers.

Next the salesperson could courteously relate the following:

1. He can explain that he realizes and understands that the customer's needs are now being satisfied by others.
2. He can explain that he represents a first-class firm that builds high-quality products, has been in business a long time, and is financially sound.
3. He can explain that his company has a strong engineering department.
4. He can share that he feels he can help the customer's company by giving faster deliveries, since his company will be trying harder for their new customer.
5. He can tell the customer that he would appreciate being given a chance to demonstrate what he can do when the customer next has an emergency.
6. He can explain that he will continue to come by to see him occasionally to make sure that all is going well with the products.

During the salesperson's initial meeting, he should try to uncover an unmet want of the customer. He should see if he could identify something the customer would like that is not now being supplied by his current vendors. Perhaps he could unearth something by simply asking if the customer is completely satisfied with his current suppliers or if there is anything the customer wished they did differently. There might be additional products or services he wishes they provided. It could be almost anything, such as in the packaging or labeling area, or something more important, such as longer life on spares or new products. What the customer reveals may provide the salesperson with a good opening to do business with the customer. It may be something that will cost the salesperson's company very little to accomplish.

Obtaining information from the customer in this area will not be easy. The customer's initial reaction will usually be that everything is fine and that all his needs, requirements, and wishes are being met.

The salesperson should bear in mind that some of the customer's unmet product needs may be unrealistic or too expensive to provide. He should probe for this information anyway. He just might find something he can supply or do that will help him break into this account. The salesperson must be careful at this stage to not overly commit his company. He would never want to mislead the customer by agreeing on the spot to do something and then later have to back out on his promise. He must listen and investigate before offering the customer anything. The customer will respect this sound and logical approach.

In following up, the salesperson should be persistent but not bothersome. He should not make a presentation and then disappear, but should continue to call on the customer on a regular basis.

The salesperson should give the customer time to consider the information. He should then send another sales letter summarizing his presentation and the reasons why the salesperson's company should be the supplier. The salesperson should remember that he will rarely get an order immediately. If too much time elapses without an order, the salesperson should repeat the presentation to the customer's contact person as well as other decision makers in his organization.

The salesperson also could offer a special concession on the product or services. If what he is trying to sell is well proven and in general use, he will obviously not have to make as many concessions as he would for a new product. However, he will still have to provide some inducement or incentive in order to convince the prospective customer to switch from his traditional sources. The salesperson must be patient and persistent. The degree of concessions necessary will depend on several things, such as:

1. **General market conditions.** If deliveries are long, the salesperson might be able to break in on the strength of shorter delivery. He still must do his selling job and convince the customer his product will work well or his services are more reliable.
2. **The reputation of the salesperson's company.** This involves not only the company's reputation, but also its standing in the industry.
3. **The track records of the salesperson's products.**
4. **The number of competitors for this account.**
5. **The customer's reasons for not doing business with the salesperson's company.** If it was due to bad product performance or personality conflicts, these will have to be sorted out. This usually requires a lot of time and effort.

At this time, the salesperson should be unusually alert for things he might provide to the prospect that will help him do his job better. Perhaps he could furnish the prospect technical reprints or maintenance information that he does not have but would appreciate. The salesperson could determine the prospect's outside interests and offer to take him or give him tickets to sporting functions or musical programs, depending on his preference.

The salesperson should put forth a genuine, sincere interest in the prospect and his company. He should do his best to demonstrate that his company is a solid, dependable supplier and that his product has valuable benefits for the prospect. At all times he should keep in mind the prospect's interests.

I cannot overemphasize the importance of perception at this point in a salesperson's relationship with the customer. The way he and his company are perceived will be decisive. Therefore, he must present and establish a good image.

The salesperson should ask the prospect to give him a chance to perform under a difficult situation, such as when unusually short deliveries or tight specifications are required. If given this opportunity, the salesperson must then make absolutely certain that he handles this order in a first-class fashion. He should not take any chances but instead should walk the order through every step of his company's system. He also should alert everyone involved that this is a new customer's order, and they must perform particularly well so as to gain this customer's regular business.

The salesperson should personally and regularly monitor the progress of the order and keep the customer posted on its progress. The salesperson should notify the customer as soon as the products are shipped. He should not leave anything to chance. Having been given a golden opportunity, he must make the most of it.

Sales Examples

Example 1

Several years ago we were trying to introduce a new model of our products but had been unsuccessful in finding a domestic customer. We then learned about a project overseas where our product would fit well. We obtained the inquiry and quoted our units. Since our product was new and it did not have any field experience, we knew we had a difficult task before us. I realized that even with all our written guarantees in our proposal, a separately written commitment from our president might also be helpful. I drafted the letter in which he pledged his personal assurance that if any problems arose with this product that he would quickly get involved and sort them out. I obtained a similar letter from our major partner. These letters were presented to this company, and a few days later we received the order.

Example 2

On this same project, we were assisted by the customer's consultant. Several years earlier, he had needed technical information. We had cheerfully provided it, even though at that time he was not involved in any project where our product was required. We expected nothing in return, but our response to him when he needed help paid dividends years later on this new project.

A salesperson must be responsive when someone asks for help. It will virtually always be rewarded one way or another. The salesperson will rarely know precisely what tips the scales in his favor. In these examples, however, the letters of commitment and the support from the consultant certainly helped our cause and were decisive in introducing this new product.

Breaking in with a new customer and selling new models of a product are very important tasks for all salespeople. They are tasks that a salesperson is expected to perform well, because all companies have *blocked* accounts, or accounts with which they do little or no business. A progressive company will from time to time introduce new products. The outstanding salesperson will be able to crack blocked accounts as well as sell new products. If he can do these well, he will always be in demand and will always have a job. The salesperson should work hard by developing and improving his skills and productivity these areas, because they are vital to his success.

Summary

To enhance his chances of being successful in introducing a new product or breaking in with a new customer, there are several things a salesperson should do. These include the following:

1. The salesperson should make sure he and his firm have exposure through trade journal advertising, by displaying at trade shows, and by joining professional groups and organizations.
2. The salesperson should make use of satisfied customer lists.
3. The salesperson should choose his customer carefully when introducing a new product. He should select a customer that is a big user of the product, has a convenient location, and that will be sympathetic and cooperative during any start-up problems.
4. The salesperson should learn a lot about this prospective customer. This includes information regarding their buying habits, the names of contact people and decision makers, and the backgrounds of key decision makers and why they have not been doing business with the salesperson's firm.
5. The salesperson must make sure he and his engineering people know precisely what the new product is expected to do.

6. The salesperson can get his executives involved at the appropriate time.
7. The salesperson should find out why the customer is now doing business with his competitors.
8. The salesperson should prepare himself mentally before the first meeting.
9. The salesperson should make a professional presentation on his new product or what he is trying to sell. He should stress his product's advantages, tailoring them specifically to the customer's needs or requirements. He should show the customer how they could benefit from the salesperson's product.
10. The salesperson should show his prospective customer his company's manufacturing facilities and introduce his key engineering and quality control people to the customer.
11. The salesperson should be prepared to make concessions on a new product in pricing, service, and warranty.
12. During the first meeting, the salesperson should try to identify an unmet need on the part of the prospective customer that the salesperson's company could meet.
13. When the salesperson is given his first order, he must make certain his company builds the product well and ships it on time.
14. The salesperson should not underestimate his task. It will not be easy, but he should not give up. The rewards are tremendous.

KEEP CUSTOMER RECORDS

Many salespeople have beautiful, complete customer records on their desks in their offices, often in a large book not suitable for traveling. This is fine when the salesperson is in his office, but it does not help him when he is making calls away from his base. Customer names, addresses, e-mail addresses, and telephone numbers should be kept only in a format that a salesperson can take with him when he travels. He could have this information on a printout, in a notebook, or stored on his laptop computer or other portable device. Whatever format the salesperson prefers, this information should always be available.

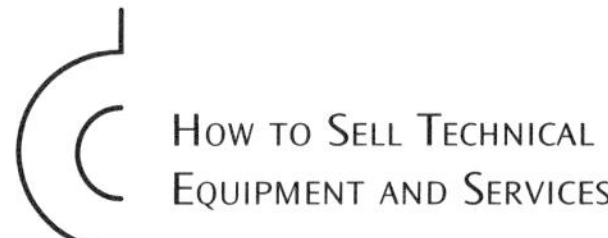

It can save a salesperson valuable time to have these customer records with him when he needs to call or e-mail someone while he is traveling or is out of his office. That can happen frequently, because as he works on an active job, he must continue with his other duties and keep his other customers happy. However, if customer information is readily available, he can quickly call to check the status of other jobs and sort out developing problems. Time is precious for a salesperson, and he cannot spend it looking up phone numbers. Furthermore, it is not always possible to obtain these numbers if he does not have them at hand. They may be located in a suburb or across a river from the big city.

Time is precious for a salesperson, and he cannot spend it looking up phone numbers.

Sales Example

Several years ago, we were in Rome working with an Italian contractor on a large job that included a steam turbine. It developed that we needed the help of the turbine vendor right away. It was rather late in the day in Rome and was after business hours in Germany, the home office of the turbine vendor. No one else had the turbine vendor's phone numbers. I checked my black book and found the card of the turbine vendor's general manager. The card included his home telephone number. We called him at 7:00 PM and explained that we needed his sales engineer in Rome early the next day. He replied that he would have him on the first plane the next morning. The sales engineer was in our meeting before noon, and we obtained the order.

If we had not called when we did, we would have lost an entire day and perhaps the order. Since the general manager lived in a suburb, we could not easily have obtained his number through information or directory inquiries.

Few salespeople can remember all of the names of the people who work for a given customer. The salesperson, of course, knows the one he is about to call on and the ones he sees often, but there will always be many he has only met once and does not regularly see. Should the salesperson run into them in the lobby or hall, or should they be unexpectedly in his meeting, he will probably be embarrassed if he cannot remember their names. This is especially true if someone is with the salesperson who must be introduced. If the salesperson has his records with him in some format or another, he can review the information briefly ahead of time. He can refresh his memory about names and other important facts he may have previously jotted down about this customer.

Occasionally, what the salesperson learns from the first person he calls on will dictate that he alter his plans and make further calls on others in this company. Having his account information with him will enable him to quickly determine his next contact person. Alongside each individual's name, a salesperson should include additional information, such as the following:

1. When and where they first met
2. Where the customer is from
3. Where the customer worked previously and how long he has been with his present firm
4. A list of products he operates
5. Any idiosyncrasies or other useful information, such as anniversaries and birthdays
6. Date of each call
7. The customer's educational background (which may not have included college)
8. Family information

The salesperson would not necessarily go in rattling off all these facts. However, a quick glance at them prior to his office visit or telephone call will enable him to better understand his customer and to be more successful selling to him. An individual's business card can be taped or stapled to the salesperson's record sheets or otherwise filed for useful retrieval. When a salesperson receives a business card, he should always add to it any information he learns, including the date. He can also store the information electronically if he prefers. However he chooses to store the information, he will be glad he took the time to do so. As he progresses through his career, he will handle many customers in different geographical areas.

These customer records should also contain addresses of the various people and, if the route is complicated, specifically how to get to offices or plants. This business record should also contain phone numbers of other vendors' people with whom he works from time to time. Keeping all of this information with him will help a salesperson work more efficiently.

A salesperson's records should also include the home and office numbers of important people at the salesperson's main office or plant, plus his counterparts in other geographic areas. Time zone differences and aggressive sales efforts will often require that the salesperson call them outside office hours.

A good salesperson will always have something with him to write on or some other way to keep notes. This could take many forms (such as a 3-inch by 6-inch leather folder with monthly replacement sections) but should have ample space for casual notes. The salesperson should keep this available, because he might receive calls at home, or he might think of something while he is away from his office that he should remind himself to do later. A good salesperson should allow for this, because some of his best thinking will be done outside his office.

The salesperson can use these same methods to keep a record of the many things he does each day. He can use his notebook, computer, or other means to remind himself to call someone or to do something next week or next month. These notes should be scrutinized carefully before being filed or deleted. The salesperson must be absolutely certain that he has kept all of his promises and has acted on all the entries requiring a follow-up. Following this procedure will greatly assist him in keeping his promises and will help him to implement ideas he thinks of when he is out of his office.

Summary

1. A salesperson should maintain good customer records and should keep them with him.
2. A salesperson should always have a good format on which to record important information and should always keep it with him.
3. A salesperson can use a notebook, laptop computer, or other convenient and portable means to record and retrieve this customer information.
4. A salesperson should keep files on all active jobs and should keep them with him.

18

Telephone Calls

The telephone can be one of a salesperson's most useful tools. To those in inside sales, it certainly is a primary tool. To use the telephone successfully and to its maximum potential requires a lot of skill.

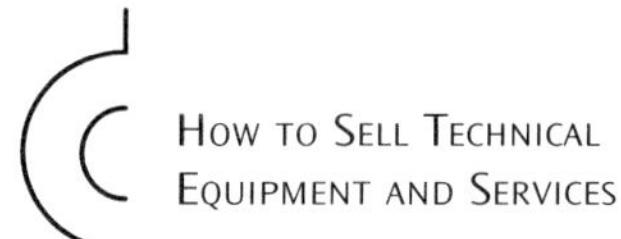

Many helpful articles have been written about how a salesperson should make and receive phone calls and how he should conduct himself on the telephone. However, there are a few important things a good salesperson must remember and practice. First, he should place his outgoing calls himself. This has the following advantages:

1. He will not leave important people waiting on the line while his administrative assistant tries to locate him.
2. He will be mentally prepared and ready to talk as soon as the other person comes on the line. He will not be rushing out of the office or thinking about other things.
3. If the prospect is unavailable, the salesperson can decide immediately whether to wait on the line, call back, or leave his number.
4. The salesperson should avoid any suggestion of trying to impress the customer with his importance. This could otherwise occur if he comes on the line only after his assistant has the prospect on the line. Some customers are very sensitive about this and are offended even before a salesperson starts talking.
5. A salesperson will impress the person he calls by being on the line and ready to talk, saving a lot of the customer's valuable time.

For calls to a customer's firm, the salesperson should politely and immediately identify both himself and his company when the other person answers. This is true whether the call is answered by an operator or someone who will recognize his voice. If the salesperson has a common first name, he should always give his last name as well. Furthermore, the salesperson should not assume that because he met a customer once that the customer will automatically remember him and his company. If there is any doubt, after giving his name and his firm, the salesperson should refresh the customer's memory with details about when and where they met. He should make it easy for the customer to recognize him and never make him feel embarrassed. Also, he should not expect people to remember his voice. People's voices are often similar.

A salesperson who identifies himself when calling a customer also helps the customer's administrative assistant if that individual answers the phone. The assistant will not have the awkwardness of asking who is calling, which helps maintain professionalism and respect for the salesperson. An assistant who knows immediately who is calling will be more likely to help the salesperson reach the customer and can assist the salesperson with answers. For instance, if the salesperson knows the customer well and is calling to make an office appointment or to ask him to have lunch, the assistant often knows if the customer is already engaged. If not, the assistant might be able to arrange either the office visit or the lunch date. By revealing that the customer has a salesperson's competitor in his office, the assistant may even help avoid an extremely awkward situation. The salesperson can often save time if he is referred to someone else for answers.

The salesperson should never ask an assistant if the customer is in until he has identified himself. Even then, it is best for him to ask, "Is Mr. Smith available?" This provides an easy out if he is in a meeting or has someone in his office, or if the assistant is screening his calls. The salesperson should never ask the assistant to interrupt his meeting.

The salesperson should never ask an assistant if the customer is in until he has identified himself.

When a salesperson speaks initially to his prospect, it is a good idea for him to ask if he is interrupting anything or if it is convenient for him to talk. It is usually not a good idea to ask if he has time to talk, because then he may think that the salesperson might want too much of his time. If his assistant is unavailable, the customer may answer the phone himself, or a temporary employee may put the salesperson's call through during an important meeting. The presence of the salesperson's competitor or even other people in the customer's company could severely restrict his replies.

If the customer is busy, the salesperson should ask if he can call back at a more convenient time. He should give the customer a chance to return his call or to designate a more convenient time for him to repeat the call. If the salesperson neglects to do these things, his customer may give him abrupt or even rude answers without the salesperson realizing why. The salesperson may not get the answer he wanted because his request was made at an inconvenient time, and the customer was not able to give his undivided attention. Other people in the customer's office may inhibit him from speaking freely.

When someone calls the salesperson's office, he should never say, nor allow anyone who answers the phone for him to say, "Who is calling?" This is offensive to almost everyone. There are more polite ways to gain this information, such as, "May I tell him who is calling?" or "Would you like for me to tell him who is calling?" If the salesperson is unavailable, his assistant should mention this first and then ask politely, "May I tell him who called?"

The salesperson should return all phone calls, even from people he does not know, like, or expect to do business with. It only takes a minute to be courteous. Just because a salesperson does not recognize a name or company does not mean that the person or company is not important. This person may have been referred by a good friend, a good customer, or one of the salesperson's senior executives. He may even be related to one of the salesperson's customers. With a minimum expenditure of time, the salesperson may be able to help him. A salesperson needs all the help he can get. A salesperson expects people to return his calls, so he should practice the Golden Rule and return calls himself.

The best approach for a salesperson is to either be in, and available to everyone, or to be out, and unavailable to everyone. When a salesperson has someone in his office, he should not answer the telephone himself. He should allow his assistant to answer the phone or let it go to voice mail. He will thus save valuable time with his visitor. Any other practice will get the salesperson in trouble sooner or later, and he will be accused of playing games. If the salesperson does not accept all calls when he is actually available, he will end up asking someone to screen out calls from certain people. Eventually the evasions will be bungled, either by the regular assistant or by someone else who answers the salesperson's phone.

Sometimes a salesperson must shut off phone calls in order to get important work done. In this case he should simply ask his assistant or whoever answers the phone to say he is in a meeting or that he has someone in his office, but they should not say he is in conference. The person who answers the phone should say that the salesperson will return the call soon. Later in the day, he should return all of these calls. He should not ask someone else to return a call for him, since he usually does not like it when others do this to him. The following list of questions is patterned after the New York Telephone Company guides for telephone courtesy:

1. When the telephone rings, does he answer promptly?
2. Does he give his name right away?

3. Does he speak directly into the mouthpiece in a normal tone of voice?
4. Does he make an effort to make his telephone voice sound pleasant and friendly rather than curt or indifferent?
5. Does he have a pencil and paper handy?
6. When it is necessary to leave the line, does he explain to the customer that he must step away and then put the phone down gently?
7. When he returns, does the salesperson thank the person for waiting?
8. When he says he will call back, does he keep his promise?
9. Does he ask necessary questions in a nice way?
10. When he receives a call for someone else, does he cheerfully offer to take a message?
11. Does he listen attentively without interrupting?
12. When the call is returned, does he express appreciation?
13. When placing a call, does he have in mind exactly what he wants to say?
14. When the customer answers, does the salesperson identify himself immediately?
15. As the call is being terminated, does he thank the customer for taking time to talk?
16. Does he wait for the customer to hang up first and then gently replace the receiver?

Here are some other tips:

1. The salesperson should proceed immediately with business and should avoid small talk.
2. On the other hand, if a customer or someone in the salesperson's own organization calls, he should not be too quick to say, "What can I do for you?" It is better to wait until the caller says what he called about. If he is trying to be friendly, the salesperson should not cut him off. To say, "What is on your mind?" right away could offend by suggesting or implying that the caller is waiting too long to get down to business. It could suggest impatience or rudeness.
3. The salesperson should have his message well thought out and should not drag it out by repeating himself.

4. The salesperson should never interrupt. Nothing shuts down a two-way discourse faster.
5. The salesperson should use short, familiar words and should not try to impress people by using strange or long words. Short words can be very effective. The overwhelming majority of the words in Lincoln's Gettysburg Address have only one syllable.
6. The salesperson should keep his message simple. He should remember that the customer can only hear what is said and cannot see the expression on the salesperson's face to tell if he is smiling or scowling.
7. The salesperson should avoid talking too quickly. He should think ahead of his prospect but not talk ahead of him.
8. The salesperson should pause often.
9. The salesperson should use words familiar to the customer. He should not expect him to understand the jargon of the salesperson's profession.
10. The salesperson should always speak in a grammatically correct fashion. Poor English can be offensive even to people who do not speak good English.
11. The salesperson's opening words are very important and usually set the tone of the entire conversation, so he should choose them well.
12. The salesperson should not repeat the customer's name too often or he will risk being offensive.
13. As a salesperson, he will not want to leave his name and number unless he is certain the prospect will return his call. If he leaves his number, he surrenders the initiative. He is then at the customer's mercy while waiting for him to call. This is certainly true when a salesperson is calling someone who does not know him well. For a salesperson to leave his number is especially dicey when he is working on a big order with someone who is very busy. The customer will be besieged by salespeople and will not have time to return all calls. In cases like this, the salesperson should leave a message that he called and will ring back later. Then he can retain the initiative and can call as often as he likes, using good manners.

14. The salesperson should be careful with the content of any messages he leaves. He should be careful to do the following:
    - He should keep messages simple and short. Complex messages will get bungled.
    - He should never include sensitive or confidential information, because his message might be seen or heard by others and thus cause embarrassment.
15. The salesperson should always identify himself when he calls, even while retaining the initiative and not leaving a number. He should remember that it is rude to repeatedly call a customer and not identify himself when he learns that the prospect is out. I was in a customer's office recently and was told that someone had called him several times the day before while he was out of town but never left a name, company, or number. The customer was obviously not impressed with this sort of conduct.
16. When the salesperson answers an outside call from a customer attempting to reach someone else in his organization, it is dangerous to try to transfer the call. Invariably the other person will be out or the line will be busy. It is usually best for the salesperson to take the number and personally give it to the correct person. Since the salesperson took the message, he must make certain the call is returned if it is from a customer.
17. The salesperson should never use subterfuge in an attempt to get through to someone who is difficult to reach. This tactic is doomed to failure in the long run. The salesperson represents a substantial company with quality goods to sell. He should not resort to trickery, pretense, or excuses.
18. When a customer calls and the salesperson is unavailable, he should not ask his assistant to quiz the customer about the call. To do so will cause the customer to expect the salesperson to have all the answers when he calls him back, and the salesperson may not yet have enough input. It is better for the salesperson's assistant not to ask why the person called. The salesperson can then call back himself so he can ask all the necessary questions.

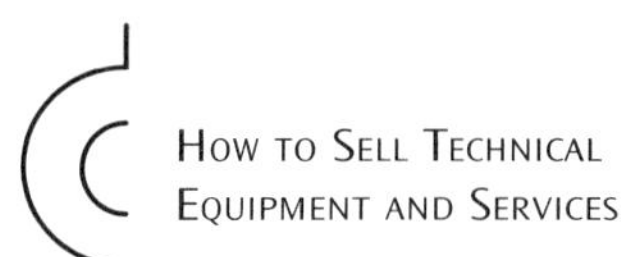

19. The salesperson should speak to everyone who answers the customer's telephone with the same respect and consideration he shows the customer. These people are very close to the buyer and will pass along both favorable and unfavorable impressions they receive from the salesperson.
20. The salesperson should not try to make jokes or be clever on the telephone, especially when talking to strangers or someone he does not know very well. It is better to be serious at all times and maintain a professional sales attitude.
21. Many people have answering machines or voice mail, and a salesperson should follow any instructions exactly when leaving a message.

Sales Examples

Example 1

Many years ago, a colleague of mine would always ask his assistant to place his calls to customers, especially to people who were hard to reach. By the time his call would finally go through, he would be out in the warehouse or the service department talking to other people. His assistant would have to run down the hall, yelling that the customer was waiting on the line. A salesperson should place all calls himself and should never allow the customer to wait on the line for him.

Example 2

A couple of years ago, I called an important engineer with an oil company. He answered the phone himself, and I immediately asked if I was interrupting anything. He said, "Yes, you are. I have my office full of people and answered this call myself only because I was expecting an important incoming call and thought this was it. Can I call you back?" A few hours later, he called back when his office was otherwise empty and he had plenty of time to talk. A few days later, he sent me in the mail a schematic diagram of the information I was asking about. His response was much more than I had expected. I believe if I had talked to him with his office full of people, he would have given me short answers and would not have provided this information, and I would not have known why.

Example 3

Once when my assistant gave me my telephone messages, she asked if I knew one of the callers. When I answered negatively, she then said that person certainly tried to give the impression that she knew me personally by quickly asking, "Is Jim in?" Apparently, she expected to be put straight through by pretending to be someone I knew quite well. She was a total stranger working for a brokerage firm. This individual was at a serious disadvantage before she even talked to me. Needless to say, I never did any business with her.

Example 4

One Tuesday, I called a major oil company and asked for someone I knew fairly well. When his assistant answered, she told me her boss was out but would be in on Friday. I asked if he would be in Friday morning or later in the day. She icily replied, "He is returning from offshore by helicopter and you can never accurately predict their schedule." She probably did not mean to sound discourteous, but it came through to me that way. I would certainly not want her answering my telephone.

Example 5

Several years ago, I received a call while I was out of the office from someone unknown to me in Syracuse, New York. I recognized neither the name nor the company. I returned the call anyway, because I think all calls should be returned. When the stranger answered, the first thing he said was that the chairman and CEO of my company had suggested that he call me for some information on China. A salesperson should always return his calls because he never knows what or who has prompted them.

The perception that customers have of a salesperson's firm is influenced to a great extent by the telephone reception they receive and the way their calls are handled. The telephone is a priceless selling tool. It can greatly magnify a salesperson's selling efforts and can save him an enormous amount of time. He should work hard toward improving his telephone manners and techniques. This work will pay handsome dividends and increase his sales.

Summary

1. Since the telephone is the salesperson's finest tool, he should learn and practice the skills to use it well.
2. The salesperson should place all outgoing calls personally.
3. The salesperson should immediately identify himself and his company.
4. A salesperson should make certain that he is not interrupting an important meeting in the customer's office.
5. A salesperson should not let anyone answering his calls to blurt out, "Who is calling?"
6. The salesperson should promptly return all phone calls, even if he does not recognize the name.
7. The salesperson should be consistent in how he answers his calls. He should be available to everyone or unavailable to everyone and should not have his calls selectively screened.
8. When calling a customer, the salesperson should always have in mind exactly what he wants to say, arranged in logical sequence. He should immediately proceed with business.
9. A salesperson should never interrupt when a customer is speaking.
10. A salesperson should use short, familiar words, pause often, and avoid speaking too quickly.
11. The salesperson should speak in a grammatically correct manner.
12. A salesperson's opening words are decisive and can set the tone of the entire conversation.
13. When attempting to reach someone who is difficult to contact, a salesperson should not leave a return message except as a last resort.
14. The salesperson should be very careful about the contents of any messages he leaves. He should keep them short and simple.
15. The salesperson should not attempt to transfer incoming calls from customers. He should take down the number, deliver the message personally, and make certain the call is returned.
16. The salesperson should always take time to think about the call he is about to place and should be mentally prepared for it.

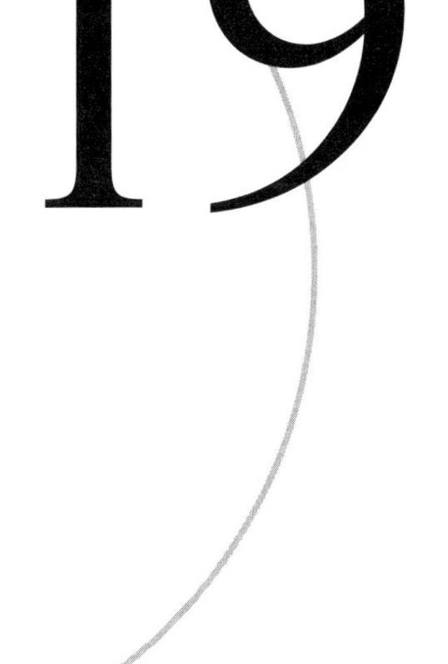

19 Don't Take Customers for Granted

Many sales are lost and severe damage can be done to a salesperson's reputation with his customers if he takes them for granted. He should not expect to be given the order because of past deeds or accomplishments.

Sometimes salespeople say things such as, “The customer owes us the next order,” or “We earned this order.” This is very dangerous thinking. It may be true as far as the salesperson’s reasoning goes, but he is not the customer. The salesperson is not making the decisions and placing the orders.

The salesperson must have the discipline to go out to sell every day and convince the customer on each and every order to place the business with him. The old adage, “What have you done for me lately?” certainly applies to customers.

Perhaps a salesperson has clearly gone out of his way to accommodate a customer during an emergency. He can and should discreetly mention that his firm specializes in this and can react rapidly as proven to the customer in the past. However, he should not think that just because they have responded swiftly or have gone to great lengths to help that he can relax or that he is entitled to the next order. It just does not work that way. If the customer is indeed indebted to the salesperson, he probably realizes that. The salesperson should not remind the customer too strongly or too frequently, or it will become counterproductive.

The salesperson should never expect individuals in a company to deliver an order to him only because of friendship, lavish entertainment, or something special he has done for them. These things should certainly help, but he must never assume that they will get him the order. He should work just as hard as if he had nothing going for him. He should do his selling almost as if he were starting from scratch. Many salespeople confuse friendship and business, and they mix them together. Virtually all customers separate the two as far as they can. Unless a salesperson is prepared for them to be separate, he will be disappointed. Even though he knows a customer socially, and perhaps even was out with him and his family the night before, he should never mention these facts in the presence of his associates. The salesperson should not trade on this. The customer may not want this generally known, and if he does, the salesperson should let him bring it up.

Many salespeople confuse friendship and business, and they mix them together. Virtually all customers separate the two as far as they can.

Perhaps an individual in the customer's organization supported the salesperson on the last order and has been favorable to his company in the past. The salesperson should never assume that he will vote for the salesperson to get the next order. The salesperson's competitor may have in the meantime been aggressively selling the customer on competitive products and may have convinced him. The salesperson should not neglect anyone or take them for granted for very long, or they may no longer be on his side. If the salesperson loses the order, he may struggle with ill feelings toward his customer. His customer may feel equally unhappy with the salesperson because the customer feels he expected too much.

Summary

The salesperson must appreciate his customers and avoid taking them for granted. He must give all of his customers his full sales efforts and service, and not rely on past deeds or friendships, or his sales will suffer.

20

Know the Industry

Many customers look forward to visits by salespeople who are well informed in their industry, because they can obtain the latest information from them about what is going on in other areas. Many executives, top management people, and engineers are so busy doing their own jobs that they miss some of what is going on in their industry. A well-informed salesperson can bridge this gap and enhance his reputation with his customers.

How can a salesperson achieve this? First, published information will not give him the complete story, but it is a good way to start. For example:

1. He could subscribe to and read the top trade magazines published in his industry. These will reveal news of expansions, new products and processes, and personnel movements. When short of time, the salesperson can ask his administrative assistant to read and mark the items in his particular interest area.
2. He can read the business section of a local daily newspaper with particular attention to the section showing new developments, new appointments, transfers, or promotions among his customers.
3. He should read a national newspaper as often as possible. This will help him remain current on developments and trends overseas as well as out of his immediate area.

Reading technical magazines and publications will also give the salesperson some idea about competitive trends. He should read all of the articles relating to his business. He also should pay attention to competitive ads or technical papers published by his competitors. These technical magazines will assist him in learning more about the subsidiary portions of his business where attendant products are used. This will also help him to identify other salespeople who are calling on his customers to sell complementary products. Knowing these salespeople will help the salesperson do his job better. They can give him additional intelligence on active projects and help him confirm or verify his own information.

Technical articles are often published by the salesperson's customers or his competitors. In either case, they can be good sources of information. If they are written by customers, they can give the salesperson insight to their thinking. During the next call, he can comment favorably on the article. Asking a genuine, intelligent question will impress the author. These articles may contain information that can help the salesperson the next time he is selling to them. If authored by a competitor, an article will almost always provide additional intelligence about his products or his organization.

If authored by a competitor, an article will almost always provide additional intelligence about his products or his organization.

Reading technical magazines in the salesperson's industry will undoubtedly keep him better informed in his profession. He will be a better conversationalist and will have additional topics to discuss besides his products. It will keep him apprised of legislation affecting his business so that he is a more intelligent voter.

To supplement published information in the industry, the salesperson should add to his knowledge by joining and attending one or two professional organizations related to his business. He should watch for opportunities to provide a speaker from his company. He should also occasionally attend conventions and technical meetings related to his industry. Visiting with customers and other salespeople at places like this will keep him current in his industry and will supplement the published information.

Making a lot of calls and having lunch with customers is still the best overall way to be well informed. The salesperson should never allow himself to get bogged down with paperwork. He must take time to see customers as often as possible. Customers will welcome his visits if he is well informed in his industry. This is particularly true of a customer's top executives.

One of the best ways for a salesperson to know his industry is to go to see his customers in their offices. While making these calls and in waiting rooms, he will encounter other salespeople. He will invariably hear news about mergers and acquisitions in his business and learn about personnel changes.

Summary

To be outstanding, a salesperson should take the time needed to become well informed in his industry. His customers will be more anxious to talk to him, and it will make him a more successful salesperson.

21

Sell In-Depth

It is extremely important for a salesperson to sell in-depth. To do this, it is mandatory that the salesperson has more than just one contact person in the customer's plant, station, or headquarters. There are many ways a salesperson can obtain the names of other individuals in the customer's organization. There are also some helpful strategies for cultivating these other people, particularly the assistants, the lower level people, and those on the fringes.

Consider a salesperson who has been assigned to an account for quite some time. The customer has given him substantial business on an ongoing basis. They like his products and have had good success using them, and he has recently submitted a sizable quote. The salesperson thinks that since they have been buying from him and the account is in good shape, he will likely get this pending order. However, the following Monday morning, the salesperson places a call to his contact in the customer's organization to check on the status of his quotation. The switchboard operator tells the salesperson that this person is no longer with the company. Now the salesperson is in trouble. This individual was the only contact that the salesperson had in the customer's organization, and he has no idea who the successor will be. The successor might even be someone that his competitor knows and has been meeting with for some time.

This scenario may sound unlikely, but it happens frequently. A successful salesperson will take steps to see that it never happens to him.

Salespeople often call only on the major decision maker with accounts they handle. No doubt the decision maker is important and much attention should be paid to him, but a salesperson should not neglect the people below the decision maker or around him. If the salesperson ignores these other people, he will always be scrambling when the top person is promoted, resigns, retires, or otherwise leaves that position. Almost invariably, someone that the salesperson has neglected will be promoted to fill this vacancy. Although the salesperson may not know the successor, it is possible that some of his competitors have been paying attention to that person and have gained an advantage.

If the salesperson calls on or knows only one person in the organization, then he has no leverage and is not giving in-depth coverage to the account. To broaden his coverage, he should generally concentrate first on the level below or around the decision maker, not above. He will always be ahead of his competitors if he knows, pays attention to, and cultivates more than just one level of employee or just one person.

If the salesperson calls on or knows only one person in the organization, then he has no leverage and is not giving in-depth coverage to the account.

There is not always time to get to know everyone well. Nevertheless, a salesperson should always treat officials of the second and third rank with the same respect as he does the top decision maker. He should give these other people the same attention, and if possible, he should call on them with almost the same frequency as he does his main contact person. He should do this with sincerity, because sooner or later their promotions will place them in positions of authority to make decisions in the salesperson's favor. When this occurs, he will have done his homework and will already have established relationships with these people and will know something about them. Before their promotions to top authority, they often do not get as much attention as the top decision maker. Therefore, they appreciate it much more. They will more often be available for lunch or dinner. Frequently, they will tell the salesperson more about what is going on and will more readily relate the status of new and active projects.

In customer meetings involving several levels of authority, the salesperson must make certain he and his colleagues respond respectfully and completely to all questions. This respect should be shown to the lowest level person just as it would to the top decision maker. After the answer is given, the salesperson should ask the lower level person if he is satisfied and if his question has been fully answered. Sooner or later this person will no doubt move up in the customer's organization and will remember the salesperson's respect and attention when he had a low-level job.

The salesperson should show attention to the number two and number three people discreetly. If the number one person will resent this or feel threatened, the salesperson should take it easy when showing attention to his subordinates or the ones around him. Usually a salesperson will not have a problem in this area if he does not neglect the boss and overdo his attention to these subordinates, and if he is sincere in his efforts.

Another reason that a salesperson should pay attention to these people before they get the top job is that when they are promoted, everyone will be showering them with attention. If the promoted people remember that the salesperson neglected them when they had lower level positions, they will likely resent any later respect he shows them, considering it insincere.

As companies are continually merging and thus combining departments, laying off people, and giving early retirements, the turnover can be high. Therefore, it is more important than ever to have broad coverage.

Furthermore, the purchasing decisions on technical or engineered products are rarely made by just one person. Sometimes these purchase decisions are made by several people or by a committee. The more people a salesperson knows in the customer's organization, the more likely it is that he will know at

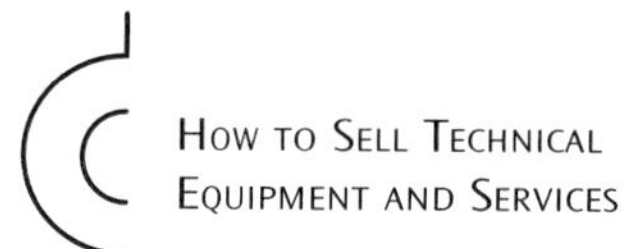

least some of the people involved in these kinds of decisions. It is very unlikely that he will know all of the individuals who are called in on a major project, but he will know at least several if he has in-depth coverage of the account.

It is also a good idea for a salesperson to cultivate people on the fringes of the decision makers. Often, they will know something about aspects of the project that can contribute to his overall job intelligence and understanding.

It is not easy for a salesperson to get to know and cultivate relationships within a customer's organization. However, there are a few suggestions:

1. As a salesperson calls on a customer, he must be alert to the people around the decision maker, the people he relies on for support, and the people who attend the meetings along with the ranking person. He also should be attentive to people who are asked to sit in on the meeting. He should be sure to obtain their names and positions so he later can go see them or at least talk to them on the telephone.
2. After the salesperson is well acquainted with his normal contact person, he should ask him for introductions to others in the customer's company. The contact person could introduce him to other buyers, engineers, or maintenance people who work in the general area of his products.
3. Occasionally when a salesperson asks his normal contact person to lunch, he could suggest that the contact person bring one of his associates. When the situation is appropriate, he could ask him to bring his boss.
4. When a salesperson is talking to his main buyer in purchasing, he should ask for suggestions concerning other people in maintenance that he should get to know. When talking to the maintenance people, the salesperson should ask them who else in purchasing he should contact. If the person the salesperson knows works in engineering, he could ask for suggestions concerning those he should contact in purchasing and maintenance.
5. Sometimes when a salesperson is visiting his customer's contact person, a colleague will come into the office. In this situation, the salesperson should not only introduce himself, but if possible, he should ask the visitor something about his job. The salesperson must be sure to remember the colleague's name. If he is someone whose duties are related to what the salesperson is selling, he could call on him later. These opportunities usually are overlooked by most salespeople.

6. Sometimes the receptionist can suggest others around the buyer or decision maker that the salesperson should contact. He should ask the receptionist who else, if anyone, his competitors come to see when they visit.
7. The salesperson should be alert at trade shows and conventions for individuals from his customers' companies. He should be sure to introduce himself and learn their names and how they relate to what he sells. He could also go see them the next time he calls on that customer. If they are not directly involved in his business, he could ask them to suggest others for him to contact. Occasionally someone in another area, such as the financial or manufacturing department, can offer valuable suggestions. If the account is assigned to another salesperson, he should be sure to pass these names to the proper salesperson for follow up.
8. When a salesperson's firm has a reception or dinner party at a convention or trade show, he should invite more than just one person from each organization. He should include some of these other people he has met. If the salesperson only knows one person, he should ask that individual for the names of others in his company who could be invited.
9. The salesperson should watch newspaper or trade journal announcements about his customers. They sometimes reveal people the salesperson should also be calling on to broaden his coverage.
10. The salesperson should obtain and study a company's organization charts. These charts will reveal who else works in the vicinity of the decision maker. It is especially important to keep and study organization charts of a company over the years. They will reveal who is moving up in the company and who might next be in the key position most affecting the salesperson's business.

The salesperson should be careful not to play favorites among the lower echelon people in the customer's organization. While it is well to try to pick out the bright stars, he should never try to be too clever in this endeavor.

The same buyer or engineer may not handle every job on which a salesperson bids. If the salesperson has in-depth strength in a company, he will be more likely to know and be in good standing with the one assigned to the new project. He will not then be dealing with a stranger. People in an organization talk to each other. If the salesperson is responsive to the people he normally contacts, that information is passed around and can be of great help as he meets others in the organization. He should remember that his reputation will precede him, rather than follow him.

Sales Examples

Example 1

Several years ago, I had an engineering friend who worked for a very small company as chief engineer. One day he called to ask for an estimate on two small machines his company would soon need for a planned project. I followed up the estimate with a quotation and showed him photographs and lists of product users indicating where we had similar units running. I convinced him that our machines were the products to buy, and he gave me a verbal order for two. I confirmed this agreement in a letter to him. He explained that the project involved several partners who had to approve the expenditure and that this would take several months.

I entered the verbal order with our factory and explained the circumstances. We proceeded on an engineering only basis. Periodically I called my friend, but the approvals were dragging. Several weeks went by. One day I ran into this chief engineer on the street during lunch hour, and since I had not checked with him in a couple of weeks, I asked him the status and if his project was approved yet. To my astonishment, he replied, "I have changed jobs and am no longer with my old firm. I meant to call you, but it slipped my mind."

I was shaken because this engineer was the only person I knew within that small organization. He said not to worry, because the president knew of this commitment. He suggested that I should call the president to reestablish contact, and I lost no time doing so. But when I called the president, he was unaware or did not remember that a commitment had been made to my company for this product. I explained that it had, and I sent copies of my correspondence to document this. We retained the order, which was firmed up shortly thereafter. I was very nervous for several days before this was sorted out and vowed to never again be caught in the same situation.

Example 2

While working my way through college, I was employed by a wholesale candy and tobacco company as a salesperson. I called on small grocery and drug stores. Often, I would have to wait to see the manager or buyer. While waiting, I would visit with the stock clerk just to pass the time, asking about his family and other things. On subsequent calls, I learned that when the buyer was sick or otherwise not at work, this lower level person would temporarily be in charge. He quite often gave me a larger order than the regular buyer did. This demonstrated to me the importance of getting to know more than just one person. I sort of stumbled into this, but I kept it in mind throughout my selling career, and it has paid big dividends.

Example 3

I once had a customer that had one man who decided on all purchases of the engineered products I sold. He was in charge of the operating department and would always politely listen to the engineering and purchasing people on any given project. But in the end, he would tell them what to purchase, and unfortunately, it was always a competitor's products, not ours. I did continue to call on him, show him photographs, and stress the benefits of our products. However, I also decided to broaden my influence base, because I realized that sooner or later, he would no longer be in that dominant position.

I began calling on his assistant, who was the number two person in the department. While he had the same school ties as his boss, he was more approachable. He had probably been ignored by the competitor to whom his boss was so loyal and committed.

Over the next year or so, I called regularly on the person who was second in command and went out of my way to make sure he knew about the latest developments and improvements with our products. I always included him in dinner parties at conventions. In all business meetings where several people from his company were present, I made certain his questions were fully answered.

About two years after I began my campaign, his boss was suddenly taken ill and soon passed away. While I certainly regretted what had happened, I suddenly found myself in excellent shape with this customer. Shortly thereafter a big job came up with this firm. This was one of the biggest projects they had ever implemented. By continuing to do a good selling job, we were awarded this big project, and I do not think the race was even close. This plant was later expanded several times, generating several other large orders for my company. Cultivating the second level of authority certainly paid off.

Example 4

One of the other companies I called on also had a strong individual in the operating department who made most of the product decisions. I usually had to wait to see him, but I was always asked to sit near his office, not in the reception

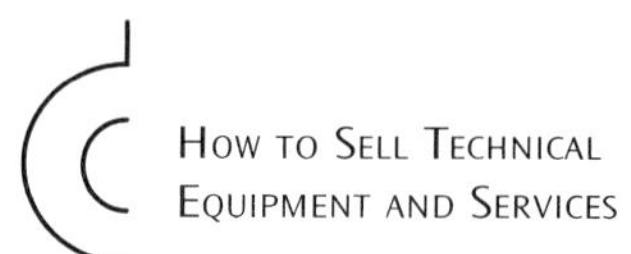

area. This senior executive had a young engineer working for him who kept his records, files, and reports. While I was waiting, I would always say a few words to this young engineer, asking him about his family and how his job was going. This situation repeated itself many times during the three years I handled the account before being transferred out of the country.

Fifteen years later, this young engineer was then a senior manager and had during these years bought a lot of our products. On one of his trips to our factory in connection with one of these orders, he asked my whereabouts. After he was told what I was then doing, he replied that I was the *only* salesperson who treated him like an engineer when he was a clerk. Years later when I started my second career, I called this gentleman. Even though he was then retired, he was extremely cordial and voluntarily sent me valuable personnel information on his former company. Cultivating customer contacts on more than one level resulted in a lot of business for my firm and helped me again years later.

Broad coverage is necessary for the survival of a relationship between a salesperson and his client companies. Presidents of large companies say the most dangerous thing that can happen to a product supplier is to depend on a single personal tie with the client company. If a client hires a product supplier because the client's president likes the supplier's president, the supplier's salesperson must take urgent steps to forge ties with the client at the lower levels. Only when he is wired in at every level can he hope for tenure. Contact with the customer should not be restricted to the account executives. It works much better to know people from the service department, engineering, research, communications, marketing, and so on. A successful salesperson gets to know the customer.

It is always best for a salesperson to broaden his efforts to reach additional contacts in a downward direction within the customer's company. If he tries to widen his circle of contacts by moving upwards in the company, he will encounter a lot of resentment. Most decision-makers and buyers are nervous if a salesperson is always calling on their boss. This makes most decision makers uncomfortable, although they may never say anything to the salesperson about it. It will, however, manifest itself in lost orders. Occasionally the salesperson will want to make an exception and call on upper level people. He should not do this on a regular basis and should not try to involve them on a specific order.

Many large purchase decisions are amazingly close, and it does not take much to cause a salesperson to lose an order. The salesperson should cultivate more than one level of contact person and more than just one or two people within the customer's organization. This will greatly enhance his chances of closing the maximum amount of business. It also will enable him to be more solidly involved with the customer and to retain this influence as people get promoted, retire, or resign. If a salesperson sells in-depth, it will increase his current business and help safeguard the account for the future.

Summary

1. It is very important for a salesperson to sell in-depth.
2. The salesperson must know more than just one contact person in the customer's plant, station, or office.
3. The salesperson who knows only one individual is always left scrambling when that person is promoted, retires, resigns, or otherwise leaves.
4. To broaden his coverage, a salesperson should concentrate on individuals around his customer's contact people or below them—not above, unless he is cautious.
5. The salesperson should show this respect to the lower level people discreetly, so that he does not offend the main buyer.
6. In meetings with the customer, the salesperson should respond to a lower level person just as respectfully as he would the decision maker.
7. Following this course will place the salesperson in a better position when these lower echelon people are promoted. He should treat those of the second and third rank with the same respect he shows the decision maker.
8. Many decisions are made by a group, so the more people a salesperson knows, the more likely he is to have several supporters on the committee.

9. There are some suggestions for a salesperson to broaden his coverage:
   - As the salesperson calls on a customer, he should be alert to the people around the decision maker. These are the people he relies on for support and the people who attend the meetings along with the ranking person.
   - After the salesperson is well acquainted with the contact person, he should ask him for introductions to other buyers, engineers, or maintenance people who work in the general area of his products.
   - Occasionally when a salesperson asks his contact person to lunch, he should suggest that the contact person bring one of his associates. When the situation is appropriate, he could ask him to bring his boss.
   - When a salesperson is talking to his main buyer in purchasing, he can ask for suggestions concerning others he might contact in maintenance. When talking to the maintenance people, he can ask them who else in purchasing he should contact. If the individual the salesperson knows works in engineering, he can ask for suggestions concerning people in purchasing and maintenance he should get to know so he can better do his selling job.
   - When a colleague comes into the office of the contact person, the salesperson should take the opportunity to introduce himself, and if possible, ask the visitor something about his job. The salesperson should be sure to remember his name.
   - Sometimes the receptionist can suggest others around the buyer or decision maker that the salesperson should contact. He should ask the receptionist who else, if anyone, his competitors contact when they visit.
   - The salesperson should be alert at trade shows and conventions for individuals from his customers' companies. He should introduce himself and learn their names and how they relate to what he sells. He should make an effort to go see them the next time he calls on that customer. If they are not directly involved in the salesperson's business, he should ask them to suggest others for him to contact.
   - When the salesperson's firm has a reception or dinner party at conventions or trade shows, he should invite more than just one person from each organization. He should include some of these

other people he has met. If the salesperson only knows one person, he should ask that individual for the names of others to invite from the customer's organization.

- The salesperson should watch newspaper or trade journal announcements about his customers. They sometimes reveal people he should also be calling on to broaden his sales coverage.
- The salesperson should obtain and study a company's organization charts. These charts will reveal who else works in the vicinity of the decision maker.

10. The salesperson should not try to be too clever in deciding who is likely to be promoted from the lower echelon in the customer's company.
11. The salesperson should be very careful about calling on his decision maker's boss. Many buyers are very resentful of this.
12. Virtually all purchase decisions are decided by a very narrow margin.
13. The salesperson should sell in-depth. This will generate more business and will safeguard the account for the future.

22

Get Along with Colleagues

Salespeople who treat other salespeople and associates well will serve customers better and get more orders.

A truly good salesperson will use some of his sales techniques internally with his colleagues. To do their jobs well, people in other departments have deadlines and job obligations, and the salesperson should respect these. He should work hard at developing and maintaining harmonious relations with people from other departments in his company. This will make his selling job easier and more productive.

To be successful in getting along with associates or customers, the salesperson should show a sympathetic regard for the feelings of others. Whatever problem he may have with other departments, its solution will be found in the relationships with the people involved. If the salesperson practices the Golden Rule, he will take a giant step toward having good relations with these groups. He should do his homework before making a request, rather than just dumping a problem on other departments and asking the people there to sort it out. He should make their task as easy as possible.

Expressions of gratitude are always in short supply. The salesperson should be sure to express his appreciation to people in other departments who do something for him. This is especially true if they do a good job, but he should thank them even if the response is routine or average. It will bring out the best in them and elicit a better and faster response the next time. The salesperson should never assume that they were just doing their jobs and that no thanks or words of appreciation are required.

Expressions of gratitude are always in short supply.

When someone does an outstanding job for the salesperson, he should make sure he tells that person and also lets that person's supervisor know. In special cases, a short note is an excellent idea, and it could even help the person get a favorable merit review. Too many people are quick to criticize but slow to praise. If the salesperson feels he absolutely must criticize, he should do so only after several mistakes or poor responses, and he should do so constructively, softly, and privately.

The salesperson should keep in mind what other departments have told him in given situations in the past so that he does not ask the same question repeatedly. Even his company's in-house people will get tired of giving him the same solution or answer on more than one occasion. They may then feel that he is using them and is too lazy to do his own thinking.

The salesperson should make sure that his requests are clear. He should not make all of them urgent but should allow a reasonable response time. He should put important or involved requests in writing. This does three things:

- It organizes the salesperson's thoughts and will help clarify his request.
- It gives the recipient the information in a written form.
- It saves the other person a lot of time, because the details will be readily available when needed.

A salesperson should also remember that someone else besides the person he is talking to may have to actually perform the task. If his request is verbal, as the assignment is passed along to others, a lot of details will be lost. A written request can easily be passed to someone else for handling.

Communicating in a written format can also help avoid misunderstandings and can improve relations at other times. It is helpful when a salesperson asks someone from another department to accompany him to an outside meeting with his customer or to attend a meeting in his own offices with the customer.

The salesperson's request should always be written, and it should include at least the following:

1. Name of the company
2. Who will be attending the meeting from the customer's organization, including their titles or their job functions
3. Date and time of the meeting
4. Topic or topics to be discussed
5. Type of products involved
6. Background information
7. Specifics concerning what the salesperson or his customer expects to accomplish
8. Any information, models, drawings, or sketches that should be brought along
9. Expected duration of the meeting

The salesperson should give as much advance notice as possible. He should never invite his colleagues to an ambush. He must question his customer so that he knows what the customer will ask, what will take place in the meeting, and what he should expect. He should then relate this information to the others in his firm who will be involved. He should not do this on the way to the meeting. He should give his colleagues this information ahead of time so they can consider the problem and formulate consensus responses that reflect company policy.

During the meeting, the salesperson should never allow his associates to get the company in trouble by committing to too much or committing the company too quickly to a course of action. If strange or unexpected questions come up, the salesperson should offer to give the replies later unless he is absolutely certain that he or his experts know the correct response. He should not hesitate to speak up and keep his specialists from getting the company in trouble. He should bear in mind that these specialists do not talk to customers every day and may become intimidated in their presence.

A salesperson needs all the help and support he can get from inside his own organization if he is to close the maximum amount of business. He should never play games with people in other departments but should be serious at all times.

It is easy for a salesperson to assume that inside people get paid for doing their jobs, so he should not have to be nice to them to get their help. Instead, he should keep in mind that most of them are very busy, and many have more work each day than they can do in eight hours. The salesperson's requests are often competing for their valuable time. By maintaining good relations, the salesperson can encourage them to give top priority to his requests and also to do an outstanding job for him.

One of the best ways for a salesperson to build goodwill with other departments is to be responsive when they ask him for help. If the accounting department asks him to sort out an overdue account, he should drop everything and help. If the manufacturing department comes to him with a problem, he should respond favorably and quickly. He should not brush them off. If the engineering people ask for help or for additional information, he should give it to them immediately. If the purchasing department asks for clarification on something they must order, the salesperson should get it for them right away.

In all these instances, the salesperson is in a good position to help. He should know his customer well and should therefore be aware of which person to contact inside the customer's organization for information and decisions. He should not ask one of his associates to call his customer to sort out problems. He should personally call them. The possible exception is when a salesperson is handling routine matters of communicating information or data. However, if a problem is present or apt to occur, the salesperson should stay involved and help his people arrive at a solution.

To make sure he receives maximum assistance and reasonable responses, a good salesperson will use his selling talents internally with his colleagues as well as externally with his customers. Many times it seems to take more of a salesperson's efforts inside his own organization than it does with his customers.

This is particularly true in large organizations in the following areas:

- submitting complete quotations on time
- obtaining products that are competitive
- reaching agreement on exceptions to specifications
- receiving competitive prices
- obtaining the delivery needed to land the order
- receiving drawings, engineering data, and specifications within the customer's time frame
- having the products shipped on time
- reaching warranty adjustments that the customer is entitled to and will accept
- obtaining required delivery on spare parts
- securing service personnel when required

Often the people making the decisions inside the salesperson's company do not have all the facts available. The salesperson should see to it that they do have those facts before he accepts a decision that will hold him back in the marketplace and prevent him from getting future orders. The salesperson should not play games with his management, but instead, he should emphasize firmly what the customer is currently thinking and what he will accept. The salesperson should remind them of current competitive moves and tactics, as well as the latest trends in the industry and marketplace. His field of expertise affords him information from outside the company that they may not have. Occasionally, the salesperson should get his customers together with others from his company for discussions in person concerning critical items. Invariably his factory people will be more impressed and swayed if they hear objections and arguments directly.

The salesperson has an awesome responsibility in his company. The salesperson is the one person who should be an expert on his customer, his industry, his company, and his products. He also should have extensive knowledge of his competitors' products and their strategies and tactics. He is the one to bring it all together so that his company will be successful in the marketplace and can maximize profits, but he needs a lot of inside help to accomplish this. The salesperson should be certain that the decision makers in his company are well aware of all the facts before they insist that he implement a decision or policy with his customer. These decisions could cost him current

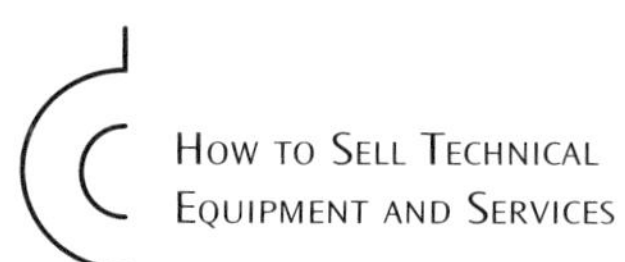

or future orders or damage his company in the eyes of the customer. He will be in a much better position to obtain favorable decisions if he has good relations inside his own company.

Internal selling covers all the internal problems that could hinder the salesperson's ability to sell the maximum amount of products to his customers. It also extends to new products and product upgrades. He should make certain his management is continuously aware of the customer's stance and the competitive climate. He should not be bashful about writing down his arguments. Words die out and are often forgotten, but a memo will get attention and also becomes part of the record. Most management executives will react more favorably if the salesperson's written arguments, positions, and ideas are reasonable. He should keep his writing accurate and clear. In cases like this, he is selling his ideas to his supervisors or other management people.

An alert salesperson is an excellent source of information on new products and product improvements. These innovations are required to assure that his company is the leader and not the follower in new developments. While marketing and engineering people may have this as a primary basic responsibility, they always need the input of the salesperson and his customers. He should provide this on a continuing basis, not only by being alert to market trends, but also by regularly quizzing his customers. He can then pass useful information to his home office people. If the salesperson has a good reputation, he will be taken seriously. He should, through internal selling, make sure these suggestions and requirements receive intelligent consideration and are not disregarded or pigeonholed.

To be successful at selling internally, the salesperson must have a sincere willingness to get along with other departments. He must expect relations to go smoothly. He should approach his dealings optimistically, even if he has had bad experiences before. He should ignore negative comments, and this requires discipline. However, the ability to ignore negative comments does not mean acceptance or agreement. In general, the salesperson should expect good things to happen, and this should be his intent on an ongoing basis. He must demonstrate a good-faith approach. If he approaches the other department with a chip on his shoulder, expecting to find fault or to have trouble, he will certainly find it.

The salesperson should allow the other department a way to save face and give them ample time to respond. He should make reasonable requests and should accept reasonable answers or responses. If the answers prove inadequate when given to his customer, the salesperson can then return and ask for more. He will return with a stronger hand because he has already consulted with his customer.

To achieve a goal of outstanding relations with his colleagues in other departments, the salesperson should strive to develop the following:

- credibility
- confidence
- believability
- a genuine and pleasant demeanor

The salesperson's attitude should inspire the people inside his organization. It should bring out the best in them. It should get them to want to do an outstanding job for the salesperson and his customers. He should keep in mind that his initial attitude and behavior as he approaches them can be decisive in the kind of response he receives. He should remember that he wants them to handle his requests first, or to at least put them at the top of their list. The salesperson should bear in mind that most company rules, regulations, and policies have wide ranges of application. If he has poor relations with the people he is contacting, he will receive the narrow interpretation of the rules. However, if he has developed good relations, they will give him the broader or wider interpretation. This can make a lot of difference.

These good relations will have the following additional benefits:

1. It will save the salesperson time, the most precious commodity he has, because his responses will come faster and without so much effort on his part. He will not then have to spend so much time convincing people to work on his requests.
2. The salesperson is more likely to receive favorable answers.
3. The salesperson will be more apt to obtain reliable, accurate, in-depth information, because others will want to help him.
4. They will go to extra efforts because they will want to be associated with a winner or a successful salesperson.
5. The salesperson's cheerful, refreshing, considerate attitude will bring out the best in them. It will inspire them and increase the overall efficiency of the company.
6. The salesperson's pleasant, cooperative, serious attitude will be contagious and will spread to other salespeople. They will observe how successful he is at getting results, and they will want to be in his position.

7. People in these departments will tell others about the salesperson, including his supervisor.
8. When working on the salesperson's requests, they will sometimes be willing to enlist the support and assistance of others in their own department.
9. These good relations will be demonstrated when these inside people are around the salesperson's customers or talk to them on the phone. The opinions that these others have of the salesperson will be subtly evident in the way they refer to him.
10. In-house people who do not respect and admire the salesperson can give him superficial replies that could cost him the order. They will work to the letter of the law rather than giving his request any extra effort.
11. Finally, when a salesperson does a good job of inside selling by getting along well with the people inside his company, he gets useful practice for dealing with his customers.

Getting along well with people is what selling is all about. This does not mean just that a salesperson should get along with his customers. It means that he should relate well to his colleagues and with people in other departments.

If the salesperson expects to be really successful, he must absolutely be good at this. He must have the ability to get along with customers with a wide range of dispositions, because they are not all alike. He will encounter a wide range of personalities among his buyers. If he cannot get along well with his own associates and other people within his company, then he likely cannot get along satisfactorily with many of his customers.

One of the best ways for a salesperson to promote good relations is to avoid criticizing people. A salesperson who says unflattering things about others will poison his own mind and reduce his selling effectiveness. Furthermore, the critical salesperson may not realize that he is harming himself. When a salesperson repeatedly says unflattering things about others, people will quite correctly assume that they will also be criticized when they are not around. It should be evident then that the salesperson can severely damage his reputation when he says bad things about others.

It is true that all of us are human, and many of us find it tempting to criticize others, especially rivals or people in other departments. But the successful salesperson must rise above this and refrain from doing so.

A salesperson should focus on praising others, even his rivals. He should say only positive things about other departments. It will make him a better and stronger person. People will admire him, and he will be more likely to receive their help. He will do a better job of selling. The salesperson should remember a principle that was mentioned previously: When a person is talking, whatever the subject, he is to some extent talking about himself. When the salesperson says negative things about other people, he is saying a lot about himself.

If the salesperson treats people inside his organization shabbily, some of this attitude on his part will show up in his dealings with customers. He might say that he would not allow this to happen, but his condescending or negative attitude will invariably resurface and manifest itself in some manner when he is responding to his customers.

The salesperson's goal should be to have a good reputation within his company. This will have many benefits:

- When the salesperson requests a new product, his engineering department will recognize that he has done his homework, knows the potential sales, and can provide reliable technical information.
- When the salesperson reports competitive feedback on a job, he will be immediately believed without question.
- When the salesperson requests help from the purchasing and accounting departments, it is immediately given, because his requests are reasonable, prudent, serious, and well prepared.
- If the salesperson asks the shipping department late in the day to get something out, they will know he has a good reason to be requesting this so late.
- When the salesperson asks management executives for price or warranty concessions, they will respond favorably.

A truly good salesperson will work hard to acquire this reputation. It will pay handsome dividends. He should work very hard at developing and maintaining good relations with other departments inside his company and should always avoid being critical. If he does this, he will be amazed at how much easier it will be for him to get his job done and to be much more successful in his selling efforts.

If the salesperson has a good reputation inside his company, he will be much more believable when he reports competitive moves in the marketplace.

He will be able to get new products developed and will be able to get more things done for his customers. He will have a better reputation with them and will close more orders.

I once asked an important customer in Canada what impressed him the most in sales engineers who called on him. Without hesitation, he said, "I want the salesman to have a good reputation and a good standing inside his own company, because then he can deliver. He can keep all the promises he makes to me, and obtain for my company fair and equitable prices as well as fair settlements on back charges."

Max DePree, chairman emeritus of Herman Miller, wrote in his book *Leadership is an Art*, "It begins with a belief in people. When we think about the people with whom we work, people on whom we depend, we can see that without each individual we are not going to go very far as a group. By ourselves, we suffer serious limitations. Together we can be something wonderful."

The evidence is overwhelming that a salesperson should strive very hard to do a good job of inside selling and must get along with the people inside his company.

Summary

1. A good salesperson will use some of his sales skills internally on his colleagues and people in other departments.
2. The salesperson's relationship with other people is critical and will be the basis of solving any problems that arise.
3. The salesperson must do his homework before approaching other departments. He should make it easier for them to respond favorably.
4. The salesperson should express gratitude to other departments.
5. The salesperson should be extremely reluctant to say anything critical of other departments. If unavoidable, he should do so softly, constructively, and privately.
6. The salesperson should not repeatedly ask the same questions.

7. The salesperson's requests should be clear and in a written form, and he must allow a reasonable time for response. He should avoid urgent requests unless absolutely necessary.
8. When asking someone from another department to attend a meeting with a customer, the salesperson should make the request in writing and give all relevant details.
9. In meetings with customers, the salesperson should protect his inside people.
10. The salesperson should be serious in his dealings with other departments and always allow them to save face when mistakes occur.
11. The salesperson must always be responsive when asked for help by other departments.
12. The salesperson should be optimistic in dealing with others inside his company. He should expect things to go well.
13. The salesperson has an awesome responsibility and should be the one to bring everything together so sales and margins are maximized.
14. The good salesperson should inspire his colleagues and bring out the best in them.
15. A salesperson who has good relations with others inside his own company will experience many benefits.
16. Getting along with people is what selling is all about. If the salesperson cannot get along well inside his company, he probably cannot get along well with his customers.
17. If a salesperson says unflattering things about others, he harms his own reputation. Most people will assume that he will criticize them when they are out of earshot.
18. The salesperson should praise others and not criticize them.
19. The salesperson should develop good relationships with others so they will respond quickly and favorably and thus allow him to deliver on all of his promises to his customers.
20. The salesperson should establish and maintain a good reputation inside his company.
21. By themselves, the individuals who work for a company suffer serious limitations. Together, they can accomplish wonderful things.

23

Whether or Not to Bid on a Large Project

Since time and resources are always limited, evaluation of large product bids is one of the most important assignments of a salesperson. A great deal of money is spent in going after the big jobs. Thus a salesperson, in consultation with his management, should review all the facts and determine the best way to proceed after the receipt of an inquiry on a large project. If the inquiry is from a regular customer, the salesperson may know immediately that he will respond. On the other hand, it may be a doubtful situation if the inquiry is not from a regular buyer. There are some important questions that a salesperson should attempt to answer prior to making plans:

1. Has this customer done business with the salesperson's company in the past?
2. Does this customer regularly buy from the salesperson's company?
3. If he has not bought much from the salesperson's company in the past, how satisfied is he with his current supplier?
4. Are there any indications that the customer is inclined toward or would prefer to buy from the salesperson?
5. Does the salesperson have any evidence that the customer would prefer not to do business with him?
6. Does this customer have any of the salesperson's products in use? If so, has the customer had good or bad experiences?
7. Can the salesperson's company reasonably expect to accommodate this customer's buying procedures and requirements, accepting his terms and conditions?
8. Does the customer have reasonable delivery expectations? Can the salesperson's company achieve them?
9. How closely do the customer's requirements fit what the salesperson can supply?
10. Does the salesperson have more or less experience than his competitors on the products that the customer has inquired about?
11. How busy are the salesperson's shops and engineering force?
12. How busy are the competitors' shops and engineering force?
13. How much potential business does this customer represent during the next five years?

If the salesperson is close to this customer, he will know about the status and timing of any large projects long before the inquiry is issued. Much of the information needed will already be in his hands. Since the salesperson will still require additional information once he has received the inquiry, he should make an appointment to visit the customer's officials. Prior to a meeting, the salesperson should thoroughly read and study this inquiry, paying particular attention to unusual provisions.

Immediately after the issuance of an inquiry is an excellent time for a salesperson to obtain the additional input required to make his decision and plan his strategy. The customer should then be eager to talk. The salesperson should do this early, because his firm usually needs all the time allowed to put together a good bid. If this customer normally buys at least some of its products from the salesperson's company, a bid will likely be expected. For a salesperson to do otherwise might do irreparable harm.

Perhaps the salesperson has not sold much to this customer in the past but has done a lot of groundwork, or *missionary work*. The customer may be inclined to do business with the salesperson, and a professional competitive bid may be just what the salesperson needs to finally obtain a project or an order.

In some cases, however, the customer has not bought from the salesperson, and the salesperson has not done much selling work to change the customer's mind. Then the salesperson has an uphill fight and some careful analysis to do before deciding how to proceed. If the customer has a lot of the salesperson's products and has had good service from them, then the salesperson's decision is probably already made. If the customer has had poor service with the products and the salesperson has not taken care of it, his chances of a successful bid will be slim.

Perhaps the customer had problems with the products, but the salesperson took care of them. If the machinery now works well, the salesperson may be in a better position than he realizes. Product problems are opportunities. If the salesperson sorted the problems out expeditiously, the customer knows he can be counted on in adversity. The customer may not know how the salesperson's competitors will react when severe problems arise.

In other cases, a salesperson may know that the customer's commercial buying habits are tough and will be difficult to accommodate. A salesperson's company may require progress payments and/or

Product problems are opportunities. If the salesperson sorted the problems out expeditiously, the customer knows he can be counted on in adversity.

escalation, and he suspects that the customer's company will not agree. While this alone may not be enough to cause a salesperson to decline to bid, it should be considered carefully before spending money on a detailed proposal.

Perhaps the customer always insists on turnkey proposals, and the salesperson knows he cannot bid this way on this project. He should explore this early by visiting with the proper customer executives to explain his position. The salesperson should do this with executives at a high enough level that he can be sure to receive accurate information reflecting the company's official posture. He would not, for example, want this decision to come from someone in the customer organization at a lower level who might not know management's current thinking in light of existing business circumstances. Only a face-to-face discussion with senior customer people will give the salesperson an accurate answer. The salesperson should, of course, always go through the proper channels in arranging these visits.

Sometimes a salesperson finds buyers who, because of their inactivity or absence from the marketplace, are not attuned to current commercial practices. Situations can change dramatically over a short time. For instance, the customers may not realize that escalation and progress payments are now in all contracts in the industry. This may not have been the case with the last contracts the customers signed or the last purchase orders they issued for products on similar projects. The salesperson should make sure that the customer understands the current business climate before he decides how to proceed.

Even if a customer has not purchased products from the salesperson lately, the salesperson should investigate the customer's level of satisfaction with his current supplier. There may be a sales opportunity.

Sometimes a salesperson has strong indications that if the quality, price, commercial terms, and delivery are comparable, the customer would like to buy from him. In this case, he should submit bid.

While doing his pre-bid investigation, the salesperson should bear in mind that he cannot be successful with every company. There are many reasons for this. Perhaps the salesperson has done a lot of work on this account, but he just cannot budge the customers. If they do not seem interested in doing business with the salesperson, he probably should not expend money on a bid. On the other hand, a salesperson may think a good technical bid could finally assist him in landing an order on this project, or even the next one. In that case, it is possible that a quotation should be made, even though the salesperson may have generated little enthusiasm.

Suppose a salesperson learns that the customer expects and can accommodate a 6-month delivery time. However, the salesperson's delivery time is 18 months, because his company has just received several large contracts. The salesperson should then investigate to see if the customer really does expect shipment in 6 months. At the same time, he should determine what delivery his competitors could make. If the competitor's delivery time is also 18 months, the salesperson knows that the 6-month expected shipment date by the customer is unrealistic. However, if a competitor can indeed make the 6-month delivery, the salesperson's chances are poor. He may decline to quote if the bid preparation cost to his company is high.

Sometimes a salesperson has an account with which he has done extensive sales work, has demonstrated his products, and has bid many times without receiving a substantial order. This might be a good opportunity for the salesperson to ask for some degree of explanation. The receipt of a new inquiry or the expectation of a major expansion is an appropriate time. During these visits, some or all of the following should be pointed out to the customer:

1. The salesperson values the customer's potential business very highly.
2. The salesperson's firm has struggled very hard to find the right combination to do business with the customer but has not been successful.
3. The salesperson feels he needs guidance or suggestions as to what he might be leaving undone or what he could do differently to win this order.
4. The salesperson should make it clear that he is not blaming anyone but himself for this failure.
5. The salesperson can explain that unless he can determine a way to improve his chances on future jobs, he is considering declining to bid on this project. This will get the attention of most customers, but the salesperson should not say this in a threatening or high-pressured manner.

The customer's response will depend on many things, the most important of which is how many competitors there are for the products required on this project. If the salesperson's company is 1 of 10 suppliers, he probably will not get much encouragement, and the customer will not be concerned if he does not bid. However, if the salesperson's company is 1 of only 2 or 3 acceptable suppliers, then he will have the customer's attention. Following the conference with the customer's executives and after extensive internal discussions, the salesperson's course of action should be clear. He will either come away from the customer's office with some support and a commitment that his bid will receive full and patient consideration, or he will be given no encouragement.

Sales Examples

Example 1

Several years ago, a customer with whom my company had done little business requested a quote shortly after the account was assigned to me. The inquiry was for major prime movers to expand a plant that had a competitor's products. Usually in circumstances like this, the customer would stay with the brand of products he had and would not mix two kinds of products in one location.

Upon receiving this inquiry, I immediately made a trip to the plant where this product would be installed. I wanted to determine our chances and whether or not the customers were satisfied with the machinery they were using. I struck gold. The plant superintendent had just been transferred there. He came from a location that used our products and was very friendly to my company. I not only learned that the customers were extremely unhappy with the current products and with our competitors, but I also learned why. The products had given trouble and they could not get spare parts and service.

The information I gathered enabled us to slant our pitches in a useful direction and to tell the operating people and the home office executives how we would handle these exact problems. We obtained the order. It was duplicated a year later with more of our products. If I had not gone to the station and investigated the situation, we might have treated the inquiry too lightly. We might have believed we had little chance for success and thus lost that order and the later one.

Example 2

One of our competitors used this approach successfully a few years ago in an overseas country. My firm had received 70% to 80% of the customer's business for all the products on a certain petrochemical process. This share of their business was unusually large, but we had pioneered the application and our units had performed superbly.

Upon receiving this new inquiry, our only significant competitor asked for a meeting with the customer. He summarized the situation and reminded the customer that we always seemed to get the order when this particular process was involved. He went on to say that since the forecast of being successful was so bleak, he really did not see why he should bid. This got the customer's attention, since there were only two or three vendors of this product with adequate experience to qualify.

The customer assured this complaining vendor that if his price and delivery were competitive, he would get the order. This vendor turned in a slightly lower price and a competitive delivery and was awarded the order. I do not think he would have received this order without the pre-bid discussions with the customer. The customer just did not want to take a chance on reducing the number of qualified vendors.

Summary

Considerable time and money can be spent in quoting on a major project. A salesperson should not take this step lightly for a company that is not a regular customer. This decision should be a consensus reached after lengthy discussions with others inside his company. It should be made only after thorough investigation and consideration, and not before the salesperson has discussed it with senior customer executives.

24

Sell to Other Divisions in the Company

Surprisingly, when salespeople are called upon to sell to other divisions within their corporation, many forget their sales know-how. They approach this situation assuming that the division owes them the order because they are all in the same corporation. While this may be true and will sometimes get a salesperson the business, usually it will fail. It is not the correct approach.

Another division of a salesperson's corporation should be approached with the same sales determination, dedication, and humility that he would use with any other customer. The fact that the salesperson's company and the other division are both members of the same organization should not alter the salesperson's methods. By thoughts, deeds, and actions, the salesperson should convey sincerely to these people that they and they alone are going to make the decision on this equipment.

The salesperson should not approach another division expecting special favors. Generally, the less he expects, the more he will get. He should humbly offer and present his products in the same way as he would to total strangers. He should give them his regular sales pitch, propose presentations by his engineers, and offer to take them to see his product in actual operation by a satisfied user. Taking this approach will pay off handsomely for a salesperson. Not only because the division will want to do business with him, but also because it will be unique. Many salespeople, when calling on a division within their own corporation, will cast aside their customary approach. They begin name-dropping and have the attitude that they are entitled to the order because they are all part of the same organization.

The salesperson should not approach another division expecting special favors.

A salesperson should keep in mind that when he goes to another division to sell his product, he may open a Pandora's box. This could occur for several reasons:

- The other division probably has historical sources of supply and may be doing business with the salesperson's competitor. They may be satisfied with what they are now using.
- The other division may have strong ties to other suppliers, such as sharing agents or participating in joint ventures.
- The other division may have the competitor's product already engineered into their system, so that substantial engineering expense would be necessary to accommodate the salesperson's product. The competitor may have a better service or spare parts organization already in place and serving them.
- The competitor's price may be substantially lower.

Sales Example

A senior executive told me he was once called by his counterpart in another division of his organization regarding a product about to be purchased. Another division within the organization also manufactured this product, but this senior executive had in the past purchased products from a competitor. His counterpart told the senior executive that he must buy this product from him, since they were both in the same organization. This senior executive was very upset over his condescending approach.

When relating this high-handed encounter to me, the senior executive said he would have canceled the project rather than be told what to buy. This demonstrates to what extent other divisions will go rather than have someone try to dictate their purchases.

Summary

If a salesperson goes in at the normal contact level with his customers and does a thorough, sincere selling job, he will receive plenty of consideration and support. He will be much more likely to be successful than if he and his executives go in at the top and start demanding the other division's business. A salesperson must do as professional and careful a sales job in this situation as he would in any other.

Don't Overlook Consultants

It is amazing how many otherwise competent salespeople completely overlook consultants in their businesses. These consultants are important for a number of reasons:

1. They are almost always experienced.
2. They have worked a long time in their occupations, usually all their professional lives.
3. They come in contact professionally and socially with many of the salesperson's customers.

4. They are engaged by decision makers who want a different or independent observation of a problem.
5. They are considered by their own clients to be unbiased in their feelings on the brands of products to buy. Their recommendations often outweigh those of in-house people.
6. They are often called in on new projects at their earliest inception.
7. They are often consulted when product problems develop and are asked to investigate the difficulties or recommend solutions. In some cases they are asked to prepare evidence or strategies for impending lawsuits or settlements concerning back charges.
8. They are often asked to evaluate and comment on the reputation, reliability, and dependability not only of the bidding firms involved, such as the salesperson's company, but also of the individual executives and salespeople.

Not all consultants possess all of these attributes or qualities. However, if the consultants in a salesperson's territory possess only a few, he obviously should keep in touch with them. The salesperson should make them aware of his products and new developments. Then when they are contacted or engaged by his customers, they will have a favorable impression and current information about the salesperson's company and products. An additional advantage is that they are likely to have significant information about the competitors' actions and strategies, some of which they may be willing to share with the salesperson.

On occasion the salesperson may lose an order without ever really learning why. There is the possibility that a consultant of whom the salesperson was unaware was cultivated by his competitor. Just a doubt or hint from a well-respected consultant can be devastating. It does not take much to increase a buyer's pervasive fear of making the wrong decision and to turn a critical decision against a company's products. The salesperson should

Just a doubt or hint from a well-respected consultant can be devastating.

remember that most purchase decisions are decided by a very narrow margin. A good report or recommendation from a consultant can often provide just the edge a salesperson needs to win the order.

Keeping in touch with these consultants should not require too much of a salesperson's time, and offering them help in their work will enhance his image with them. Besides sending technical information to them from time to time, it may be sufficient for a salesperson to give them an occasional telephone call or invite them to lunch. Time and money spent in cultivating consultants have produced dividends far in excess of their costs.

Sales Example

We were working with a consultant and attempting to introduce a new product in a remote location. It is usually tough enough to sell something new in one's own backyard, but it is much more difficult 11,000 miles away from one's factory. We were extremely surprised to be given the order, which was very important to us. Later, the consultant told me that on decision day in the final meeting, the general manager who was approving the purchasing decision asked the consultant how long he had known me. The consultant replied that he had known me for 20 years.

It is hard to pinpoint all the reasons why one's company received an order, but in this case, the consultant's answer certainly helped. One of the reasons I had good relations with this consultant was because I was responsive and had provided him with information about our products. I had kept all my promises when he was not buying anything, and I expected nothing in return. On one occasion I helped him when he was called upon to be an expert witness and needed photographs and specifications of our products. It only took a few minutes of my time to be helpful, and years later it paid big dividends.

On another occasion, a consultant who had been engaged by the customer to evaluate the engineering aspects concluded that our product had a basic shortcoming. We knew this was wrong, but we did not try to discredit him or tell the customer he did not know what he was talking about. Instead, we invited him to our factory at our expense to talk directly to our designers and engineering specialists. I met him near his home base and traveled with him to our headquarters, arriving in a snowstorm in the early hours of the morning.

We showed him our drawings, went over our method of calculations, and produced a list of successful similar units. We thus were able to convince him that our product was soundly and correctly designed. Shortly thereafter, he withdrew his objections and gave his blessings to our product, and we were awarded the order. We might well have lost this contract if we had fought the consultant rather than winning him over.

Summary

A successful salesperson will not overlook consultants. They often are very influential with a salesperson's customers.

26

Business Attire

The way a salesperson dresses can greatly influence how successful he is. Clothes say volumes about a person. While the proper attire varies widely in industry, a salesperson should be careful always to dress properly and in good taste. He should not overdress, but he certainly should never underdress, either. If the salesperson's customer will be wearing a coat and tie, by all means, so should the salesperson. If he is in doubt, he should wear them. If does not need them, he can always take them off, but if he is not wearing them and the occasion calls for them, it will be a problem. In addition, the salesperson should make sure his shoes are always well shined.

The salesperson should not be anxious to dress too casually. If casual dress is appropriate, certainly he will want to dress that way, but he must be sure he does not dress too casually. Also, he should make certain his executives and colleagues, when accompanying him, are made aware ahead of time what attire will be appropriate.

Customers like to do business with salespeople who look successful. They do not like for someone who is an obvious failure to come into their offices and try to convince them to buy his products. They tend to think that if a salesperson is really capable, and he really knows his business, he should look successful.

Customers like to do business with salespeople who look successful.

Clothes should be unobtrusive and never loud. Among many reasons for this, there is also a practical one. People remember too easily a loud coat, tie, or suit. Conservative clothes in good taste can be worn more often. They must, of course, always be clean and well pressed. While a salesperson might prefer to wear the latest fashion, occasionally the senior people resent this. A salesperson needs all the help he can get, so he should avoid offending anyone or creating unfavorable impressions with poorly chosen clothes.

Clothes can also give a person confidence. Sometimes a salesperson knows ahead of time that he is going to have a rough session or will be meeting a demanding customer. He should give himself that extra bit of lift by wearing his best suit, the one in which he feels the most confident.

Perhaps a salesperson flew a long distance to see an important customer or to participate in an important sales meeting or conference. For the flight during the night, he dressed in comfortable, casual clothing. He had his brief case with him, but his checked luggage was not on the turntable when he arrived. Time was short, so he scurried to buy shirts and ties he did not need and did not like. There was no longer any way that he could present himself properly dressed as he had carefully planned. Worse yet, the time he so urgently needed to calmly attend to the last-minute details was wasted.

These things do happen. It is preferable for a salesperson to appear at these meetings properly dressed, even in clothes he has worn during the entire flight. A salesperson should never travel by plane casually dressed when on his way to see customers unless he is carrying his luggage in the cabin with him. Checked luggage too often is delayed or lost. Furthermore, he will often encounter customer executives on these flights. Since he is in sales, he should always look his best.

Sales Examples

Example 1

At one time I traveled overseas on a regular basis. For these weekend overnight flights, I always wore a tie and coat. Many other businessmen wore casual clothes on these flights, and I came to envy them. On my next trip, I decided to dress casually. Upon arrival at my destination, my checked luggage was missing. We were to leave by car early the next morning to call on an important customer, and a coat and tie were mandatory. I was in a stage of panic. I could imagine attempting to stop along the way very early the next morning to buy a dress shirt and tie, delaying our arrival and purchasing items I otherwise did not need and would never wear again. Fortunately, my luggage arrived at my hotel around midnight, but I never again put myself in that situation.

Example 2

I recall still another time arriving at an overseas airport at 8:00 AM and meeting one of our salespeople to take a three-hour flight to another country to conduct our business. I asked where his coat and tie were, and he responded, "In my checked luggage." This was highly inappropriate. First, his luggage could go astray, and second, it meant that even if his gear did arrive with us, we then would have to go to the hotel so he could change before proceeding with our sales calls.

Summary

A successful salesperson will purchase and wear suitable, conservative business attire. These clothes do not need to be the most expensive, but they must be of good quality, fit well, and be in good taste. A salesperson should always look ahead and make absolutely certain he has the appropriate clothes with him for the sales calls he will be making. He should not take chances or gamble with this vital requirement.

27

Entertain Customers

Many good books on etiquette are available, and no attempt is made here to cover everything in that category. Instead, a few suggestions are offered to assure that the salesperson reaps the maximum benefit from the money he spends entertaining his customers. These suggestions are on the conservative side, and they are designed to please and satisfy by far the majority of a salesperson's customers. The salesperson wants to be sure his customer enjoys the encounter and will accept his invitations again in the future.

Most customers resent overly lavish entertainment. Many companies have strict rules about it, and the salesperson must be sure to abide by them at all times. He should not, however, invite his customers to low-budget lunches or parties. He certainly does not want to be openly extravagant, but he should not cut corners. If he is short of money, he should have fewer parties and invite customers to fewer lunches. When he does invite them, he must make certain it is a first-class affair.

Most customers resent overly lavish entertainment.

The salesperson should bear in mind that most of his customers are busy. Their time is limited, and they must establish priorities in how they use it. They will, therefore, accept his invitation only if they enjoy his company and really want to be with the salesperson and his wife, when spouses are being included. Otherwise, they will decline with weak excuses. If spouses are included in the event, the salesperson should make certain this is clear to his customers.

I remember once inviting on short notice an important couple to dinner in London. During the evening, I told the wife how pleased I was that they were not busy when I called and were able to join us that evening. She replied, "We were busy, but we wanted to see you and your wife." This was certainly an exception. I am not suggesting that customers will regularly break other engagements to accept the salesperson's invitation. How strongly they want to be with the salesperson, though, will greatly influence their decision. Usually, those who really want to accept his invitations will find the time or will encourage him to call again. They might even suggest an alternate date.

Many people will not accept a second invitation after not having enjoyed the first occasion with a salesperson. A salesperson should never argue with the staff in a restaurant, keep his guest out too long, or take them to places they do not enjoy. He should carefully plan any lunches, dinner parties, or cocktail parties for his customers. It is worth a salesperson's time and effort to make sure these special occasions for his customers are hosted well.

The salesperson should not waste valuable time for lunch with his colleagues. He should arrange to be with a customer, because it will greatly increase his effectiveness. He will have to work at this, because if he is very busy in his office, it will be lunch time before he realizes it. He should make lunch dates a day or so ahead. When time is short, he can choose a customer close to his office. If the salesperson is traveling, he should consider where he will be at noon or in the evening and make plans with a customer.

The salesperson should be conservative enough in his planning that he will be on time. He must be certain that the meeting times and places are clearly understood by both himself and his guests. If a date is made a few days ahead of time, he should be sure to confirm it on the designated day. Most customers keep diaries and will not forget, but if a customer does forget, he will be embarrassed. The salesperson will always find it to be advantageous to assume the responsibility of confirming the arrangements. If he does this it will avoid the awkwardness of misunderstandings. The salesperson should always make these arrangements personally, except in an emergency. His customers will appreciate his personal touch.

The salesperson should select a convenient place where the customer wants to go. If the customer has a favorite place, the salesperson should offer to take him there. If he has no favorite, the salesperson should choose a good restaurant, but not necessarily the most expensive one. He could offer his customer one or two choices to indicate what he has in mind. If the customer does not select one, then the salesperson should do so. The salesperson should keep the length of the lunch within his time frame and thus avoid a reputation for keeping people out to lunch too long. He should be conservative in the kind of restaurant he selects. He should not pick one that serves only one kind of food unless he is positive his customer prefers that kind of food and that the restaurant does it well.

If it is possible, the salesperson should call for his customer. Sometimes, however, it may be more convenient to meet him at the restaurant. The salesperson should always be on time and should wait in the reception area unless it is necessary to save their table. He should not order refreshments until the customer arrives. He should also tell the customer ahead of time who else will be along. Instead of making unfavorable comments, the salesperson should be sympathetic if the customer is late. The salesperson should avoid talking about religion or politics and should keep his sales pitch to a minimum. He could make a few carefully chosen, informal comments well into the lunch, but never the first thing. The salesperson should always express his appreciation that the customer took time to join him.

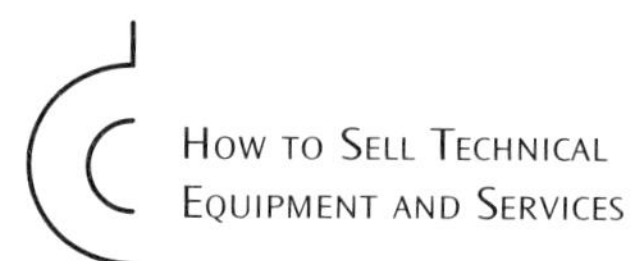

For dinner, it is not usually possible for a salesperson to arrange transportation for his customers in large cities. This should only be provided when it is easier for them. A customer might not want the salesperson to come to his house to pick him up, since he would feel obligated to invite the salesperson in, and that might not be convenient.

If the salesperson has invited several couples for dinner and he is considering an unfamiliar restaurant, it is a good idea to scout it out in advance. To make things go smoothly, he should order the food and wine ahead of time. If he does order the food, he should not go way out. He should play it safe and order the food that the restaurant specializes in or will do well. For a starter, he should always order something that can be served at room temperature. This allows for greater flexibility as to when they actually sit down for dinner. It will avoid upsetting the restaurant staff if they do not sit down exactly on schedule. The salesperson should order food that is not fattening and that everyone will like. For a group that is not too large, he could allow each person to make his own selection, but he should not do this with large numbers when time will be limited.

Even for a small group, it is better to have a private room. In addition, it is better to have cocktails in one room and then move to another for dinner. The salesperson does not want his guests to be standing among the tables to be used for dinner. For cocktails, he should insist on a large enough space for people to move around freely.

The salesperson can use place cards to show people where they will sit, and this is usually an excellent idea for larger groups of guests. He should arrange the place cards for guests from his own company somewhat evenly among his guests that are customers. He should separate the members of company groups. It is usually a good idea to seat a man and his wife apart, but a salesperson should be careful with this, because some couples do not want to be separated during dinner. The salesperson should be alert to see with certainty that everyone is served promptly. If someonc is slighted, he must attend to the situation quickly and graciously.

The salesperson must make arrangements ahead of time as to how he will pay the bill. If the restaurant does not accept his credit cards, he should have the cash available, or perhaps if he gives them notice, they will accept his check. He should always pay the bill as unobtrusively as possible. He should excuse himself from his guests so that he can examine his bill and ask any necessary questions entirely out of their hearing. He should never have an argument with the restaurant staff in the presence of his customers if he wants them to be his guests again. If the salesperson runs into difficulties with the service, he should excuse himself and go sort it out privately.

As soon as the salesperson knows for certain that he will attend a convention, he should make dinner arrangements with some of his customers. If the meeting lasts three days, he should make plans for two nights, and if it lasts five days, he should make arrangements for three nights. This will leave him some free time to spend with people he might see unexpectedly at the convention. He should always take his personal stationery with him so that he can write out invitations to people he meets unexpectedly, especially if he cannot reach them by phone. During a convention, a salesperson can rarely find people in their hotel rooms.

The salesperson can usually find out ahead of time who is going to a convention by inquiring among his customers. As he attends certain conventions over a period of time, he will know who goes regularly. His information can be increased by collecting registration lists of the various conventions and by having his office assistant tabulate during the off-season who went from various companies. He will have a good list for future use.

A genuine invitation sometimes reaps dividends even though it is declined. Perhaps an important person who regularly attends a certain convention tells the salesperson he does not think he will attend this year. The salesperson should send him an invitation anyway if he is having a dinner party. The customer may change his mind and go at the last minute. If he does go, the salesperson will have shown good manners. If the salesperson fails to do this, he may find that he has invited the customer's colleagues and excluded the customer. If the customer appears at the convention and does not have an invitation to the salesperson's party, he may then be reluctant to come.

All of these invitations should be in writing so that there will be no misunderstanding about the date, time, and place. Initial invitations can be verbal, but should be confirmed in writing with everyone who accepts. Just prior to departing for the convention, the salesperson should verify any acceptances to avoid surprises. He will not want to tell his executives that he has the customer's important executives coming to dinner and then have them not show up.

It is very important that the salesperson make these dinner arrangements ahead of time. His customers will be flattered that he would ask them early. He should never wait until he arrives in the convention city to try to line up his customers. By then it will be too late. They likely will be booked up by the salesperson's competitors, or they will have run into old friends. They might even have made plans of their own to attend local events.

The salesperson should extend these invitations personally and be careful about promising to include his executives. If producing his executives will enhance his chances of obtaining commitments from influential customers, he should be sure to secure a firm promise from his own executive so that he does not bow out. He should put his acceptances and plans in writing to all parties both inside and outside his company and should remind his executives as the time approaches. By the same token, if the salesperson has promised his executives that a customer's important executive will be present for his party or dinner, he must be sure that person is indeed planning to attend. He should not promise before he gets a firm acceptance. Once he has the commitment, he should confirm it in writing to avoid misunderstandings. He should verify it again a few days before the convention.

If the dinner party is being held in a city that is unfamiliar to the salesperson, it is important for him to book the restaurant or club reservation early by phone. He must confirm the arrangements in writing to a definite person, so he must always be sure to obtain this person's name. A week or so before the occasion, he should have his assistant call again to be sure everything is in order. The salesperson should inspect the location immediately upon his arrival. He should talk to the manager and tell him exactly what he expects. He should tell the manager that he is bringing important customers, and that he is willing to pay extra if necessary for ample portions, good food, and good service.

Before selecting a restaurant, the salesperson should check with several sources to be certain he selects a good place. He should not take just one person's opinion. Again, he must make previous arrangements regarding how he will pay his bill.

If the salesperson gives a large reception or party, he should check everything out ahead of time even more thoroughly. Most clubs, even though they are otherwise very experienced and capable, will not have enough of the best provisions unless the salesperson insists. He should tell them that he does not want to run out of food, that he expects them to prepare plenty, and that he will pay extra to obtain adequate servings.

If the salesperson arranges for a bar at his party, it should always be across the room and away from the entrance to prevent the crowd from blocking the door. He should be sure the room is large enough for people to circulate in but not so large that guests suspect that he prepared for many who did not want to come. If the salesperson is having a seated dinner, it is best to serve cocktails in a separate but adjoining room or a room nearby. This reduces likelihood of guests sitting down at the dinner table prematurely.

The salesperson should ask for and obtain acceptances ahead of time so he will know how many people to expect. If some of the guests do not show up, he should remove the extra places. He should never have any extra tables or even extra places. He should count his guests as they arrive and count the prepared places to make sure when they sit down that the numbers exactly match. It is much better to have to set up additional places than it is to have empty chairs when the guests sit down to dinner.

It is a good idea to have a guest book for them to sign to give the salesperson a record of who attended the event. Name tags are a good idea, but they must be large enough to be read several feet away without anyone needing to be very close to a person to see his name.

The salesperson should be sure the bar has soft drinks for people who do not want anything stronger. He should serve these with the same enthusiasm that he would serve hard drinks and without unfavorable comments. If he knows that some of his customers prefer a special drink, he should have it on hand for them.

As a host, the salesperson should be at the door when the first guests arrive. This is very important. If he has top executives attending the convention, he should especially invite some of them to be there at the beginning to greet the guests. The first part of the evening is always the best. If the executives arrive late, they will never see everybody. They do not have to stand in the receiving line all evening, but they should stay long enough to greet the majority of the guests, especially those who come early. If important guests arrive, the salesperson should make sure they are introduced to his top executives.

As incredible as it seems, elaborate receptions have been given by large, responsible companies with no one at the door to greet the guests when the party began. Someone from the salesperson's company, preferably the salesperson if he is the host, should be near the door all evening to greet late arrivals and to say good-bye to the departing guests. Some guests will feel uncomfortable if there is no one at the door for them to say good-bye to and to thank.

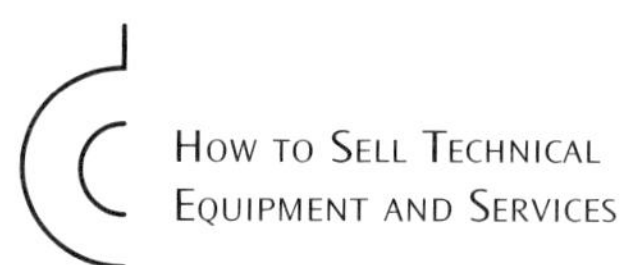

Sales Examples

Example 1

Once while traveling overseas with my wife, I asked the local manager to invite an important customer and his wife to dinner. The manager and I arrived with our wives at the agreed restaurant. When the customer arrived, he was alone. Even though I did not understand the local language, I could tell by what was said and the look on the customer's face that he had not understood that his wife was included. The manager had delegated this invitation to someone else, and the arrangements were bungled. What was to be a pleasant evening was diminished by this serious mistake. The salesperson should extend dinner invitations personally and should not delegate this task.

Example 2

On another occasion, I had planned a dinner party during a convention on the Riviera. Reservations had been made by telex well ahead of time, but the afternoon before our gathering, I went to the restaurant to sort out the logistics. I made all the arrangements, ordered the food and wine, observed the rooms we would be in, and inspected the seating arrangements. As I was about to leave, I asked if they accepted credit cards and was told that they did not. I swallowed hard but told the restaurant manager not to worry, I could handle the situation.

Before going back that evening to meet my guests, I rounded up all the cash I thought I would need. When I arrived at the restaurant, the manager called me aside and cordially told me I could pay the bill by personal check if I chose. I was astonished by his change in attitude between our afternoon meeting and my arrival that evening only three hours later. He was apparently persuaded to accept my check by my earlier telex reservation and by the professional way I had outlined the details concerning the good care I wanted them to give our customers. Handling this situation directly and taking time to come to the restaurant ahead of time changed the manager's attitude, and the service was outstanding. Years later I was still being complimented on the splendid setting and service.

Summary

Entertaining business associates has been widely accepted as an extremely desirable practice. Unspoken tensions and unwanted inferences invariably fade in the atmosphere of a capable, gracious host. Social functions are a means of extending a positive image both for the salesperson and his company, and some of the aura they create will follow into the marketplace. The salesperson should take these gatherings seriously and plan carefully so that they are successful.

III

Making the Pitch

28

In the Customer's Office

One of the most important events of a salesperson's career occurs when he is in a customer's office and has a chance to promote his products and his company in a personal meeting with his customer. This is what he has been preparing for, sometimes for a very long time. Now that he has his chance, he wants to do all he can to make the visit successful. The salesperson wants to leave the customer with a favorable impression of himself, his products, and his company.

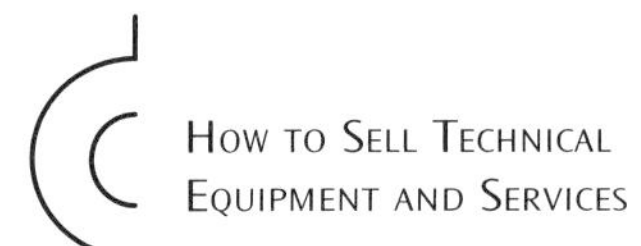

Before leaving to call on a customer, a salesperson should be sure he is well prepared. It is very important that he establish ahead of time exactly what his mission is and what he is going to say to the customer. He should have the points committed to memory in the order that he wants to introduce them.

The salesperson should always have an appointment. He should never drop in on a customer regardless of how well he knows him. So as not to be late, he should allow ample travel and parking time. If the route to the customer's office is unfamiliar, he should leave quite early. In fact, he should arrive at the reception area a few minutes before his appointment. However, he should not allow the receptionist to announce him early, even though some receptionists seem anxious to do so. The salesperson is due at a certain time, and he should make sure his host is not called prematurely, since he is probably busy and may not be prepared to receive the salesperson early. The salesperson should be sure he is announced to the person with whom he arranged the meeting, not necessarily the senior person who will attend the meeting.

If the salesperson is bringing a delegation, he should make certain the prospect knows this in advance and should make sure everyone is announced by the receptionist. If there are more than two people, the salesperson should have a written list with exact titles to read from when he makes introductions in the meeting. Afterwards, he can give this list to the customer.

The salesperson should make sure he enters by the reception desk so that he is properly logged in and announced. This may seem obvious, but some salespeople will take liberties with this when calling on customers they know well. A salesperson needs all the help he can get to maximize his sales. Thus he should not put up roadblocks to his success by violating the customer's rules.

When walking from the reception area to the customer's office, a salesperson should not peer in doors or open them. He should not otherwise stop along the way to visit with people whose doors are open, unless of course they call out to him. This may sound ridiculous, but many buyers report this crude behavior.

The salesperson should avoid being late, or he will quickly acquire that reputation with both customers and colleagues. When a salesperson is late, he is often put on the defensive by his customer. This is always a poor way to begin a meeting, and it is devastating for a meeting in which a delicate or difficult topic will be discussed, and the salesperson is already on the defensive. On the other hand, if the customer is tardy, the salesperson should not make any remarks about it, even in jest. He should be sympathetic, because his customer is probably overworked. He should express appreciation that his customer has taken time to meet with him but should not dwell on it.

Customers vary, and not all react alike. Some want a few sociable words. The first thing a salesperson should do is to tell the customer that he appreciates his taking the time to meet. If the salesperson has had a recent order from the customer, he should thank him again for the order. However, he should quickly turn the conversation to new business. The salesperson should not be the one to persist in idle conversation. The customer may want to talk about football, hunting, fishing, or something else. If so, the salesperson should try tactfully to delay such conversation until after he finishes his business, and then only if the time still allows. One way a salesperson can move quickly to business is to say, "I know you are busy, and we do not want to take too much of your time."

The salesperson should not be the one to persist in idle conversation.

If a salesperson is calling on a customer for the first time, then he should take a few minutes to be sociable. Again, he should not take too long, or he will use up too much of his allotted time. With those customers he already knows, he should get straight to business.

I once had a customer I knew well both socially and professionally. I always made an appointment before going to see him. As I crossed the threshold of his office and before I even sat down, he would ask, "What's on your mind?" I never thought it rude—in fact, it taught me a valuable lesson. I always came prepared to proceed immediately with business. A salesperson does not want to appear cold or unfriendly, and since customers vary, he should play this by ear. In general, a salesperson should do his best to make the most of the sales time with his customer.

Many things can happen as soon as a salesperson goes in a customer's office that could damage the impression he is trying to create and cause the meeting to end disastrously. The salesperson should be careful what he says first, because his opening remark or statement usually sets the tone and direction of the entire meeting. He should never start off on a negative or controversial note.

A salesperson who begins the meeting by volunteering whose office he just left can misdirect the thrust of his entire discussion. He could end up being asked what others told him during his previous meeting. He may then find himself giving out information rather than receiving it. Furthermore, the last person the salesperson saw could be this man's competitor, his enemy, or someone that he just does not like. If a salesperson is asked whose office he just visited, he should certainly answer honestly. However, he should not volunteer this information unless it is important to do so or unless he would otherwise mislead his customer.

All of the salesperson's comments should be positive and upbeat. They should demonstrate that he is proud of his company and its products, reputation, and policies. If the salesperson has colleagues with him, he should make certain he tells the customer immediately what their specialties are and why they are attending the meeting.

When a salesperson enters an office, he must bear in mind that the telephone on the customer's desk is like a time bomb. Even though the salesperson has made an appointment, the phone can ring at any time and can result in the customer having to leave the office and cut short the meeting. I have been in a customer's office many times expecting the visit to last 30 minutes. However, after 5 or 10 minutes, the phone rang, and the customer announced that he had to go to his boss's office due to an emergency. Because I had gotten right down to business and related my sales points, the time was not wasted.

The salesperson should remember that a verbal sales effort is, at best, inefficient for two reasons:

- Speakers take far too much for granted. They assume they are being heard and understood, but they usually are not.
- Listeners do not pay very much attention to the speaker. Most customers have many other things on their minds, such as their immediate tasks, crises at home, and problems with their own jobs.

For these reasons, the salesperson should always repeat several times the important points he wants to get across. If he does not, he will be astonished how many people will fail to hear, understand, and remember important facts. He should not be afraid to repeat salient features and important benefits several times. He should keep his comments short and choose his words for maximum impact. He should always have photographs to show. If he is relating numbers, he should have them in a format that he can show his customer during their discussion and then leave it with him.

The salesperson should remember the importance of having his customer see as well as hear what he is saying. He should be sure that the customer sees the numbers or facts he is presenting. From the many studies that have been made, a salesperson should bear in mind that a customer who both sees and hears the information will retain much more of it. Photographs and written figures will greatly assist in accomplishing this.

Many times when reviewing the loss of an order, I learned to my astonishment that the customer bought competitive products because of a feature our product also had, perhaps even better. I had just failed to mention this benefit often enough for it to be understood and remembered. I did not show him as well as tell him.

After getting down to business, the salesperson should be sure to talk in a way the customer understands. He should avoid in-house or trade terms that the customer may not recognize. Few customers will stop a salesperson to tell him they do not understand. They will just allow him to continue talking.

When promoting a specific product, the salesperson should begin the discussion with his product's strategic benefits. He should have them well organized in order of importance. He should follow his mental agenda in the order of rank and leave the less-significant items for last.

In the discussion of a subject, the salesperson should occasionally stop to allow his prospect time to react and comment. He should not move too quickly to new topics but should pause and ask for the customer's reaction as a precaution against receiving the wrong impression. The salesperson may think the customer has accepted his arguments and understood what he related when this was not the case at all. The customer may not have had a chance to express himself.

Many people are timid and will not react immediately or speak at once, so the salesperson must always allow time for reactions. He should gauge the reception and interest by the number of questions his statements, comments, and graphic material are generating. If he does not receive many questions, the customer is probably not too interested. Another reason to pause occasionally is to allow the salesperson to collect his thoughts and to give his colleagues a chance to make clarifying or additional comments and to participate in the presentation.

The salesperson should constantly monitor the reaction of his customer and set the pace of his presentation based on this input. If the customer is getting restless or impatient, the salesperson should speed up and perhaps shorten his stay. If the customer is asking a lot of questions and showing genuine interest, the salesperson can expand on his prepared presentation.

A salesperson should remember that often it is not what he says that matters so much as how he says it. He should speak softly and sincerely. He should avoid strident tones and should not exaggerate. He should make eye contact with the customer and not look at the ceiling or around the room. He should try to hear what the customer is leaving unsaid.

In the event that the salesperson has many things to discuss, he should cover the easiest and most agreeable items first before moving to the unpleasant or perhaps controversial points. In order to be successful in this area, he will have to study the items ahead of time and arrange them advantageously. He should place the easiest and least controversial topics at the top of the list, leaving the more delicate topics to the end. He should get agreement on the easy points first and always leave difficult subjects until later. Otherwise, he may not even be able to settle the easy ones.

To show proper respect, the salesperson should address his remarks to everyone in his audience. The person whom the customer asked to sit in on the meeting may have more to say in the decision than the contact person. The salesperson should pay close attention to all of the customer's people and answer their questions just as seriously as he would those of his host. He should always assume that everyone in the meeting will have a lot of influence, and then he will not slight anyone.

When a salesperson goes to see a customer, he should always have something important to say. He should never start by saying, "Well, what's new?" or "When are you going to give us an order?" Invariably, someone in the salesperson's firm has recently had a big order someplace in the world, and the salesperson can relate this information to the customer. If the salesperson is unsure of the customer's exact interests, he should show him pictures of his company's facilities or his newest product. Everybody likes to look at pictures. Sometimes the pictures the customer sees will remind him that he will need products like this later. The salesperson may flush out an inquiry that is still way on the back burner. By showing photographs that cause the customer to think about the salesperson's products, the salesperson may find out that he has a new project coming up. The salesperson will then know about it before his competitors.

Since the salesperson plans to show photographs, he should be sure to have them organized and in the order that best presents his products and his sales points. If the salesperson is using a bulletin to show photographs or to make a point, he should have it properly marked so that he can easily find his place. He should not keep his customer waiting while he fumbles around. Also, he should always place the photographs or bulletins carefully in front of his customer, never pitching them across the desk. I mention this because one of my senior salespeople did this once. We were calling on a customer in Australia and wanted to show him photographs of our products. This salesperson actually pitched the photographs across the desk. He probably meant no offense, but I was astonished.

The cost of having a salesperson in a customer's office can be staggering, especially if extensive travel is involved. The interval with a customer in his office is a very strategic time for a salesperson, the most crucial in his career. It is what selling is all about. Like an actor on a stage, the salesperson must know his role and play it well.

The salesperson must *never* interrupt while the customer is speaking. Interrupting is bad enough socially among friends, but it is inexcusable for a salesperson to interrupt a customer who is trying to say something. It indicates that the salesperson is more anxious to talk than to listen. Interrupting demonstrates gross disrespect and has no place in a salesperson's repertoire. Sometimes a salesperson is very intent on getting his points across, but he must exercise self-control and avoid interrupting. Occasionally a customer may misunderstand something the salesperson said and may be responding based on an incorrect impression. Even then, a salesperson should only intervene if he can do this with discretion, good manners, and apologies.

Some of the worst interruptions occur when a salesperson starts up again after he has stopped talking but waits just long enough for the customer to begin his comments or response. The customer thinks the salesperson has had the floor and now it is his turn. To interrupt when the customer is part of the way through the first sentence is unforgivable. It demonstrates insensitivity and a total lack of respect, and it will usually cause the customer to clam up or to rephrase what he was about to say. As related previously, some people, when interrupted, will not finish what they were saying even if requested to do so. This is very important to remember. If the customer is interrupted, he may have second thoughts concerning what he was about to tell the salesperson, and it may have been very important. The salesperson thus misses valuable feedback or commercial intelligence.

If there are several people in a salesperson's group, one person should be the spokesperson, with the others supporting the topic under discussion. Usually this is the salesperson, unless he has senior executives along who have agreed to assume this role and who have been properly briefed. The salesperson should avoid questions from his side that abruptly change the subject and upset his prepared agenda. Many meetings have become thoroughly disorganized by irrelevant questions or the abrupt introduction of a new topic by the salesperson's own people before the topic at hand is even finished.

This is not to say that the other members of the sales group should not ask questions during the meeting. They should ask questions if the statements by the customer are not clear, or if they require additional information. If the topic is important, it is usually a good idea to ask many questions, because the more questions that are asked, the better everyone understands. Other members from the salesperson's firm should not answer key questions that he puts to the buyer, even if they think they know the answer. Usually the query is being made for a reason. Perhaps a question has been asked for clarification or verification and should be answered only by the customer. On the other hand, if the salesperson is asked a question that he cannot answer, he should say that though perhaps he should, he does not in fact know the answer. He should write the question down so he can look into it and get the answer for the customer. He should not bluff and try to answer when he does not know. He should keep all of his promises.

Before changing subjects, it is a good idea for the salesperson to be sure that the customer has ample chance to comment on the statements he has just made. He may speak right out, but he may not. Either way, the salesperson should provide that opportunity. He should ask the customer's opinion on what he has explained. He could ask if the customer has any comments to make, or he could ask what his reaction is. The customer still may not say anything, although most of the time he will comment if he is given the opportunity.

A salesperson must never get into an argument with a colleague in a customer's office. They must present a united front and should never expose internal disagreements. If a salesperson must correct or change something a colleague has said, he should do so diplomatically.

While it is fine for a salesperson to call his host by name, he should not repeat it too often, or it loses its impact. In fact, the constant repeating of a person's name can become irritating and monotonous.

The salesperson must also be careful to avoid inflammatory words. Some words are controversial, stir resentment, and should be avoided. *Unfair* is one of them. The following examples demonstrate first the importance of a professional approach when entering a customer's office building, and second the danger of using words like *unfair*.

Sales Examples

Example 1

I once went to another city to call on a customer with the local salesperson. This salesperson had recently retired from a senior position at this firm. We arrived at the customer's offices, parked in the parking lot behind the building, and went in the rear entrance. The next thing I knew, we were obviously right in the middle of the executive offices. Becoming nervous, I immediately asked where the reception desk was. When I was told that it was at the front of the building, I suggested we go there and enter officially and properly. The local salesperson protested that he always came in that way and that it would be all right. At my insistence, we made our way to the front area of the building and registered with the receptionist and were properly announced. I might add that this local salesperson had done very poorly selling to this customer. No doubt this lack of observing the rules was one of the reasons.

Example 2

I once went with a colleague to call on the purchasing agent of a very good customer. This was the first time I had met this gentleman. Prior to our meeting, my associate had heard that this company had had severe problems with one of our machines and was considering trading it in and buying a competitive unit. This was a very serious situation and was unprecedented in our industry.

Shortly after we sat down, my associate asked about this, and the purchasing agent answered that they were indeed thinking about doing this. My companion said that we had not been given ample opportunity to solve the problem and that this would not be fair. The purchasing manager replied that his company was always fair in its dealings. My companion was even more distressed and made additional comments. He concluded by saying that for the customer's company to change vendors would just not be fair.

The customer, raising his voice, said, "I told you earlier that my company is always fair in its dealings with vendors." By then, my associate was also becoming very upset and gave still additional arguments why they should not trade our unit in on a competitive product. Unfortunately, he ended by saying that to do so would just not be fair. That was the last straw. The purchasing agent stood up, pointed to the door and said, "Out! Get out of my office!" The next thing I knew, we were on the street. I was devastated and was quite sure we both would be fired before sundown.

My colleague called the purchasing agent later that day and apologized. They eventually became good friends and often got together and laughed about the incident, but it was never funny to me. It made a lasting impression, and I have always avoided using the word *unfair* in discussions with customers. I also do my best to avoid all inflammatory or emotionally charged words.

The salesperson must exercise care when referring to his product models unless he is sure his customer is familiar with them. It is better to speak in terms the customer will readily understand. If the model is new, he should make sure that the customer is familiar with it, or he should explain before he starts referring to it. A salesperson should never put the customer in the position of having to ask him to clarify what model he is talking about. The customer may be hesitant to ask and may not say anything, even if he does not fully understand what the salesperson is saying. Salespeople who are extremely knowledgeable in their product lines and who talk about them many times every day will often use model numbers too quickly. They need to remember to elaborate, identify, or explain. Also, the salesperson should never talk in a condescending manner, regardless of how much he knows about the subject or how much of an expert he is.

The salesperson should never talk about religion or politics with customers. These are dangerous areas and should generally be completely avoided.

It should go without saying that the salesperson should not smoke, put his feet on the furniture, or otherwise behave as a casual guest in the customer's office. He also should not be too hasty in accepting coffee or other refreshments. Unless the salesperson is sure that the offer is genuine, he should not accept, especially if the meeting is almost over or if he can detect that the customer is anxious for him to leave. A good gauge and something that will help the salesperson make a decision is to ask the customer if he will be having coffee or whatever is offered.

A salesperson should be polite and should not stay too long. Buyers repeatedly say that they appreciate salespeople who can be brief gracefully. If the salesperson leaves before he wears out his welcome, it will be much easier for him to get in to see the customer the next time. He should stay, of course, as long as the customer is asking questions and showing interest. However, he should not overstay his welcome and force the customer to say, "Well, I'm sorry, I have to excuse myself," or "I'm glad you stopped by." If a salesperson waits that long, he has stayed too long and may have trouble obtaining the next meeting. The salesperson should be very alert to his customer's responses. If the customer's interest is waning, the salesperson can be sure he has begun to think about other things. It would be better for the salesperson to depart and come again another time.

The salesperson should never look at his watch while the customer is talking. Often he can fix the time by looking at someone else's watch in an unobtrusive manner.

The salesperson should never allow his own office to refer other customers' calls to him while he is in a customer's office. Almost always something delicate must be discussed, and he will not want others to overhear. Furthermore, the salesperson should not answer his cellular telephone while in a customer's office. It is best for his office to just leave word at the customer's office for the salesperson to call when the meeting is over so he can receive his messages.

If at all possible, the salesperson should leave the client's premises before returning telephone calls. If it is absolutely necessary for the salesperson to call from the customer's premises, he must keep his conversation brief. Also, if he is using the customer's telephone line, he should never sit down at his desk to make a call. He must stand up and out in front of the desk, not behind it.

The salesperson should make a list of any promises that he made and be sure to keep all of them. He should later confirm all important points covered. He should get his information across and then depart, leaving the customer with a good impression so that he will be welcome the next time. The salesperson should have materials to leave with the customer, such as pictures, tables, or graphs. He should thank the customer once again for taking time to meet.

Summary

The time a salesperson spends in a customer's office can be pivotal. Therefore, he should be sure to follow these guidelines for meetings at the customer's office:

1. The salesperson should establish a clear mission and know exactly what he wants to convey and to accomplish, and he should be prepared.
2. The salesperson should always have an appointment.
3. The salesperson should be on time. If he is not familiar with the area, he should allow extra time for travel and parking.
4. The salesperson should always enter through the public entrance.
5. The salesperson should never allow the receptionist to announce him early.
6. The salesperson should make sure he is announced to the person who set up the meeting.
7. If the salesperson is bringing others with him, he must be certain the customer knows this ahead of time and is aware of how many will attend. He should make sure they are announced also, if possible.
8. At the start of the meeting, the salesperson should identify his colleagues and their areas of expertise from a prepared list that he can later give to the customer.
9. After being announced, the salesperson should proceed promptly to the meeting area. He should not open other office doors or otherwise stop to visit en route.
10. If the customer is late or keeps the salesperson waiting, the salesperson should not make derogatory comments.
11. The salesperson should get right down to business.
12. The salesperson must be careful what he says first, because his opening remarks usually set the tone of the entire meeting.
13. The salesperson should not volunteer information about whose office he just visited.
14. The salesperson should address everyone in the meeting and show them all attention, not just the senior person or boss.

15. All comments should be positive and upbeat.
16. If the salesperson has colleagues with him, he must make sure they are all introduced from his prepared list, identifying their specialties and pointing out why they are in the meeting.
17. The salesperson must state important features and benefits of his products more than once.
18. The salesperson should move immediately into his message, remembering that the customer could receive a telephone call at any moment and then have to quickly end their meeting.
19. The salesperson should discuss the easiest things first and should make sure more controversial points are brought up last.
20. So that much more will be retained, the salesperson should make sure the customer sees as well as hears what he is presenting.
21. The salesperson should use photographs, graphs, and charts to get his message across. He should have them well organized.
22. The salesperson should avoid talking constantly or moving from subject to subject.
23. The salesperson should talk in terms that the customer can easily follow, avoiding in-house or difficult terminology.
24. The salesperson should stop occasionally and give his customer time to react and to make comments.
25. The salesperson should allow the customer time to ask questions, especially before changing subjects.
26. The salesperson should speak softly and sincerely.
27. The salesperson should never interrupt a customer when he is talking.
28. The salesperson should not abruptly change subjects.
29. The salesperson must constantly monitor his customer's reactions. He should set the pace of his sales presentation based on the customer's input.
30. The salesperson should not repeat the customer's name too often.
31. The salesperson should avoid inflammatory words.
32. The salesperson should never expose internal disagreements.

33. The salesperson should explain any new models the customer may not be familiar with in straightforward terms and in a patient manner. He should never be condescending.
34. The salesperson should use good judgment in accepting refreshments.
35. The salesperson should not stay too long and should not drag out his departure.
36. The salesperson should not take outside calls while in a customer's office.
37. The salesperson should always show appreciation for the time granted.
38. The salesperson should make a list of any promises made.
39. The salesperson should confirm any important points covered.

Identify the Real Decision Makers

Although it is not always easy to ascertain, a salesperson should always make sure he is selling to the person or persons who will make the decision about the purchase of the products. Many people will claim to be the decision makers, when in reality they are only conduits to the people who will actually decide. Also, many who are very influential will deny they have much to say in the final decision. Sometimes the salesperson's products are quoted directly to end users who will analyze bids, issue the purchase order, and have the products installed.

There will be times when a salesperson will bid to a contractor. Sometimes the contractor will possess a turnkey arrangement, wherein he makes all products decisions, not usually subject to the ultimate user's review or veto. At other times, the contractor has some sort of *fixed-fee reimbursable* arrangement. In this case, he issues inquiries, accepts and analyzes bids, and makes recommendations to the end user, who makes the final decision on which product to purchase. Identifying the decision maker thus depends on the manner in which the project will be handled.

Identifying the decision maker when no contractor is involved is sometimes easy for the salesperson. At other times it is not, because some customers are not anxious for salespeople to know this information. Often the purchasing departments are very strong and insist that the low bid be purchased. Even though they may tell a salesperson that they make the final decision, this is not always true. The salesperson must investigate and determine this for himself, which he can do by quizzing various people inside the company. He should be sure to talk to more than one person.

Valuable input can also be obtained from other salespeople selling ancillary products to this customer. This information takes time to develop and is best collected between projects. Even though the salesperson isolates the decision making to the engineering or operating department, he still must identify the most influential people among them.

Again, this requires the salesperson to question many people. The salesperson should ask several individuals inside the company to outline the route an inquiry follows within the organization. The salesperson should know its route from the origination until bids are received and analyzed, and a purchase order is issued. What he learns from this will indicate where he should concentrate his sales pitches.

A salesperson must be alert to promotions, demotions, and organizational changes in the customer's organization. These can dramatically alter who has influence. A salesperson would not want to ignore someone who has been demoted or moved sideways. However, he will want to make sure he devotes attention to and takes care of the new people who will now be in more influential positions.

A salesperson must be alert to promotions, demotions, and organizational changes in the customer's organization.

A decision maker's counterparts in similar companies can be good sources of information. They often know each other, talk about mutual problems, and visit in trade organizations and seminars. They are usually willing to help a salesperson if approached gracefully.

The purchasing people frequently receive the bids, but sometimes they are only channels to the engineers and the real decision-makers. The purchasing people are rarely engineers. However, they often welcome a salesperson's direct discussions with their engineers under certain conditions. Usually the salesperson must keep them fully informed and must have their permission to pass technical information directly to the engineers. The salesperson should obey all their rules and send directly to the purchasing department all information or commercial items such as prices, warranties, and terms and conditions.

The salesperson must also understand that official, binding commitments can usually come only from the purchasing people. This is usually a tightrope walk and requires a great deal of skill on the part of the salesperson. He must follow the job aggressively with the decision-making engineers and at the same time avoid stepping on the toes of the purchasing department. Most intelligent, hard-working salespeople will properly address this problem, keep everybody happy, and get the order.

One trap that is easy to fall into is for a salesperson to write back directly to an engineer or technical person who asked a clarifying question on the bid, especially a commercial question. This often upsets the purchasing people, even if they receive a copy of the letter. The salesperson usually must send correspondence following meetings, phone calls, or direct visits. Thus the best approach is for him to ask the person requesting the information to explain the proper avenues for the salesperson's letter of confirmation. The salesperson should point out that he wants to avoid bypassing anyone or violating the company's rules and should ask for the person's guidance. This should keep everyone happy and prevent damage to his selling effort.

Special attention should be given to identifying the decision makers when an engineering contractor is involved. If the contractor has a turnkey arrangement, the contractor's engineers working with the purchasing people will almost always have the final say. The decision makers then will usually be found in the mechanical, process, and/or purchasing departments of the contractor. The salesperson will find extremely competent and knowledgeable people in all three areas, and he should follow all groups closely. The purchasing people working with the process and/or mechanical group will usually make the decision.

If the contractor has a fixed-fee reimbursable arrangement, then the salesperson must target all of the following:

- the contractor's mechanical or process group
- the contractor's purchasing department
- the end user's operating, engineering, and purchasing people

In this case, the end user's engineering department may not get too heavily involved because they have hired a contractor to do the engineering, selecting, and recommending. The salesperson must verify this, however, so he does not overlook anyone.

The end user's operating group will often be strong on the scene and should be followed closely. In this case, the ultimate user is reimbursing the contractor for products purchased and frequently dictates what to buy. If the end user selects the higher bids, the money comes from his pocket. The end user will be more concerned with reliability, efficiency, maintainability, and availability of spare parts. His people must operate and maintain the products throughout the life of the plant, whereas the contractor usually disappears after the plants are commissioned.

A good approach on projects such as this is for the salesperson to ask the contractor and end user's people to tell him who is going to make the ultimate decision. Ordinarily, the contractor's mechanical department recommends the products. The end user's firm approves or rejects, since it is paying, with the contractor's purchasing department not taking a strong hand.

The best procedure is to work simultaneously on the contractor's mechanical and/or process group and the end user's people who will influence or make the decision. In this manner, a salesperson will have all bases covered. For the salesperson to work only on one or the other risks having his products rejected by one group or the other, sometimes for insignificant reasons. If the salesperson ignores the contractor and works only on the ultimate user, the contractor will be unhappy. He may, when his recommendations are rejected or changed, counter by contending that the salesperson's products cost more to install or do not meet the specifications. He may even say he cannot guarantee the plant if the end user insists on selecting or vetoing product selection. The salesperson must sell to both the contractor and the ultimate user, assuming all the time that both will make the decision.

Most contractors get nervous when the salesperson calls on the ultimate user. The salesperson should let them know that he does not expect anyone else to do his selling for him. Therefore, he hopes they understand that he is only trying to do his job. He should also explain that his competitors likely are calling on the end user, and he must also. If it is explained in this manner, and the salesperson keeps the contractors posted on what he is doing, they will usually understand.

Sales Example

Sometimes people will play games in this area, and occasionally a salesperson's competitor will have done a better selling job to the other party. An example occurred when we were working a job years ago and clearly had the best products for the application. We thought the end user would make the decision. We also felt we had the end user sold, because he was familiar with our products and had had good luck with them. For these reasons we had neglected the contractor and had spent all our selling time with the end user.

During the latest stage of this job, we went by one day to see the end user. His engineers explained that they clearly favored our equipment, but that the contractor wanted extra money. The contractor claimed that our product cost more to install and hence would require adding money to the contract.

While we were in the engineer's office, the plant manager came in asking how the selection process was going. The engineers revealed to him that they wanted our product, but the contractor wanted more money to install it. We explained that they were being misled and explained why our solution was no more expensive to install than the competition's design. We gave precise reasons. The manager proceeded to say that before awarding the order to the contracting firm, this firm had agreed that the price would be the same regardless of what brand of product was selected. While we were in the office, the manager called the head of the engineering contracting firm to remind him of this arrangement. The manager said he wanted his people to have our product without any extra price. The contractor agreed, and we received the order.

The point is that a salesperson must keep in touch with and concentrate on the people who have the final say. We had been concentrating on the end user, and in this case, the end user had the most authority. However, we should have also done our selling to the engineering contractor to keep him happy.

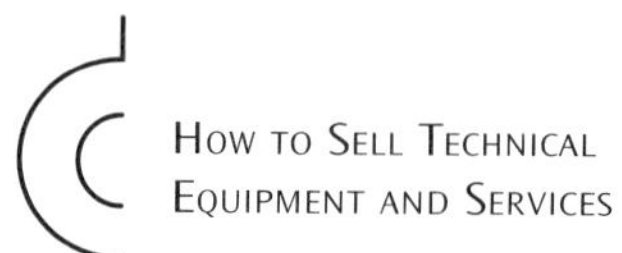

Summary

The end user will not always have the most influence. Therefore, the salesperson must work very hard to determine where the strength lies. Sometimes it is shared, but the salesperson must know this if he is to work on projects successfully. It will require a lot of hard work for a salesperson to establish this. His task will not be easy, but being successful in this area will pay rich dividends through the orders he will obtain.

30

Sales Presentations

Aggressive, sales-oriented companies will always be searching for opportunities to give presentations on their organizations and their products. These exhibitions are unique opportunities for a salesperson to promote his company, experts, services, and products to prospective buyers. If a salesperson's firm is not well known to his customers, this is an excellent vehicle to enhance its image. Even if the company is already well known to the salesperson's customers, this is an unusual opportunity to promote a specific product or a specific project.

Often the presentations given under these circumstances can be decisive. They will either enhance or detract from the image of the salesperson's firm. It is, therefore, very important that these be well prepared so the salesperson can promote his company and its products and services. A salesperson should always be alert for chances to conduct these presentations to groups in the customers' organizations.

Sales presentations should not be last-minute exercises. They should be scheduled well in advance so the salesperson's own experts will have ample time to think about what they will say and prepare a good speech. The salesperson should alert his inside people concerning what he is arranging and what he is hoping to accomplish. He should keep them posted as he finalizes the date and contents of the presentation.

Unfortunately, sales presentations are often imprecise, unorganized, and dull. A successful salesperson should never allow this to happen to his presentations. If the show is to be given to a group of people, long before the actual event, the salesperson should visit with the customer's person in charge to determine the following:

Unfortunately, sales presentations are often imprecise, unorganized, and dull. A successful salesperson should never allow this to happen to his presentations.

1. **The audience.** If the group will be large, the salesperson should obtain a written list of the people who will attend, together with their exact job titles and areas of interest. It is very important to know the area of primary interest so the salesperson will know what to concentrate on and which of his experts to bring to the meeting. If he does not know this, his presentation will have to be general. A salesperson should remember that everyone in the audience will be wondering what is in it for them. He should keep this in mind as he prepares his presentation.
2. **The exact date, location, time, and duration.** The salesperson should remember to ask how much time will be allotted.

3. **The size of the room and available equipment.** The salesperson should ask what equipment can be used and if a speaker system needs to be employed.
4. **Meeting room preparation.** If the group will be large, the salesperson should ask if he and his presenters could have access to the location just before the meeting in order to set up. This will give the salesperson time to become familiar with the room and to make certain everything is in order before the audience arrives.

Armed with this information, the salesperson should meet with his experts and the other people in the company who will participate. The salesperson should observe the following rules or precautions as he plans and later gives his presentation:

1. The salesperson should analyze the expected audience and decide, at the very least, what will interest the strong, outspoken, or important members of the audience. He should consider what they might want answers to or consider important.
2. During this planning stage, the presenters should be empathetic and project themselves into the customer's shoes. They should ask, "If I were the customer, what would I want to hear?"
3. Based on the above and taking into consideration any current project or one on the horizon, the salesperson should decide what he wants to accomplish and set his goals.
4. The salesperson should always stress the reliability of his products and services. However, if labor savings, expandability, or efficiency will be important to the customers, these should be stressed. If the customer is not familiar with the salesperson's company, the salesperson should give this background information. This information should include his company's size, test facilities, manufacturing space, and the number of employees, engineers, and machine tools. The salesperson will also want to address his company's quality assurance program and explain to what codes his products are manufactured.
5. The salesperson's presentation should be well planned, expertly written, and organized to accomplish his objectives. It should be well rehearsed on his own premises long before the meeting, so he will have time to correct any shortcomings.

6. The salesperson should arrange the meeting to cover the most important things first. If he is stressing advantages over the competition, he should put indisputable items first. Then he can progress to what he believes to be less-important items. He should be alert and responsive to his audience, however, since what he considers somewhat insignificant may be important to some of the attendees. If the salesperson suspects this, he must be prepared to elaborate. He should spend as much time as the customer wants on these items of demonstrated interest.
7. At least some of these presentations will probably be made by the salesperson's experts, who may not be sales oriented. Thus he should arrange ahead of time to review what they plan to say and make sure it is worded to prove his point in language the customer will understand. This should be done in advance of the scheduled presentation to allow time for modifications.
8. The salesperson should omit any comments that will distract from his objective. He should not merely list features of his products. Instead, he should show how these features benefit the customer, especially where dollar savings are possible.
9. The salesperson should make sure that descriptive, solid, confidence-giving words are used, avoiding inflammatory language. Some words damage a salesperson's cause, even when used sparingly or spoken in jest. For example, a salesperson should not refer to a particular feature of his products using counterproductive words, such as *tricky*, *dicey*, or *risky*. He should carefully select words that will prove his points.
10. The salesperson should never introduce a new term or topic without explaining it unless he is certain his audience understands it. He should not use initials without properly identifying them unless he is sure everyone in the audience will recognize them.
11. In explaining changes, the salesperson must be sure to establish benchmarks. He must explain what has changed and why. He should give concrete reasons related to what better serves the customer or show why the modified model is a better value.
12. The salesperson should have good lead-in slides or pictures that are not too busy. The salesperson should avoid starting off in the middle of a story. He must be certain the narration makes sense and is easily understood. If the salesperson stresses that his products or parts are

light in weight, he should be sure to point out why this is better. Conversely, if he says his products are heavy, he must explain why that is desirable.

13. The salesperson must make sure all charts and graphs are properly labeled, even though they may be on very familiar subjects. Someone in the audience may not understand and may be too timid to ask. In a large group, the amount of knowledge will vary. The salesperson must try to be clear to everyone.
14. The salesperson should avoid in-house terms that mean little or nothing to customers. He should not just mention a model number but should relate the information to what the customer will readily understand. Following the explanations, model numbers can be used, because they will then be identified.
15. The salesperson must be certain that all of his materials are properly arranged and that he knows how to operate any equipment he will be using.
16. If the salesperson is using a product bulletin to illustrate a point or show a feature, he should have the pages accurately marked for convenient retrieval.
17. The salesperson should make sure presentations are given slowly, clearly, and concisely, with ample time for questions on each subject or topic as he proceeds. He should stop occasionally to ask if there are any questions, since many people are hesitant to interrupt. By the time he finishes the entire presentation, many people may have forgotten their questions.
18. The salesperson should summarize his advantages, placing unassailable items first. If his products have a unique feature, he should say why they are best.
19. When the salesperson is not making the presentation, he should sit in the audience and watch the reactions of key people to determine how well the presentation is being received and understood. He should not hesitate to ask the speaker to repeat an important point. The salesperson should be alert and sensitive in these areas. He must pay attention to the junior people to make sure they also are receiving his message, since they are tomorrow's bosses and future decision makers. If they ask questions, he must make sure they are adequately answered.

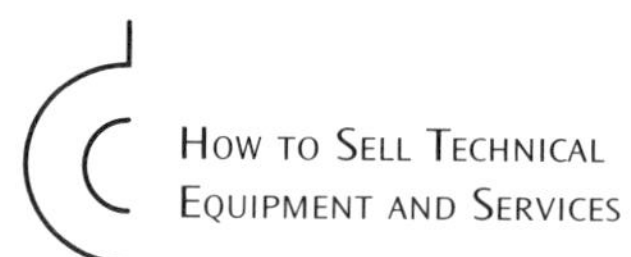

20. When making the presentation, the salesperson must stay within the time constraints. If the customer allows three hours for the presentation, the salesperson should be sure to complete it in three hours. He must have benchmarks so that he knows how far along they should be after certain intervals of time. That way he can speed up or slow down to finish on time.
21. The salesperson must make sure the presenters speak loudly enough so that all the audience can hear.
22. The salesperson should have ample copies of at least the summary or highlights of his presentation to pass out to all of his audience. This is particularly true of curves, charts, and detailed explanations of complex matters. These handouts should not contain proprietary information but should include adequate text to document the important points. These could include, for example, the reliability, compatibility, expandability, efficiency, or advantages of the products. The salesperson should also include general write-ups and photographs of his company, facilities, and people. This information is best passed out at the conclusion of the presentation. Otherwise, people will be fumbling through it during the meeting.
23. The salesperson should use original prints rather than poor-quality photocopies of photographs or bulletins. The same applies to curves, charts, and graphs if they are in color or if copying them will minimize their effectiveness.
24. The salesperson should anticipate questions. Long before the meeting, he should ask knowledgeable people in his company who are involved in this project to write down the questions that could be anticipated for this meeting. Then they should agree on the best answers. The salesperson should compile these questions and the accepted answers so that everyone in his delegation will have them for the meeting. He should be prepared. The plant or home office people should know what questions were asked during previous similar presentations, so he should ask for this information. This makes a good starting point in compiling a list of questions. If it is an existing customer, the salesperson should know his audience well enough to identify those who are likely to ask certain questions.
25. The salesperson's team should give thoughtful responses to all questions and should never get upset or display annoyance, even if someone asks a dumb question. (Actually, to a salesperson, there are no dumb questions.) If the salesperson does not know the answer,

he should readily admit it with a promise to send a written reply, and then he should do it. The salesperson should make notes, obtain the answer, and send it to the customer. He should not try to fake or bluff an answer but should always respond factually and forthrightly, never in a condescending way. A salesperson should never insult or embarrass anyone who asks a question. Otherwise, he will shut off the dialogue and create an enemy.

26. Someone in the salesperson's organization should be assigned to write down all questions asked, along with the replies given, for later review and future use.

27. The salesperson must be sure his presentation is well organized, so that the story he is trying to present flows freely. It must be precise and should contain brief summations at the end that emphasize the salient points.

28. It is imperative that the salesperson avoid exposing any internal disagreements, even mild ones. If he must converse with one of his colleagues, he should do so privately. The salesperson's team must always present a united front to their audience.

29. The salesperson should prepare a list of all members of his delegation, together with job titles and areas of responsibility. He should hand out copies to each member of the audience, and before the meeting ends, he should obtain an accurate list of attendees and their job titles. This is important, because rarely will the actual attendance list be the same as the one given to the salesperson prior to the meeting. This actual list will enable him to identify any important people who did not attend the presentation. The salesperson will want to go see them later and give them a summary of the presentation.

30. A salesperson should be prepared to start on time. His spokesperson or the person in charge on his side should begin crisply by:
    - thanking them for taking the time to attend
    - outlining what the presentation will cover and its expected duration
    - introducing the salesperson's team

31. At the conclusion, the salesperson should ask for further questions. He should then summarize quickly, emphasizing a key feature or point, and express appreciation for their attendance.

A company's day-to-day business can be greatly influenced by a well-planned presentation on the salesperson's company and its products. New customers can be convinced to try the products. Large jobs are decided to a great extent on information put forth during formal presentations. The salesperson must make sure his are always professionally done. This takes much thought and work, and they must be done well if he is to be successful.

The salesperson should avoid the *good old boy* approach regardless of how well he knows his audience. The people in the audience are professional people taking time off from their other duties to hear about the salesperson's company and products. Their time is valuable. The salesperson should be certain he always gives them well-prepared, professional presentations, so they will feel their time was well spent. They will then be more inclined to buy from him.

While the points I have outlined apply when several people are involved, many of these can be put to good use when a salesperson is visiting with just one or two customer people in their offices.

Sales Examples

Example 1

An expert presentation helped us close a big order several years ago. We were involved with a large American oil company that was planning to buy products for installation overseas.

We asked for time to give a technical presentation, and they agreed. We then asked whether or not they had any special questions. As a result, we were given a long list of questions they wanted answers to, and a date was set for our meeting.

We spent several days formulating our replies for the meeting. We also put together a story woven around their questions that stressed the unique and outstanding features of our machines. We had our experts in the meeting, and not only answered all of their written questions, but also many others triggered by the remarks we made while telling our story.

A few weeks later, we were awarded a very large order, which proved immensely important to our future sales in this market area. Later, we were told by the key decision maker with this company that the ball game was over at the conclusion of our presentation. By then, all of his delegation had decided that our machines were by a wide margin the best for the job. Our performance was decisive, since we had answered all their questions.

Example 2

On another occasion, a sister division in my organization spent considerable time and money giving a presentation to a major oil company. Later, a good friend who was a senior manager with this customer and attended the meeting volunteered that the presentation was a disaster because of the *good old boy* approach taken. This customer obviously expected a professional approach, which he did not get.

A salesperson should give a lot of thought to presentations. They present unique opportunities to increase sales.

Summary

1. A salesperson should always look for opportunities to give sales presentations.
2. They are excellent vehicles to promote the salesperson's product and his company.
3. They should be well planned so they are not last-minute fire drills.
4. Most presentations are disorganized and pretty dull.
5. Before deciding what to present, the salesperson should evaluate his audience and determine what he wants to accomplish.
6. The salesperson should make certain the material is properly organized.
7. If the group will be large, he should inspect the meeting room ahead of time, if possible.
8. The salesperson should not use in-house terms or model numbers without defining them.

9. It is important that a salesperson choose his words carefully, avoiding inflammatory phrases.
10. The salesperson should make sure he knows how to operate any equipment that he will use in his presentation and that the information presented is easy to read and understand.
11. Presenters should not speak too rapidly.
12. The attendees should be given a chance to ask questions during the presentation.
13. The presenters must keep within the allowed time frame.
14. The salesperson's team should anticipate questions and have answers ready.
15. The salesperson should make a list of all questions for future use.
16. The salesperson should give the customer a list of the names and job titles of those in his delegation.
17. The sales team should answer all questions cheerfully.
18. The salesperson should be sure to thank attendees for taking time to hear his presentation.

31

Strike a Responsive Chord

Salespeople make wide use of computers in their business, and so do their customers. Even though most people in the customer organizations use computer, virtually all of the buying decisions are still made by people. These people have likes and dislikes, as well as prejudices and idiosyncrasies. To be successful, a salesperson must learn to identify these traits among his customers. Having learned them, he must then slant his sales efforts to best satisfy and accommodate their preferences. He must strike a responsive chord with his customers.

With expensive capital goods, as well as with minor items, the fear of making a mistake or buying the wrong product is uppermost in the customer's mind—it is pervasive. Before the customer signs the order, requisition, or recommendation, he must be convinced that he has made the right decision. He must be convinced beyond doubt that less risk, or no risk, is involved in buying the salesperson's product and dealing with his company.

It follows then that product reliability, efficiency, and dependability should be the salesperson's strongest sales arguments. He should support his efforts by taking his customers to visit his company's facility and the plants of satisfied customers. The salesperson could also give the customers a list of others who use the products and arrange phone calls or other conversations with satisfied users.

The important decision to buy technical products is not usually arrived at quickly. The customer goes through a slow process that involves input over many weeks or years. A company's public image is not gained overnight, either. If a company has an unfavorable image with a customer, it will not be changed without an enormous amount of work. It usually also entails the passage of time, sometimes many years, or even a generation. Sometimes the people who have the bad impression must retire or pass away before the roadblocks are removed. Sometimes the company's image problems do not vanish even then. The people who disliked the products or the company may have been outspoken and spread this distrust or unfavorable image to superiors, subordinates, and colleagues.

A salesperson should never allow his customer to consider his products as only equal to competition's products as far as reliability, efficiency, and performance are concerned. He must concentrate on the differences and demonstrate why these differences make his products more reliable. He should then continue emphasizing why his products have the highest reliability, efficiency, and performance. He must give concrete reasons to support his arguments and never forget these in his subsequent sales pitches. By this point, the salesperson should have already demonstrated that the order is in better hands if placed with him, because of the personal attention he will devote to it. The salesperson makes himself the difference and will save the customer money by making certain he is well satisfied.

The salesperson next should concentrate on other features, because not every customer will be influenced by the same second- or third-most important attribute. He should bear in mind that there are often many unique features of his products when compared to those of the competition. He must know them well and promote them vigorously. Customers will always try to equate his products with the competitors' products and then buy the lowest priced products. The salesperson should never concede this. He must repeatedly point out why his products are better and document why they are more efficient or reliable. The availability of quick delivery and service are always important. Sometimes these are decisive reasons in product selection.

The salesperson should be alert to the customer's responses during these discussions and should concentrate his remarks in the areas in which his customer responds and shows interest. He should ask questions about the customer's concerns and ask if he has adequately responded to them. The salesperson should allow time for the customer to respond. He should not assume that he has convinced the customer—he must ask questions to make sure. The salesperson should practice empathy and put himself in his customer's shoes and consider what he will look for and expect when committing to purchase from a certain vendor.

In the early stages of a job, a salesperson should identify the customer's main concerns and chief interests. The salesperson should carefully note the customer's response when asked what is most important to him when reaching a purchase decision. The salesperson may not always be given an accurate list, but it will be better than one put together without the customer's input. In their initial meetings, the salesperson should ask a lot of questions about what the buyer looks for in this of type product and what features he considers important.

The salesperson should have a mental checklist of things to mention in order to gauge reactions, but he should not review them in a rapid-fire fashion. He should mention one item and ask a few questions about how the customer feels about that item. If there is no reaction, or if the customer shows little interest, he should mention another. Eventually he should bring up everything on the list, but he may need to space the questions out over several meetings.

The salesperson should not stop or be discouraged if the customer says price is the only thing considered. He should concede that price is certainly important. If the customer insists that price will determine the order, then the salesperson should ask how the customer decides on a vendor if two or more

If the customer insists that price will determine the order, then the salesperson should ask how the customer decides on a vendor if two or more suppliers have the same price.

suppliers have the same price. This will flush out what points the customer values after price. It may be wise for a salesperson to ask several people in the customer organization what factors will be evaluated and what priority each will be given. He should always keep in mind that fear of making a mistake will be uppermost among the customer's concerns, even if it is not mentioned. The salesperson can also ask his customer what he thinks buyers or maintenance people in other companies put first in evaluating this decision. People often answer more truthfully if they feel they are giving opinions that can be attributed to others.

It can be surprising which features of a salesperson's product a customer will consider important—features the salesperson may undervalue or overlook. It is often astonishing what turns out to be the deciding factor in giving an order to a vendor. By probing for a responsive chord, the salesperson will find out what the customer is receptive to and what gets his attention. The salesperson can then amplify on these points and thereby raise the customer's opinion of his product. The salesperson's products will no longer be seen as equal, but superior. Thus he will help the customer justify the price, if it is slightly higher, or the longer delivery time, if it is longer.

As mentioned previously, the salesperson should not hold back when considering his list of advantages. He must not be too fast to make judgments for his customer, because not all decision makers think alike. Usually these buying decisions are very close, with minor points or features many times making the difference. The salesperson must work hard to determine in each case what interests the customer, what he responds to, and what influences him.

The reputation of the salesperson is often decisive. Frequently, however, the reason given for buying elsewhere is something the salesperson considered to be minor, but the customer did not. The customer apparently equated products from the salesperson and his competitors in terms of reliability, efficiency, performance, and risk before considering less-important features. The salesperson must continue to probe until he learns what else interests the customer. In doing this, he must emphasize all the other attributes of his product and his company. Eventually, he will strike a responsive chord, and when he does, he must amplify this point and repeat it often.

With today's high labor costs, a salesperson should look for ways to save the customer money in this area. Faster delivery of spare parts will reduce the inventory he must carry and will speed up his turnarounds, saving him money. Downtime is always very expensive. If possible, the salesperson should use comments from satisfied customers to document that his product has a higher efficiency and will minimize downtime.

A salesperson should keep in mind that he may not always know when his price is high. It is best for him to assume early on that it is, and to start his campaign to stress his outstanding advantages over a long period of time. By the time the salesperson knows for sure that his price is high, it is usually too late to convince all the decision makers of his product's superior features and advantages. Having seen a lower price from a competitor early on, they may well have begun to lean in that direction early in the process.

A salesperson must be aware that the customer is not always looking at, or at least should not be allowed to look at, initial price only. He will often evaluate installed costs. If appropriate, the salesperson should look for ways to help the customer save money on installation. He should investigate how the customer will evaluate installation costs of various vendors' products, especially if it will be a unique situation and if fieldwork will be unusually expensive.

During the sales calls and discussions, the salesperson should continue to probe for features that will appeal to the customer. He should do this as he works on a specific quotation, but he should keep on asking questions even between projects, since the customer will usually say more then. Gentle persistence in this area will pay handsome dividends.

Sales Examples

Example 1

Once while working on a project that involved installing products offshore, I learned of the customer's concerns by listening carefully during the course of several meetings. He was concerned about offshore installation delays due to high costs of labor and support products, such as heavy lift cranes. He was concerned that the pieces would not fit properly when being assembled offshore, or that pieces would be missing, causing him expensive delays. I proposed the following solution:

1. We would identify the service engineer to be used on this job.
2. We would have him on hand at our plant during the final assembly and testing of the product.

3. We would have him work with the customer's engineers and construction people in planning the shipping, the logistics, and the composition of offshore transportation loads for the job site.
4. In concert, they would decide how to best package the product for shipping, taking into consideration the offshore assembly requirements.
5. This same service engineer would be on hand when the product was moved offshore and would remain on hand during assembly and commissioning.

We knew the customer would be impressed with this approach. To our astonishment, in the evaluation we were given a credit of $500,000 for this service! (I would have guessed its worth at one-tenth of this amount.) With this plan, which we put in writing, we clearly removed our unit from a direct comparison, enabling us to overcome a price disadvantage. When the customer had asked our competitor how he would handle this concern, he just shrugged.

Even the way the company packages its product or the way it is prepared for shipment will be considered especially important by some buyers. The method of packaging may enable the customer to store the product safely for a longer period of time before installation or usage.

Sometimes because a salesperson's company has always followed a certain procedure, he assumes all of his competitors do the same. The point is that as a salesperson is searching for a responsive chord with his customer, he should not reject even minor possibilities.

Example 2

At one point prior to the development of the compressor piping pulsation analog, we had a customer who had his own in-house method of eliminating pulsation. The customer used choke tubes in the gas piping installed on the compressor skid package. Discovering this, we fabricated his piping into the skid exactly in accordance with hand-drawn sketches the engineers provided. We built dozens of units from these sketches and often received orders without competition. Our competitors were for a long time unaware of this customer's special requirement. By learning of his unique requirement, we had struck a responsive chord that benefited the customer and resulted in continued sales.

Example 3

Another customer wanted threaded studs for all flanges and covers on his unit, rather than cap bolts, which were standard and used by all vendors. After we found out how strongly the customer felt about threaded studs, we provided them, and thus received many orders.

Example 4

One of our customers liked a lot of flexibility in the sizing of his compressor cylinders. This allowed him to fully load his units at various suction and discharge pressures, and even by bringing gas in between stages. Because we discovered this and accommodated his desires, we beat out the competition for years. The customer did not readily volunteer this information, but by asking a lot of questions, we learned of this preference.

If a customer really wants to give a salesperson the order, this is a clever way he can go about it. He just fails to reveal to the competition these pet requirements of his.

A salesperson does not have to give these extras away if they add substantially to the cost. Customers are usually willing to pay a reasonable price for these extra things. We charged for the service person on the offshore platform project, for the choke tubes, for the special studded trim, and for the oversize compressor cylinders. The point is to discover these hidden, unmet wants, and to satisfy them.

Summary

The salesperson must search for, and be continually alert to, what interests his customer. When he identifies and recognizes these points of response, he must take them seriously and give well thought-out replies to each and every one. He should then repeat these comments to every individual even remotely involved in the decision. He should put these comments in writing for even greater emphasis and clarity. A salesperson who strikes a responsive chord will close a lot more orders.

32

The Initial Response Can Be Decisive

A salesperson should, of course, always be striving to obtain new customers. He should always be striving to take excellent care of existing customers and expanding the business he does with them. He should also be alert to limiting his company's exposure against cancellations, back charges, and returned goods, while at the same time expeditiously sorting out product problems. A salesperson can take a giant step toward doing a good job of this and accomplish virtually all of his objectives if he keeps in mind that his initial response can be decisive.

A salesperson must be ready to help a prospective customer and should not make a bad impression with poor answers early in his conversations. If he receives a call from someone looking for a small part or something that his company does not make, he should be sure that he is not only cordial but also as helpful as possible. He should be responsive.

If the salesperson's company does not make the item, he should not insult the customer by the way in which this information is relayed. He should do his best to help the customer locate what he is looking for. The salesperson can suggest other places to call or consult with his colleagues or engineering group if he does not readily have this information. Obviously he cannot spend all day on something like this, but usually it does not take much time to be courteous and helpful. It has been my experience that sooner or later a person is rewarded for anything he does for customers.

If the salesperson's company does not make the item, he should not insult the customer by the way in which this information is relayed. He should do his best to help the customer locate what he is looking for.

A salesperson should keep in mind that while this customer may not be in the market now for what his company sells, this person may be a prospective customer and should not be antagonized. The salesperson should leave the customer with a good impression of himself and his company. This will facilitate the possibility that the customer will call again when he needs something the salesperson can supply. Since perception means a lot in the customer's mind, the salesperson should make sure he leaves a good impression.

Occasionally, existing customers call for something the salesperson's company does not make or for a small order. Not all sales will be for large amounts, so a salesperson should be grateful for small orders and not just courteous to people who give him big orders. He should never give a negative impression by the tone of his voice or by displaying impatience. The salesperson should keep in mind that the first thing he says may turn the customer against the company, or at least make him feel less favorably toward the salesperson and his firm.

For example, perhaps a customer calls asking to return material the salesperson knows was custom made for him. He should say immediately, "Sir, we manufactured those items expressly for your company. They are peculiar to your units or your project. They will not fit just anywhere. We wish we had other uses, but we don't at this time. However, I will discuss this with management and check to see if we can find other uses for the items and whether or not we can give any credit at all. I will get back to you." A salesperson should never mislead the customer by failing to point these things out in the initial conversation. Otherwise he may mislead the customer into thinking he can return custom-made products or parts for full credit.

If a customer calls to cancel an order, a salesperson must be very careful how he answers. If he has had the order a few hours or even a day or so, there may not be much to be concerned about. However, if the salesperson has had the order several days or weeks, and especially if it is for custom-made items or items the salesperson's company is obtaining from an outside supplier, he should discreetly remind the customer of that. If the part is being made in the salesperson's plant, the salesperson should tell the customer that in order to meet the delivery requirements, the salesperson already had to order material, release engineering, and start other related work immediately. The salesperson should respond that he will investigate to determine the impact and to see how much financial exposure his company has and will call the customer back.

A salesperson should never treat a cancellation casually, especially if it is for engineered or special products. He should immediately raise the possibility of cancellation or restocking charges under these circumstances. He should never mislead the customer by giving the impression that there is no problem if the customer cancels. The salesperson does not want to alarm his customer unnecessarily, but he should alert the customer to the possibility of cancellation charges. In some cases, the salesperson's company may have already spent money on engineering.

Occasionally, the customer may only be considering or thinking about terminating the order. He may just be fishing. He may not really want to cancel the order but has been instructed to call and discuss the impact. By asking a few questions, the salesperson can determine how serious he is. If the salesperson says there is no problem and indicates there would be no charges, the customer may proceed with canceling, since he thinks he can do so without incurring any liability. If, however, the salesperson immediately raises the possibility of cancellation charges, the customer may reconsider and go back to his colleagues and superiors with this information. The salesperson may end up retaining the order only because of his alert initial response.

Suppose one of the salesperson's customers calls and says that the product he was sold failed prematurely. A salesperson should not say, "We are always hearing that," "We told manufacturing that they should do a better job," "All of our customers have trouble with that product," or "Engineering under designed it." To do so is to dig a big hole for the salesperson's company. Instead, the salesperson should ask a lot of questions.

The best response is for a salesperson to reply, "We are very sorry to learn you have had trouble. We have very high engineering design and manufacturing standards. We inspect our goods thoroughly and have had excellent success with this product in other locations. We will investigate and get back to you. We will either send someone to determine what went wrong or ask you to return the part for inspection." The salesperson should not commit to a specific action until he has had a chance to discuss it internally. He should never indicate that this is a chronic problem or that the product is poorly designed. A salesperson should never reveal in-house disagreements or problems at a time like this, or at any other time, for that matter.

Sometimes a salesperson has sold products to a customer without any specifications, and later someone in the customer's organization mentions that certain specifications apply. The salesperson should immediately point out that he was unaware that these specifications applied to this job and ask the customer why he thinks they do. The salesperson should never engage in discussions on these specifications and how they relate to his products on this order without first pointing out firmly that he was until now unaware they were involved. The salesperson should point out that they were not taken into consideration when pricing and quoting and do not apply to what the salesperson's company is building.

If a salesperson does not make this clear, he risks becoming hopelessly entangled. It will become very difficult for him to reestablish his correct position that the specifications just do not apply as this point. He should, of course, offer to accept a copy of the specification for review by the engineering department. He should explain that they will investigate to determine the impact and to quote a revised price and delivery if the customer wants it built to the new specifications.

There are other times when the salesperson's initial response can be decisive, such as the following:

1. When a customer or colleague has finished a comment or statement, the speaker will be turned off by a put-down comment or if the salesperson quickly changes the subject without asking a clarifying question or in some manner indicating he heard and understood what was said.
2. When a customer voices an objection to buying a salesperson's products, the salesperson should acknowledge the comment and ask additional questions. This will provide him with more time to think about his reply and might show him additional areas to attack or comment on. The salesperson's initial response should be conciliatory, with a follow-up that stresses the advantages to the product and answers the customer's specific objection.
3. A salesperson should respond to late shipments, wrong items shipped, items sent to the wrong address, or incorrect invoicing with a sincere apology first, not with excuses. He can then explain that his colleagues work very hard to avoid these problems. Also, the salesperson can offer to watch particularly for procedures on future orders to make certain these errors are not repeated. He should close his comments or response by voicing his understanding that the customer is unhappy and then apologizing again. He should ask what else he could do to help correct this problem.

Most of us have encountered problems in our personal lives with purchases or with service. When we complained, we were quite often more upset with the answers or comments received than we were when the original events occurred. This is because of the poor initial response of the offending firm or organization. It can be devastating to customer relations.

Without question, the more experience a salesperson has, the easier it is to give the proper response initially in situations like these. However, a salesperson should be alert and strive from the beginning to do a good job in this area and especially to not mislead customers.

A salesperson should ask a lot of questions so that he fully understands the situation. If it is a new request and if he has any doubt about how to respond, then he should tell the customer in a nice way that he has not encountered

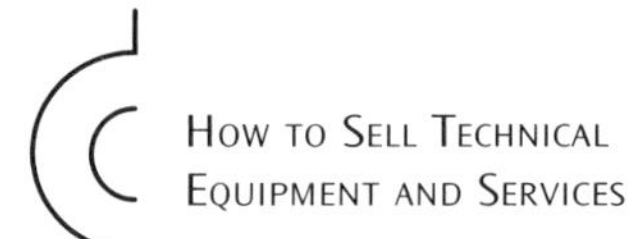

this situation previously. The salesperson should explain that he will discuss the problem with the proper people in his company and get back to the customer. The salesperson should never hesitate to say that he does not know the answer and that he must discuss it with his management. It is much better for a salesperson to say that than try to bluff and say the wrong thing and then later have to dig himself out of a hole.

This is an area in which many young, inexperienced salespeople have difficulty. They just do not like to admit that they do not know all the answers. This may be a normal reaction, but a good salesperson should guard against it. Since new problems are always coming up, and since situations are constantly changing, not even senior salespeople will know all the answers. A salesperson should not feel that it distracts from his image to say he does not know something. His customers will respect him for taking this approach and so will his management.

A salesperson should always put forth a sympathetic attitude but never commit the company to too much or say too much. Otherwise, he will then mislead his customer and leave a bad impression when he comes back with something less than he first indicated. He will also lose credibility. Remember, too, that people hear what they want to hear. They will interpret a person's initial remarks in the way most favorable to their own cause.

A salesperson should always be extremely alert when he is on the telephone talking to customers or when he is in the customer's office. To the customer, he is the company, and they place a lot of importance on what he says. The salesperson, therefore, must always be vigilant, careful, and extremely aware of what he utters. It is almost like an actor on stage—all eyes and ears are on him.

A salesperson must keep in mind also that some customers, although not many, will deliberately bring up a problem without warning, hoping to lure the salesperson into a premature and favorable response. When this happens, the salesperson may be reluctant to say he does not know the answer and may respond prematurely, to the detriment of his company. A salesperson should not be caught in this trap.

If something new, strange, or unusual is mentioned, a salesperson should just say that he is not prepared to give answers immediately. Instead, he should ask a lot of questions and get all of the details so he can discuss this with his management. Then he can be sure when he calls back that he will be giving the optimum response—one that is accurate and has the full backing of his company. He will then handle this in the best interests of his firm. He will not have to backtrack on anything said initially and will not be second-guessed by anyone inside his own organization.

A salesperson should also keep in mind that there are almost always several groups or layers of people involved in a customer's organization. Rarely is it a one-man show. When a salesperson tells the contact something about how he plans to solve a problem, the customer usually tells others in his own company, such as his superior, colleagues, or those in a different department. If the salesperson later downgrades or reverses what he initially said, the customer, in turn, will have to go back and alter what he has told a lot of people. This can sometimes be difficult, because word spreads quickly under these circumstances. If the contact loses face, the salesperson looks bad also. The salesperson and his company lose credibility. Consequently, the salesperson's initial response should be the best one for the company and should be a consensus response to which his company will adhere.

For example, suppose a salesperson's firm has just closed several large orders so that lead times are very long. A customer wants to buy custom-made parts or items the salesperson does not have in stock. If the salesperson immediately announces that he is sold out of that part for six months, he may turn his customer away and into the arms of his competitors.

His correct response would be to say nothing about how busy he is. Instead, the salesperson should determine what delivery the customer really needs and expects, together with the quantity required, so it can be discussed internally. The salesperson should explore this first through the normal channels inside his company, but he should not hesitate to go to top management when he is about to lose an order because of long delivery.

When this is called to management's attention, they can usually arrange a better delivery by authorizing overtime, expediting castings, or by subcontracting. A salesperson should not accept a routine answer in situations like this. He must insist that top management get involved. If it turns out that the salesperson still cannot provide the required delivery to get the order, he will have done all that was possible. He brought it to the attention of his superiors, and no one can later fault him for mishandling and giving the wrong initial response.

Sales Examples

Here are some actual examples of how initial responses can be decisive. I will relate 10 examples, all of which are true.

Example 1

A customer called to say that some of the products he bought failed inspection. Without checking with anyone, the salesperson told him to ship them back to the plant for examination and analysis. When the products arrived back at the plant, the salesperson learned that the engineering department would have preferred to send their own person to the customer's jobsite. This would have allowed the inspection and evaluation to be carried out jointly in the customer plant and in presence of the customer representatives. The salesperson could have avoided this situation if, after receiving word of the problem from the customer, he had discussed this internally before responding. His initial response was not the best way to solve this problem for his company.

Example 2

Years ago I received a call from the division manager of a large oil company who had just learned that one of our units had failed offshore. His first question was, "Who is going to pay for this casualty?" I responded by saying that I was very sorry about the breakdown, but we were working furiously to solve the problem. Our top priority was to get the parts required to the jobsite, along with a serviceperson, so the unit could be repaired and placed back in operation and once again earn money for his company. When the unit was operating again, we would sit down and reach a mutually satisfactory settlement. His response was, "That is all I wanted to hear."

Later we sat down and settled this problem with minimum financial exposure to my firm. My initial response could have been, "We understand the unit was overloaded," "We understand you used bad oil," or, "We understand you have lousy maintenance." These poor responses would have put him on guard that he was going to have trouble obtaining a fair settlement. My company would have lost in the final discussions, because the customer's records and his documentation of the events surrounding the failure would have been better than ours. His people had operated the products and were with them around the clock.

Example 3

We were meeting with customers in Africa who had trouble with a product we had sold them. We agreed to repair a part on a no-charge basis if they would pay the freight to our factory in the United States and back. They agreed. Someone with the customer's company mentioned insurance. My colleague immediately said, "We will take care of that." I interrupted to say that since they were arranging for and paying for the transport, they should take care of adequate insurance coverage. They had no objections and agreed. Later we learned that since this country was in a war zone, the insurance on the shipment was $50,000! This is something we almost gave away by making the wrong initial response.

In negotiating with a customer, a salesperson should never agree to do something at no charge or to provide replacement parts or products free without first knowing the cost to his company. It almost seems redundant to mention something so basic, but this rule is violated often, to the sorrow of those involved.

Example 4

We were discussing a large job with the Soviets in Moscow. At one of our meetings, the vice president in charge of purchasing pushed a telex across the table to us. He said, "From this message, you will observe that we can buy the products required on this project from your competitor for 60% of your price." Without even looking at the telex, we responded, "They are overcharging you. They are usually 50% of our price."

This competitor had indeed quoted one-half of our price on a previous job, so our comment was valid. The purchasing vice president was unable to conceal his astonishment, because he expected us to be on the defensive, to make excuses, and to go away and try to get him a better price. We received the order one week later because we did not panic when confronted with what the customer thought was a dramatic display of a price reduction by a competitor. Our initial response was instrumental in getting the order.

Example 5

I was confronted at an overseas trade show by the president of a large international company. He advised me that we were charging his firm the same price for products FOB (free on board) our factory in the United States that he paid us in his own country where freight, duty, warehouse fees, and other fees were included.

My response was that of course we charged the same price and had been doing so for many years to my knowledge. The reason was that we wanted to encourage his company to use the local warehouse rather than buying in the United States. His response was that they certainly did not want to do anything to destroy the local warehouse.

I used this argument repeatedly throughout our long negotiations with this company. This approach saved us a substantial amount of money in our final settlement. My initial response to this accusation greatly enhanced our negotiating position and may have been decisive.

Example 6

Many years ago, I walked into a shoe store and asked if they had any Scotch-grained leather shoes. The salesman responded by saying, "Nobody wears Scotch-grained leather shoes any more." I replied, "I do," and walked out. I went down the street and asked the same question at another shoe store, and they said of course they had them, and that they were one of their best sellers. I bought two pairs and never again returned to the original shoe store.

Example 7

On an airline flight some time ago, the flight attendant came by to offer me something to drink, and I asked if she had any apple juice. Her response was, "Oh, I wish we did." This was the most polite *no* I had ever received and left me with a very favorable impression of her and that airline. This was a superlative answer, especially since she could have said, "No one drinks apple juice anymore," or "Of course we don't have any." Her warm, considerate response almost made me glad she did not have any apple juice.

Example 8

It was the day prior to a sales meeting. The arrangements had been made several weeks earlier, but I called the hotel banquet sales office to verify the plans and to check on the meeting room arrangements. I was put in touch with the person handling our meeting. I identified myself and told her that I would like to come over and inspect the room assigned for our use the following day. She burst out laughing.

Puzzled, I asked what was so funny about my request and explained that I just wanted to make certain our arrangements were suitable and adequate. She responded by saying the hotel was completely full and how busy and snowed under they were. I then said, "I assume you currently have a meeting going on in the room assigned to us tomorrow, and I will settle for an unobtrusive peek." Reluctantly and at my insistence, she checked and found that the room was not then occupied. I was allowed to have a look and ended up making substantial changes to the way it was to be set up.

The point is that her initial response was terrible—about the worst I had ever heard—and dramatically lowered my confidence in the hotel. A response like this when the facilities were being booked would have caused me to look elsewhere. As it turned out, the hotel did a good job, and the arrangements were satisfactory. However, the initial response raised many doubts in my mind and made me apprehensive.

A salesperson should remember that laughter is fine at the proper time, but he should be careful when he laughs and make certain it is appropriate. The salesperson should not laugh when his customer is serious.

Example 9

Another time, we had sold products to a firm in the Middle East. The firm had made progress payments on this machine, but prior to its completion and shipment, the country had a revolution. The firm stopped the payments, but we went ahead and finished the products and put them into storage. Several years later, we sat down to discuss the delivery of these products, the balance on the invoice price, plus storage and financial costs.

Since at the time the products were sold we had a sales representative in this country, we consulted with him to verify the residual amount of commission we still owed on this sale. We submitted an amount that the representative agreed to in writing. We finished our negotiations with the customer, reached a settlement on the balance due, and shipped the products. We paid our representative the residual amount he agreed we owed.

Four or five months later, this sales representative called from overseas to say that he had just discovered a side letter agreement on this job which indicated that we still owed him additional commission. My response was, "It's too late." When he asked why, I said, "One year previously, we came to you and asked you to sign off on the remaining amount of commission due. You signed off in writing, and we made a settlement with the customer on that basis. It is now too late to reconsider and discuss additional commission."

Later, this agent did indeed send a copy of the letter signed by our local salesperson indicating agreement to pay additional money. However, the home office had not authorized and was unaware of this supplemental transaction. Since the representative had already signed off on what we owed him, it was simply too late to discuss any additional money. The representative accepted our reasoning, and my company saved a great deal of money due to the proper initial response.

Example 10

We had sold a large order to one of our customers and as usually happened, they asked for several extra items. We gave them the prices and received a verbal authorization to proceed. In our letter conveying the prices, we confirmed their instructions to proceed to supply these extras. We proceeded to order and ship all extra items.

All of this happened in October and was handled by one of my salespeople. In May, seven months later, I received a call from the customer who wanted to talk to me since the salesperson was out of the office. He began by challenging the various prices given in the October letter, saying that they were too high. I listened politely until he finished, then I said, "What is the date of that letter?" He replied, "October 17." I said, "What is today's date?" He responded, "May 27." I reminded him that last October we had submitted these prices and had been authorized to proceed. Since our October letter clearly documented this, I felt it was too late to discuss prices now. He replied, "I guess you are right."

Thus far we have dealt with a salesperson's responses to his customers, but these principles apply equally to his conversations with colleagues, supervisors, and vendors as well. The tone of a salesperson's entire conversation or meeting is set by his opening words, his initial reply, or his first comment.

Initial responses, like the beginning of a paragraph or speech, make the most impact. They sometimes lock a person into a given position or posture. They create the perception people have of the salesperson and his firm. Most individuals, after hearing just a few words, tune the salesperson out and essentially hear no more. Others think the salesperson has agreed to a favorable settlement when he did not.

A salesperson must always be on the alert when he is on the telephone, visiting in person, and when he is in the presence of customers or colleagues. He must work hard to make certain he gives the correct initial responses, because they can be decisive.

Summary

1. A salesperson must always be ready to help a new or existing customer and should never offend the customer with his initial comment or response.
2. If a salesperson's company does not make an item requested, he should not insult the prospect by the way he relays this information. He should take time to suggest alternate sources.
3. Sooner or later, the salesperson is likely to be rewarded for the things he does for his customers.
4. A salesperson must keep in mind that the person he is talking to could later be in the market for what he can supply.
5. A salesperson should be grateful for small orders. Not all orders can be big.
6. The salesperson's firm almost always incurs immediate costs on custom-made products. If a customer calls to cancel, the salesperson should always mention the prospect of cancellation charges.
7. When a customer calls to report problems with products he has purchased, the salesperson should express sympathy and ask a lot of questions. He should never make unfavorable comments about shortcomings of his products.

8. If a customer calls to say that specifications apply to an order already entered, the salesperson should always raise the prospect of additional charges.
9. The salesperson should respond favorably by asking questions
   - during normal conversations;
   - when a buyer voices objections;
   - when problems with his firm are reported.
10. When encountering a new or unusual request, the salesperson should
    - listen carefully;
    - ask a lot of questions to obtain complete details.
11. Regardless of his experience level, the salesperson should never hesitate to say he does not know the answer and that he has not encountered this situation before.
12. A salesperson must remember that people hear what they want to hear. They will interpret his initial remarks in the way most favorable to their own cause.
13. A salesperson must always be alert to his initial response when he is talking to a customer, whether in person or on the telephone.
14. A salesperson should be aware that a few customers will unexpectedly confront him with startling requests or revelations in an attempt to lure him into an initial, rash commitment.
15. A salesperson should bear in mind that many layers of people are often involved. If he passes out incorrect information, it will spread quickly, and the damage is difficult to control.
16. A salesperson should be slow to turn down orders because he cannot make delivery. He should investigate fully and involve top management before losing a sizable order because of delivery delays.
17. A salesperson should never agree to do something or furnish a part at no charge unless he is absolutely sure he knows the cost to his company.
18. A salesperson must be careful when laughing to be sure that it is an appropriate response.
19. A salesperson must be careful with initial responses. Like the beginning of a speech or a paragraph, they make the most impact.

33 Respect the Chain of Command

Often when a customer has a poor relationship with a vendor, there is a good reason. In most cases, it was because someone at the vendor's company, perhaps long ago, went over someone else's head trying to get an order. They may have told the top-level people things that made the lower echelon look bad, perhaps causing them trouble or embarrassment. When this happens, people often have to retire or leave the company before the vendor's position improves. Even after the offended person leaves or retires, the vendor will usually still have problems. The individual may have said many bad things about the vendor's firm that were heard by the young engineers and others still associated with the company.

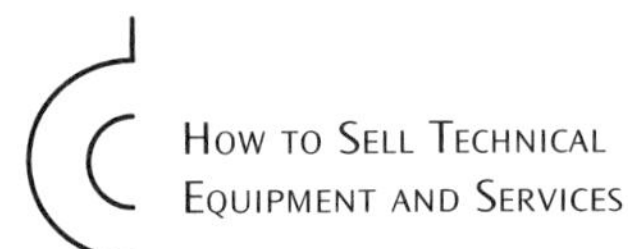

In most cases today, committees make large capital purchase decisions, rather than just one person. However, one or two people usually either dominate the committee or greatly influence its decision. There are, of course, exceptions, such as a company owned by one person or a company whose president personally makes all the big decisions. The salesperson should always work through the proper channels and be very cautious about going around people or over their heads to reach these decision makers.

Sometimes, after repeated efforts over a long time with large publicly held companies, a salesperson feels he is being treated unfairly. In this case, he should consider going to a higher level. He must find a way to get his story across to the person actually making the decisions. Occasionally, regardless of the consequences, the salesperson has to take the bull by the horns and go to the top-level executive. This is the course of last resort and should be attempted only after all other efforts fail. Because customers vary, the salesperson must evaluate the situation thoroughly and reach a consensus with his supervisors, taking into account the risks involved.

One approach with these large companies is for a salesperson to talk to the customer's purchasing people, project engineer, products engineer, or other principal people in the customer's company. The salesperson should explain to them that he understands that his competitor is talking to the customer's upper-level executives, and while he has not done this himself, he does need guidance. If the salesperson's relations are good with those people, and they favor his products or are sympathetic to his cause, they will usually give him good advice. They will either tell him to go see the senior executives, or they will say that he does not need to do so. If his relations are good and he has done his selling job with these lower echelon people, he should abide by their recommendations, at least on this current project.

If the salesperson follows this procedure and loses the order, he should consider changing tactics next time. However, if he does go to the top on the next job, he will be able to explain that he stayed away previously and lost the order. If the salesperson does visit with senior executives, he should report back to his usual contacts what he told these people. This is especially important if something unusual or out of the ordinary was discussed or if they requested anything special.

The comments outlined above are not limited to those occasions when a salesperson is working on closing an order on a large project. He should work through the proper channels and respect the chain of command at all times. When it is necessary to see people above the level of his normal contacts, he should reveal his plans to his contacts and ask for their guidance. He should keep them informed about the result of his efforts. Although there are always exceptions, following this procedure will work with most customers.

There are salespeople who cannot stand selling to just lower level people, and eventually they will call on the top-level people without good reasons. They refuse to limit their normal dealings to the people handling the day-to-day details of the business. Often it is just an ego problem. Some salespeople feel more important if they are calling on senior people, but this mind-set should be avoided at all costs.

Some salespeople feel more important if they are calling on senior people, but this mind-set should be avoided at all costs.

Sometimes a salesperson meets with upper level executives because the salesperson has known the executives for quite some time. Before they were promoted, these executives were the correct people to contact. If this is the situation, the salesperson must be very careful in the way he calls on both levels of authority. Even in situations like this, I feel a salesperson must make certain that he always calls first on the lower level of the customer's people. He should call on them more often and always send information to them. Any discussions on new products or new developments should always occur first at this lower level. A salesperson should never let them find out from their bosses about these things. In business or social meetings when both groups are present, the salesperson should defer to the lower level people and give them appropriate attention.

Sales Examples

A good example of what can happen when a salesperson fails to respect the chain of command is found in the following true stories.

Example 1

My firm had just lost an enormous order in which I was not involved. The products were to be installed offshore. I also called on the same engineers, but only for products purchased for use in other world areas. Shortly after the loss of this large order, I asked the leading engineer, his boss, and his colleague to lunch. During lunch, in an effort to do a little forecasting, I asked if any large projects would be coming up soon with their firm in my area. The lead engineer replied, "After the last project, I hope we never have another."

I said how sorry I was that my company did not receive the order on that recent project. His response was astonishing. He said if I had been handling the job on my side, we would have received the order. He continued to say that the decision had been made to buy our product, but we blew it.

When I said I understood there were problems, he said, "Of course there were problems, but you and I could have worked them out." I replied, "But I thought the financing of another vendor was a problem, and that you had requested my firm to underwrite this financing."

"That was not an issue and had nothing to do with the decision," he said. He also added that our salespeople calling on him on this recent project never really believed that he was the decision maker.

From inside my firm, the only thing I was later able to learn was that we did go over the engineers' heads and have meetings with top executives in their partner's organization. This occurred without asking for guidance and without keeping the lower level informed. To make matters even worse, this very large order was duplicated five years later, but the customer again purchased the competitive products because of savings in duplication, a common industry practice.

Example 2

Many years ago my firm was having trouble selling to a large oil company. Investigations by the salespeople then calling on this customer revealed that the trouble likely originated several years earlier. At that time, our executives learned we were about to lose a very large order. They went to the president and over the heads of several individuals, including the manager of the department that evaluated and purchased all of the products.

Our executives were unsuccessful in their appeal to the president. Furthermore, we deeply offended the department manager. He not only never again bought from us, but he also regularly told all of his young engineers how unethical we had been by going over his head. Only after this manager retired years later were we able to again sell to this company. Even then, we never received the share we should have had, which was a residual effect of this miscalculation by our senior people.

It seems that in some companies, salespeople are encouraged to concentrate on the executive level in order to do their selling job. Soon these companies acquire a reputation for routinely going around the established chain of command. This reputation is unpopular and counterproductive. A salesperson should make certain his company never falls into this category.

Summary

An enormous amount of business has been lost by salespeople and executives who went around the people they were supposed to contact. This problem often exists when a salesperson must, to sell his products, deal with both purchasing and operating people. The salesperson should get to know how his customer operates and how they want things handled. He should get to know the individuals and handle the account to maximize his business by keeping all parties happy and respecting the chain of command.

Avoid Aggression and Condescension

Even though a salesperson's products may greatly outsell all others, and even though his prices are lower than competition's, he should take it easy when he tells this to his customers. In general, customers do not like a salesperson to talk in strident tones and brag about how great his company is. A salesperson must practice humility. If his products are much better than the competition's, his deliveries are shorter, and his prices are lower, the chances are good that the customer will already know. A gentle, softly spoken reminder will suffice. It can be counterproductive for a salesperson to take too strong a position or to make statements and assertions too firmly. It can cause the customer to be resentful. A salesperson should remember that how he says something is more important than what he says.

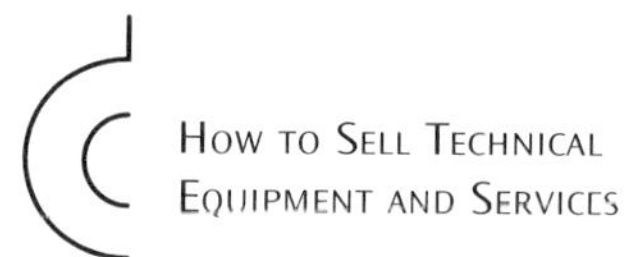

Sales Example

A senior buyer overseas told me that he had just switched jobs and joined a company as a senior buyer of heavy products. In his previous job, he had been chief purchasing agent for many years and had a lot of authority. A senior salesperson with a products firm who was well acquainted with this senior buyer had been working for some time on a big job with this company, and he dropped in to see this senior buyer. At this point, the salesperson had already been talking to others in the organization and felt he was in a commanding position. Right away, this salesperson told the senior buyer, "You may have had a lot of stroke at your previous firm, but you do not have nearly as much influence here." The salesperson continued in an arrogant tone and acted as if he already had the order for the products on the current project.

This senior buyer told me he consequently went about his job to make certain this salesperson did not get this order. He did it by feeding pricing information to the competitor, so the competitor was able to make the low bid and win the order. Besides being incredible, this shows what can happen when a salesperson acts arrogantly and talks down to a customer.

A salesperson should avoid going into a customer's office and making arrogant statements about his products or his company. It is much better for him to relate this information in less aggressive ways. He could use phrases like, "We believe we do it best,""We think our quality is exceptional," and "We would like a chance to prove it to you." Customers are smart and knowledgeable people and generally know the marketplace very well. The salesperson should not offend them by being overly aggressive or condescending.

People basically do not want to be told they are wrong, even if they are.

The same thing applies if a salesperson is an expert in a given field. He should not talk down to his customer, who may not be an expert in this category. He should not give the impression of being a know-it-all. The salesperson should remember that the customer has the decision making power. It is possible for the salesperson to be right and still lose the order. People basically do not want to be told they are wrong, even if they are. People do not like to be talked down to or otherwise made to feel uncomfortable. The salesperson should speak in gentle tones and never pin anyone in a corner. He should consider the customer's feelings and allow him room to save face.

For example, perhaps the salesperson is an expert in thermodynamics or metallurgy and enters the room quoting numbers and equations to prove his point. His customer will be uncomfortable if he knows less than the salesperson does about this, especially if the information is related in an overbearing way. While the salesperson should be an expert on his products and in his field, he must always remember to use soft words and practice humility as he relates his sales information and tries to sell his products. He should always allow the customer some maneuvering room and should not try to overpower him by quoting facts, figures, and equations. The salesperson might be right, but he will usually lose the battle, and the next order as well.

Summary

1. The salesperson should speak softly.
2. The salesperson should tell his story sincerely but without boasting.
3. The salesperson should not be a know-it-all.
4. The salesperson will sell more if he does not come on too strongly.
5. The salesperson should not appear arrogant.
6. The salesperson should consider the customer's feelings.

35

Demonstrate the Products and the Facilities

A salesperson should keep in mind that fear of making a mistake is uppermost in a customer's mind when selecting expensive capital products. It is also in his thoughts even on smaller purchases, such as spare parts or modifications. It follows that if a salesperson is to obtain orders, he must demonstrate that his products will perform in a superior fashion and with less risk than the competition's products. To be convinced to buy a salesperson's product, the customer should see it being built or in use. This is especially helpful if it is new or if he is not familiar with the product or the company. It is a good idea for customers to see the machines in person, even if they are already familiar with them. The customer will always learn something new on a plant visit.

The customer who is not already using the salesperson's products can see them in operation in only two places. One is at another customer's plant, and the other is at the salesperson's factory, usually on a test stand. If a customer unfamiliar with the products refuses an invitation to go see the machinery without a good cause, the salesperson should pay attention. This may tell him a lot. The customer may not seriously be interested, and if he asked for a bid from the salesperson, it was only to check prices. On the other hand, many customers will consider an installation visit as a very important factor in the products decision. They may disregard sales presentations and letters and may base their decision almost entirely on seeing the machines successfully operating and evaluating endorsements from satisfied users.

A salesperson should plant the seeds early when considering inviting people to visit his facilities or to go see his products in another customer's location. He should suggest the visit but not try to tie them down immediately to a specific date. He should also point out that it could be arranged so that the customer is away from the job a minimum amount of time.

After waiting a few days, the salesperson should bring it up again. By this time, the customer will have had more time to think about the logistics and, hopefully, will show some interest so that the trip can be finalized. If he still puts the salesperson off, the salesperson should wait longer and bring it up again. It is possible that in the meantime, the salesperson's company will have given the customer good service on his inquiries or orders. If the salesperson has always been responsive, the customer should then be more interested in arranging a visit. If not, the salesperson should try to determine what is behind the customer's lack of interest in visiting the facilities, especially if he is not buying from the salesperson. If, however, he is giving the salesperson orders, the subject should be dropped for the time being.

Because it will be in use under field conditions, observation of the salespersons' product in actual operation in a user's installation is obviously much better than at the factory.

Because it will be in use under field conditions, observation of the salespersons' product in actual operation in a user's installation is obviously much better than at the factory. It will have gone through the commissioning stage and will have accumulated operating time. The prospective customer can quiz unbiased management, engineering, and operating personnel as to areas of interest. These could include performance, reliability, ease of installation and maintenance, and availability of spare parts and service. From what the customer sees and hears during these plant visits, he can better visualize what the machines will look like in the plant he is planning to build. It will also provide an opportunity for the prospective customer to converse with the operating people about other matters not directly related to the salesperson's products.

Before scheduling a visit to a customer's installation, the salesperson should carefully consider which operating site to select, assuming he has several places available. There are a few guidelines he should follow. Obviously he should select the plant that will give him the best recommendation, one that has had minimum difficulty, and one where the products are performing well. The salesperson should select models similar to the ones the customer plans to purchase.

The location of the plant visit should be reasonably accessible, and the salesperson should make practical travel arrangements. Before the salesperson schedules the plant visit, he should call the maintenance or production manager, or whoever is closest to the operation. The salesperson should verify that there are no problems or complaints with his products. This cannot be overemphasized. He must not rely on anyone else to make this call, even if the location is in another area or in someone else's territory. He must obtain the necessary permission and make the calls.

There are several advantages to the salesperson being responsible for these arrangements. It will give him a chance to talk directly to the person he will later meet when accompanying the prospective customer to the installation site. It invariably will make the visit go smoother. He will have the important advantage of being reassured that he has chosen a good location and that he will receive a cordial reception. The salesperson should ask this person what troubles he has had, if they were fixed promptly, and if he has any residual complaints. The salesperson should also ask him if he would recommend these products to a prospect. If he answers negatively, the salesperson should avoid that location and find a better one.

It is far better for a salesperson to discover this while on the telephone than it is for him to learn about problems during a visit after he has spent time and money to travel there. More importantly, the salesperson usually will have only one chance to take his customer to an installation site. Therefore, it must be successful. The salesperson should obtain and record the office and home telephone numbers of the plant representative who will host or coordinate this visit. This will enable him to promptly communicate if plans change, delays occur, or if any hitches develop on the way to the plant site.

If the salesperson has done his homework and has selected a location that has had good service from his machinery, his participation in the plant visit can be minimized. He should arrange to point out salient features to each member of the visiting delegation, working from a prepared list of important features. The salesperson should be careful not to overlook anyone in the group. He may not be certain who has the most influence.

The salesperson should listen very attentively during the discussion period with the plant operating people when questions are asked. He may have to clarify some of the answers given, so he should write down all questions asked and the replies given. This will give the salesperson additional clues to concerns the prospective customer has as he moves toward a decision. The salesperson should, however, allow the prospective customer time to talk privately with the host. Otherwise he may feel the visit was rigged and may not be entirely satisfied.

Following this plant visit, the salesperson should ask the prospective customer about his impressions and determine if he has any additional questions generated by this inspection. The salesperson will have a good opportunity to remind the customer of the advantages of his machinery and to relate them to what they have just seen.

When the salesperson arrives back at the office, he should call his host to thank him for his hospitality. He can also ask what the host thought about his customer's impression of what was seen and thus can learn of any comments the customer made to the host. Later, the salesperson should thank the host in writing for his cooperation.

If the product offered is new, perhaps the only place it can be seen is in the salesperson's factory during manufacture, on the test stand, or during final assembly. Obviously, this does not provide as good an opportunity as an operating plant visit. If selected, however, the salesperson should first have a thorough office briefing to describe to the customer what he will see before taking him to the manufacturing or test area. If the unit is undergoing testing, the salesperson must make sure it is running when his customer is there. He should have it checked out ahead of time so that there is no delay.

The salesperson should provide the customer with a schedule or an agenda and should include a set of test data. He also should include in this packet photographs, a list of product users, and other appropriate information and specifications on the products. However, he must not include any proprietary information. On the test stand, the salesperson should point out important features to each of his visitors, not neglecting anyone. The top specialists should be available, and at least some of them should be at the test stand, with the rest available for the question-and-answer period to follow. The salesperson should confer with his people ahead of time to make sure that what they plan to say is to the point and properly worded. He should provide ample observation time, and if possible, take pictures while the customer is observing the products.

It can also be important to have prospective customers visit the manufacturing facility even if there is not a unit the salesperson can show on the test stand. Often the salesperson's facilities will be better than his competitor's facilities. Even if they are equal, there are benefits to having them meet and visit with the engineers, quality control personnel, manufacturing people, and executives. This will always enhance the salesperson's prospects on the next order.

When scheduling these visits, the salesperson must be certain all of the proper people at his factory are alerted. He must provide these people with not only the date and time of his visit, but also with a written list of his customers, along with their correct titles. He should identify their primary interests, since these may vary.

The salesperson should verify ahead of time that all arrangements are in order. He should directly advise the designers or engineers about points or features that should be stressed. Again, he should not do this through an intermediary but should talk directly to the factory people who will participate. The salesperson should confirm in writing everything he tells them. He should also quiz his engineers on the advantages and features of this product. After all, if they created it, they must have had certain design parameters in mind to beat the competition. These advantages should be pointed out to the prospective customer long before the trip. Then during the session with the engineers and designers, they can be emphasized and amplified.

The salesperson should ask someone from the manufacturing section who is intimately acquainted with all of the products currently moving through the shop to conduct the plant tour. The salesperson can thus provide the customer with correct and specific information on what he is observing. Insofar as possible, customer's names should be tied to the products viewed.

The quality control section of most plants is very impressive, and most customers are sensitive to quality. The salesperson should alert the person in charge of that vital area so his customers will be well received and properly impressed.

Following the shop or test stand visit, the salesperson should arrange a meeting in a quiet room. There the customer can have any questions answered by the test people, designers, engineers, and executives. The salesperson should note all questions and answers in writing for later confirmation and use. If questions are asked that cannot be answered on the spot, he must get the reply later and send it to the customer. He should not forget this vital aspect. It is also very important that he ask his president or chief executive to meet the visitors and possibly have lunch with them. They can assure the customers of the company's support and commitment. This is mandatory.

Finally, on a trip of any kind, whether to the salesperson's factory or to an operating facility, the salesperson must ascertain that all of the transportation logistics are properly arranged. It is fine to have the office assistant or the travel people do the arranging, but the salesperson must verify that there are no slipups with any aspect of the arrangements. He should be certain that automobile trips are not too strenuous and will fit practically into his time schedule. He should also allow time for delays and for rest stops.

The salesperson's customers are important people whose time is valuable. If they have agreed to spend two days with the salesperson, they do not mean three. A logistical breakdown can make the trip a disaster. Therefore, the salesperson must personally and thoroughly check all arrangements to ensure the trip will be successful. He should keep with him both the office and home telephone number of the coordinator in his factory so that he can readily communicate if plans change. After the completion of the visit, the salesperson should write notes thanking the individuals who participated. Again, he should not overlook anyone.

The importance of having customers visit a salesperson's own facility will vary depending on how big the company is and how good its reputation is in the industry. Plant visits and shop tours will greatly improve a salesperson's chances on the next order, even if his company is very big and already has a fine reputation.

If the salesperson's company is small and not well known, these plant visits are mandatory if he is to sell to most customers. After visits to plant facilities, I have heard such comments as:

- "We never seriously considered your company until we saw your facilities and met your management people."
- "We had no idea you had such a fine facility. If we had visited years before, you would have received a lot more business from us."

Sales Example

At one time we quoted two of our products to be barge mounted and to operate at very high pressures. The potential customer had not previously bought any of our products. We knew that if we were to obtain the order, we had to take the two key decision makers to see some of our units operating in a similar environment. We arranged the trip, hiring a boat to take us to see similar units operating on barges. Thus the potential customers were able not only to see our machines operating but also to observe auxiliary products. Both decision makers were able to quiz operators directly to ascertain that our units performed satisfactorily. This trip, lasting less than two days, also enabled these decision makers to get to know us better.

By making sure all the elements of the trip were well planned, the visit went off without any hitches. The customers were impressed with what they saw and gave us the order a few days later. The field trip to see this product was decisive.

Summary

1. A salesperson should show his products operating in a satisfied customer's plant.
2. A salesperson should show his products in his company's factory on the test stand. He should also show the plant facilities.
3. The salesperson must carefully check all arrangements so there are no problems.
4. The salesperson must be certain all members of the customer delegation have their questions answered and that he points out the salient features to each individual.
5. The salesperson should write thank-you notes to his host, his factory members, and the customer's people who took time to make the trip.

36

Sales Letters

There is a common misconception that sales letters are written only for a specific quotation or on an identified project. Actually, a salesperson should consider all letters written to his customers to be sales letters, not just those concerning product benefits and features. In all of his correspondence, the salesperson should create a good impression of himself and his company, with the goal of increasing business with the customers. In his letters, the salesperson should always be selling, although sometimes he is striving to regain the goodwill of a customer. In this chapter, we will deal with those sales letters specifically promoting the company's products.

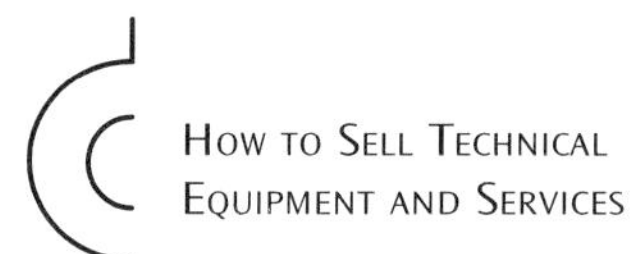

A salesperson deals constantly with people who must be brought around to his way of thinking concerning his products, and his persuasive efforts can be verbal or written. Usually he will attempt to persuade verbally, but often written words increase his chances of success. A written effort can be honed to better achieve the objective. A salesperson should use sales letters to sell goods and keep them sold and to sell himself and his company to the customers, as well.

The sales letter, then, is but one of the elements of a selling effort. When well written, though, it can be the catalyst that insures or cements the sale. An outstanding sales letter is not often due to flashes of imagination. Instead, its words are carefully chosen by disciplined minds. They are diligently produced, no matter how casual they appear in the finished letter. It is not easy for a beginning salesperson to write outstanding sales letters, but he should consider them carefully and strive to improve them.

Sales letters are written primarily to convince customers to buy a salesperson's products. Thus the salesperson should carefully and thoughtfully compile a compelling list of benefits to include in the letter. Sales letters should also promote the salesperson's company and its facilities, engineering expertise, and people. They should enhance the customer's perception of the salesperson and his firm.

Customers generally form their opinions of the salesperson and his company over a long period of time, based on the following:

- quality and performance of parts or products
- how the salesperson and his company handle problems
- pricing policies
- delivery or shipment record
- reputations of the salesperson and his colleagues
- the salesperson's business attitude
- what they hear from their sales representatives
- what they hear from others
- the facilities of the salesperson's company
- the salesperson's correspondence

The customers' impressions are primarily created by what the salesperson says, along with his actions. These can include the handling of their orders, complaints, or problems, as well as what they hear from others. All of these, together with the salesperson's correspondence, have a profound impact on the customer's perceptions of the salesperson and his company. Sales letters should always create a favorable impression.

When selling custom-made products or products with heavy engineering input, a salesperson should ask his engineers or designers why they designed the equipment the way they did. A salesperson should understand why their design is better than the competitor's design, and engineers and designers will often know more about competitive products, as well. Consulting with them will add to a salesperson's knowledge of the product. It will also reveal additional selling features and benefits that can enhance the contents of his sales letter.

This information should be reflected in the salesperson's rough draft of his sales letter. He should show it to his engineers and ask them to verify the technical accuracy of his comments. This often will flush out still more technical reasons why their design is better. It will also insure that the salesperson's comments are factual and easy to understand. A salesperson should bear in mind that most engineers are very conservative and tend to downplay even the outstanding features of their designs. A salesperson must be more positive and optimistic. He should not overstate or misrepresent, but neither should he be bashful. He must extol the features of his products while being careful to write factually.

Every well-written sales letter has the potential to influence the customer's impression of the salesperson's company and products and could influence the customer's purchase decision. There are some important guidelines a salesperson should remember:

1. Sales letters should always be well written, with absolutely no spelling errors or mistakes in grammar.
2. Sales letters should always have a specific subject, such as the quotation number and the customer's requisition or inquiry number, and perhaps the plant location. If the letter does not relate to a specific inquiry or proposal, then the salesperson should tie it to the name of his products, the customer's project, or perhaps to a recent meeting or discussion. This will aid the customer in immediately knowing what the letter is about and will help him to file it in the proper place for easy retrieval.

3. A salesperson should use the recipient's full name, not his nickname, when writing the sales letter. He should also verify that the company's name is correctly spelled and that he has the correct address. If in doubt, he should call and verify this information.
4. The sales letter should immediately discuss the business without any frivolity or personal comments. If the salesperson knows the recipient very well, even socially, he should never indicate this in a sales or business letter. The addressee may not be anxious for his colleagues to know how well he knows the salesperson. They might accuse or suspect him of not being completely objective in his product decisions. Sales letters often become part of a permanent record and should be professional.
5. The sales letter should always be factual and should never include anything that is doubtful or that cannot be proven.
6. The correspondence should never be overpowering or aggressive but should use soft language. The salesperson should use phrases such as *we believe*, *we think*, or *customers have told us*, rather than making flat statements that can offend customers.

Many otherwise competent salespeople avoid or postpone writing sales letters that delineate the features and benefits of their products. There are many reasons for this. Some salespeople procrastinate or are lazy, while others hesitate to put much of anything on paper for the customer. A successful salesperson will not be characterized by these failings.

Writing sales letters to customers on a given project has the following advantages:

1. They organize the salesperson's selling strategy in print. To write a good letter, a salesperson must order his thoughts, perhaps do research, and even make calculations. This will provide an outline of strong points to stress and will help distinguish the salesperson's products as he calls on his customer in person or by telephone until the job closes. A well-written sales letter should sharply focus the entire job strategy.
2. A sales letter gives the customer written reasons why he should buy the product, why it involves less risk or is more efficient, and why it will give less trouble. It will demonstrate that the product will save money in the long run on this particular project.

3. The customer will have the letter to use in discussions with his colleagues and superiors, hopefully to convince them the salesperson's product is best. A committee often will make the final decision. It is helpful if the members can read the important product points, rather than being forced to rely on memory, other people's comments, or their own notes.
4. Sales letters provide a reminder to the buyer of what the salesperson has already told him verbally. During the closing stages of a job, decision makers meet with and talk to many vendors. Often they honestly confuse who said what and even forget most of what they heard. It is always astonishing to observe how little of verbal communication is retained after one or two days. These letters will dramatically increase the amount of information retained by the customer.
5. A well-written sales letter demonstrates that the salesperson has thoroughly analyzed the customer's inquiry, and knows his own products, as well as competitive products.
6. A sales letter can also convey information to decision makers who are otherwise not accessible to the salesperson. He can send copies directly to them when appropriate, but he must make sure it is appropriate. He should take care not to offend anyone, and if in doubt, he should discuss it with his customer's contact person.

A salesperson should begin by writing down all of the reasons his product is best or unique. Having done this, he can carefully arrange them so that the unassailable point is placed first, followed by the second best reason, and so on. If a salesperson lists a weak or questionable reason first, his letter will probably receive little consideration. The customer will reject the statement and will stop reading or at least stop absorbing. If, on the other hand, the first reason is solid and acceptable to him, he will keep reading, and the letter is more likely to create a favorable impression.

A salesperson must think carefully about each reason and be realistic. He should not kid himself or try to deceive the customer. Often he will need to study his own bulletins, as well as his competitors' publications, to refresh his memory and insure accuracy. His reasons should always be customer oriented and show benefits. For example, he should not merely say that the metallurgy is better. He should say specifically what it is, point out why this is more advantageous, and demonstrate the benefit this provides to the customer. If his product is heavier, he must show why heavier is better. If it is lighter, he should show why it is lighter and why that is better.

If permissible, the salesperson should send an original letter to each of the key decision makers. He should not always rely on copies, because someone may feel slighted. How the salesperson should then proceed will vary from customer to customer. He should consider the people and personalities involved in each case and avoid offending anyone.

If permissible, the salesperson should send an original letter to each of the key decision makers.

Copies of all sales letters should be kept on file so that on the next job, the salesperson will need only to update them as the product changes, the job varies, or as new selling advantages occur. Bulletins, photographs, charts, graphs, or tables should be included with the letter. If the salesperson has told a customer about an outstanding feature, he could refer the customer to a certain picture on a specific page of the bulletin. The salesperson can also point out to the customer any attachments to the letter, where he will find the specific supporting data or photographs described in the letter.

In these sales letters, as in all presentations, the salesperson is not merely selling machinery or products, but also peace of mind. Customers do not buy just products, they buy solutions, or what they hope the products will do for them. The salesperson should promote his unique product features and demonstrate why he is the most reliable person to provide the product needed.

A sales letter should not be too long or complex. Many people put aside a letter that is laborious to read. The salesperson should use short paragraphs and leave a space between reasons for buying his products. He should always tabulate data, since a nicely prepared table is easy to read. If comments on one aspect will be too long, he should consider placing them alone on a separate sheet and refer to it in his letter.

The salesperson must choose his words carefully to convey confidence, trust, and reliability and to convince the customer he will have no risk, or less risk, with the products. The salesperson should choose synonyms carefully, using a thesaurus if needed. If selling internationally, the salesperson must keep in mind the background of the customer, since certain words will translate better than others. A sales letter must be firm and positive, without any strident tone. It should never be flippant or casual but should always be serious. Selling is a serious business.

If a salesperson has more than six or so good reasons for buying his products, then he should consider writing two letters, and waiting a day or so before sending the second. On subsequent office visits with the customer, he could go through these letters, answering questions and amplifying his reasons. If the customer questions any of the salesperson's points, he should provide additional evidence to support his claims. Usually product decisions are made by a very narrow margin, and there is no reward for second place. Often, listing salient features in a letter can help tip the scales in the salesperson's favor. Sales letters help the salesperson organize his thoughts and make his discussions with decision makers go more smoothly, since he will stress the salient points during subsequent meetings.

Sales Example

In 1965 we received an inquiry from a company for a large number of our units. Prior to submitting our proposal, we made an appointment with the key executive with this company and went to see him. During our discussions, we asked him what factors his people would consider and evaluate on this project. Without hesitation, he replied that he would make certain they carefully considered delivery, service, availability of spare parts, and price.

When we submitted our bid, we included a sales letter outlining exactly how we would handle service and spare parts. We identified the location of our service people and warehouses. We gave bar charts, spelling out our manufacturing and assembly schedules for each unit. We indicated what percent of our total shop capacity this order would represent, and we promised monthly progress reports. In later meetings with the customer, we reemphasized all of these points, and we finally received the order for all of these products. This was due largely to our efforts at outlining our program in a good sales letter. This program was geared toward what the customer told us would be evaluated and would be important to him and his people.

A salesperson must be alert for opportunities to send sales letters to his customers. If the project drags out, he should send more than one. Also, if he has another project the following year, the salesperson should start over, because by then the buyer will not retain much information. He should tailor the letters to the particular inquiry, product, or project, and should never treat them lightly. A sales letter should be given careful thought and should contain well-chosen words. The salesperson should prepare an initial draft and then revise it until he is certain it will achieve its purpose. Often it is best for the salesperson to put it aside until the next day, when he will likely have new ideas or insights.

Writing good sales letters should be a priority to a salesperson, and he should always deliver accurate information with confidence-giving words and correct spelling and grammar. Good sales letters will pay handsome dividends and bring in many more orders.

Summary

1. All letters written to customers should be considered sales letters.
2. In all of his correspondence to customers, the salesperson should attempt to create a good impression of himself and his company so as to increase the amount of business received.
3. Sometimes sales letters are written to regain the customer's goodwill.
4. A salesperson deals constantly with people who must be brought around to his way of thinking about his company's products.
5. Usually he will accomplish this verbally, but written words will often increase his chances of success.
6. The salesperson should use sales letters to sell goods and keep them sold.
7. Sales letters are only one element of the selling effort, but when well written, they can cement the sale.
8. The impact of an outstanding sales letter is not because of flashes of the imagination. Instead, the wording of sales letters is carefully prepared by a disciplined mind.
9. It is difficult for beginning salespeople to write outstanding sales letters, but they should give them a lot of thought and continually strive to improve them.

10. A salesperson must analyze his product carefully to compile a list of product benefits to include in his letters.
11. The sales letters should also promote the salesperson's company, its engineering, its manufacturing expertise, and its people.
12. Customers generally form their perceptions of the salesperson and his company over a long period of time based on the following:
    - product quality
    - pricing policies
    - the handling of the customer's problems
    - the delivery record of the salesperson's company
    - the reputation of the salesperson and his colleagues and the impressions they give
    - the salesperson's business attitude
    - the salesperson's management
    - what they hear from the salesperson
    - what they hear from others
    - the facilities of the salesperson's company
13. The impression a customer has of the salesperson and his company is influenced by what the salesperson says, and especially by what he does.
14. When selling engineered products, the salesperson should visit with his engineers to learn why they designed the products the way they did.
15. The useful product benefits that a salesperson learns should be reflected in the draft of his sales letter. He should show it to his engineers to verify its accuracy.
16. A salesperson should not overstate or misrepresent, but neither should he be bashful.
17. The following are suggestions for good sales letters:
    - They must be well written with no spelling or grammatical errors.
    - They should always have an easily identified, meaningful subject.
    - Full names should be used, not nicknames.
    - The salesperson must make sure the customer's name is correctly spelled.

- The letter should immediately get to the point.
- Sales letters must be factual and not overly aggressive in tone.
- The sales letter should use soft language.
- The salesperson should revise the letter until he is satisfied he has done his best.

18. Sales letters have the following advantages:
    - They help organize the selling strategy on a given project.
    - They give the customer written reasons why he should buy the product.
    - He can use the sales letter in discussions with his colleagues.
    - Letters remind customers of what the salesperson said and help the customer avoid confusion with competitive products.
    - Letters prove a salesperson has analyzed the inquiry and given thought to what was quoted.
    - Sales letters can convey information to decision makers who are not otherwise directly accessible to the salesperson.
19. When preparing a letter pointing out benefits, the salesperson should consider the following:
    - The salesperson should list all the possible benefits.
    - He can then organize them according to importance, listing the unassailable point first.
    - He should think carefully about each benefit and be realistic.
    - He must keep in mind the customer's requirements and his point of view.
20. If permissible, the salesperson should send an original sales letter to each decision maker. He should use good judgment about doing this, so he does not offend anyone in the customer's organization.
21. The salesperson should retain copies of all sales letters in a file to use on future projects.
22. The salesperson should not hesitate to include applicable photographs or bulletins.

23. The salesperson should remember that customers do not merely buy products. They buy solutions to their problems or requirements, which provide peace of mind.
24. Sales letters should be brief and concise, using short paragraphs and active, descriptive words. If the subject is lengthy, the salesperson should write more than one letter.
25. The wording of sales letters should convey confidence and trust.
26. A sales letter should not contain a lot of facts in its sentences. The salesperson should tabulate this information for clarity, using separate sheets for detailed explanations.
27. A thesaurus may be helpful to select the words that give the right impression.
28. After sending the letter, the salesperson should go through it with the customer during their next encounter by telephone or in the office. The salesperson should observe the customer's reactions and use the feedback to improve future letters.
29. The salesperson should be alert for opportunities to send sales letters to his customers.
30. Many purchase decisions are close. A well-written sales letter can often tip the scales in the salesperson's favor.
31. Good sales letters pay handsome dividends and bring in many more orders.

37

Protect the Home Office People

Many salespeople tend to believe that all home office people are infallible experts on practically everything in their fields, and thus they know how to answer all questions. This is not necessarily so. Virtually all are excellent design engineers, problem solvers, marketing specialists, or manufacturing people. However, they are generally accustomed to talking internally to their colleagues within their own companies. Most of them rarely see customers except on the factory's home ground or in the factory's offices. When a salesperson transports them a few hundred or a few thousand miles, he could be surprised by the answers they give in the strange and unfamiliar atmosphere of a customer's office. Some of them are awed by customers and react in a completely different manner in their presence.

For such meetings involving his company's experts, the salesperson should not allow his home office people to flounder in any way when speaking or get in over their heads with a customer. When these experts are accompanying the salesperson, he should have a written agenda covering what he will discuss with the customer and how he will answer certain questions in the meeting.

The salesperson should brief his experts ahead of time. Unless he already knows them and their qualifications, he should try to evaluate their depth of knowledge and determine how they will respond. The salesperson should not do this while traveling to the meeting or in the customer's lobby. This briefing should occur in the salesperson's own office, a conference room, or a hotel meeting room before going to the customer's office. He must plan and allow ample time for thorough discussions. If these company experts are coming to the meeting from out of town, he must insist that they arrive in time for a strategy session. This will require discipline and good organization but will be worth it.

The salesperson should brief his experts ahead of time.

Having arrived in the customer's office, the salesperson should be in control of the discussions. If strange, unusual, or difficult questions arise, he should not hesitate to interject by saying, "Let us think about that and get back to you," or "We did not expect that question and are not prepared to answer." Of course, this requires good judgment on the part of the salesperson. The salesperson should not embarrass his expert, but neither should he allow the specialist to say too much or to say things that will damage or obligate the company unnecessarily. The salesperson should promise a quick reply. When the reply is later given, it can adhere rigidly to company policy and guidelines.

These home office or headquarters people will accompany the salesperson to help him do his work. The salesperson is obligated to prevent them from being embarrassed or having to answer questions that they should not be answering. His failure to protect them could cost the company money and damage their own careers.

The salesperson wants to always protect his home office experts. By the same token, he should never allow them to pass out inflexible answers or information that will cause him to lose an impending order. The salesperson may feel they were instructed to give these replies, and the replies may even be correct. However, he should never allow these answers to be final and to cause him to lose the order without first rechecking their validity at the highest level.

Sales Examples

Example 1

As mentioned previously, our company learned a valuable lesson in not readily agreeing to undertake a commitment without knowing its cost. In a meeting with an overseas customer, we were finalizing the return of a very large machinery part to our factory for repair. Since it was under warranty, we had offered to do the repairs free, provided the customer paid the ocean freight to our plant and back. Agreement had been reached on these items when the question of product insurance came up. My colleague from the home office, thinking this was a minor cost, volunteered that we would arrange this.

Since I realized we did not know how much it would cost, I suggested that since the customers were arranging the transportation, they should also arrange for insurance coverage. They readily agreed. Later we learned that the insurance cost $50,000, since this country was then considered in a war zone because of a nearby civil war. Avoiding this insurance cost saved the home office person and me a lot of embarrassment. He thanked me many times over the years for keeping him out of trouble.

Example 2

We had been given a tentative order pending the resolution of specifications and performance satisfactory to the customer. After two weeks of wrestling around with and studying these requirements, we went to a meeting with the customer to discuss our answers and proposed solutions.

The customer had originally requested a working pressure of 1,100 pounds per square inch (psi), but our factory preferred to limit this to 1,000 psi. When we told the customer this, the leader of the customer's delegation said, "We cannot firm up the order based on 1,000 psi; it must be 1,100 psi." Faced with cancellation of this order, I told the leader, "We will check again with our factory." One of the engineers from our factory interjected, "It will not do any good to check. We have already investigated, and 1,000 psi is the limit." I repeated to the senior man that we would still check again before allowing the negotiations to collapse. My colleague again repeated, "It will not do any good to check again." By then I was very distressed with him, but since I had excellent relations with this customer, I kept the negotiations open by telling the customer we would call our factory and be back to him right away.

We left the customer's office and went back to our local office. I then called one of our top executives and told him that unless we could make the working pressure 1,100 psi on these units, we would not receive the order. He said he would investigate with the engineering department and get back to me. He called back in 10 minutes to say we could meet the customer's requirement, and we kept the order.

The salesperson should also keep himself out of trouble, because as a salesperson, he should never allow an order to slip away unnecessarily. If a salesperson is about to lose an order because of failure to meet the customer's requirements, he should check with his top executives to make certain that his position is correct and final.

He should never allow lower level people to cause him to lose an order. By following this procedure, he is still protecting these colleagues. He is protecting them from being second guessed by top management after the loss of an order.

A salesperson has a lot of authority and responsibility. His main responsibility is to get orders, and to do so, he should never hesitate to go to the top people in his organization for final decisions before an order is lost. A salesperson never wants to lose an order and later be told that if he had gone higher in the organization, he would have obtained the necessary concession to obtain the order.

Summary

The salesperson should closely monitor the conversations between his customers and his home office people when they accompany him to meetings. He must protect them and keep them out of trouble, but he should not allow their inflexible responses to cost him an order.

38

Avoid Cutting Corners

If a salesperson had a crystal ball that would reveal the exact things he had to do to get an order, he could reduce his workload dramatically. He could then do only the minimum necessary to receive the order, and no more. Unfortunately, such a forecaster is not available. Thus the salesperson should never hesitate to do everything he can that might help him get the order. If a salesperson does this, he will be more successful. It will set him apart as a superior salesperson.

If a salesperson continually presents new ideas or new thoughts, he will usually be admired by his customers for being resourceful and innovative. Often these items that require extra effort from the salesperson will reveal new information of which his competitor is unaware. Even if the customer rejects some of his suggestions, the mere rejection or refusal will very often reveal new intelligence or feedback not otherwise uncovered.

If a salesperson continually presents new ideas or new thoughts, he will usually be admired by his customers for being resourceful and innovative.

Suppose, for example, that a salesperson is working very hard to get an order requiring extremely short delivery. The salesperson might tell his customer that he will assign an additional expediter or a project manager to the manufacturing cycle. The customer might then reply that the short delivery time is no longer required. Although the customer had not intended to deceive the salesperson, the altered requirements had not been revealed to him previously. The situation may have just changed. Because the salesperson was trying to come up with additional reasons why the customer should buy his product, he flushed this information out.

Often these new inquiries or suggestions will tell the salesperson more about how he stands on the job and perhaps will bring out the real reasons he is not the preferred vendor. The salesperson had perhaps been led to believe that his delivery was a problem, but now he knows that it is not so important. Instead, there are other reasons the customer is hesitating to buy from him. Conversely, the salesperson may have thought a very short delivery had given him an edge. Now he has learned that his apparent edge is gone. He then must concentrate elsewhere if he is to regain the advantage and be successful.

Sales Example

This extra effort paid off once when several of us were working on a big job that had dragged on for months. Toward the closing stages, I attended a technical conference in Tokyo. During lunch one day, I went by our local office to pick up messages from my home office. One of the sales engineers working on this job back in the United States had sent me a telex. He told me that the president of the customer's overseas company where the products would be used was attending this conference. This man would then travel to Hawaii to meet the domestic people so that a purchase decision could be made. The wire gave me the gentleman's name and asked me to contact him and discuss our sales points.

The technical conference had drawn a crowd of several hundred engineers and executives. Since I did not know what this man looked like or where he was staying, I almost threw the telex away in disgust. Instead, I went back to the hotel where the sessions were being held and decided I would try to find this individual. By this time, the afternoon meetings were underway. I went to the meeting rooms, looked in, and realized there would be no way to locate him in the crowd.

I walked past these meeting rooms once, and as I turned to go back by, a gentleman walked out. I tried to read his name tag and thought that it looked like the name of the man I was trying to locate. Unsure, I followed him to the next room, where conference papers were spread out on tables. I went on the opposite side of the table he was facing, so that I could clearly read his name tag. To my astonishment, he was indeed the man I needed to see!

After introducing myself, I quickly told him why our products would do the best job on his project and why he would have less risk buying our machinery. He was polite and listened. I asked where he was staying, and we parted. I went to my room and wrote down on my personal stationery what I had just told him about the reasons he should have for buying our products. I determined his hotel room number, took the letter to his room, and pushed it under the door. That night when we met unexpectedly at a cocktail party, he said, "I read your letter before the ink was dry." After his meeting in Hawaii, we received the order.

I do not know how much my perseverance at the technical conference helped us get the order, but it certainly did not hurt. One additional important decision maker had met me, heard from me, and read why our product would involve less risk and do the best job for his company.

It is easy for salespeople to say that one does not have to do certain sales tasks, or go see yet another person. However, a successful salesperson should leave no stone unturned. He should not give up and must keep searching for new ideas that will put him in better shape to get orders.

When a customer requests information, the salesperson must make certain he responds adequately. He should not give a short or shallow reply but should consider all questions seriously and give complete, thorough answers. After the customer has read the reply, the salesperson should ask if he has been responsive and if the customer has what he needs to do his job. He should follow this same pattern in all that he does. The salesperson should establish a reputation for being thoroughly responsive. He should do this when striving for the order, after he receives the order, and even if he loses the order. He should show this courtesy to customers and colleagues alike.

SUMMARY

Perhaps a lot of luck is involved in selling. However, I always found that the harder I worked, the luckier I got.

39

Solicit Help from Others

No salesperson personally knows every one of his present or potential customers. Many other people will know these other people and organizations more thoroughly, and they may have a long history of dealing with them. In addition, the salesperson should have many friends who are also selling.

He should not hesitate to ask for help and guidance when he must sell to people he either does not know or does not know well. Most people will be willing to help if a salesperson approaches them properly, especially if he has helped them in the past.

A salesperson should not consult with just one person. He should solicit input from several people before beginning work on a large project with a new or unknown customer. The questions he asks these other people will vary, depending on his knowledge of the prospective customer. For example, he could ask for names and titles of key people and important decision makers who strongly influence product purchases. He could inquire further about their experiences and backgrounds.

The salesperson might ask for introductions, but he should be careful about this. Introductions can get involved and complex. Furthermore, customers might strongly associate the salesperson with the person who is making the introduction. This is not always to the salesperson's advantage.

If these potential customers are strangers to the salesperson or his company, he should request a meeting in writing, especially if he feels that a telephone request might be rejected. A handwritten note will sometimes be very effective. The salesperson should request a meeting but say that he will call to settle on a convenient time. His call will then be better received.

If the salesperson's division is part of a large corporation, he should not overlook valuable contacts that some of these other divisions may have with the potential customer. This may help with an account he is trying to break into or even with one that has historically done business with his company. This may not always be easy to track down.

If the salesperson knows his customers well, he will know what they buy and whether or not some of his corporate divisions are substantial suppliers. If they are, he should immediately get in touch with the division sales manager or salespeople and compare notes. He should ask for information about the buying habits of some of the important people he does not already know. However, the salesperson should not ask them to do his sales job for him and should not impose. He should feel free, however, to ask for commercial intelligence. This could include information such as who influences purchasing decisions or has the final decision, who are the policy makers and what are their backgrounds, and who are the *fast horses*.

The salesperson can save time by consulting with division people within his own corporation. In soliciting this help or assistance, he should make it easy for these people. He should pick a convenient time and go to their offices. The salesperson should try to do this in a planned, organized fashion. He should avoid requests for assistance on a crisis basis, when it is an imposition, or when a big job is going down the drain. Also, he should not overburden these sources.

During meetings with salespeople from other divisions, the salesperson should try to find some way he can help them in return, making the exchange of information mutually beneficial. If he knows his business and is a good salesperson, there will be some accounts with which he can assist them. The salesperson may know important decision makers in some companies better than his colleagues. If this is the case, the salesperson should consider meeting periodically to share information. For instance, they could arrange to meet every two or three months, depending on the situation. He may want to ask these division people to help him get an appointment but should not lean too heavily on them. Again, he should not expect them to do his sales job.

If a salesperson's colleagues assist him, he must never let them down or embarrass them in any way, or he will permanently shut off a valuable source of information and help. He should be sure to express his gratitude. He should keep them informed on his progress and let them know if he wins or loses the order. If the salesperson obtains the order, he should give them some of the credit; but if he loses it, he should blame only himself. It is very important for a salesperson to let his colleagues know how he progressed. He should not ask for help and then remain silent about the outcome, or they might turn down his next request.

If a salesperson's colleagues assist him, he must never let them down or embarrass them in any way, or he will permanently shut off a valuable source of information and help.

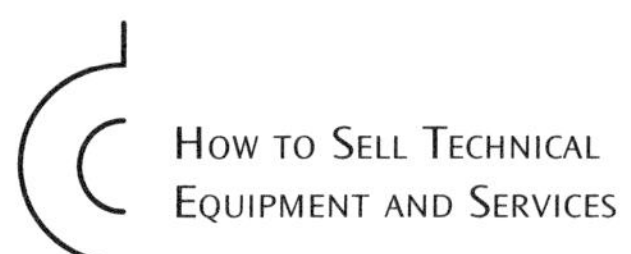

Summary

Properly developed relationships between salespeople in different divisions of a large corporation can be mutually beneficial and a great overall asset to the organization. If a salesperson solicits help from others who know his customers, he can save a lot of time and glean much useful information.

IV

Closing the Deal

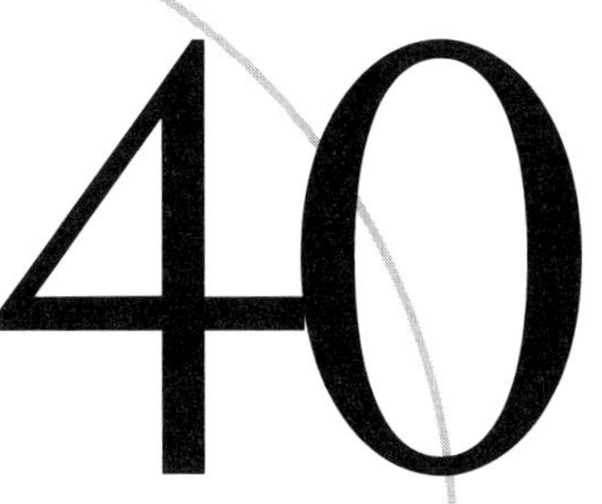

Ask Questions

The man who can't ask, can't learn.

–Proverb

Most people think that asking questions is a very simple exercise requiring little skill. However, this is not true, especially when one is gathering intelligence and finding out the status of a job or trying to discover what a customer is thinking about his project, your products, and perhaps even your competitor. Most individuals value answers more than questions. By doing so, they overlook the tremendous importance of the sort of questions essential in obtaining accurate information and in problem solving.

There is an art to asking questions, and a good salesperson will master this art. Once mastered and faithfully and skillfully used, it is a powerful sales tool. It is worth your deepest study, constant use, and continued evaluation. A salesperson who asks questions skillfully accomplishes the following objectives:

There is an art to asking questions, and a good salesperson will master this art.

1. He acquires useful information.
2. He uncovers objections to his products that the reticent buyer has not openly revealed.
3. He can make sure his prospective customer is listening.
4. He can make sure the customer understands what he is saying.
5. He can often get the customer to agree with him in what he is explaining.
6. He can encourage the customer to participate in the discussion so that the dialogue is two-way and not a lecture.
7. He can learn the customer's motives and objectives and learn which are the most important to him.
8. He can help the customer reach a decision to buy the salesperson's products.
9. He can build rapport with the customer. The customer will enjoy being around the salesperson, especially if the salesperson asks questions and listens sincerely to his responses.
10. He can develop a clear, accurate picture of the current situation.

The salesperson can accomplish these 10 goals if he learns the different kinds of questions and applies them proficiently. He should do this when he prepares and delivers his presentation or as he goes about his job calling on his customer, delivering his sales pitches, and responding to the customer's needs.

There are several different kinds of questions, but there are five that are important when selling technical products:

1. **Direct question.** This could include what, why, when, how, where, and who.
2. **Indirect question.** Instead of asking the prospect what delivery he expects, the salesperson could say, "If I knew what delivery your project required, perhaps we could meet it."
3. **Confirmation question.** The salesperson asks this question to get the buyer to agree with him. He could say, for example, "Am I correct that you are now happier with your product quality than you have been in previous experiences?"
4. **Feedback question.** The salesperson repeats something the buyer has said to him when he wants to confirm it and to make absolutely sure he has asked the right question and has received the right answer.
5. **"Swivel" question.** A technique recommended by James Bender in his book *How to Sell Well* (McGraw Hill, 1961), this helps the buyer reach a decision by offering unconsidered alternatives. Suppose a buyer has no in-depth knowledge of the salesperson's new-generation equipment and prefers to stay with a competitor's tried and true older model. The salesperson could say, "Your loyalty to the older model is certainly understandable. However, which would be better for your company—a unit that could lower your production downtime and raise profitability with fewer maintenance requirements, or an older unit that requires more downtime and has higher maintenance needs?" In another example of a swivel question, a salesperson could ask, "Would you like to order the 5 units already quoted, or would you prefer to take 10?"

Often a salesperson can be misled when he asks a direct question a certain way, receives an answer, and then assumes he found out what he was attempting to learn. Customers or others will answer his question as asked, but the answer may be misleading if he did not ask the right question. On particularly important subjects, after receiving the answer, the salesperson should rephrase the question one or two additional ways to be sure he understands the customer and there is a meeting of the minds. Otherwise, key words that are used by customer to mean certain things might mean the same thing to the salesperson. Unless the salesperson rephrases the question and asks it again, he may be misled, even though not necessarily intentionally. In rephrasing the questions, he could start with phrases such as, "Are you saying..." "Do you mean..." or, "I understand you are saying..." and thus better understand the customer.

For a salesperson to assure himself that he is obtaining correct answers, it is also an excellent idea for him to ask more than one person. This is not to suggest that he does not trust or believe the original source, but because he will usually get a different slant if he talks to several people. Usually he will get additional in-depth information from others, i.e. second and third sources.

Asking several people questions about the same subject is similar to plotting a moving ship's position on a navigation chart. If a ship is steaming into a harbor, and a person on board takes a compass reading on one object on the beach and plots that reading on a chart, his vessel is somewhere along that line. If the person takes a reading on a second land object and plots that on the chart also, the ship is somewhere near the intersection of the two lines. If the person can plot a reading taken on a third onshore marker, he can much more accurately define the position of the ship as very near the intersection of the three lines. Plotting subsequent readings taken on additional onshore objects would even more exactly locate the craft's position.

This is similar to what occurs when a salesperson is gathering intelligence while working on a project. The more knowledgeable sources he can check for information, the more accurate it is apt to be. He is not necessarily trying to question the credibility of his original source, but he is trying to discover all he can and verify his information. Sometimes a salesperson learns only scraps of information from several sources, and it becomes necessary to verify these elsewhere to avoid being misled.

To establish and maintain credibility, a salesperson must never pass along unreliable information to his associates, his superiors, or his customers. To insure he has trustworthy input, a salesperson should ask the question several different ways. He should also question as many people as he can who will have knowledge about the job, project, or subject. When a salesperson has only one contact within an organization, he cannot easily verify information. It is, therefore, mandatory that a salesperson develop more than one contact in an organization.

If a salesperson is calling on a customer during an important project, and he wants to be positive that he obtains accurate information, he should write down his queries ahead of time. He must be very careful with his wording so that he asks the right questions. These important questions should be written down before going to a meeting and committed to memory. It is not a good idea for a salesperson to pull out a list of questions in a customer's office and write down what the customer answers. That will annoy the customer and make him think that he is talking to a reporter. He will be much less likely to give the salesperson the information he wants. Instead, the salesperson should commit the answers as nearly as he can to memory. As soon as he leaves the customer's office, he should record the answers before he forgets what he has learned.

Another thing to bear in mind in asking questions is that many people will answer questions the way they think they ought to reply, rather than the way they are really thinking. This is particularly true when safety, price, and efficiency are concerned. Some will say they always buy the lowest price. Others will maintain that they place quality, efficiency, or long service life first. People may feel they should answer a certain way to all questions relating to these subjects, even though deep down the answers do not reflect their actual reasoning or business practices. It has been my experience that customers quite often decide early on whose products they want to buy, and then they justify their decision.

An example of this occurred many years ago when a large automobile manufacturer placed multiple choice questionnaires in their dealers' showrooms. These questionnaires asked prospective customers to indicate what features they ranked first, second, and third in importance in the purchase of a new automobile. Safety emerged as the feature most often placed first. This was long before seat belts, air bags, padded dashboards, and other safety items were available on cars. The automobile company suspected the answers did not accurately reflect people's preferences. So they rewrote the questionnaire and asked what the prospective customer thought his neighbor or his friend put first in buying automobiles. The winning answer then came back as styling, and the motor company knew that at that time, styling was precisely what sold automobiles.

It follows then that a salesperson has to be careful in the way he questions a customer so that he is not misled by the reply. It will occasionally be better to ask the customer what he thinks other people in the industry are going to put first when selecting products. Or he could ask the customer what others might buy next year or three years from now, or what they are going to do under certain other conditions. Since the salesperson is asking the customer what he thinks other people are going to do, he will often get his answer disguised in a roundabout way. The customer can answer the question and attribute his reply to his friends or to other people. His answers under these circumstances will be more likely to accurately reflect his own true feelings.

The salesperson should avoid asking questions that can be answered with a *yes* or a *no*. They usually do not tell the salesperson enough information. He should ask questions that will involve more response from the customer.

Questions should be asked at intervals during a meeting, and at a pace that does not make the customer uncomfortable. By the same token, the salesperson should not be afraid to ask questions, and he should not assume he knows all the answers. Even though the salesperson may have been in the business for quite a while, times change, conditions vary, and prospects can think and believe very differently.

The salesperson should use good judgment when asking important or crucial questions. He must be sure the atmosphere is appropriate and the customer is not in a hurry and is in a receptive frame of mind. Otherwise, he may get short answers and unfavorable replies. Sometimes customers are intimidated by the salesperson and will give misleading impressions. Therefore, if a salesperson expects to receive accurate answers to his questions, he should select the proper atmosphere, keep an open mind, and not prejudge the answers.

If the question the salesperson wants to ask his customer is on a delicate subject or will involve substantial effort on the customer's part, he must choose his initial words very carefully. He should think them through ahead of time. He should phrase his first question so that he draws out the customer and should not ask for too much initially. He should use discretion and probe cautiously, asking for more information if his customer warms to his questions. If the salesperson asks for too much immediately, or if the customer gets the impression the salesperson will put him or his people to a lot of trouble, he may shut down and not answer.

On the other hand, if the salesperson tells the customer that he needs help and then moves prudently, he will usually obtain most of what he requests, assuming that his requests are reasonable. The salesperson should make it easy for the customer to respond favorably by keeping all initial requests modest and approaching him judiciously at a convenient time to talk.

Salespeople too often approach an active job with a customer assuming they already know the answers to most of the questions because of past experience with this company or others. In reality, it is surprising how many times the situation has indeed changed and the customer is moving away from his historical position. Even though certain questions will sometimes sound naive and a salesperson feels that he ought to know the answers, he should not make assumptions but should ask questions instead.

One of the biggest mistakes a salesperson can make is to assume too much. The other common miscalculation is to jump to too many conclusions upon the receipt of a few scraps of information from the customer. These scraps can conjure up all sorts of scenarios in the salesperson's mind based on past experiences and situations. Certainly in some instances, the salesperson can accurately expand his understanding of the big picture from the information received, but he should not do this too quickly. He should resist the temptation, ask for more details, and ask clarifying questions that focus on the current situation, unhampered and uninfluenced by past situations. This will also keep him from taking too much for granted from initial, general, and perhaps shallow comments.

The salesperson should always make certain his questions are based on a genuine effort at seeking information. Many people pretend to ask questions when they actually want to answer their own questions. Sometimes they want to make a statement on the subject. This is quickly obvious to a salesperson's customers or colleagues and will be counterproductive.

As a salesperson follows an active job or tries to close an order, he must make certain his questions are clear and as brief as possible. He should not make a speech when asking a question, or the customer will be confused about what he is really asking. Most salespeople have been in large meetings where someone ostensibly was asking a question but instead gave a long, rambling speech with the question hidden somewhere. The salesperson must avoid this and should ask his question clearly in as few words as possible. Then the salesperson should stop talking and allow his customer or colleague to respond. He should not interrupt. He should let the customer answer and then ask any qualifying questions.

Often a salesperson has colleagues with him in his meeting with the customer. In this situation, other members of his group should not ask a new question until they are sure the original questioner does not need to ask a follow-up question for clarity. The salesperson should also give an indication that he understood the reply by acknowledging the response in some manner before moving the conversation forward.

When asking a customer these questions, a salesperson should not abruptly change subjects and jump from one topic to another. He should change subjects gradually and with transitional comments so that the conversation moves smoothly and logically from one phase to another. If the salesperson hops from one subject to another, it will confuse the customer. Disjointed questions will generate disjointed responses. Furthermore, if a salesperson switches suddenly

from subject to subject, the answers will usually be hard to keep straight in his own mind. It is far better for him to ask questions progressively on a subject and then move on to something else.

Other members of the sales team should be careful not to answer questions that the salesperson directs to the customers. The salesperson is questioning his customer because he wants his input, not that of his own colleagues. Also, there should be no side conversations.

It is important for a salesperson to ask a variety of questions when making a sales presentation to his customer. All too often the salesperson gives his sales pitch and carefully outlines why the customer should buy his product, but he then fails to stop occasionally and ask the customer for his reaction. Sometimes a salesperson goes on at length and even changes subjects without slowing down or pausing to ask the customer what he thinks about what has been said. He assumes the customer is listening to everything he said and is being convinced to buy his product. In reality, the customer has tuned him out. At such a time, the salesperson should stop listing features of his products and reasons to buy. Instead, he should ask the customer what he thinks of what he has been saying. The replies will often astonish him.

Sales Example

Once we were working a big job when the plants were full and the deliveries were long. Our customer was in Alaska and had a logistical problem in that he could only ship goods into the North Slope during a narrow two- or three-month period each summer. If the product missed this shipping window, it was delayed an entire year. The customer was planning to buy 30 or 40 large pieces of machinery, and being good salespeople, we wanted all of the business.

During a previous meeting, this customer had expressed doubt that we could build all of these products within his required time period. For this second meeting, we did our homework on machining hours, machine tools, assembly hours, test personnel, and shop schedules. A home office executive came for the meeting armed with many graphs, charts, and facts. He spent several minutes carefully outlining how we would go about building all of these products and ship them to make timely deliveries for the customer's construction schedule.

The executive gave his presentation, which was a good one, but as soon as he uttered his last word, someone in our group asked a question or made a comment about an entirely different subject. The conversation immediately went in a different direction and away from our delivery presentation.

I finally slowed down the discussion and said to the senior member on the customer's side, "Sir, at our last meeting, you expressed doubt that we could build all of these products and meet your delivery schedule. Today, our market manager gave a presentation, carefully explaining that we have the shop capacity and the machine tools to build these products when you need them. Now that you have heard our explanation today, do you feel that we can build all of it to meet your schedule?" He replied, "No, I still don't think you can build all of it." If I had not asked this question, our delegation would have left the meeting thinking we had the customer convinced that we could meet his schedule. By finding this out, we were able to repeat key portions of our presentation in an effort to accomplish our objective.

When making a sales presentation, a salesperson should stop after each point or so and gauge the customer's reaction by asking a question before continuing.

Another time to ask questions that is often neglected by salespeople is after receiving or losing an order. Salespeople rarely ask enough questions at these important times. If a salesperson loses, he is often too busy licking his wounds. If he received the order, he is often too busy celebrating. Under both conditions, however, a salesperson should ask a lot of questions—not immediately, but after a few days. If the salesperson won, he should be quiet and enter the order. He should not ask questions then, or he may talk the customer out of the sale. He should wait a few days or weeks until there is no danger of losing the sale by asking questions.

If the salesperson lost the order, he should determine the following:

- He should determine why he lost.
- He should decide if it was due to price, delivery, technical shortcomings, or vendor preference.
- If the price was high, he should ask if a competitive price would have won the order.

If the salesperson received the order, at the appropriate time he should determine the following:

- He should determine why he won.
- He should ask if it was due to a lower price, his company's superior engineering, or technical features.
- He should ask if it was because of the delivery time.
- He should ask if it was because the customer preferred to do business with the salesperson and his firm.

The salesperson will often be astonished at the answers he eventually gets, both when he wins and when he loses. Either way, the true reasons are rarely what he thought they were.

In both cases it is very important to know how the salesperson's bid ended up in terms of price. This will help him on future jobs, although it is usually not easy to determine. Customers are often reluctant to reveal the price they paid or to tell the salesperson very much even if they gave him the order. If the salesperson lost, it is usually best to ask if the decision was based on technical aspects, price, delivery, or vendor preference. If he is told which of these it was, he can concentrate on that area and learn as much as possible, but he should not allow himself to be misled.

If the customer says price was the deciding factor, the salesperson should not assume that it was the only reason he lost. He should ask to be sure, since he may have lost in more than one category. Also, the customer will almost always say price was the reason the salesperson lost, because by saying this, he gives the impression that he saved his company money. He may also believe he lets everyone save face. He thus allows the salesperson to blame his competitor for cutting the price or to blame his management for high prices.

In trying to determine how much too high the bid was, assuming the salesperson did lose on price, he should never ask directly how much too high the bid was. The customer will almost always say he cannot reveal that. It is more useful for a salesperson to ask if his bid was *substantially high*. If the answer is positive, the salesperson could throw out a figure of 10%. By offering a figure and gauging the reaction, he can usually determine whether his bid was 5% high or 15% high.

In conclusion, questions are powerful sales tools. They have many uses besides obtaining information. They help a salesperson gauge attitudes, uncover objections, obtain reactions, and enlist participation in his sales presentation. They help him develop an accurate understanding of existing situations. They also help him build a better relationship with his customer. Questions are excellent substitutes for high-pressure sales tactics. They help the salesperson streamline and pace his sales presentations. Used wisely, questions raise the salesperson's popularity with his customers. Asking the right questions at the right time is decisive to a salesperson's success. He should pay close attention to this task and work hard to sharpen his skills in this vital area.

Summary

1. There is a real art to asking questions, and it requires skill.
2. Asking questions is a powerful sales tool.
3. By asking questions, a salesperson achieves the following goals:
    - He acquires useful information.
    - He uncovers latent objections.
    - He can make sure his prospect is listening.
    - He can make sure his prospect understands what he is saying.
    - He can get the customer to agree with him about what he is explaining.
    - He can encourage the customer to participate in the discussion.
    - He can discover the customer's buying motives.
    - He can help the customer reach a decision.
    - He can build rapport with the customer.
    - He can develop a clear, accurate picture of the situation.
4. There are five different kinds of questions that are useful. These include direct, indirect, confirming, feedback, and swivel questions.
5. The salesperson should carefully phrase his questions so the answers will not mislead him.

6. The salesperson should repeat the answers the way he thinks they relate to his question.
7. The salesperson should question more than one person in the customer's organization.
8. On large orders, the salesperson should list and memorize important questions prior to the meeting.
9. The salesperson should write down answers as soon as he leaves the buyer's office.
10. The salesperson should remember that many prospects answer questions the way they think they should, rather than the way they actually feel.
11. The salesperson should ask his prospect what others think about his products.
12. The salesperson should avoid questions that can be answered with just *yes* or *no*.
13. During a meeting, the salesperson should pace his questions so the buyer is not intimidated.
14. The salesperson should use good judgment when asking important or crucial questions.
15. When approaching a delicate subject or asking the customer for information involving substantial effort on his part, the salesperson should carefully choose the moment and his initial words. He should not initially ask for much and should be sure the time is convenient.
16. The salesperson should not assume he knows all the answers because of previous experiences.
17. The salesperson should not assume too much from the initial answers.
18. The salesperson should not relate initial responses too quickly to past situations.
19. The salesperson should ask clarifying questions to make certain he understands.
20. The salesperson should make sure his questions are genuine and not use them as platforms for speeches.

21. The salesperson should slow down his sales pitch and ask his customer's opinion about what he has heard. He should gauge the customer's reaction to see if he made himself clear. His arguments may require repeating
22. A salesperson's colleagues should not answer questions that he asks the prospect.
23. The salesperson should not jump around from subject to subject, but should ask questions in a logical sequence and obtain the answers before moving to the next question.
24. After losing an order, the salesperson should ask intelligent questions and listen to the replies.
25. The salesperson should determine why he won the order, but only after he has safely entered it.
26. The salesperson should try to determine the winning price level.
27. Questions have many uses besides obtaining information.
28. Questions are good substitutes for high-pressure sales tactics.
29. Handled properly, questions help build better relations with a salesperson's customers.
30. Used wisely, questions raise the salesperson's popularity with his customers.
31. The salesperson must work hard at asking the proper questions and listening to the answers.

Be a Good Listener

Todo esta dicho ya, pero como nadie escucha es preciso empezar continuamente.

(Everything has been said—but since no one listened, I must start over again.)

—Unknown

In 1973 I went with the local manager to call on the maintenance foreman of a large overseas oil company. On his desk was a plaque with this inscription in Spanish. Since I did not read Spanish, I asked him what the inscription said. He said it epitomized his life history, and then he translated it for me. After I heard the translation, I told our host that it also epitomized my life history, and it still does today. People just do not listen. People, in general, do not know how to listen. Most people are lousy listeners, but a salesperson cannot afford to be a poor listener.

Throughout most of history, listening has been the only medium of learning. On the other hand, reading has served as a primary tool of learning for only a few hundred years. The written word is slow compared to the spoken word, which makes listening increasingly important in the current age of speed and fast communications. Compared to the written word, the spoken word has greater persuasive power. Among other reasons, this is because listeners are more vulnerable than readers. All kinds of studies indicate that people are much more influenced by what they hear than by what they read. Hitler led a literate country to its downfall not merely by what he wrote, but by what he spoke.

Visual learning, or reading, has been the favored method of instruction in schools, while listening skills often have been neglected. This is poor preparation for functioning well on the job later in life. It is estimated that people listen at about 25% efficiency. However, many decisions are influenced greatly by the way that people listen. This could include decisions such as what foods people eat, the medicines they take, what they wear, the moral codes they adopt, or how they vote.

According to the book *Are You Listening?* (R. Nichols, L.A. Stevens. McGraw Hill, 1957), 100 technical workers in 47 states were asked to rate reading, writing, speaking, and listening in order of importance on their jobs. The results were: reading, 4%; writing, 11%; speaking, 22%; and listening, 63%.

The listener is often only one of several people listening in the same situation. Reading, however, is usually done alone. The reader can choose his own surroundings and set his own pace. Listeners do not usually enjoy that luxury.

The listener must adjust to the pace of the speaker and surroundings and often must tolerate distractions naturally found when other people are present. A reader can stop and reread a difficult paragraph. The listener, on the other hand, usually has only one chance to hear a speech or a conversation. There is rarely an instant replay. This demonstrates how important it is for a person to be a good listener.

Effective listening requires patience to hear the speaker out. When interrupted, most people will hesitate, back away, and often rethink what they were about to say. This can be very critical to a salesperson gathering feedback, either on an active job or to find out why he just lost an order.

Effective listening requires patience to hear the speaker out.

Some salespeople in these circumstances, after hearing just a few words, interrupt and then move in with all sorts of disclaimers, excuses, or statements that shut off any further information.

One of the worst kinds of interruption occurs when the listener just wants to slip in a few words. This breaks the speaker's train of thought and can be very disrupting in the flow of vital competitive feedback.

Although it has probably not occurred to most people, effective listening requires a lot of courage—courage that not all have mustered. When someone listens completely to another person's ideas, he opens himself to the possibility that some of his own ideas might be wrong. Most people fight change and deep down feel that if they listen too attentively, they might be forced to change their minds. Based on their experiences and education, people form mental pictures of the way things should be in the world around them. When there is a possibility of hearing something that might change these images, selective deafness often occurs. This may explain why salespeople sometimes find that buyers do not really want to listen to their sales pitches. It also means that salespeople have to be skillful in their presentation so the buyers will listen. Sometimes listening is a social activity, but at work, it is a serious duty.

Listening is a skill that can be improved through training and practice. Children are taught in school how to read, how to write, and how to speak, but no one teaches them very much about how to listen. This is rather surprising, because being able to listen is extremely important for success in all walks of life, especially in sales. It is valuable when a salesperson is gathering information, and it is extremely significant when he is in a customer's office. It is important when he is on the telephone talking to a customer, and it is important every waking hour of his life. Surprisingly enough, most people, not just salespeople, are very poor listeners.

The Four Elements of Listening

According to Nichols and Stevens, there are four important elements of listening:

- sensing or hearing
- interpretation
- evaluation
- response

There is much more to listening than just *hearing*, which is the physical part of listening. Hearing or sensing only means that the person has received the message. The three other parts of listening are also very important.

The second part is the *interpretation* of what was sensed or heard. Do the speaker's words mean the same thing to the salesperson as they do to him? Often the backgrounds of the speaker and the listener are vastly different, including their vocabularies and experiences. It is easy for a misunderstanding to result concerning what is said by the speaker and what is understood by the listener.

The next element of listening is *evaluation*. This is when the listener weighs the information and decides if and how he will use it.

The last element of listening is the *response*, which is the result of the first three elements—what was heard, what was understood, and the evaluation of it.

To be a good listener, a person must convey to the speaker that he is indeed listening. It is easy for someone to spot a person who has not heard a word that was said to him. He seems to look around the room waiting for the speaker to stop talking so that he can quickly say what he thinks. Most speakers detect this quickly, and a salesperson should never give this impression. A good salesperson absolutely must learn to be a good listener. There are books written on listening, and there are other ways that this can be cultivated.

One of the best ways that a salesperson can demonstrate that he is indeed listening is the way he pays attention to the person speaking. He should look at the person speaking and make him aware that he is following what he is saying. The salesperson should not squirm, continuously move around, or make noises, but should give the person speaking his full attention.

At this time the salesperson should remain silent, but he should remember that there are several kinds of silence:

- There is the cold, chilling brand of silence.
- There is the demanding kind of silence that says, "OK, I am listening—try to sell me something."
- There is the neutral kind of silence.
- Finally, there is the warm, receptive quality in some forms of silence that indicates understanding and a desire to hear more.

Obviously, a salesperson should project the warm, receptive form of silence.

To be a good listener, a salesperson should have a respectful, receptive attitude and be genuinely interested in what the speaker has to say. If he maintains this attitude, the visible reactions will take care of themselves, even though there are dozens of visual clues that convey understanding between listener and speaker. Most people have developed a keen sense of whether or not someone is listening to them.

A salesperson's response to a speaker determines how much he learns from him. Encouraging reactions help the speaker reveal what he has on his mind. They keep him talking. From the salesperson's reactions, the speaker takes his bearings. If a salesperson demonstrates inattention by looking at his watch or shuffling papers, he will shut the speaker down and may lose valuable information and insight. The salesperson should never allow his eyes to wander around the room. He should look at the speaker and be alert at all times. This applies to all the members of his group while they are in a customer's office. Everybody should listen attentively.

An impolite comment or an unfavorable question will also stop the flow of information from the speaker. While a salesperson is listening, he should not allow himself to become confused by trying to memorize every number and fact related. Some will be important and should be remembered. However, the important thing is for him to grasp and understand the ideas and thoughts being spoken and to give the speaker his attention.

A salesperson can also make the customer realize that he is listening if he asks clarifying questions about what was just said. He should do this rather than asking an unrelated question or saying something the moment the speaker halts. Even if the salesperson is very anxious to get a point across or to change the subject, he should first ask a question or two about what was just said. This will demonstrate to the customer that the salesperson was listening and that he understood what the customer was saying. Only then should he proceed.

The one occasion in which a salesperson absolutely must be a good listener is when a customer is voicing objections to buying his products. The salesperson should hear the customer out, ask follow-up questions, and *listen*. The more a salesperson learns about the customer's objections, the better he will understand them. Once he understands them, he will be more likely to overcome them. The salesperson should also learn to listen between the lines, because not all customers voice all their real objections. Often, much is left unsaid that is important, perhaps decisive.

Another time in which it is vital for a salesperson to be a good listener is when a customer is hot under the collar and upset with the salesperson's firm. He should hear the customer out without interrupting before asking clarifying questions. It is the best way to defuse an explosive situation. When a salesperson does comment, he must make sure what he says conveys without a doubt that he heard what the customer said. His first comments should indicate understanding and sympathy with what upset the customer. Then he can proceed with clarifying questions and explanations.

There is a good way for a salesperson to gauge how good a listener he is. He should estimate at the end of each visit with a customer or colleague, either in the office or on the telephone, how much time he spent talking and how much time he spent listening.

Listening and understanding are vital. A salesperson must be able to understand what the customer is attempting to communicate directly and indirectly to him. This could be either in response to the customer's questions or generally about his company, the salesperson's firm, or the other topics under discussion. This requires not only intense listening, but also a good understanding of people and human nature. Moreover, a salesperson should always be careful to remember the context in which words were spoken if he is to later reflect an accurate picture of what was said. He must also remember the sequence and time frame in which things were said in order to have a clear and accurate understanding of what transpired.

To better understand what is being spoken, a salesperson should keep in mind something about the person talking. To a large degree, when people are talking, they are talking about themselves. The speaker's words will subconsciously reflect his inner feelings, preconceptions, assumptions, background, and prejudices. This is unavoidable and not to be condemned, but it should be kept in mind as a salesperson tries to understand what he hears.

A salesperson should not allow these facts to cause him to automatically doubt the speaker, his motives, or the accuracy of what he is saying. They should be kept in mind simply to help the salesperson more realistically interpret and understand what is being said. The salesperson should be sympathetic and understanding without judging the speaker too harshly. Otherwise, the salesperson will misunderstand the message and either shut the speaker off or severely restrict the communication.

Too many salespeople are concerned with talking about their products to listen to what the customer needs. A bad salesperson does not listen or seem to care about the customer. He will not retreat from his own agenda long enough to talk about the customer's problems, his requirements, and his product preferences. This type of salesperson is overbearing and pushy, has preconceived notions, and quickly shoots down all of his customer's objections. He talks about the technical specifications of what he is selling rather than its benefits to the customer. He does not listen and hear what the customer is trying to say. This kind of salesperson is doomed to failure.

A good example of poor listening by most people is what happens when several individuals from the same company attend a meeting with a customer or with their own colleagues. When they later meet to discuss what they heard in the meeting, they will invariably have as many versions as there were people in the gathering. Sometimes there is such a divergence that it seems certain that some of the individuals must have been in a different meeting altogether.

Sales Examples

Example 1

Several years ago, I attended a meeting with two other senior people to discuss a problem and to make recommendations toward a solution. One person was designated to write a summary of our meeting and to follow through to the conclusion. Several days later I received a copy of the summary. After reading it I was puzzled, so I called one of the other participants. I asked him if the group had a second meeting that I did not attend, since I did not recognize anything in the summary. He said that there had been only one meeting, and he was equally perplexed. The author of the summary had apparently heard what he wanted to hear, not what actually transpired in the meeting.

Example 2

In 1945 Vice President Truman became president upon the death of President Roosevelt. President Truman later told his biographer that in 1945, shortly after he was sworn in as president, one of his cabinet members said that

President Roosevelt had upon several occasions promised him that he would be the vice-presidential running mate in the previous election in 1944. Therefore, he would have succeeded President Roosevelt as president.

Later, President Truman told a reporter that this did not surprise him at all, because this person had always heard only what he wanted to hear and had his own version of every conversation. Truman went on to say that this individual was so intoxicated by the sound of his own voice that he literally heard only what he wanted people to say, not what they actually said.

From these two examples, it should be obvious that poor listening habits are widespread, cut across economic and political boundaries, and are not restricted to just uneducated individuals.

As mentioned previously, people in general are poor communicators verbally. If a salesperson is to avoid mistakes or misunderstandings, he must cultivate good listening skills. He should ask clarifying questions to greatly encourage the speaker. It will not only indicate to the speaker that the salesperson is listening, but it also gives the salesperson additional feedback concerning the discussion. A great way to get acquainted with people is to ask them thoughtful questions about their careers, where they grew up, how long they have been with their company, and where they worked previously. Then the salesperson must listen while they are talking.

When a salesperson asks questions and listens, it makes his customer feel good about being around the salesperson or talking to him on the telephone. He will feel important and will respond more favorably.

Example 3

Several years ago, we were working on a large project in the Soviet Union. Other firms were involved and their presidents were leading the discussions. Following the conclusion of one of our negotiating visits, I was traveling to London, and at the Moscow airport encountered one of these presidents. The plane was not crowded when we boarded the flight, and I sat down across the aisle from him. As soon as we were airborne, he asked me to move over and sit by him. I began the conversation by asking a question about his career, and where he grew up. When he finished responding, I asked another question, and continued asking questions during the remainder of the three and one-half hours of the flight. I made a few comments, but mostly I asked questions and listened intently to his replies.

Upon our arrival, he was met by his London manager. A week or so later, I had lunch with this London manager. During our meal, he asked, "What did you do to our president on the recent flight between Moscow and London? He said you were the best conversationalist he had ever met." The only thing I had done was to ask questions, listen, and let him know that I was listening. Even today, because of the answers I received, I probably remember more about this president than 98% of the salespeople who ever called on him, even those who saw him over a long period of time.

Improving Listening Skills

To be a good listener, a salesperson should practice the following nine suggestions:

1. He should listen for ideas and not necessarily facts, even though facts are certainly important when the customer is talking about the salesperson's current bid, new projects, or problems with his products.
2. He should judge the content and not the delivery of what is said.
3. He should listen patiently, even if the subject initially appears dry or uninteresting.
4. He should not jump to conclusions. Occasionally, salespeople hear the beginning of what someone says and then conclude that they know all the rest and stop listening. Later, these people feel certain the customer actually said what they only assumed he was going to say. The speaker will feel he was misunderstood—and he was.
5. He should keep listening with an open mind, because he could be wrong in his initial conclusion.
6. He should not let his prejudices and emotions interfere with what is being said. He should not become distracted by inflammatory words that set in motion his thoughts, past memories, and emotions. All of these will seriously hinder his ability to listen effectively.
7. He should concentrate on what the speaker is saying. He should not sit stiffly with his jaws clinched but should be relaxed and attentive. If he concentrates, it will be obvious to the speaker.

8. He should adjust his note taking to the speaker and the situation. Sometimes it is appropriate to take notes, and other times it is not. Usually, it is inappropriate for a salesperson to take notes in a customer's office unless he is writing down data. If he otherwise takes notes, the customer will feel he is talking to the media and will be intimidated and may not say very much. The salesperson should use good judgment.
9. He should actually work at listening. A good salesperson will strive to be a good listener by practicing the suggestions just enumerated. If he does these things well, the speaker will sense this through feedback from the salesperson's nods, questions, and comments.

There are some additional suggestions to help a salesperson better understand his customer:

1. He should analyze the buyer's temperament and not react to his words only. He should decide what kind of person the customer is. This takes time, and it means that the salesperson must become well acquainted with the customer.
2. He should be certain of the meaning of the customer's words. Words are not always used the same by everyone. In asking clarifying questions, the salesperson should use what he considers to be a synonym of the customer's word to make sure they are talking about the same thing.
3. He should listen beyond their words for their intent. Some sarcastic people in early meetings or encounters will try to scare or intimidate salespeople. The words themselves often count less than the intent behind them.
4. A salesperson should not be a wishful listener and only hear what he wants to hear. He should not read too much into what someone says casually. Some salespeople take a casual remark as a firm commitment when it was not meant that way at all. If a salesperson thinks what he is hearing is a promise or a commitment, he should verify his understanding of what he heard by repeating the idea in his own words. He should do this not only with customers, but also with his colleagues.

5. A salesperson should work at improving his auditory memory so he can recall more of what he hears. This can be done by having someone read short paragraphs to him in phrases, stopping occasionally, and asking him to write down what he just heard. Doing this regularly will greatly increase how much he retains of what he hears.

A salesperson spends virtually all of his time communicating with people, both customers and colleagues. It is a very important part of his job, and his very success depends on how well he communicates. By being a good listener, he will take a giant step in being successful in this critical area. If he really wants to be an outstanding salesperson, he must spend time working at improving his listening skills. The payoff will be dramatic.

Summary

1. Most people really are poor listeners. To be a good listener, a salesperson must at all times convey to the speaker that he is indeed listening.
2. It is easy for a customer to recognize when a salesperson is not listening.
3. A salesperson can demonstrate to his customer that he is listening to him in many ways:
   - He should pay attention.
   - He should make eye contact with the speaker.
   - He should hold still and not fidget.
   - He should have a respectful attitude.
   - The salesperson can ask clarifying questions or make responsive comments. He should avoid quickly changing the subject.
   - He should maintain a warm, receptive silence.
4. The salesperson must listen very carefully when he is in the following situations:
   - The customer has voiced objections to buying from him.
   - The customer has problems with the salesperson's products or his firm.

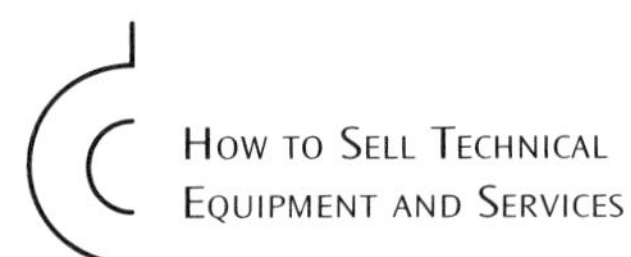

5. To understand clearly what has been said:
   - The salesperson should remember something about the speaker and his background.
   - The salesperson should remember the context in which something was said.
   - The salesperson should remember the sequence in which events were related.
6. The salesperson must *never* interrupt. When people are interrupted, they often have second thoughts and will not complete what they started out to say.
7. The salesperson should listen for ideas.
8. The salesperson should judge content and not delivery style.
9. The salesperson should listen patiently.
10. The salesperson should not jump to conclusions.
11. The salesperson should not stop listening when he disagrees.
12. The salesperson should not allow emotions to interfere.
13. The salesperson should concentrate on what is being said.
14. The salesperson must make sure he knows the meaning of the speaker's words.
15. The salesperson should listen beyond the words for what the speaker is leaving unsaid.
16. The salesperson should not be a wishful listener and only hear what he wants to hear.
17. The salesperson should work at increasing his auditory memory.
18. Throughout most of history, talking and listening were the only means of communication. Reading is a relative newcomer.
19. The spoken word is faster than the written word. This is very important in this age of speed and fast communications.
20. The spoken word has more persuasive power than the written word, because listeners are more vulnerable than readers.
21. People are influenced more by what they hear than by what they read.

22. At school, children are taught to recall what they visually learn, often at the expense of developing good listening skills.
23. A person's listening skills greatly influence virtually everything he does in his daily life.
24. Listening usually occurs in the presence of others and must compete with distractions.
25. Listeners must adapt to the pace of the speaker.
26. A listener very often has only one chance to hear a conversation. There very rarely are any replays.
27. Listening requires patience.
28. Interrupting is devastating to the listening process.
29. Listening requires a lot of courage, because what a person hears might change his mind. When faced with this, many people experience selective deafness.
30. Listening is a skill that can be improved through training and practice.

Finally, there are four elements of listening: hearing, interpretation, evaluation, and response. Communications are a vital part of selling, and being a good listener is crucial to being a good communicator. A salesperson must focus on being a good listener and spend time each week in order to be an outstanding salesperson.

42

Gather Intelligence and Feedback on a Job

Gathering product and commercial intelligence is a vital and continuing responsibility for a successful salesperson. When he is working on a specific job, obtaining accurate and reliable feedback is mandatory. He must know what is going on, how the customer is thinking, how his company stands competitively, and what his competitors are doing. This gives the salesperson confidence that he is aiming his sales pitches properly and covering the right points as he fine-tunes his sales strategy.

If with good feedback a salesperson is not convinced he is making progress, he should find out why and alter his tactics. The salesperson should mentally put himself in his customer's shoes and determine what the customer would expect and do in these circumstances given his objectives, constraints, and background. This information hopefully will allow the salesperson to reevaluate the strategy he has been following and to take the necessary corrective actions.

A salesperson must always promptly report and explain any sudden or unusual change in a customer's thinking or approach on a given project. How quickly and thoroughly he can do this is a good indication of how close he is to the customer. It also reveals how much he knows about the current project and how well he is handling the account on an overall basis.

It is very important early on to narrow down just who the major competitors are. If at the beginning there are many bidders, the salesperson will have to sell against all of them. By asking questions, the salesperson might be able to trim this list down to one or two serious contenders. Then he can focus on which of the product's features and benefits to accentuate and can emphasize how his product is superior to those of the one or two competitors.

During the quotation or bid analysis and the buying cycle of a large order, a salesperson's management will expect him to always know what is going on. This is one of the best barometers of how good a salesperson he is. It reveals how well he is working the job as well as how he has taken care of the account in the past. The salesperson will have the account in good shape if he attends to some important factors. He should convince the buyer that he will handle this order better than anyone else, and he must develop and cultivate good sources of information. In the closing stages of a potential order, the salesperson should talk almost daily to someone involved on the project. That way, when management asks for a report, he will know precisely what is going on that day and will be able to quickly and accurately report on the project's progress.

If a salesperson encounters long periods during which he cannot find out what is going on, this is usually bad news.

If a salesperson encounters long periods during which he cannot find out what is going on, this is usually bad news. It often means the job is moving away from him. The customer is almost always talking to someone. If it is not the salesperson, it is probably the competitor, who is in better shape and is slated to get the order. These silent periods and information blackouts should be taken very seriously, because virtually every time they mean unfavorable news is coming.

A salesperson should remember not to leave his number if the customer is out or does not accept his call in the closing stages of a job. During these periods, the customer will be inundated with calls from salespeople. The salesperson should leave his name and say that he will call later. By doing this, he retains the initiative. If he leaves his name and number, and the buyer does not call back, he is to some extent left stranded. Occasionally during the later stages of a job, more intelligence can be obtained by phone than through office calls, since visiting will probably be restricted. The decision maker will plead that he is too busy to see anyone, and many times he is even too busy to talk on the telephone.

One of the best ways a salesperson can enhance his intelligence on a current quote is to ask for the order. He will often be astonished at the reactions he will receive. This technique will flush out objections to the bid—objections he probably did not already know about. He should ask for the order early on so that if there are serious objections, he still has time to do something about them. If he waits to ask for the order until the customer is about to make a commitment, he may not have time to send additional information or refute allegations his competitor has made. The salesperson should gather job intelligence directly from the customer by asking for the order.

If a contractor or consultant is involved to advise or assist the ultimate user, he will usually be a good source of information. People with the end user, contractor, or consultant who are not directly and openly engaged in a given project will sometimes reveal more than those more directly involved. Those individuals directly responsible will be talking to many vendors and must guard more closely what they say.

It pays for a salesperson to be innovative as he tries to obtain additional feedback and intelligence on a project or a key order. He should not just call and ask when a decision will be made or what is new, because these questions can often be answered in one or two words. He should always come up with new wrinkles or new suggestions. For example, he could offer to commence engineering, order castings, start machining, or in some other way begin to work on the order to save delivery time and ship sooner. As mentioned previously, these offers will often ferret out objections and reveal problems not otherwise known to the salesperson.

On a large project, it is important to determine if there are any partners. Often there are many, but usually one is the operator and is probably evaluating, selecting, and buying the product. However, minority holders must be kept fully informed. They usually receive all of the important correspondence and usually must vote or sign off on what is purchased. A smart salesperson will identify the partners and go see some of them. These minority shareholders are often small companies, and sometimes they are one-man offices. Calling on them can be a rich source of information for the salesperson and another way to verify what has been obtained elsewhere. Usually the operator, the group soliciting and analyzing the bids, will not object to a salesperson calling on the partners. If there are objections, the salesperson should explain that he assumed his competition would visit them also and that he was acting in self-defense.

Sales Examples

Example 1

Several years ago, we were working a large project involving many partners. The major shareholder was the operator. As operator, this firm would send out the inquiries, receive the bids, analyze them, and make recommendations to all the partners.

Engineers and purchasing people in the operating company were very tight-lipped and would not reveal much about what was going on. I obtained from the operator a list of the various partners. In examining this list, I learned that a small firm located in the town in which I lived owned a minor interest.

I called on this small firm to ask how the project was moving and was astonished at the friendly reception. This engineer did not receive much attention and was anxious to talk. He gave me a complete rundown on the exact status and, more importantly, what vendor the operator preferred. This enabled us to more accurately direct our sales pitches to show how and why our products were better than the one the operator favored.

This was an important discovery because it allowed us to focus more or less on just one competitor—the one favored. We otherwise would have diffused our efforts by attempting to combat or to sell against the other two or three competitors. We were successful, due largely to having this intelligence from a minor shareholder.

Another source of intelligence is someone who has left the customer's company and has taken another job. This is especially true if he occupied an important position in the decision-making chain in his previous company. Sometimes he will tell a salesperson about any political difficulties, enemies, or particular problems with the salesperson's product acceptance. He may even tell the salesperson who favors the competition and who does not. It is surprising how much a salesperson can learn from this source—a source most salespeople never think about or pursue.

The salesperson's approach here should be one of a sincere desire to see how the employee is doing in his new job and how the salesperson can help. It is likely that the employee will still be in the same industry and may indeed still be a potential source of business. After the salesperson finds out about the employee's new job and offers to be of assistance, he can then approach the subject of the previous company. The former employee may not say very much. The salesperson should not expect him to reveal all the skeletons in the closet. The things that he may reveal, however, can be of tremendous assistance as the salesperson continues to work with the company in question.

A salesperson should always gather intelligence without violating a confidence or breaking any of his own company's or his customer's rules. Gathering intelligence is made much easier if a salesperson remembers two things. The first is that most people like to talk. The second is that the more friends a salesperson has in the company and in his industry, the more sources he has. Since the people selling ancillary products are good sources, the salesperson should always be friendly with them, treat them courteously, and answer any questions he can for them. He should take time to help them once in a while. To make friends, the salesperson must be one, and no one in his lifetime has ever accumulated too many friends.

Project intelligence comes from many sources. Visiting with other salespeople who sell similar things (not competitors) will often help a salesperson. He may learn something about the project or something about the customer's likes and dislikes that perhaps he would not have been able to find out on his own. Customers are on guard about pumps if they are talking to a pump salesman. However, they might not be quite so much on guard about pumps when talking to someone selling subsidiary products. Consequently, a salesperson may find that the salespeople selling products incidental to his own products may be good sources of information.

Example 2

We were working a large offshore job for turbine-driven centrifugal compressors. I was very friendly with the turbine salesperson who was in good position to get the turbine order on this project. The customer held a meeting to decide what kind of products to buy, but the salesperson handling the job was unable to determine the outcome. When he told me this, I offered to see what I could learn and called the turbine salesperson. I began the conversation by asking him about a job in Alaska, in which I had little interest, so he would not recognize my keen interest in the job offshore in the Gulf of Mexico. After he discussed the job in Alaska, I asked him, "What ever happened to the job in the Gulf of Mexico?" He immediately told me that he had the order not only for the turbines but also for the compressors to be built overseas. I asked how long he had had the order, and he said about one hour.

Armed with this intelligence, we were able to go back to the customer and point out the advantages of buying domestic rather than imported products, and we turned the job around. This early feedback from a salesperson who ordinarily sold only ancillary products was vital. We otherwise would not have learned about this foreign purchase until it was too late to do anything about it because of the tight secrecy lid the ultimate user had placed on the job.

As related earlier, another source a salesperson should consider is someone who has been transferred to another job within the same company. This person may no longer be actively engaged in evaluating the salesperson's products. However, he likely will stay in touch with his former colleagues and often will know much more than one would expect. The salesperson should go see him and take him to lunch. He can be a valuable source of intelligence. It will also show sincerity, since the salesperson should not suddenly stop calling on someone just because he was transferred out of the immediate interest area. The employee will often return, usually in a higher position.

A salesperson should take time to be friendly with the salespeople handling things relating to the salesperson's products. They can be very valuable sources of information. Occasionally someone who sells other items to the customer may have a better rapport with that customer than does the first salesperson. The ancillary products salesperson may have developed particularly strong friendships or closer relationships with certain key people. Perhaps the first salesperson has been busy working in other areas and has not dealt with these people long enough to have developed a similar connection.

Visiting with other salespeople (not competitors) calling on the same customers gives a salesperson another slant on the job. He can often find out from these individuals how fast the job is moving or whether he is getting the correct input from his sources. It is also another way of verifying information he already has. The salesperson should use the telephone extensively in talking to these people. Customer waiting rooms also provide an opportunity to pursue this knowledge. Industry conventions offer still another avenue, and attendance at professional society meetings will place a salesperson in touch with other salespeople.

Because different lead times are often involved on a job, certain products must be committed first, with others to follow. Talking to the salesperson who sells the products that must be purchased first is an excellent way for a salesperson to determine how fast a job is moving. It can reveal any delays or postponements. The salesperson should also talk to people in the customer organization who will be working on the satellite portions of the project. They often will provide valuable information such as timing, which vendor is favored, and chances a job will be approved.

Summary

Having complete, accurate intelligence, and following up and acting on it, will set a salesperson apart from most others. It will enable him to close a larger share of orders. A salesperson should work hard all the time to develop good sources of information and to obtain accurate, up-to-date intelligence.

Be Careful in Making Assumptions

The more experience that a salesperson gains, the more knowledgeable he should become, and the easier it will be for him to make assumptions about his customer. The salesperson may assume he knows what the customer is thinking about purchases or what the customer's reaction will be in a given situation. However, customers vary, and most of them are constantly evaluating new information. The customer's people, ideas, and even their priorities are constantly changing.

For these reasons, to gauge a customer's current position, a salesperson should not hesitate to ask questions. He must be careful about making assumptions. Time passes so rapidly that he may think he knows a customer's reaction, while in reality, it may have been months since they discussed important subjects. There are many times that a salesperson should remember to visit with his customers to understand their current thinking. Such times occur when the salesperson receives a new inquiry, a problem arises as he works on a project, or when he prepares his forecast.

There are many times that a salesperson should remember to visit with his customers to understand their current thinking.

It is usually not too difficult to learn the customer's current attitudes, so the salesperson should not be afraid to ask again. He can review in his mind what he understands about their ideas on important issues and can ask if their opinions have changed. Most people are quite willing to answer questions as long as the salesperson is not probing too deeply into their private business.

The salesperson also must be careful not to make too many assumptions about his own company's attitudes and positions. If time has elapsed since these have been reaffirmed, he should not be afraid to ask about them. This is particularly true in the case of new inquiries for products that the salesperson's current product line does not include. Even if the salesperson's company has refused to quote before, he should still give them another chance to do so. Sometimes his company may be monitoring a given market, and even after refusing to quote for several years, they will suddenly agree to bid into this new area. The salesperson should not be caught refusing an inquiry only to learn later that his firm was interested and would have responded.

Furthermore, the salesperson should not assume he knows what models his competitors will quote on a given project. He may think he knows because of what he has previously observed, but he should verify this if possible. This is not always easy, because his customer may not want to reveal this information. Other salespeople quoting auxiliary products on this same job may know, since their products must dovetail with those of the salesperson or his competitors.

The salesperson must know accurately what his competition quoted if he is to sell successfully against them. It is important for him to avoid assumptions and ask questions.

This is also true as the salesperson analyzes a new inquiry. Perhaps the customer is still asking for an expensive trim or feature for which the salesperson now has a good substitute. The salesperson should not assume the customer will refuse substitution just because he has in the past. The salesperson should explain his position and ask again. The same procedure should be followed when he makes his sales calls, pitches, and presentations as the project unfolds. He must remain alert and ask questions. Instead of assuming he knows why the customer is reacting the way he is, the salesperson should ask and be certain. He should make assumptions very carefully.

44

Overcome Objections

There is hardly anything in the world that some man cannot make a little worse and sell a little cheaper, and the people who consider price only are this man's lawful prey.

—John Ruskin

"Your price is high," is the most common objection salespeople encounter. This one seems to be voiced the most often, but there are others. In order to successfully overcome objections, the salesperson must know about all of them. Some customers will quickly voice all their concerns. Others will not say much and will disguise their misgivings by discussing the price. It is, therefore, up to the salesperson to flush out all of the objections and not to settle for the price objection alone.

To do this will require a lot of skillful probing on the salesperson's part and will usually involve preparing a list of questions to ask the customer about the products and the quotation. These questions should relate to the various aspects or features of the products and proposal and should be worded to determine the customer's opinion of these features and the salesperson's offering. He should not assume he knows these answers.

Early in the meetings with the customer, the salesperson should not hesitate to ask the buyer what features he is looking for or what he expects from a supplier. Some of the questions should be phrased so that the answers cannot be just *yes* or *no*. These one-word answers can be very misleading, because they do not explain or elaborate. A salesperson will invariably learn more if his questions must be answered with an explanation. The customer's responses will usually indicate his acceptance or rejection of the product's characteristics. Hopefully, if his questions cover enough territory, they will identify most of the objections. The salesperson should also remember that opinions differ from one customer to another. It is important that when working on a special project, the salesperson knows the objections that apply to the products or parts under discussion.

For example, if a salesperson says his product is built to a certain code, the buyer might say that this quality is not needed or required. Or perhaps the salesperson points out that a certain part is removable while the unit is in operation. The response might be favorable, or again it might reveal that all of the competitors' products also have this feature. (The salesperson should avoid the latter situation by studying his competitors' products and knowing how his products differ.)

By going through this list of questions with the decision maker, a salesperson can usually receive a pretty good indication of how he stacks up against the competitors. In instances where the customer does not like one of the product's features, the salesperson can explain why it is included. If the customer rejects the explanation, and if the feature is objectionable to them, the salesperson might be able to eliminate it, depending on the individual case.

By asking the decision makers these questions, the salesperson hopefully will flush out latent objections. He should keep in mind that not all customers will readily and quickly voice all their concerns. A salesperson must usually uncover them after a lot of effort. Too often the important or serious objections do not surface until after the order is lost. Quite often the customer who remains unconvinced

Too often the important or serious objections do not surface until after the order is lost.

does not want to reveal all his misgivings. He might think that the salesperson will successfully overcome them, and then his real reasons for not buying from the salesperson will be weakened. This might make his buying decision more difficult to justify. Many of these individuals will smile, be very cordial, and buy from the competitor. It should therefore be obvious that if the salesperson is to receive the order, he must be sure to bring out into the open all serious objections and then successfully overcome them.

The prospect with no objections also can be a big problem, because it is difficult to know what he is thinking. If the salesperson is unable to elicit any objections, he should ask for the order. This will usually reveal any objections.

In selling, it is always important for a salesperson to be constantly aware of various objections his customers are likely to raise when he is making his sales pitch. They may say the price is too high or the delivery is too long. They may claim the efficiency is low, parts purchased previously had poor quality, or they received poor service on previous orders. Perhaps the salesperson's products may be new, and his company has not built them before. Or the customers may say they are completely satisfied with their current suppliers.

A salesperson should approach objections in any of these areas as follows:

1. He should listen to the objections carefully and hear them out without interrupting. Then he should repeat the comments in his own words—not necessarily the buyer's words—and assure the buyer that he has understood the objections.
2. He should not make assumptions but should ask questions to make certain he completely understands the reasons behind the buyer's objections. He may know, but he should ask questions in order to be sure.
3. He must control his temper.
4. He must recognize that some objections are stalling techniques.
5. He can use today's objections as honing tools to make tomorrow's sales talk sharper.
6. He should use *you* instead of *I* in discussions.
7. He should reduce broad objections to specifics.

8. If there is the slightest doubt that his response will be rejected, he should support his answers with the testimony or experience of a third party.
9. For use on future jobs, he should tabulate for his files all objections encountered on a given product and his solid, organized, and careful answers or explanations.

Long before objections start, the salesperson should have established himself as a specialist who knows the most about the products. He should be seen as the person who will follow the customer's order through the complete manufacturing and delivery cycles better than anyone else. This includes engineering, manufacturing, shipping, and commissioning. This is best done through deeds, that is, by his performance on previous orders.

The salesperson should have previously convinced the customer of the uniqueness of his engineered products, their many outstanding features, and why they are the best for the job. A salesperson with superior products, who is obsessed with taking good care of his customers, is in an excellent position to answer and overcome any remaining or residual objections.

An alert, well-prepared salesperson will think about objections well ahead of his phone call or visit to the customer's office and will know the correct responses from memory. Often this includes consulting with his colleagues and with engineering people for their input. The salesperson should never be surprised when a prospect raises objections. Many times when he brings up these doubts, the salesperson can turn them to his advantage by immediately and thoroughly answering them. The customer may just be fishing. As mentioned previously, he may even just be trying to give excuses that are not the real reasons for a refusal to buy the product. These may be excuses, but they are completely valid in the customer's mind.

A salesperson should ask a lot of questions about any objections. They often cover up hidden feelings and will, upon investigation, tell him a great deal about how the customer is thinking and what he is considering foremost in selecting the product. The importance of the salesperson asking questions about the customer's protests cannot be overemphasized. Often the salesperson will not know the whole story until he asks many, many questions.

It is also very important how the salesperson answers these doubts. If he acts surprised, confused, or hesitant when objections are raised, the customer will immediately suspect that the objections are valid. Conversely, if the salesperson is well prepared and has previously rehearsed the explanation of these objections, he will be able to give clear, convincing, concise, and prompt responses. For example, a salesperson may be asked if his company has built a certain model of product that is close or similar to his other products. If his company has not, the salesperson should say so. At the same time, the salesperson can use the following procedure:

1. He can point out how close the subject model is to his other models and explain that his engineers used the same design criteria and parameters.
2. He can reemphasize how many of the other sizes his company has built and how long they have been in satisfactory operation.
3. He can present a list of satisfied users of other models. He should have letters from satisfied customers on hand to show his prospect.
4. He can tell the customer how many design engineers his company has engaged in this work and how many successful new or modified models or sizes they have already engineered, designed, and introduced.

The salesperson's responses should be offered without the slightest hesitation or excuse. They should be spoken with complete confidence, although without arrogance. They should be explained with an attitude that the salesperson is pleased to be able to address these objections. It is astonishing how often salespeople will allow a customer's doubts to place them on the defensive, destroying their sales efforts.

As explained previously, the salesperson's initial reaction can be decisive. Therefore, the more prepared he is for these objections, the better his chances are for giving the customer satisfactory answers. The salesperson should not merely respond and assume he has overcome the objections, however. After he has made his points, he should ask more questions to make sure the customer is satisfied with what he has said. If not, he should explain further. If the salesperson has no more information to use, he should tell the customer that he will get back to him with further details.

A salesperson should never take objections lightly and should always answer honestly. There is no such thing as an unimportant objection. All questions should be treated seriously and not ignored or rejected out of hand. Once in a while a salesperson encounters a question that he has not heard before, and he does not have a ready response. In this situation, the salesperson should simply tell the customer that no one has raised that issue before, and he will get back to the

customer with a reply. First, the salesperson should make sure he understands the objection. Then he must obtain an accurate and substantive response from his experts. He should not bluff or try to improvise an answer.

A salesperson must work hard to overcome objections. Failure to do this is one of the biggest mistakes salespeople make. It is far better to take objections too seriously than not seriously enough. A salesperson who takes objections seriously will certainly answer adequately. Many salespeople have found that during the various stages of negotiations on a job, they heard certain doubts or protests expressed by the customer and treated them too lightly. To their sorrow, they did not adequately overcome them and thus lost the order.

In most cases, the answers a salesperson gives to a customer should be confirmed in writing so that the buyer has on hand a printed rebuttal or explanation. In that manner, when the customer is deciding what to buy, he has explanations to the questions he raised. A salesperson who puts these in writing accomplished several things:

1. The information is in print so the customer does not have to rely on his memory or his notes when he is in the final meeting to decide whose products to recommend.
2. It will enable the customer to pass this information along to other interested people in his company, to his superiors, or to others who will participate in the decision.
3. It will organize the salesperson's thoughts. It is one thing to relate the explanation to the customer verbally and another to put it in writing. The task of writing out the explanation will most likely enable the salesperson to present his case more clearly. If the response is complex or involved, he should ask his colleagues, his boss, or someone from engineering to read the draft so that a consensus response is submitted. The salesperson also should choose confidence-giving words.

One of the objections encountered most frequently is that the price is too high. This objection could signify one or more of the following:

1. This could be a negotiation technique to attempt to obtain a lower price, although this should not be assumed too quickly.
2. The price may indeed be high.
3. The desire for the product may be too low.

4. The salesperson may have misinterpreted the customer's specifications or requirements and quoted more than his competition. In other words, his price is high, but for a reason—he quoted a different bill of material.
5. The customer has not compared the salesperson's product on an equal basis with his competitor's product. Perhaps he has not discovered that the salesperson's product has stainless steel, where a competitor uses much cheaper carbon steel. Perhaps the salesperson included everything the customer specifications called for, but the competitor left something out, either deliberately or through an oversight.

Buyers often erroneously cite price as the reason for not buying, because that does not assign blame. The customer does not then have to explain why he did not buy from the salesperson, and it might make a salesperson feel a little bit better about losing the order. He can blame others and not himself. He can even conclude that he did his sales job, but his company just could not be competitive. He can even blame his competition for cutting the price.

When a customer says that the price is too high, what should be done? First, the salesperson should respectfully remind the customer that a price is high only if the identical item can be obtained elsewhere at a lower cost. He should then point out his product's features and benefits and explain how his product is different. Next the salesperson should, if possible, go through the quotation with the customer in detail to show that he has included everything specified. He can make sure that he has not quoted more than the customer wanted.

The salesperson also can ask if the customer's requirements have changed since the inquiry was issued. In other words, he should make sure he has quoted to the customer's specifications and that the customer is still in the market for products as called for in the original inquiry. (Requirements sometimes change after an inquiry is sent out, and the customer does not always notify all the bidders of the changes.) The salesperson should then ask the customer if he has indeed compared the salesperson's technical quote to others. He should find out if the customer is certain the competitors quoted the same things in accordance with the specifications.

The salesperson should go through his benefit list thoroughly and point out the salient features, asking which ones can be omitted so he can offer a lower price. Often, this will flush out specifications or features of the salesperson's product that the competitors' products do not have. If a salesperson knows his competitors' products well enough, he can pick out some features their

products lack. After asking if he can leave some of the features out, so as to lower the price, the salesperson can select other features and ask the same question. This will often make the customer nervous about ending up with a product that is missing something useful or necessary.

Sometimes the customer refuses to leave anything out of the quote. After completing the previous steps, the salesperson should report any remaining pricing discrepancy to his pricing authority. It may be that the customer will accept a price change. If that is possible, the salesperson should ask his pricing specialist to review recent price levels on similar jobs sold or lost to review the cost margins and selling price to see if the price can be adjusted.

Sometimes the final price remains high when compared to a competitive bill of material. Then the salesperson should reemphasize the superiority of his products, especially from a reliability standpoint, and should repeat his product's features and benefits. The salesperson sells peace of mind, not just products. He must convince the customer that his unit has greater protection against breakdowns because of higher quality and because the design is more conservative. If possible, he should give examples of people who bought cheaper parts or products and suffered long outages.

A salesperson should also work at convincing the customer of the mutually beneficial importance of his company's long-term profitability. He should point out the dangers of always squeezing to obtain rock-bottom prices. A customer who does this may have fewer choices in the long run because some firms will be forced out of business. This can result in longer deliveries or with the remaining vendors providing less quality. Sometimes comments such as these appear to fall on deaf ears. They should be courteously made in any case, because they can later influence a customer's attitude or posture during negotiations.

Sometimes it is necessary to reduce a price, but a salesperson should bear in mind that cutting a price without changing the scope of supply has three effects:

1. The purchaser wonders if he got the lowest price possible.
2. The seller wonders if he got the highest price possible.
3. The reputation of the products tends to suffer. The very act of cutting the price is an indication that perhaps the value was not there in the first place.

No one is really completely happy with a price reduction. Many customers consider a lower price an indication of lower quality. A reduction in price is often an indication to the purchaser that the seller has some doubt as to the quality claimed for the product.

Sales Example

Once when we were working on a project in the Soviet Union, we had bid against specifications, as had all of our competitors. The job dragged out over several months. In the final stages, as usual, the Soviet negotiators kept trying to beat our price down. We looked at our margins and decided we could go no lower. The Soviets persisted in asking for a lower price. Finally, we asked if we could again review with them the bill of materials or scope of supply to make certain we were not quoting more than they wanted.

When this was done, it turned out that several items and requirements had been eliminated by their engineers over the last few weeks, but no one had gotten around to telling us. Once we knew that the bill of materials had shrunk, we looked again at our costs and decided we could make a price reduction. It was adequate, and we received a very large order. If we had not verified the scope of supply, we would have lost this order.

When quoting a product, the salesperson must verify, both initially and toward the end of the process, that his company has not quoted more than the customer wants. Requirements can change, especially if the job drags out over a period of time.

The salesperson should go through this exercise to make sure the customer is properly evaluating his bid. Even so, he should never admit that his engineered products are only equal to those of the competition. The salesperson should remember that his products were designed by his company's engineers. Competitive units were designed by a completely different team. There is much pride among designers to do things differently. Only in the broadest terms are two products engineered by separate design groups identical, even if they both meet the specifications. The salesperson's products will invariably be different and will possess unique, exclusive features. He should convince the customer these features are better.

Prior to the receipt of the customer's inquiry on a given project involving engineered products, the salesperson should have been emphasizing the exclusive features of his product. They should then be converted into meaningful customer benefits no competitor can match. If the salesperson knows his competitors' models, he will know the salient features of those products. He will then know how his product is unique and different. The salesperson should ask his design engineers why they approached the solution the way they did. Often he will learn that his product is simpler and hence easier to maintain than the competitors' products. Perhaps removing a given part for maintenance requires less time on the salesperson's product. This saves labor, which can be translated into dollars. The competitor's more complicated solutions often gain nothing.

The salesperson should concentrate on the differences in his products and thereby remove his products from a direct comparison. It will then be difficult for the customer to say his price is high. As pointed out earlier, the price of the product is high only if the identical item can be obtained elsewhere at a lower cost. It will not always be easy for a salesperson to find a long list of differences, but he can always find some. Sometimes one is enough. That is why product knowledge is vital. The more ways a salesperson can demonstrate he is offering something unique and advantageous, the less the customer will think about price.

Here is a sobering thought for a salesperson to remember. If his firm always had the lowest price, most reliable products, and best delivery, it would not need salespeople. It would only need to advertise and hire a room full of people to open orders, because it would get them all. Salespeople are employed to overcome objections. That is a big part of their job. A salesperson must work hard at improving his skills in this area.

Sometimes the salesperson's product is critical to the operation of a plant. When it is out of service, the plant is down, and the salesperson should begin early to steer the customer to thinking about the cost of downtime rather than the lowest price. He should determine before the meeting the customer's cost of downtime. He could then calculate, for example, what a 1% difference in the price of the product means to him in downtime. He might be able to show that his products would have to operate only a few hours more each year to more than overcome a cheaper price.

A salesperson must learn to always address this concern, because he will not always be told the price is high. He may learn this only after the order is lost. It is best for a salesperson to assume his price is high and face the problem head on. In many cases, cost of downtime is hundreds of thousands of dollars per day.

Perhaps the outage figure is $200,000 per day. He can emphasize that avoiding only one or two days of downtime, which the customer can do by selecting his superior product, will offset between $200,000 and $400,000 of initial cost. If the life of the project is 10 years, a price difference of $200,000 figures out to be $55.00 per day. The salesperson should prove to the customer that the extra reliability built into his conservative design is worth more than $55.00 per day. Combined with the peace of mind the customer gets with the salesperson's product, the difference is much more than offset.

Efficiency can also be used to offset a higher price. If the salesperson's product is more efficient, he should point out that it will use less energy. The savings he calculates and demonstrates to the customer will in many cases offset a much higher price. The salesperson should not overlook this important aspect.

Fear of buying the wrong capital goods looms large in a customer's thinking. The salesperson can use efficiency savings and cost of downtime to offset an initial high price and get the order. Perhaps the salesperson's company has better service and spare parts accessibility. If so, he can also point this out. He should assure the customer that his products, when down for emergency or routine maintenance and overhaul, can be put back on line quicker and minimize the cost of this outage. Many times his company will have service people more closely located to the job site. This will save downtime in an emergency.

An outstanding salesperson will convince the customer that he is the difference, that the dedicated service and attention the salesperson will devote to him will be worth the higher cost of his products. The salesperson must help the customer by promptly sorting out problems, being available and responsive, and quickly resolving any warranty difficulties. He should demonstrate that the customer will actually save money by purchasing products from him, even at a slightly higher price.

This objective should dominate the salesperson's thinking, because rarely will he have the lowest price, best delivery, and highest efficiency. Furthermore, this is his chance to demonstrate his superior performance as a salesperson. An excellent measure of a salesperson's competence is the number of orders he closed by overcoming price, delivery, and even performance problems to bring in orders he was not really expected to get. He made himself the difference and tipped the scales in his favor.

The salesperson should, therefore, work very hard to do an outstanding job of taking care of his customers. If the customer has problems, the salesperson should not give up until they are solved. He must listen carefully to all objections raised and ask questions to reveal unspoken objections. He should keep a list of all objections and work out satisfactory responses, memorizing them so he can overcome future objections before they cost him orders. He must make himself the difference.

Summary

1. "Your price is high" is the most common objection, but there are many others.
2. In order to overcome objections, the salesperson must know about all of them.
3. Not all customers will immediately volunteer all of their objections.
4. The salesperson must ask enough questions to flush out all objections.
5. He should ask the buyer what feature he is looking for or expects from a supplier.
6. He should phrase most questions so that they cannot be answered with a *yes* or *no*.
7. He should never assume he knows all of the buyer's objections.
8. The salesperson should stress features he considers to be important in order to bring out objections he otherwise would not know about.
9. He should ask enough questions to flush out latent objections that otherwise will come out only after the order is lost.
10. Some customers will not reveal all of their objections because they do not want the salesperson to overcome them and eliminate their intended reason for not buying from him.
11. A salesperson should beware of buyers who just smile, listen, and remain cordial. If a prospect has no objections, the salesperson should ask for the order. That will usually flush out any objections.
12. The salesperson should try to anticipate with each customer and on each quotation what objections are apt to be voiced and have his responses ready.

13. The salesperson should approach objections by doing the following:
    - He should listen to the customer without interrupting. He should repeat back the comments in his own words and obtain assurance that he has understood the customer's objections.
    - He should ask questions to make certain he completely understands the reasons behind the buyer's objections, never assuming he knows all of them.
    - He should keep his temper under control.
    - He should recognize objections as stalling techniques.
    - He should use today's objections as tools to hone tomorrow's sales talk.
    - He should say *you* instead of *I* in discussions.
    - He must reduce broad objections to specifics.
    - If there is the slightest doubt that his response will be rejected, he should support his answers with the testimony or experience of a third party.
    - For use on future jobs, he should tabulate and record all objections encountered on a given product, along with his well-organized, careful answers or explanations.
14. Early in his dealings with his customers, he should establish through his actions that he is a dedicated expert in his field. Orders will be better off with him than with anyone else.
15. He must listen and take all objections seriously. There are no unimportant objections.
16. Some objections mask hidden feelings, and upon investigation, will reveal to the salesperson a lot about how a customer thinks.
17. He must answer all objections calmly, clearly, and convincingly, without any hesitation.
18. He should have a good explanation if he has not built the product before.
19. He should confirm in writing all responses to objections.

20. When a customer says the price is too high, it could mean one or more of the following:
    - It is a negotiation technique to attempt to obtain a lower price.
    - The prices may indeed be high.
    - The customer's desire for the product is too low.
    - The salesperson misinterpreted the customer's specifications or requirements.
    - The customer has not compared products on an equal basis.
21. A customer thinks that telling the salesperson that he lost the order because the price was too high lets everyone off the hook.
22. When the salesperson does, indeed, have a higher price, he must sell his product's superiority and peace of mind, not just the equipment.
23. Reducing the price should be done reluctantly because of the following negative effects:
    - The purchaser wonders if he got the lowest price possible.
    - The seller wonders if he got the highest price possible.
    - The reputation of the products tends to suffer, because the very act of cutting the price is an indication that perhaps the value was not there from the start. No one is really completely happy with a price reduction.
24. If a project drags out, the salesperson must periodically verify that the buyer has not changed the scope of supply.
25. The salesperson should never admit that his engineered product is only equal to the competition's product. The salesperson's product will invariably be different and will possess exclusive features no competitor can match.
26. A salesperson must demonstrate cost savings in higher efficiency and less downtime.
27. A salesperson should concentrate on the differences and thus remove his products from direct comparison.
28. If his firm always had the lowest prices and the best deliveries, they would not need salespeople.
29. A primary function of a salesperson is to overcome objections.
30. The salesperson should concentrate on making himself the difference.

45

Get the Supervisors Involved

The salesperson has the direct responsibility for the customer. He is the first line of contact with customers and should know what is going on at all times. The supervisor, on the other hand, usually oversees several people and has other duties as well, so that he cannot always know when one of his people needs help. Thus the salesperson must always be alert for potential problem situations. He must not hesitate to ask for assistance and guidance when problems loom on the horizon or are on top of him. A danger signal occurs whenever the profile is suddenly raised on a project on which he is working, and senior customer people start getting involved. When this happens, the salesperson should also sound the alert and involve his supervisor.

Many talented, aggressive salespeople would prefer to do their jobs entirely on their own without any outside help. While this is an admirable trait, it is not always the best overall approach. One of the biggest reasons salespeople do not involve their superiors is because they feel that by so doing their position in the company is diminished. Actually, the opposite is true. The involvement of a salesperson's superiors enhances his standing both with his customer and within his own organization. It demonstrates that the salesperson has sound judgment, and it will also protect him from the *go-it-alone* syndrome. I have always been suspicious of salespeople who never asked for help and never wanted their customers to know anyone but themselves. It demonstrates a shortsighted, selfish attitude, and in some instances, an attempt to cover up shortcomings.

One of the biggest reasons salespeople do not involve their superiors is because they feel that by so doing their position in the company is diminished. Actually, the opposite is true.

Situations for Supervisor Involvement

As a salesperson goes about his job, there are many instances in which it is appropriate for him to involve his supervisors. These include the following:

1. Unusual or new situations that the salesperson has not encountered before
2. Involvement of high-level customer executives on a current order, project, or warranty problem
3. Inability to obtain the price or the delivery needed to get a new order
4. Problems with delivery on a job going through the plant

5. Customers visiting the salesperson's plant
6. Serious problems of any kind with an existing order
7. To strengthen the bond between the salesperson's firm and his customer and to better establish it as a reliable, dependable supplier
8. To allow executives to better understand the customer's problem and the salesperson's selling obstacles with the customer
9. To gain access to the customer's top management
10. To introduce people in the salesperson's management organization to the customer, so he is familiar with the people who will help him if problems arise

A salesperson's superiors should be able to help him in all of these instances, both inside and outside the firm, for the following reasons:

1. It is part of their job.
2. They invariably have had more experience and have often previously encountered the situation the salesperson now faces. They can offer problem-solving solutions.
3. They will have more influence in dealing with other departments inside the salesperson's organization and can enable him to short-circuit normal handling.
4. They can deflect some of the flack encountered when the salesperson attempts to put an order on the fast track.
5. They can get involved in making decisions as the situation unfolds and enable the salesperson to better and more quickly reach a consensus decision. It minimizes later second-guessing.
6. They will better know the rules and policies so the salesperson will be more apt to be acting within his firm's guidelines and rules as he tries to cut corners.
7. They will often have recent beneficial knowledge or input the salesperson does not have. Being higher in the organization, they will have a broader horizon.

Assistance within the sales organization

Internal help should be asked for any time it is needed. A salesperson should not be bashful about asking for it. If he is in doubt, he should ask for help. As he goes about his selling job, he will regularly encounter situations within his own organization in which he will be given routine answers when he needs specialized answers. He should never settle for routine answers from low-level people who are sticking to the rules, especially when he knows they will cost him sales. As a salesperson, he should know better than anyone what is required to maximize sales and keep the company growing. After he has tried diligently, but unsuccessfully, to obtain answers through normal channels, he should involve his superiors. He should not give up until he gets what he needs and what is in the long-term best interests of the company.

There are important situations in which the salesperson is most likely to require this kind of help. These will involve the following:

- obtaining information to meet a quotation deadline
- obtaining competitive prices
- obtaining delivery necessary to get the order
- bringing a project back on schedule with delivery on a current order
- resolving field problems when the equipment is out of warranty

The salesperson knows better than anyone else what is needed in these situations. He is the one who must lobby for what he needs. He must first work through the established avenues but should not hesitate to involve his superior if the effort falls short. I cannot overemphasize the importance of following this course of action. A salesperson *must not* settle for answers that he knows will cost him business.

Customer visits

The salesperson will always want to alert his superiors and involve them when his customers will be visiting the salesperson's facilities. This is best done in writing, and the salesperson should give the date, time, and names and titles of individuals, together with the purpose of the plant visit. The salesperson can later set up times for his superiors to meet the customer's people, which in some cases will be adequate, or to sit in on any scheduled meeting if he thinks their presence will help.

Trade shows

If a salesperson's superiors or executives are attending trade shows, he should give them maximum exposure. At the booth or in his hospitality suite, he will want to be sure they are introduced to all of his important customers. It is even better for a salesperson to arrange dinner meetings with some of his best customers. These must be planned well ahead of time for maximum benefit and to ensure that the supervisors can meet with the customers.

Meetings with top-level executives

Finally, the salesperson will, from time to time, want to arrange visits in the customers' offices for his superiors. His executives should not be taken just to see the top-level people in the customer's organization. They should also be introduced to the level of people the salesperson normally contacts. In fact, before requesting high-level meetings directly, the salesperson should go through his normal business contacts and ask for their suggestions and help. The salesperson should explain that he is not attempting to circumvent anyone but is trying to establish broader relationships between the companies so they can work together on a mutually beneficial basis.

If a salesperson asks his normal contacts to help set up the meetings, they will likely be asked to attend. If not, at least they will know what is going on and should not be offended. If they do not attend, the salesperson should consider taking his management people to see them separately. If that is not possible or practical, he should at least brief them right away on the outcome of the meeting and advise them of any agreements or promises made.

There are times with virtually all customers when a salesperson needs high-level involvement in order to break into an account or to increase the company's share of business. Arranging a meeting high up in the organization can often facilitate this. The salesperson should generally arrange these contacts and meetings on an orderly basis when no large project is being considered or is even on the horizon. Last-minute attempts to involve top executives who are strangers usually prove counterproductive and can be disastrous during the final stages of a large project. These top-level meetings should be systematically arranged when it is mutually convenient and between large projects.

Preparation for Top-Level Meetings

Before a top-level meeting, the salesperson should make the appropriate preparations. These important tasks include the following:

1. The salesperson should correctly establish and confirm in writing both to his customers and to his superiors the exact date, time, and place of the meeting.
2. The salesperson should give his senior people a written list of people they will see, together with exact titles and responsibilities. He should include as much background information as possible.
3. The salesperson should brief his executives on the account in general, including the nature of the customer's business. In particular, he should identify any new projects coming up and any problem areas, together with their current status. He should list in detail any ideas or points he wants to emphasize and prepare the wording he would suggest. The salesperson's executive can change it, but he should be told exactly what should be said.
4. The salesperson should be sure he knows the correct meeting location and how to get there quickly. He should not fumble around. If the location is unfamiliar, he should take time to make a dry run to locate it ahead of time.
5. The salesperson should arrange the schedule so that he has plenty of time to reach the first appointment on time.
6. If the sales team is going from place to place to see several individuals or more than one firm, the salesperson should schedule the meetings so there is ample time for each session and plenty of time to travel from one location to another. He should watch the clock and leave each office in time to maintain his schedule. He should be the one to monitor this. He cannot be bashful, but he must be courteous.
7. The salesperson should make sure that it is agreed in advance which person from his side will lead the discussions. This does not mean that others cannot ask questions or make comments, but someone from the sales team should be designated to guide the meeting. There should be no side conversations.

8. If there are several people in the sales group, the salesperson should prepare a written list of names and titles to hand over to his customer at the proper time.
9. The salesperson should make sure his sales team knows the proper attire, if there is any doubt.
10. Just before the visit time, the salesperson should personally verify the appointment to make certain there is no misunderstanding.

Here, as always, the salesperson should have a game plan and carefully and thoughtfully decide what message he wants to convey. On these occasions, his executives can get across to the customer's management certain salient facts or features about his company and its products. They can help the salesperson establish credibility, reliability, dependability, and a basis for better cooperation. Later, when business is being negotiated, perhaps phone calls can be made that may help. Salespeople should be careful about this and not rely too much on top-level assistance in this area. The salesperson should personally attend to his selling job at all levels and should do it well, without too much executive help.

When a meeting is planned between these executives, the salesperson should be sure to put in writing some brief points he would like his senior people to make. This should consist of an agenda with the most important things at the top, listed in descending order of importance. The salesperson's briefing should include salient facts about his customer and his company, unless they are already well known. He should also include details about the current business he is doing with this customer, together with any problems.

The salesperson's executives may not say to the customer what the salesperson suggests, but he should not be bashful in asking. His executives will usually welcome his input and suggestions. The salesperson should remember that they are busy and often not as sales oriented as he is. Clearly the salesperson's ideas and suggestions are more likely to be presented if he prepares a written outline or brief than if he just makes verbal suggestions on the way to the meeting.

The salesperson should provide the relevant information about the customer and his visit to his superiors well before the meeting, not in the car on the way to the appointment. He should, however, have the names and titles of the customer's people on a small card to hand to his executives in case they left their list behind or do not already know them. Titles are very important to most people, so the salesperson should make sure they are right. Otherwise, he will offend someone.

The salesperson should be sure the office of the executive he is going to see is aware of how many people he is bringing. That way the customer can decide ahead of time where he will greet the sales team, whether in his office or in a conference room. Upon arrival, the salesperson should give the receptionist the names of all of the sales team, not just his own name. He should use his prepared list. If the sales team is early, he should not allow the receptionist to announce their arrival until the time of their appointment.

The salesperson must remember that once in the customer's office, the opening sentence by his side can set the tone of the entire meeting. He should immediately get down to business and be sure that this is done in a positive way. If the salesperson's company has been receiving a lot of business from this customer, the salesperson's most senior person should express his appreciation. If the salesperson's company recently received a large order, they should be sure to thank him.

Sometimes the sales team will visit a customer with whom the salesperson's company does little business, and the salesperson is trying to improve his company's share. He should commence by telling them something about his firm and his company's recent successes, and then he should relate this to the customer's business. The customer's executives will already be wondering how this discussion can benefit their company and what is in it for them and their firm. For this reason, the salesperson should explain what his company could do to benefit them. He should then get the customer to talk about his business and his problems. Everyone likes to talk, so the salesperson should let the customer have plenty of time. The salesperson will often be told more at this level about future plans that will affect his business than he has learned from his normal customer contacts.

The salesperson's overall objective is to maximize the amount of business his company does with this firm. Thus his senior executive should, at a suitable time, ask the customer what could be done to increase the amount of their business. The reply can be very helpful and should be noted and followed up on.

Members of the sales delegation should remember the following:

- They should never interrupt the customer when he is talking.
- They should not answer questions put forth by someone on their own team. They should allow the customer to answer.
- They should not abruptly change the subject but should make sure the current topic is finished before shifting to another. No one from the salesperson's side should come in too quickly with a question on a different subject.
- They should not engage in side conversations.

The salesperson should always attend these meetings, because this exposure to upper-level executives will enhance his status with that customer. Also, some customers will resent the salesperson's absence from the meeting. He is the one who regularly calls on them, handles their orders, answers their complaints, and must in the final analysis implement agreements reached during these discussions among executives. The salesperson should very closely monitor the dialogue and not hesitate to discreetly make clarifying comments if he observes that a misunderstanding is about to occur. If the salesperson does not understand agreements being discussed, he should not hesitate to ask clarifying questions. Otherwise he should be unobtrusive, and he should never try to dominate the meeting.

If any promises are made or agreements reached, the salesperson should make sure the participants understand the other side's position and what is being agreed to. Usually there is not a complete understanding the first time an item is discussed in such a meeting. Executives from both sides will often talk at once, each reaching his own conclusions. The salesperson should repeat each agreement and obtain concurrence from both sides. He should write them down, and once he is back in the office he should promptly confirm in writing all agreements and make certain all promises are kept. Before mailing the letter, he should ask his executives to review it to make sure he has accurately covered the agreement. He should never include any agreements that were not discussed and resolved. The salesperson also should follow up on any new strategies devised as a result of these meetings.

Sales Examples

Example 1

One of our salespeople was asked to set up a meeting for our president with a top official of a major oil company located overseas. This meeting was arranged for a certain date, and our president traveled from the United States on that basis. When he arrived at this oil company's office, he learned there had been a mix-up, and no meeting was possible.

Example 2

As a division president, I was traveling in Southeast Asia with our local manager. While we were calling on the engineers on a new project, we were asked to come to the office of the managing director. The managing director expressed his appreciation for our visit to his company and for our assistance to his engineers. This meeting gave me an opportunity to point out that the engineers had a problem with a current project. They were attempting to justify new equipment but were hung up over a large inventory of spare parts for the old version. I told the managing director that his people were trying to buy the new systems from us but that the spare parts inventory was a big stumbling block. He replied, "That is no problem." I told him that his engineers certainly felt it was a big hurdle. He repeated that it was no problem.

A few days later, we were given the order for this equipment, because the inventory problem had suddenly disappeared. I am not sure it would have disappeared so quickly if we had not had the opportunity during our meeting to point out the difficulty to their top executive. As division president, my attendance at the meeting allowed us to be invited to the managing director's office, which otherwise would not have occurred.

Example 3

I was asked one time to set up a meeting between one of our executives and the chief engineer of a large company. My firm had been doing some work at a high level with the company and had involved them on a large project. We felt we had done them a lot of favors and, therefore, expected something in return—namely, more business. I arranged the meeting and accompanied our executive, but we were greeted very coldly by the chief engineer. He obviously did not feel any obligation whatsoever to us as the result of our recent collaboration. He was, in fact, antagonistic and hostile. It was the coldest meeting I ever attended.

The point is that I did not ask our top executive enough questions ahead of time to find out from him why he thought this company was beholden to us. If I had, perhaps the conversation could have been steered in a different direction, so that we could have gotten our point across and increased our business with this customer. As it turned out, it was not a useful meeting. Meetings between executives can be disastrous unless they are well prepared and well planned.

Example 4

One of our customers had broken a crankshaft and needed a replacement on an urgent basis to get his machine in operation. The customer inquired through our spare parts department and was given a delivery date of six months. I became involved, went to a senior vice president, and then obtained a delivery of three months, which greatly enhanced our position with the customer. If I had not gotten involved, the delivery time would have remained six months.

Example 5

One of my colleagues had stopped working on an order because the factory told him that they could not ship until December, and the customer required October delivery. When one of the top executives learned of this, he told the salesperson to go get the order and let him worry about the delivery, because we could indeed make it in October. The salesperson obtained the order based on October shipment, and we met our committed delivery. If the executive had not gotten involved, this business would have been lost.

Example 6

We sold equipment in Southeast Asia and gave the customer two prices: $5.8 million if they made progress payments, and $6.4 million without progress payments. Even though we received the commitment overseas, the formal purchase order had to be written and issued domestically. When the local purchasing people got involved, they started trying to renegotiate the contract with the salesperson handling the account. When I learned this, I insisted on attending all subsequent meetings.

The customer's contention was that we were charging too much interest and, therefore, we had too high a price if they made no progress payments. I told the customer that we quoted the people overseas two prices, and they had chosen the higher price with no progress payments. I told them I would still give them the same choice, but they could not have the best of both worlds, that is, a lower price and no progress payments. If I had not gotten involved, I am quite sure we would have ended up making concessions that would have cost us money.

Example 7

We had received a very large order in October calling for progress payments and escalation. The order was received directly from a large American oil company, which later turned the project over to an engineering concern on the West Coast. This firm began to try to renegotiate the contract. By the time I became involved, seven or eight months had passed. I attended the meeting on the West Coast and gave everybody a chance to say everything they wanted to say. Then I told them that at the risk of losing the order, we had rejected these same requests before receiving the order last October. I further commented that they surely did not expect us to make these concessions now that we had had the order in our hands for seven or eight months. This ended the conversation, but if I had not gotten involved, surely a concession of some kind would have been made.

Hopefully, if a salesperson arranges these meetings, does a good briefing job, and gets his story across, he will impress the customer favorably. Furthermore, the salesperson's executives will come away from these sessions with suggestions on how he can better handle this account and obtain more orders. These top-level visits can do a lot to improve the overall relations between the two companies and, if conducted properly, can increase the amount of business with that customer.

Summary

A salesperson should involve his superiors

- when he foresees a potential problem or when he has an actual problem;
- when customers visit his plant;
- at trade shows and conventions;
- by scheduling meetings in the customers' offices.

The salesperson should never feel that involving his executives diminishes his status in any way. It will actually enhance his standing both with his customers and within his own company.

46

Seize Sales Opportunities

A salesperson should never make himself a bore by selling with every breath, because soon customers may either dread seeing him or ignore him. However, a salesperson should be ready to seize golden opportunities and discreetly make his points to important people he may not normally have a chance to see.

Chance encounters may catch a salesperson unprepared, and he may miss an excellent opportunity. A salesperson may run into someone he does not normally see because that person is too high in the customer's organization. In these situations he should be ready to quickly say a few key words about his products and his company. Certainly, he would not want to give a full sales pitch to a top-level executive at this point. However, a few key phrases or reasons why his products are best and involve less risk could tip the scales in the salesperson's favor. This is especially true if a big job is in its final stages. This is always a good time for a salesperson to point out how closely he will follow his project through his organization and why the customer is better off buying from him. He must be sincere in these comments and must always follow up and deliver.

A salesperson should memorize several versions of his sales pitch on each product and model. The first version is the full-length and full-size format, given in formal presentations in a customer's office, or in a meeting room when there is sufficient time and opportunity. There also should be at least two other versions, with each substantially shorter than the full-length one. The shortest version should be very brief, with just a few important comments that will not bore or delay even a chief executive during chance encounters. The salesperson could say:

- The reliability of his products is the best available.
- He is offering well-proven products.
- His product's efficiency is higher than competitive units.
- His company has sold many of these machines.
- A certain company just chose his products.
- His product delivery is timely.
- His company has plenty of shop space.
- His company just opened a warehouse or a service center in the area in which this product will be installed.
- His company just signed a new three-year labor contract and thus has no union problems.

Chance encounters may also give a salesperson an opportunity to ask questions.

Chance encounters may also give a salesperson an opportunity to ask questions. They can vary and should be tailored to each situation. They can enable the salesperson to discreetly identify new angles to develop with the people he ordinarily contacts. The salesperson should be prepared for these unpredictable encounters. A response to short, courteous comments at such times can be very revealing. The salesperson should have in mind questions suitable for such occasions. The salesperson could ask his customer the following:

- Will you move ahead quickly with this project?
- Will your people make a decision soon?
- Do you or your people have any objections to our product?
- Have you ever been closely associated with our products?
- Have you ever been closely associated with competitive products?

These brief sales pitches will also be useful during social, courtesy, or protocol visits when top executives from the salesperson's company visit the senior executives in his customer's company. This should occur on a planned basis and preferably not while an active job is unfolding. The salesperson cannot and should not expect his company president to do his sales job for him. However, he can prepare a few key sentences that he would like to have mentioned, or *threaded in*, at the top. He could even mention these himself if he is at the meeting. Although these comments should be brief, they can be very effective if well chosen.

Summary

The salesperson should take advantage of unexpected encounters to get his points across. The contest for a big order is almost always very close, and minor points can tip the scales in the salesperson's favor. The salesperson should have a very concise version of his sales talk ready to discuss with a customer at short notice. He should always be ready for an opportunity to get his sales points across.

47

Close the Sale

Although many words have been written on the subject of closing a sale, most are useless to a salesperson whose customers are engineers and top executives. They tend to abhor even the slightest pressure. The salesperson must be very careful, or he will not only lose the current order but any future business as well. On the other hand, many salespeople who do an otherwise satisfactory job never get around to asking for the order. Consequently, they do a lousy job of closing the sale.

The salesperson is usually selling to a committee, or at least, a committee must often ratify the purchase. Thus he must be certain that he has done his selling verbally and in writing over a long period of time to all the members he can contact.

Most professionals make up their minds gradually over an extended period of time. Sometimes they virtually already know what they will buy when the inquiry is issued because of past experiences and impressions, especially of the salespeople involved. Even so, the salesperson should remember that fear of making the wrong purchase decision is uppermost in the minds of the decision makers. All of a salesperson's previous sales pitches should, therefore, have been directed toward assuring them that the salesperson's company will deliver as promised.

At this point the salesperson should have already demonstrated to the customers that his product is the most conservative, the most proven, and the most efficient. The salesperson should have convinced them that his product is more likely than all the others to do the job best, offering the least risk, the least downtime, and the lowest maintenance costs. Having done all this, the salesperson should then do the following:

1. He should ask for the order.
2. He should ask if the customer has any objections to his proposal, product, delivery, or any other aspect of business. He must listen carefully and patiently to the response. By listening attentively to make sure he understands, and by asking questions about the customer's misgivings, the salesperson can go a long way toward answering any doubts. The salesperson should take the customer's objections seriously and should not downplay as minor any objections that the customer considers to be major. The salesperson should answer each objection satisfactorily and completely.
3. The salesperson should ask for a letter of intent to tie down the price and delivery, pending ratification by the committee or board of directors.
4. The salesperson should ask for a verbal commitment.
5. The salesperson should offer to proceed with the engineering and settlement of details to save delivery time, assuming the customers are leaning his way. With their approval, he could get drawings released early, order castings, and hold the price firm.

The reactions a salesperson gets when he makes these inquiries can be extremely revealing. These inquiries will often flush out serious problems the customer has with price, delivery, or even product reliability. The reactions are a good gauge of how the salesperson stands on the project.

When the salesperson asks for the order, it is very important for him to do so discreetly and without any pressure. Alternately, he could offer to proceed as outlined above as early in the discussions as possible. This should be done just as soon as the salesperson has completed his sales presentations and he feels that his customer has had time to analyze the bids. The salesperson must use all of his resources at this time, because the race with his competitors will almost always be very close. There is no reward for second place, however, and it is small consolation to a salesperson to learn that he lost the order by a narrow margin.

If the prospect has not yet been convinced to buy from the salesperson, he will in all probability bring up one of his stock resistance phrases. This could include such comments as, "Your price is too high," or "Your price is higher than the competition's price." Then the customer will sit back and watch the salesperson squirm while responding. Many times the buyer is not serious; he is just stalling or sparring. He wants more time to think and more reasons to make a specific product choice. The customer usually will not make up his mind until the salesperson satisfies him on every point.

The customer usually will not make up his mind until the salesperson satisfies him on every point.

A salesperson should expect resistance to making a purchase commitment and should take it in stride. He should never fear or dislike resistance on the part of the customer. The salesperson should be prepared to recognize and handle it in a friendly fashion. Doing this will help him make the sale.

The salesperson must overcome each effort at resistance courteously and patiently with facts based on his product knowledge. He should move the discussion to an unassailable feature of his products if he does not know the answer to one of the customer's objections. However, the salesperson should never bluff or ignore the problem. He must obtain the correct answer from his experts and then respond. He must show the customer what is in it for him, but he must do this discreetly so the conversation does not get stuck on

the resistance. He should offer again to put the product in production so as to speed up delivery and avoid delays in the schedule. He can point out that a day's delay in entering orders for castings or forgings or other long lead-times items can result in a week or longer delivery delay.

When a salesperson is given the indication that he is the successful vendor, he must strike fast. He must get something in writing immediately to secure the order. Too many things can happen to upset his order unless he proceeds decisively. The salesperson should ask for a fax of intent or an order number, or he should send a fax to his customer confirming his verbal agreement. If the salesperson receives this verbal assurance by phone, he should schedule a meeting right away to complete and finalize the order.

The more discussions the salesperson has with his customer, and the more correspondence they have exchanged, the less likely it is that his order will be cancelled. Nevertheless, the salesperson should stay in close touch every day until the formal purchase order is received. He should never allow periods of silence, even after he receives a verbal order or even a purchase order number.

48

How to Know When to Stop Selling

Knowing when to stop selling is one of the most important duties of a salesperson. It is usually decisive and is difficult and frustrating for a salesperson to do well. There are many factors a salesperson should evaluate before taking this step.

Before stopping his sales efforts, a salesperson should first exhaust all of his resources and ingenuity thinking up new proposals to offer or reasons for additional discussions with his customer. He must mentally review the job in great detail, examining all aspects of the project. He must analyze the inquiry, his proposal, his strategy to date, his customer's reactions, the competitive products offered, his competitor's actions, and any feedback. Doing this will hopefully remind him of something else he could do to favorably influence the job in his direction.

There are other steps a salesperson should take before ceasing his sales efforts. The salesperson should keep repeating the salient features or outstanding advantages of his products, showing how they will benefit the customer. The salesperson must show the customer how he will profit if he buys from the salesperson. The salesperson should repeatedly stress why the customer's risk is less with the salesperson's machines, and how his products are uniquely better. The salesperson should remember that the fear of buying the wrong thing is pervasive among decision makers.

The customer usually remembers little of what he has read or heard only once. The salesperson must keep repeating his product's outstanding advantages and the benefits they provide the customer. He must put these benefits in writing and send them to the key people. The customer meets with many salespeople and hears many sales pitches during the unfolding of a large job. He usually forgets much of what has been verbally presented.

By the salesperson's actions and during his many conversations with the customer, he should have demonstrated that he would look after the customer's order better than anyone else. The salesperson hopes to convince the customer that his service during and after the sale would make the difference.

Unless the salesperson has already committed his company to these benefits, there are other things the salesperson could offer:

1. The salesperson could offer to train the customer's operators or maintenance people in the salesperson's plant and give presentations on maintenance at the customer's job site or other location.
2. The salesperson could offer to appoint a project manager to continuously monitor the job throughout the engineering, manufacturing, and commissioning period.
3. The salesperson could provide monthly progress reports as the job moves through the manufacturing cycle.

4. The salesperson could take the customers to another job site to observe the product in use and to hear from contented users.
5. The salesperson could have satisfied users call the customer with testimonials, or he could give the customer additional names to call to verify the reliability of his product.
6. The salesperson could offer to follow the job personally through his plant to help avoid any delays.
7. The salesperson could accompany the customer's representatives to all production or engineering review meetings.
8. The salesperson could offer new energy-saving or noise-abatement provisions in his products.
9. On large or complex jobs, the salesperson could offer to assign an experienced serviceperson to this project. He could offer to have the serviceperson on hand during the final stages of assembly and testing. He could also have this same person work with the customer's people in the packing and labeling of various components prior to shipment. Finally, he could designate this same person to follow the products to the job site and remain during installation and commissioning.
10. Some of these concessions will require management approval. If so, the salesperson should obtain approval prior to offering them, but most of these do not represent any great additional expense to his company. These approvals may not always be easy for the salesperson to obtain. If he feels strongly that they will help him get the order, he should not give up. Often management will rush in with concessions when the job is going down the tube. The salesperson should convince management to make these moves while they will still do some good. The salesperson must be reasonable and discreet in his requests, but not bashful.

All of these efforts are designed to enable a salesperson to keep a dialogue going with the customer and allow them to meet regularly. This gives the salesperson the following advantages:

- He will be able to repeat his product benefits and features.
- He will be able to submit any new incentives he can offer.

- He will keep himself, his company, and his products in front of the customer so the customer will not forget. Hopefully he will be the last salesperson the customer sees before a purchase decision is made.
- The salesperson will be on top of any changes or shifts in the job requirements.
- If the salesperson continues to visit the customer, he will be able to monitor and hopefully to discover early any commercial moves or actions by his competition. Also, the salesperson may see his competition or evidence that he has been there.

The salesperson should always try to be certain that he is the last one to talk to the decision makers before their final meeting to make a purchase decision. Research shows that the last inputs are the most influential and can indeed be decisive. The last salesperson to discuss his product gains points and has the best chance of receiving the order.

Every day is important during the closing stages. Thus the salesperson cannot afford periods of blackouts when he does not know what is going on. If they do occur, it is usually bad news for the salesperson. If his competitors are behind, they may be catching up. The salesperson must, therefore, keep in touch and keep plugging away without allowing long periods of inattention. Even if he thinks he is ahead, he cannot let up or his competition will catch up and pass him. He must keep in touch with his customers.

Research shows that the last inputs are the most influential and can indeed be decisive.

When a salesperson calls his customer during this critical time, either for a meeting or for a telephone discussion, he should not leave his number unless it is absolutely necessary. The salesperson should avoid this, if possible, because it leaves the initiative with his customer. The customer may or may not call back, and the salesperson might be left to wait and worry. It is better for a salesperson to tell the customer's office assistant or the answering machine that he will be away from the phone and would prefer to call the customer back later. Of course, the salesperson can only use this procedure for a limited time. If the decision maker is still unavailable, the salesperson may eventually be forced to leave his number.

When the salesperson calls, he should always have something else to offer or say. He should not merely ask where the job stands. The salesperson can always leave a few comments on the customer's answering machine.

Occasionally, phone conversations are better than face-to-face meetings, especially if the salesperson is in good shape with his customer. The closing stage of a job is traumatic for the customer, also. He is being barraged and pulled at from all sides. Often, the customer can and will tell the salesperson more on the phone than he will in person. It may be awkward for him to be seen in a meeting with vendors at this crucial time, or it may even be prevented by company rules. The salesperson should keep this in mind. These guidelines may vary, and face-to-face meetings should, of course, be arranged when possible. However, the salesperson should not overlook using the telephone at this crucial stage.

The decision may have to move through several approval levels. If appropriate, the salesperson should try to monitor its progress at each level to keep it on track and determine if the decision is going in his favor. At this time he should always keep in touch with the people favorable to his cause, even though the action may have moved out of their immediate area. They will still follow the project and will usually be consulted, especially if a decision is reversed or even if a reversal is being considered.

Even when all of these avenues have been exhausted by the salesperson, it can be difficult for him to know when to stop selling. His inclination and training are to not slow down until he has received an order number, a letter of intent, or very strong indications that he will get the order. On the other hand, there is a limit to the effort a salesperson can put into one project. It is possible that the salesperson is receiving no feedback and the customer is showing no interest. Perhaps the customer refuses to see the salesperson or to return his calls. If the salesperson has the feeling he has lost, then perhaps he should let up, back away, and move on to more productive efforts. However, before doing so, he should ask for the order. He will usually be astonished at what new information this will flush out.

While a salesperson may not always get the order, his chances are best if he has done his homework and has taken good care of the customer over a long period of time. The better he has done his job in this regard, the easier it will be for him to follow the job in the closing stages, and the better his chances of success.

The salesperson should not neglect other salespeople outside his company who are also calling on this customer. Sometimes they will hear or learn something he will miss. It is a good idea to stay in close touch with them at this time. Early knowledge can enable the salesperson to take corrective steps to avoid losing the order. He may learn through these sources that the decision is going against him, even though the customer is not ready to tell him directly. With this indirect knowledge, he can decide whether to renew his efforts or to reluctantly curtail his activity on this project.

49

Report the Status of Active Jobs

A salesperson is constantly called upon by his supervisors to give the status of active jobs, particularly the larger ones. Most of these jobs drag out over several months. The salesperson should be careful that he does not report the situation too optimistically. The reasons for this are manifold:

1. The situation is usually fluid and can change rapidly because of many things, including price-cutting or other commercial moves by the salesperson's competitors.
2. Delays can allow competitors time to catch up.

3. If the salesperson reports the situation as overly favorable, he can become overconfident, which could reduce his sales intensity, dedication, and effort. The salesperson may even take too harsh an attitude with the customer when additional information or concessions are requested.
4. The initial impression can be misleading, even to the most experienced salesperson. For example, he may receive a very favorable response from his first discussions on his original bid. However, as other people and customer departments examine his quotation in more depth and analyze the competitive bids, this could change quickly.
5. It destroys a salesperson's negotiating position with his management. Perhaps the salesperson reported that his proposal was the favorite and would probably receive the recommendation, and then later asked for a price reduction, better delivery, or other concessions. It will be much harder for the salesperson to obtain any concessions if he has already reported an extremely favorable position on the project. Management may conclude these additional concessions are unnecessary. The salesperson eroded his bargaining position with management.
6. The salesperson's optimistic attitude might be communicated unintentionally to the customer, who has the final say and might resent an overconfident salesperson.

Another important reason that a salesperson should be guarded in his reports is because each time his information is repeated upward in his organization, it will become more optimistic. If he reports that the situation looks favorable, after this has been repeated upward in his organization two or three times, it will sound as if he has the order. Then if the salesperson does not get the order, he really will be criticized. Some will even say, "You had the job sold and then you let it get away."

The salesperson's reported account of how he stands on a job should always be much less favorable than what he really thinks it is.

The salesperson's reported account of how he stands on a job should always be much less favorable than what he really thinks it is. His report should be guarded. He should never report that the situation looks really good until he has been told he is successful and the order is being written for the salesperson's product. This caution is necessary, because any potentially negative information included with an extremely rosy report will be ignored. Only the favorable or optimistic portion will be heard and repeated. Furthermore, it is almost impossible to keep everyone fully apprised as events unfold on a job. Therefore, if a salesperson downgrades his chances when talking to others, he will be in a better position in the long run.

Summary

The salesperson should, of course, follow all large projects very closely so that he always knows their current status. However, he must be careful how he reports this information internally. He should be guarded in his reports and should not be overly optimistic.

50

Practice Discretion

A big order or project involving a lot of products is like a jigsaw puzzle, and no one has all the pieces. The salesperson does not, and neither do his competitors. However, one small thing accidentally or indiscreetly revealed by a salesperson might help the competitors fill in or complete an entire crucial area of the puzzle.

A salesperson must be very careful what he says outside his company during the active stage of a big job. Most professions span small areas. While the salesperson may not be talking directly to his competitor, he could easily be talking to someone who is his competitor's good friend. A salesperson must be cautious when talking in waiting rooms, reception areas, airport or hotel lobbies, or restaurants and bars. He must show discretion when talking on cell phones, in restrooms, on airplanes, and whenever other people are close by. He should even be careful not to speak too loudly when talking on the telephone in hotel rooms. Some walls are very thin.

While the salesperson may not be talking directly to his competitor, he could easily be talking to someone who is his competitor's good friend.

It can be difficult for a salesperson to be quiet, especially if he has learned good news and feels he is in good shape on a project. He may innocently relate this to another salesperson or specialist who is calling on his customer. Unfortunately, this person could be a friend to his competitors. This bit of information might cause his competitor to intensify his efforts or make a commercial move, such as reducing the price, which could cost the salesperson the order.

These dangerous conduits are not always in the sales and marketing areas. The salesperson should caution other people in his organization against passing information along to the salespeople who call on them. A lot of salespeople call on his organization, often in the purchasing and manufacturing departments. Vital information can leak through this channel and get back to his competitor. Most sales engineers are on guard with other salespeople, especially competitors. However, they sometimes talk too freely with other professionals they meet inside and outside their own company. Usually there is little danger, but a salesperson should not take chances. The salesperson should think before he reveals details on an active job and should probably talk about other things.

There is even a limit to talking to people inside a salesperson's own company. He should choose carefully which people he entrusts with information about the latest job status. As he works a large project, especially in the closing stages, he should keep quiet even within his own company. He should tell only his superiors and the others who absolutely need to know.

Even when a salesperson receives a large order, he should not broadcast it too loudly or too quickly outside his own company. He should let the competitor find out independently. The salesperson should wait until the products are in production and far enough along so that the order is safe from cancellation. Some competitors run in and slash the price when they learn they are losing the project. The salesperson should not help them by telling them he has the order. Furthermore, the customer does not always want the news spread around. It does not serve the salesperson to broadcast this information. He should be discreet and keep quiet about the progress of an active job and all orders placed with him.

Sales Examples

Example 1

On one job, we were able to reverse a decision and sell our products because we learned from the successful salesperson right after the order was placed that he had been selected. The customer was still unwilling to reveal the chosen vendor, but the salesperson who had received the order said too much and talked too soon. There were other special circumstances, but without this early warning, we would have been unable to use this information to reverse the decision for a substantial order.

Example 2

On another occasion, I was working a job and faced the usual fierce competition. One company had always received all the orders. In the closing stages, the customer's project manager called and invited me to his office. Once there, I was announced by the receptionist and took the elevator to the sixth floor. As I got off the elevator, I was hailed by my chief competitor, who apparently had just left the project manager's office.

Almost breathlessly he said, "You had better be ready to answer some real tough questions." He went on to enumerate all of the things he had just been asked. Then he added, "I did not know any of the answers and must go to my office to obtain the information."

I replied by saying, "Those are tough questions," and hurried to the manager's office.

This gentleman always wanted to say a few words about hunting, fishing, and the weather. I listened, but all the time I was mentally preparing my replies to the questions I knew I was about to hear. Sure enough, he asked me exactly what my competitor said he would ask. Because of the few minutes' warning, however, I was able to accurately and calmly answer all his questions.

The project manager wrote down my replies, and when he finished, he said, "I am astonished that you could give me all the answers immediately. I just asked your competitor the same questions, and he had to go to his office to develop the answers."

We received this order—our first with this customer—partly because the competitor talked too much.

Many customers realize that knowledgeable salespeople are good sources of information because they travel extensively to call on other customers in the industry. The salesperson must, therefore, be discreet in what he repeats in conversations with his customers. Usually, it is not important who said something. Therefore, it is almost always advisable for a salesperson to leave the names of specific companies or individuals out of a repeated conversation or a story. The possible exception is if the salesperson has learned the information from published sources.

The salesperson also should avoid repeating bad or unpleasant news. He should concentrate on relaying positive or complimentary news and information. He should not gossip or pass along unfavorable information. Even though a salesperson was not told that something was confidential or should not be repeated, he should not necessarily repeat it freely. He must use good judgment and common sense, and he should take time to stop and think. If the information could possibly cause anyone any embarrassment or unhappiness, he should not repeat the information. A salesperson never wants to have a reputation of repeating bad or unpleasant information about someone.

Summary

- A salesperson should keep quiet about details of an active job.
- A salesperson should never repeat these details outside his company.
- Inside his own company, he should tell only those who absolutely need to know.
- Even after receiving an order, a salesperson should not talk about it too soon. He should wait until he is sure the order cannot be canceled.
- The salesperson must be discreet in what he repeats among customers, and even then, he should leave names out of the conversation.

V

Follow Up

51

Obtain Performance Feedback

To be successful, a salesperson must be able to obtain valuable feedback from his customers. This requires that he ingratiate himself with his customers so that his customers want to help by giving him information they do not give to just anyone.

How can a salesperson accomplish this? Here are a few suggestions:

1. He can help the customer do his job better or more easily.
2. He can respect the customer's time.
3. He can respond promptly to all the customer's requests.
4. He can demonstrate keen interest and willingness to go out of his way to assist the customer when there is a problem.
5. He can develop a close relationship with the customer and become a person the customer can talk to in confidence and trust not to reveal the source of any sensitive information given.
6. He can demonstrate that he is a person of integrity and trust.
7. He can develop a good rapport with his customer. A salesperson with good customer rapport receives useful, accurate feedback and a lot of orders.

Sometimes a salesperson calls on a customer for years and never obtains any information except that which is issued formally. Another salesperson will obtain very valuable information after just a few months. To be outstanding, a salesperson must receive good feedback from his customers in the following areas:

1. **Products sold.** This allows a salesperson to monitor the performance of the products and correct any problems.
2. **Active jobs.** A salesperson needs feedback on sales he is trying to close.
3. **The company's image.** The salesperson needs feedback on his company's overall image with his customers so he can obtain testimonials.
4. **Low-producing or inactive accounts.** The salesperson needs feedback on accounts in which he is receiving little or no business.
5. **New applications or products.** The salesperson needs feedback on new applications for what he now sells or new products or services his company could provide.
6. **The competition.** The salesperson needs feedback concerning his competition.

Feedback to Pursue

Products sold

If a person expects to be successful in selling, he must maintain close contact with his customers so he can obtain useful feedback on products he has sold or is trying to sell. This process should start long before the sale, so the salesperson can be certain he understands what the customer expects from his products. This is very important. If the customer purchases a product expecting it to do something it was never designed to do, and cannot do, the salesperson is in real trouble. The customer will lose large sums of money, but the salesperson will suffer the most as a consequence of this misapplication. The smarter, the more sophisticated, and the more experienced a salesperson's customers are, the easier it should be for him to avoid this pitfall. However, a salesperson must be more careful with the less-experienced customers.

Since the salesperson knows his product well and is familiar with its capabilities and limitations, it is his responsibility to make sure he offers the right product for the job. He can thus avoid unrealistic expectations from the customer, misapplications, or outright mistakes. This can be done only through continuous feedback and interchange of ideas prior to product selection and prior to submitting a quotation.

This feedback should continue after the product is sold and while it is being engineered, installed, and commissioned. It should intensify after start-up and during actual operation. The salesperson should report any shortcomings or defects immediately to the appropriate levels in his company. Minor shortcomings or improvements may be too late to rectify on this order, but they can often be reflected with little or no additional cost in all units manufactured later. The salesperson also should occasionally visit the plants where his product is in service. He should ask the people who look after it daily what maintenance, installation, or other problems they have and what improvement suggestions they can offer. This should be an ongoing exercise. It is not something a salesperson should do once and then forget about.

When applicable, the salesperson should also visit with the customer's engineers who formulate the plant design, and perhaps the draftsperson who put the drawings together. These people may have ideas for product improvements.

For example, they may suggest that with certain minor changes, the product could be easier and less expensive to install. Sometimes the salesperson can initiate changes that cost his company very little, or nothing, but will save time and money for the customer. This will be to the salesperson's distinct advantage on future jobs. It will demonstrate to the customer that the salesperson is not merely concerned with obtaining the order. He also cares about how his product operates, how it can be installed more economically, and the service received from it. This can give him a competitive edge, since it will indicate he is in sales for the long term, not just to make a sale today.

When a salesperson sells to a new customer, it is even more important for him to call often after his product is installed to see how it is doing. This will impress the customer, since it makes the salesperson stand out among other, less-dedicated salespeople. Most salespeople get so busy that they never take time to call the plant after products are installed to ask if there are any problems with what was supplied. The salesperson will make points with his customer when he does something for him or shows interest when there is not an order pending. It shows good faith and a sincere attitude.

If a customer has a problem with the product, the salesperson should be the first to know so that he can sort it out. If he stays in touch with his customers and has good feedback, problems can usually be solved with a minimum of damage to his reputation. A salesperson never wants to hear about his customer's problems with the product from a third party, either inside or outside his company. If a salesperson's superior learns about a product problem before he does, it usually indicates that the salesperson has not developed and maintained good relations with that customer. If the salesperson does not learn early about troubles and unfavorable reports, and quickly deal with them, the results can be devastating. A salesperson with good feedback will be the first to know and can quickly initiate the necessary corrective action.

If a salesperson's superior learns about a product problem before he does, it usually indicates that the salesperson has not developed and maintained good relations with that customer.

Many home office people view complaints as a nuisance that wastes the time and effort of many people. The salesperson, however, must respond to all unfavorable reports, because his attitude can turn adversity into advantages for his company. Trouble, properly and promptly handled, can be a blessing in disguise. Complaints can actually enhance the reputation of the salesperson and his firm, but only if they are learned about early and sorted out quickly. The salesperson should make it easy for his customers to register their displeasure. He should go see them or contact them frequently so that he will receive useful feedback. Toll-free numbers will help a salesperson's customers. They can call to register complaints at the time they occur, which will generate a greater response than waiting for complaint letters or verbal comments made much later.

Active jobs

This topic was covered in a previous chapter, but a few additional suggestions are given here. Some of the most vital feedback a salesperson is expected to obtain is on an active job after he has submitted his quotation and while the customer is moving toward a decision. This is the time when a salesperson needs a lot of friends who will, without violating their company rules, help him by letting him know how things stand with the quotation.

Sometimes a salesperson can salvage an order if he promptly learns that his competitor has lowered his price, improved his delivery, modified his warranty, or otherwise made his bid more attractive. This is also a time when the salesperson should very carefully phrase his questions so that he is not misled by the replies. The quantity and quality of the feedback a salesperson obtains is a good indication of how well he has been handling the account. It also indicates how many friends he has and how well he and his company are perceived by the customer. If the salesperson is receiving almost no feedback, that is usually bad news. Usually some other salesperson quoting the job does know what is going on in the decision process.

This feedback on active jobs can be obtained in direct meetings with the customer. However, there are times a salesperson can learn more on the telephone. Buyers, engineers, and others may not want to be seen often with the salesperson while bids are being analyzed, but they will usually talk to him on the phone.

The company's image

A salesperson should be continually looking for ways to improve his company's overall image with his customers. He should always be on the lookout to obtain testimonials supporting the high quality of the products, the good designs, or its on-time deliveries. If a customer has had success with a salesperson's products or his company, he should ask for a letter commending his firm. This will not be easy to get, because most companies have policies against any sort of endorsements. Sometimes, however, they will give written reports or letters. The salesperson should, therefore, always be on the lookout for people who will give him these invaluable documents. Alternately, he should identify people who will give him verbal recommendations. If he is unable to get written endorsements, verbal recommendations are the next best thing.

If a salesperson does pinpoint people who are willing to give good recommendations, he should not pass out their names and phone numbers indiscriminately. When the occasion arises and he wants to rely upon one of these people, he should first talk again directly to the individual. He should remind the person of his willingness to help with a recommendation and ask if it is permissible for the prospective customer to call. The salesperson should also ask when it would be a convenient time for the call. This will give the salesperson an opportunity to remind the individual of some of the outstanding features of the product. In this way the salesperson will help him give the prospective customer a good report. This will prepare the individual to receive a call and will help ensure that it does not occur at an inopportune time.

Useful feedback from customers will help a salesperson accumulate testimonials that can be used to sell his products. A firm should, of course, never be quoted in writing without permission. However, a salesperson can leave names out and speak in more general terms. For example, the salesperson could say that "a leading energy company manager said..." and in this way promote his company and its products.

Feedback can also be used in a company's trade journal ads. Results from operating plants can be obtained by sending service people to observe and report on the customer's reaction to the products. Reports during maintenance or annual turnarounds are very valuable. Accomplishing this will require intensive follow-up and perseverance on the salesperson's part. Questions should be asked and follow-up done with customers even on a company's best products. Nothing is so good that it cannot be improved. A salesperson must be alert to possible improvements and make certain those inside his company do not ignore this information.

In order to obtain in-depth feedback, the salesperson should occasionally ask his customers if they are having any trouble with his company in the invoicing area. Sometimes difficulty in this area goes on for some time without salespeople hearing about it. This can occur because invoices, credits, and payments are handled directly between accountants and financial people in the selling and buying organizations.

Low-producing or inactive Accounts

A salesperson should be particularly alert to obtain feedback from a customer with whom he is doing little or no business. Someone has found the key and is selling to them. Someone is doing all the right things and obtaining a lot of business. The salesperson should find out why.

In attempting to find this out, he should ask more than just one person. He should ask several people, and not just those in the purchasing, engineering, and operating departments, why their company buys from the competitor. If the salesperson perseveres, he will eventually learn his competitor's secret and thus determine what he must do to obtain orders or increase his share of business.

The salesperson should list of all his accounts that have a high potential but a low share of business. Then he should formulate and diligently execute plans to increase that business.

New applications or products

In the course of serving his customers, the salesperson should always try to foresee what is around the corner in his business so he can possibly offer new products or services. He should study his customers and try to identify new trends in what the customers will purchase. This is best determined by continually asking questions about expansion plans, operating procedures, or changes in purchasing practices. Customers' needs and requirements continue to vary. They will often be in the market to purchase items they are not now using that are similar to what the salesperson's company produces. The salesperson should be alert to this, because often he can uncover new opportunities for his company. Good feedback will tell the salesperson what items the customers are now buying elsewhere or what new products they will be purchasing that he might be able to supply.

The competition

The salesperson should also monitor what his competition is up to in the marketplace and report this to his superiors. A salesperson who obtains good feedback will always know what his competitors are up to so as to keep his management appraised. A salesperson should not be obsessed with his competition, but he should closely and continuously monitor what they are doing. Timely and accurate information in this area not only can often help salvage a current order but also can influence his strategy on future projects. It is important for a salesperson to have useful feedback about his competitors.

The value of feedback

Feedback can often be valuable in changing a salesperson's operating procedures as well as his products. He must continue to ask questions and solicit his customers' input in these areas. At the very least, it demonstrates that the salesperson cares about his product and customers. His customers will reciprocate a lack of respect and concern on the part of the salesperson, and soon they will not buy from him. If a salesperson does not care about his customers, all too soon his customers will not care about him.

Sales Examples

The following are some examples of how good feedback resulted in a lot of business.

Example 1

We were working a job several years ago and had been asked to bid again on the project. I was waiting until the last minute to turn in our price to reduce the danger of leakage. Just prior to the deadline, I received a call from someone telling me what price level our competitor had submitted. This person was not with the customer organization; instead, he was with the engineering contractor who would install the products. I never knew why he called, but apparently we had befriended him in the past, and he wanted us to receive the order. We did, based on his feedback.

Example 2

Until 25 years ago, all compressors in certain processes of petrochemical plants were reciprocating. My company had worked closely with an engineering contractor who wanted to build increasingly larger plants. Toward this end, my company introduced centrifugal compressors in this process, and as a result, obtained more than 70% of this business during the next 20 years. Good feedback on new trends in our industry enabled us to scoop the competition. Our lead was so great, the competitor never recovered. The salesperson who did this made a valuable contribution to his company.

Example 3

Historically, compressor cylinders on pipeline compressors were linked in a manifold with a suction and a discharge bottle several feet above and below the cylinders. All customers were experiencing continuing pulsation problems and ran many field tests to investigate the cause. A lot of formal research was done on this problem. We had good feedback from these tests and research and discussed the results internally with our designers. Our engineers determined that the shorter the risers on the connections to these bottles, the lower the pulsation. As a result, we designed special compressor cylinders that incorporated the pulsation bottles within the compressor cylinders. This enabled us to sell a lot of products we would not otherwise have sold. This new product came about because of good feedback from our customers.

Summary

To be outstanding, a salesperson must have good feedback on the following:

- his products
- active jobs
- his company
- low-producing accounts
- new applications or products
- his competition

52

After Obtaining an Order

Some salespeople, after obtaining a large order they have worked on for many months, spend too much time rejoicing and telling everyone about this success. Certainly, this is a time to celebrate, but it should be brief. A salesperson should quickly return to reality and get back to work on this job as well as the next. He should keep quiet about this order outside his company until he is sure no one can upset the decision.

On the order just received, the salesperson should show gratitude to everyone involved in the customer's organization. He should not keep this too limited, because usually many more people participate in the decision than he realizes. Gratitude is in short supply in this world, so the salesperson should be generous with his thanks. On large or special orders, he should thank those most closely involved by sending a note, handwritten if at all possible or by e-mail. He should do this even though he may already have thanked them verbally. The salesperson should be sure he does not leave anyone out. He must not be concerned that he might include someone who did not support him.

The salesperson also should show gratitude to the people in his own company who helped. He should show his appreciation to the application engineer, the engineering people, and especially to the young people in his organization who participated. This builds confidence and mutual respect and makes them feel more a part of the team. This will pay off handsomely when the salesperson needs their help in the future, and it is likely that he will.

A customer's anxieties build up after a large order is placed. The customer will be wondering if the product will work properly, be delivered on time, and if he selected the right product. The salesperson should make certain by his actions, his attitude, and by his factory's output that he sends the right reassuring signals to the buyer. This will help the salesperson keep the order sold and places him in a good position to obtain the customer's next order. He should not change in demeanor or attitude now that he has been given the order. He should show the same humility as before he received the order.

The salesperson must be certain he knows exactly what the customer purchased and what he expects it to do. The salesperson should also be sure the customer knows exactly what he bought and what it will do. This may sound elementary, but because of genuine misunderstandings, many orders for custom-made products turn out to be nightmares. The customer may be mad at the salesperson and his company, while the salesperson's factory people may be unhappy with the customer, with the order, and with the salesperson.

The salesperson should build and maintain a reputation for obtaining clean orders, or orders that do not leave details unspecified.

Hoping to clear up any problems after the order is received, some salespeople deliberately leave certain areas vague during the quoting and negotiating stages. This may be tempting, but it is a bad approach. Often these unspecified items are not sorted out until much too late. At this point, both sides are too far into the process to bail out, and in the end, one or both parties are angry and upset. The salesperson should build and maintain a reputation for obtaining *clean* orders, or orders that do not leave details unspecified.

Often a large job drags on for weeks or sometimes months, with many revisions both to the proposal and to the customer's specifications. All of these changes and modifications should, of course, be confirmed in writing by the salesperson as they occur. Even so, there may still be many letters and faxes to reconcile. The salesperson must be sure that these are reconciled against the bid specifications, the quotation, the purchase order, and his field requisition confirming to his factory what to build.

If it is a large order for custom-made engineered products, the salesperson should schedule a meeting as soon as possible between his technical people and the customer. He must be sure they agree on what was sold and what was purchased. After scheduling this meeting, the salesperson should prepare an agenda and send it to the customer, so it can be agreed on in advance. The customer can add any requirements he has. This will help the salesperson decide which people from his company, in addition to himself, should attend. It will also assist the customer with his manpower planning.

It is important that all areas of the job be discussed so as to eliminate misunderstandings and gray areas. Settling these details is vital. Most deliveries are tight, and in the customer's mind, the delivery clock starts immediately. The sooner the salesperson's manufacturing department knows what to build, the earlier they can begin. With engineered products, a certain amount of engineering must be done. Thus the technical details must be settled and agreed on immediately so that the engineering department can complete its work and tell the manufacturing department what to make.

The salesperson should insure that careful, complete minutes are kept as the discussions proceed. These minutes should be agreed to and signed, preferably before the meeting adjourns. Otherwise, everyone goes back to their offices, gets busy with other duties, and the formal minutes are delayed, sometimes too long.

A good approach is for the salesperson's company to prepare a revised quotation, reflecting all changes to the original bid specifications and indicating exactly what was purchased. This document can now be labeled *exact basis of order*. This revised quotation will become a very valuable document as the

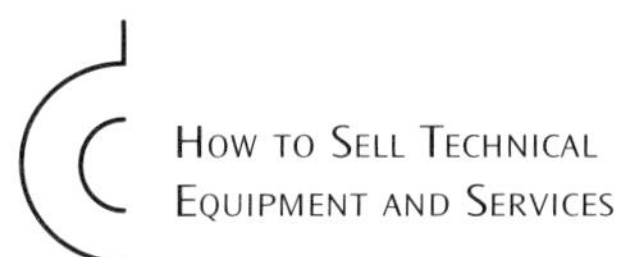

product is being manufactured, tested, commissioned, used, and even long into its operating life. If possible, a salesperson should send it by e-mail for convenience in reproducing copies.

Many subsequent orders have been lost because of unsatisfactory engineering and delivery performance on a previous contract. Sometimes poor delivery performance can be traced to late settlement of vital engineering details. This prevents the manufacturing department from knowing precisely how to proceed. Customer drawings are often late if important engineering information from the customer is delayed. Once lost, time is difficult to make up in a manufacturing cycle. Despite all precautions to the contrary, both customers and vendors tend to minimize this important consideration. In reality, it usually will cause delay. The salesperson must assume that it will cause delay and must settle all details promptly.

The salesperson should carry out the preceding steps expeditiously and in a businesslike, courteous manner. He should never change attitudes abruptly toward his customer just because he has the order. He should cordially but firmly point out that if he is to meet his delivery commitment, manufacturing must know what to build. Thus he must quickly settle all engineering and commercial details. If the customer is slow in providing this vital data, the salesperson should advise him in writing that unless it is produced by a certain time, the delivery time will have to be extended. This will usually get results. The salesperson should always remind the customer he is trying to sort out the engineering details to avoid late delivery. The salesperson must maintain the position that he is promoting the customer's cause and has his best interests at heart.

If the customer changes the specifications after the order and requests something more expensive, he should pay the difference between what was quoted and what he now wants. However, the salesperson's firm should not take advantage of the customer. Most customers are willing to pay more for legitimate changes when the subsequent charges are reasonable and when they are properly documented with explanations. This extra cost must be pointed out immediately after the change request is received. The salesperson must always be alert to new specifications or to changes in existing specifications that involve extra money. If any kind of change is requested, the possibility of extra cost should be mentioned. In no case should a salesperson proceed with a more expensive modification until the customer clearly knows the cost and possible delivery impact. The customer should authorize the change and extra charge in writing first.

If optional products were quoted, a salesperson should never proceed with any of these unless authorized by the customer. The salesperson should insist that the customer make up his mind quickly on these items and should never try to guess what he will purchase. That would put the salesperson in a no-win situation, because if he guesses wrong, he will be blamed and suffer the cancellation charges. If delivery is about to be impacted, he should let the customer know this in writing but should make certain that the customer (not the salesperson) selects the options.

If the customer's paperwork moves inordinately slowly, the salesperson can offer to send him a message by fax, letter, or e-mail advising that he is, as agreed, proceeding with the changes as outlined. He should conclude his correspondence with a phrase such as, "If this is not in exact accordance with your understanding, please notify us immediately."

It is very important for a salesperson to avoid misunderstandings. As a vendor, he will virtually always be blamed when misunderstandings occur. Enormous amounts of money are wasted each year because of these misunderstandings, with the manufacturer building one thing and the customer expecting something else. A salesperson should never allow this to happen.

The salesperson should not merely submit the engineering information to his plant and forget it. He must follow up with the contract engineer who is handling the job to see if he has any questions. The salesperson should ask the contract engineer to confirm that he has everything he requires from the salesperson and the customer, and that he understands it. If he does not, the salesperson should sort it out promptly by obtaining supplemental information from the customer.

The salesperson also should ask the contract engineer for assurances that this order is moving expeditiously through engineering. If the engineer has encountered a delay in his area, the salesperson could offer to assist him in removing any bottlenecks. The salesperson who obtained the order has a strong hand in sorting out any associated problems that arise anywhere in his organization. He should be alert and help avoid any delays on the order, and he should not hesitate to involve his top management if he observes delays occurring.

The salesperson should quickly answer any questions his factory asks about this order, because they may hold up the order until his reply is received. He should always be responsive to any questions put to him by his engineering, manufacturing, marketing, or commercial people.

After all the details have been sorted out and manufacture is underway, the salesperson should at a convenient time ask the customer the reasons he had for selecting his product. The salesperson may think he already knows the reasons, but usually he will not know all of them. This information could help him with the next sale, not only to this customer, but to others. Thus the salesperson should ask many questions in this area and should ask more than one person, so that he can obtain all of their reasons for selecting his product. This will enable him to fine-tune his sales pitches on the next similar job and to stress the advantages this customer considered paramount.

If at all possible, the salesperson should also determine which competitor was second choice, who was placed in the third position, and so on. He should discover, if possible, why the others lost. This is the ideal time for a salesperson to obtain feedback, and this information will be extremely valuable to him on the next project involving similar products and the same competitors. He should keep this information in his sales kits for future use. He can then be sure that on subsequent projects, he will focus more effectively on his competitors' shortcomings.

Some customers are reluctant to say why they gave a salesperson the order, so he should usually ask these questions in private, perhaps to just one individual. If he feels that the person may not want to tell him too much, then he could ask why the person thinks other companies buy this kind of product from the salesperson's company. This will often enable the individual to camouflage his reasons for buying the salesperson's goods. If a salesperson asks more than one person, he will improve his chances of obtaining accurate information.

Summary

After a salesperson has obtained a large order, there are several things that he still must do. First he should remember to be quiet about this order outside his company until he is sure no one can upset the decision. Then he must remember to thank those involved in the customer's company as well as his own. If there is any doubt, the salesperson should err on the side of thanking too many people, not too few.

Next the salesperson must set up meetings between his engineers and the customer so as to accurately and in detail develop the project according to the customer's specifications. He should prepare an agenda and send it to the customer for any additions. This will insure that all areas of the job can be discussed so as to eliminate misunderstandings and gray areas. Changes in the specifications could cause extra expense and delayed delivery, so all details must be carefully agreed to in writing as soon as possible.

After insuring that his engineers have all the information needed to proceed, he should frequently check on the status of the project to make sure that it stays on schedule. Finally, the salesperson should ask people in the customer's organization for feedback concerning the purchase decision and his competitor's products. This could help him in his future sales efforts.

53

After Losing an Order

Success has many fathers. Failure is an orphan.

—Unknown

When the salesperson receives a big order, people often come out of the woodwork to remind him how much they assisted him. When he loses an order, however, no one ever comes forward to volunteer how much they contributed to the loss.

When a large order is lost, the first thing for a salesperson to do is to find out as much as he can about exactly what was purchased and from whom. He should try to learn why the customer did not buy from him, why they bought what they did, the delivery time, and if possible, the price.

If a salesperson is not able to quickly get an accurate reading on exactly what was purchased and why, it usually indicates he was not close enough to the customer and the project. He must be able to develop this information despite a policy on the part of some customers to not divulge immediately what was purchased. If he has the account in good shape and knows enough people, he should be able to put together a pretty accurate understanding. If he cannot do this entirely from the customer, then he should use supplemental details from other sources.

Losing a large order usually should not come as a big surprise to a salesperson. A good salesperson will be close enough to the customer to detect which way the project is tilting long before the order is lost. The salesperson must be the first in his organization to learn about the loss of a major order. He never wants his superiors to hear about it from other sources. If it is a very large project or order, word of its loss will spread very fast. The salesperson never wants to learn about it from his competitors, either. Unless the salesperson learns about this loss firsthand and immediately, he is not handling the account well and is not very close to the decision makers.

Losing a large order usually should not come as a big surprise to a salesperson.

Finding out all the details surrounding the loss of an order is not easy, but the salesperson must do it. This is one of the times he will need good sources of information, because the decision maker himself rarely will tell him the real reasons. To make the salesperson feel better, the decision maker often will give him only some of the reasons and only part of the story. Usually he will be told that his price was too high or his delivery was too long. He should not fully believe this, because it is rarely the complete story.

If the customer says it was due to the price, the salesperson should ask if he would have received the order if the prices had been identical or if his price had been lower. Sometimes the salesperson would not have been given the order even with a competitive price, but he will never determine this unless he asks. Of course, it may be against company policy for the customer to reveal the exact sum paid. However, even the other reasons the salesperson lost the order will scarcely be revealed right away. Thus he must keep digging to put the complete story together, which could require many days to accomplish.

Even if it is difficult to obtain this information, he must keep trying, since it will impact other current projects and will help him correct his past shortcomings. The salesperson should report these details promptly to the proper individuals in his organization. As soon as he learns the order is definitely lost, he should advise other field offices that were involved so they will stop working on the job. The salesperson must then follow up as soon as possible with a written lost order report.

Regardless of what he learns, the next thing a salesperson must do is to look in a mirror and ask himself what he did wrong, what he left undone, or what he should have done differently. This soul-searching requires that he honestly and sincerely consider the answers to these questions.

Every salesperson, if he truly wants to be successful, should keep searching for ways to improve. There is no better way to do this than to learn from past failures, such as losing an order. After losing an order, he should consider the following:

1. Why did he really lose the sale?
2. Where did he go wrong?
3. What should he have done differently?
4. Did he have sufficient product knowledge?
5. Did he submit his best price?
6. Did he know his competitors' products well enough?
7. Did he offer the correct product?
8. Did he convey adequate information on his company?
9. Did he get the customer to visit his company's manufacturing facilities?
10. Did he really understand the customer's needs?
11. Did he handle the customer's objections properly?
12. Did he ask enough questions?
13. Did the customer seem annoyed by the salesperson's personal mannerisms?
14. Did the salesperson adequately utilize other groups in his firm, such as engineering, manufacturing, or management?

Above all, when a salesperson loses an order, he should not start blaming other people, other departments, the customer, his boss, his competitors, or anyone else. Doing this keeps the salesperson from addressing the real problem of what he did wrong inadvertently or what he did not do at all. To blame others when he loses an order is to rationalize failures and shortcomings. If a salesperson follows this approach, he will never correct the basic things he is either doing incorrectly or leaving undone.

The salesperson should never go to the customer making unsubstantiated accusations as to why the order was lost. The salesperson may think he knows, but the customer has access to more information. The customer talked to all the vendors, analyzed the bids, and knows what the salesperson offered as well as what his competitors quoted and any concessions they made.

SALES EXAMPLES

EXAMPLE 1

To illustrate this, I would like to relate a true example. The purchasing agent of a very large American oil company told me that after his firm had awarded a very big contract from among four proposals, one of the losers requested an appointment to see him. When the losing vendor entered his office, he immediately said in very strong language, "You have always awarded jobs like this to the lowest bidder, but you didn't this time, and I want to know why." He appeared very confident and certain that his company had submitted the low bid and should have received the order. The purchasing agent was caught completely off guard but replied that he would look into the matter and get back to him. A review of the quotations revealed that the lowest bidder had indeed been awarded the order. The purchasing agent documented this by exceptionally showing the loser the various prices in the bid tabulation.

It turned out that the four bidders had in the past, it appeared, acted in collusion and took turns being the low bidder. It was apparently this complaining vendor's turn to be the low bidder, but one of the other companies had double-crossed him and undercut his price. The protesting bidder thus not only created problems with the customer, he also inadvertently confessed to engaging in unlawful acts.

The point of the example is that a salesperson should not go charging in to make accusations when he loses a job. He does not have all the information that the customer has.

Example 2

In another instance, the losing salesperson told the customer that he would be fired because he lost an important order. The customer felt this was revolting behavior, because this salesperson had in the past received a lot of business from this customer. The decision maker told me this tactic drastically lowered this salesperson's reputation with him and would cost him future orders.

Example 3

On still another occasion, a salesperson upon losing an order told the decision maker, "You owe me the next order." The customer reported this to me and added that this behavior seriously diminished this losing salesperson's chances on all future orders, because the salesperson was owed nothing.

Example 4

Many years ago an order was going away from our company. Our sales executives asked our president to call the president of the customer's company, which was a major U.S. oil company. They wanted our company president to make a plea for the customer's president to overrule his engineers and to award the order to us. This oil company president responded by saying that with this tactic, we not only were ending our chances on the current order, but also were seriously damaging and jeopardizing our prospects on all future orders with his company.

It might make a salesperson feel better if he realizes that he is rarely fully to blame when an order is lost. It is usually a combination of events, but the only way he can get his own house in order is to accept total responsibility for the loss of the order. He should make a written list of what he should have done differently and what else he should have done to get the order.

He should talk to as many of the people involved as possible, and if it was a big job, there will have been many people involved. He should ask a lot of questions to determine what went wrong with his quote and to determine why they did not select his product but bought what they did. From the information gained, he should make out a lost order report.

Lost Order Reports

A salesperson should keep a master list of lost order reports on all sizable jobs he loses, and he should make a separate list for his major customers. Periodically he should review the master list of lost order reports to refresh his memory on what he did wrong or what he failed to do on the quotes he lost.

Before commencing work on the next big project with any major customer, the salesperson should review his lost order reports for this particular customer. He should look for any patterns and for factors that are repeated. This will indicate to him what, in his best judgment, he should do differently this time. He should examine these carefully so as to avoid past mistakes by himself or anyone in other departments within his firm. The salesperson should also review and take into consideration any successful projects he has had with the company.

This lost order file will also assist him in writing memos to the various departments and to his supervisors to suggest and recommend corrective actions on all future jobs. If quality has been a problem, he should remind the engineering and manufacturing departments. If delivery has been the culprit, he should take this up with manufacturing. If pricing has been the reason, he might want to remind people in management of this.

Having this master file will enable him to cite specific examples as he attempts to get the various problems sorted out before quoting and before planning his sales strategy on future projects. Past problems with specific customers should be addressed as he quotes on a new inquiry. If delivery has been a negative factor, he should promise status reports if the delivery is long. If quality has been a problem, he should get his management people to agree on extra inspections. If pricing has caused orders to be lost, the salesperson should review the pricing closely with his supervisors before submitting his new bids to this customer. If customer unfamiliarity with the salesperson's products or his shop has been the reason for losing orders, he should invite this customer to visit his company's manufacturing plant. The salesperson could also give him a list of satisfied customers who have bought and are using these particular models. He could take the customer to see the units in operation.

Losing an order is a very traumatic and lonely experience for a salesperson. Even so, he should not be a sore loser, regardless of any extenuating or unfair circumstances surrounding the loss. The salesperson should control his emotions and investigate to determine the real reason the customer did not buy from him. He should win with class, and he should lose with class.

For the salesperson to tell the buyer that he has made a bad decision will only harm his cause in the future. One of his best responses is to say, "Of course we are very disappointed that we were not awarded the contract, but we don't blame anyone but ourselves when we lose an order. We respect your judgment. We think our product is superior, but we should have worked harder and convinced you that ours was best. We appreciate the opportunity to work with you, and we will work even harder on the next job." A salesperson must be able to handle the loss of an order maturely and should accept the blame. At the same time, he can ask for suggestions on what he should do differently on the next project he bids to this prospect.

The salesperson must be objective as he works on his next inquiry, vigorously implementing corrective actions so he will be successful. A salesperson should accept the blame for a lost order, but he should also find out why he lost in the past and take corrective steps. This will increase the number of orders he obtains in the future.

Summary

1. A salesperson should never expect others to share the blame when he loses an order.
2. When a salesperson loses an order, he must immediately find out the following:

    - which competitor won the order
    - what was purchased
    - why the customers did not buy from the salesperson
    - why they bought what they did
    - the approximate price paid

    The salesperson must have good sources so he can determine these things.
3. If the salesperson cannot obtain very much information at this time, it means he does not have many friends in the customer's organization.
4. Losing a large order should not come as a surprise if the salesperson has the account in good shape.

5. The salesperson should be able to detect when an order is slipping away.
6. The salesperson must be the first in his organization to learn that an order is lost, and he must learn this immediately. He never wants his superiors to hear this from other sources.
7. News of a lost order usually spreads very fast.
8. Determining all the details will not be easy, but the salesperson must do so.
9. The decision maker will rarely give the salesperson the complete story. He will need other sources to fill in the puzzle.
10. The salesperson will usually be told his price was too high or his delivery was too long.
11. The salesperson should never believe that price alone was the reason. If price is given as the reason, he should ask if he would have received the order if he had been competitive.
12. The salesperson should consider the following:

    - What did he leave undone?
    - What did he do wrong?
    - What should he have done differently?

    He must be honest with himself as he considers these factors.

13. The salesperson should also consider the following:

    - Why did he really lose the sale?
    - Did he have sufficient product knowledge?
    - Did he know his competitors' products well enough?
    - Did he offer the correct product?
    - Did he convey adequate information on his company?
    - Did he get the customer to visit his company's manufacturing facilities?
    - Did he really understand the customer's needs?
    - Did he handle the customer's objections properly?
    - Did he ask enough questions?

- Did he do anything to annoy the customer?
- Did he adequately utilize other groups in his firm, such as people from engineering, manufacturing, or management?

14. The salesperson should not blame others when he loses an order. This merely rationalizes failures and does not allow him to improve by correcting his own shortcomings.
15. The salesperson should keep a master list of lost order reports to review occasionally and to learn from.
16. The salesperson should not be a sore loser.
17. The salesperson should not approach his customer with accusations.
18. Before quoting on a project for this customer again, the salesperson should review the reasons he lost other orders and should take the necessary corrective steps.
19. The salesperson should learn from losing. He must convert the knowledge gained from losing orders to successes on future quotes.

54

Avoid Misunderstandings

It is helpful to avoid misunderstandings in all walks of life, but it is extremely important in commercial matters. If a salesperson sells expensive products, misunderstandings can cost an enormous amount of money. Even worse, they can cause irreparable damage to relations with his customers. When technical or commercial information is passed to a customer, it should be confirmed in writing, even though it may seem at the time to be minor. The salesperson should bear in mind that people tend to hear what they want to hear, which can result in misunderstandings.

When misunderstandings occur, they not only cost a lot of money, but even worse, tempers flare, and customers get upset. This usually costs the salesperson business by creating bad feelings. Although the salesperson may be right, he will lose if the customer does not agree and if there is nothing in the record to document the salesperson's position. Not only will the customer not purchase products from the salesperson, but the customer or engineer may be embarrassed to have acted on the misunderstood information. There will have to be subsequent corrections or retractions. Confirming in writing any technical and commercial information goes a long way toward avoiding misunderstanding.

Apart from protecting his own company and avoiding damaging customer relations, the salesperson never wants to contribute to a dispute inside his customer's company. The salesperson does not want to cause a buyer or an engineer to lose face or respect or place them in a bad light with their colleagues, their bosses, or their upper management. A major misunderstanding could cost a contact person a raise, a promotion, or even his job. It could also cause the loss of lives in a plant. This can happen even though the information the salesperson gave him was accurate.

If the customer misunderstands verbal messages, the vendor will be blamed by association. It can happen even if his relations are good with a customer and even if he is highly respected. Consider, then, what can happen to a salesperson whose customer relations are poor or if his reputation with the customer is already shaky.

When receiving verbal information, either in person or on the telephone, a salesperson must listen carefully and make notes. He should repeat the facts as he understands them to make certain that he has understood correctly.

When giving information verbally, either in person or by telephone, the salesperson must take care to be clearly understood. He should not ramble but should arrange the information in a proper order in his notes and use them when speaking.

It is also important that a salesperson be clear in his written communications. Generally, it is better to keep sentences short. He should take time to write well and to carefully modify and correct the letter. The salesperson should think through and consider what he wants to convey. He should imagine that he is the recipient and consider what will go through the customer's mind and what questions will arise as he reads the message, given his environment and circumstances. The salesperson should feel free to change what he first wrote, especially if others in his company do not understand the message as written.

Such care is essential when a salesperson is confirming technical and commercial data to customers. It is equally important when he is confirming information received by phone inside his company. This will help avoid misunderstandings. People often mislead others verbally, even though they intend no malice. Even if we don't like to believe it, some people play games with verbal conversations and deliberately leave things unclear. Sometimes there may be a genuine lack of understanding or some muddled thinking by the other person. The salesperson must be sure that important facts are put in writing. By doing so he will enhance his reputation with his customers and his colleagues.

Even if we don't like to believe it, some people play games with verbal conversations and deliberately leave things unclear.

The salesperson should not depend on the other person, even in his home office, to confirm a telephone conversation when important information is relayed. He must do it himself. It is easy for a salesperson to overlook details such as these when he is in a hurry to make a deadline and receives information by telephone with assurances that the other person will confirm. Often he will go about his sales duties, and then days later he will realize the information was not put into writing. By then it may be too late, because conditions could change and memories may have dimmed.

During the closing stages of a project, events move very rapidly. The people within a salesperson's company often must obtain approvals from higher up. With so much information being passed by telephone, all the ingredients for misunderstandings are present.

During these telephone conversations, the salesperson must make notes and be sure details are clearly understood. He must not just hear what he wants to hear. He should ask that important numbers and facts be repeated, and he must be positive that he understands fully and accurately. He should always assume the responsibility for confirming the information that he has received by phone. He must take this very seriously. He should never put anything in a confirmation message that he did not sincerely understand at the time he received the information. If he made assumptions, he should indicate them clearly and be scrupulously honest about them, as in all dealings both inside and outside his company.

If a salesperson is out of his office, he should call and dictate a confirming fax, letter, or e-mail covering any important information received while he is traveling. If he waits until he returns to his office, it can be too late. He should not hesitate to send a fax or e-mail when time is important. It requires strict discipline in order for a salesperson to stay current with this correspondence. It is easy for a salesperson to fall into a habit of not confirming information, and he may get away with it for a little while. However, sooner or later he will fall victim to misunderstandings because important information was not put into writing.

Whether to use confirming letters, faxes, or e-mail messages must be decided each time. The decision must be based on how quickly the information will be used and sometimes on other factors, such as whether or not the recipient travels and how long mail will take to reach him. If the recipient is located overseas, mail could require weeks. Cost must always be kept in mind, but the salesperson should not get into real trouble by trying to save a few dollars.

When communicating with customers or even inside your own organization, keep in mind that all organizations have internal politics and occasional jurisdiction disputes; therefore, a lot of thought should be given before sending critical or derogatory messages to customers. Messages in print acquire a life of their own, can be widely distributed in the customer organization, and can be carefully preserved and read and re-read as the years pass. They can be used by one department to the detriment of a rival department and you suffer by being the sender.

To avoid misunderstandings, it is therefore much better to verbally discuss disputed or emotional topics rather than going into print.

Sales Examples

Here are some actual examples of how misunderstandings can arise.

Example 1

A warranty problem existed on products installed and operated in a plant. The salesperson arranged a meeting attended by his management and the customer's executives. In order to make a correction, the salesperson's company agreed to replace certain parts that had to be manufactured, which would require six months. This was offered with the provision that the customer's company would install the parts at their expense. The customer's management people accepted the offer.

Six months later, the salesperson shipped the material to the customer's job site. Shortly after it arrived, the customer's contact person called and asked when the salesperson would send the necessary labor to remove the old parts and install the revised ones. The salesperson was astonished. He was sure the agreement called for his company to furnish the new parts but for the customer's company to supply the labor and installation. Furthermore, considerable expense was involved. He checked the records and discovered that this important agreement was not confirmed in writing. This lack of paperwork created a no-win situation for the salesperson.

Example 2

The salesperson received a tentative order for products that he agreed to engineer in order to save time, although he did not yet have a firm order from the customer. The firm order was pending and could not be issued by the customer until governmental approval for installation was received. A few months later, the salesperson's factory was running short of work and called to check on the status of the unconfirmed order. The salesperson called the customer, who authorized the salesperson to proceed to build the product.

Six months later when the product was finished, the factory requested shipping instructions. A call to the customer revealed that he had no intention of firming up the order, since governmental approval was still pending. The records were checked, and the salesperson discovered to his dismay that the verbal instructions from the customer to proceed with the order were never confirmed in writing. Again, this was a terrible situation for the salesperson and his company, brought about by a lack of paperwork.

Example 3

There was a chronic warranty problem on a new design that had stretched out over several years. The salesperson had been unable to solve the problem. The customer was very unhappy, but he also represented a huge potential for additional sales. A meeting was held with executives from both sides present and the salesman's company agreed to the return of the product. Some months later when the solution was to be executed, it developed that the customer thought he could remove and return the product and receive a cash rebate. The salesperson's people insisted that they only agreed to issue a credit memo upon the return of the products, which could be used solely against the purchase of new products from their company. The salesperson checked his records and discovered that the agreement was never put into writing.

Example 4

Early in my career while I was an application engineer, a customer called requesting the working pressure of a product he had purchased earlier from us and had in operation. I obtained the information from our engineering department, called the customer with the numbers, and then confirmed our conversation by letter. About one year later the same engineer called and said, "Can you tell me again the maximum working pressure of my product?" When I gave him a figure, he replied, "I thought you told me a much higher number last year." I answered, "No, I gave you the number verbally at 600 psig and confirmed it by letter." I went to my files, made a copy of my letter, and sent it to him again. If I had not initially confirmed the correct number, my company could have been held liable in case of an accident. Even worse, a severe accident could have cost lives and could have gotten the customer in trouble with his company.

Agreement Details and Confirmation Letters

Sometimes the higher the level of people in a customer meeting, the more likely a dispute or a misunderstanding will occur. This is due to several factors. First, the top two executives often both talk at the same time, with each saying how he thinks it should be and neither listening to the other. Second, if there are junior members in the meeting, they are sometimes reluctant to speak up and admit they do not understand the agreement. They do not want to ask these senior people to repeat the agreement terms so as to confirm them. In nearly all cases, when the terms are repeated during the meeting, the details are modified. Both sides think of implications or clarifications that were not readily apparent or considered at the time the statements were made.

There should be a specific person designated to write down any agreements. The junior salesperson, or whoever is designated to the task, should not hesitate to speak up, ask questions, and make notes. He must keep on asking questions until the agreement is clear to him, and the participants agree on the terms. It is a mistake for a salesperson to wait until after the meeting to try to sort out the details. He will then have at least as many versions as there were attendees in the meeting. It sometimes appears that a few senior people just do not want to be closely tied down and prefer to leave things vague. In all but a few rare cases, this is a mistake, and trying to set ground rules for this scenario is difficult, if not impossible. Furthermore, the salesperson's top executives may not call regularly on customers and may not feel at ease. The salesperson can be of tremendous help at times like these, even though he may be outranked.

The salesperson should never include anything in the confirming letter that was not agreed upon. If in doubt, the salesperson should call the customer and clarify any items before writing the confirming letter. The salesperson should also ask the appropriate people within his company to read and sign off on the draft. Detailed data should be tabulated, and the letter should be written with short, clear sentences. The salesperson and his company have the most to lose due to misunderstandings. The salesperson can be in danger of not only losing the present contract, but also any future business.

Summary

1. The salesperson should confirm in writing all important information given to or received from customers.
2. The salesperson should confirm in writing all important information received from or given to others inside his own company.
3. The salesperson must listen carefully when receiving verbal information. He should repeat it to make sure he understands it correctly, rephrasing it if necessary to remove all doubt.
4. The salesperson should not just hear what he wants to hear and then stop listening. He must be honest at all times and should never play games and try to confirm something in writing that was not agreed to by both the buyer and the vendor.

5. When giving information verbally, either in person or by telephone, the salesperson must take care to communicate clearly. He should organize his facts and comments in a logical order.
6. If the salesperson receives important information while traveling, he should not wait until he is back in his office to confirm it.
7. In meetings with customers when the salesperson's executives will be present, there should be a clear understanding ahead of time concerning who is appointed to confirm the agreements reached.
8. The designated person must repeat the important points discussed to make sure both sides are in agreement before the meeting is adjourned.
9. The salesperson should confirm the agreement immediately, using clear, concise language. He should show the draft to his executives who attended the meeting for their approval.
10. As a vendor, the salesperson has the most to lose in case of misunderstandings. The salesperson can avoid them by promptly confirming in writing all important information.

55

Obey the Rules

A salesperson should always strictly obey the rules, not only those of his own company but also those of the firms with which he does business. This may seem obvious and redundant to people in a book on selling, but it is surprising how many otherwise competent salespeople overlook or ignore this vital part of selling successfully over a long period of time. If the customer has specific hours that salespeople can call, by all means, the salesperson should observe these hours unless he has specific authorization to deviate from this rule. If, during the course of a large, drawn-out job, the customer decides that his people are not to see salespeople during certain days, he should stay away.

If a salesperson's customer has rules about how long the engineer or the people he calls on can be away for lunch, then the salesperson must get them back to their offices within the allotted time frame. He should keep track of the time carefully and be sure he has them back on time. If they come back late with the salesperson, someone will see them or otherwise learn about it and pass this information along. The salesperson's image will suffer. If they have company rules against drinking at lunch, then the salesperson should not tempt them. If rules exist about gifts and entertainment, he must adhere strictly to these regulations.

In some cases, the customer's people will readily go along with breaking the rules. If they want to do that, let them do it with other salespeople. A successful salesperson will not cooperate with breaking the rules and let himself be guilty by association. The salesperson has more to lose than the customer's employees do. A salesperson needs everything to go in his favor. He should not pile up negative impressions by disobeying rules that his customer has established.

The salesperson should also obey the rules within his own company. Disobeying or disregarding small rules often leads to breaking more important restrictions. When customers learn that a salesperson disregards his company's rules, they may come to expect him to bend or break the rules for them. However, if he has a reputation for scrupulously abiding by his company's rules, the customer will be less likely to expect him to disobey or disregard them. The customer will also have more respect for the salesperson.

When customers learn that a salesperson disregards his company's rules, they may come to expect him to bend or break the rules for them.

Customers like to deal with a salesperson who has a good reputation and solid influence within his own company, so that his firm will support the commitments he makes. Surveys show that customers respect and are more apt to buy from salespeople with good reputations inside their own companies. Customers will know they can trust the salesperson and rely on his word and his agreements. This is very important to individuals who make vital decisions for their organizations. If a salesperson has a poor reputation within his own firm, the customer will soon know this and will be reluctant to buy from him. The customer will sometimes learn about it from other people in the salesperson's firm through comments that they make about him. Obeying his company's rules demonstrates a salesperson's loyalty and integrity, which his customers will admire and respect.

When negotiating with the customer on a warranty adjustment or in any other important area, the salesperson's management will often instruct him to make certain points in his presentations or negotiations. The salesperson must always be certain he understands his instructions and the reasons for them. If he does not understand, he should ask questions. During his meeting with the customer, the salesperson should make sure to include all topics or points suggested by his management. He must fully support his company's position. He should never present these points timidly and should absolutely not give even the slightest indication that he does not agree with them. He should support his company's position vigorously.

If the salesperson has any reservations about the posture his management has suggested he should take, he must iron this out before the customer meeting. He should not be bashful if he disagrees with the initial settlement put forth by his executives. Since he is the salesperson handling the account, he will be more familiar than anyone else with all the details and where the blame and responsibility rest. He must make sure his management is aware of the customer's current thinking about the problem. He should work with his management to obtain an offer that he can support. It should be fair to both sides and one that the salesperson feels his customer will accept.

Following the customer meeting, the salesperson must be sure to report to his superiors that he presented the points or put forth the arguments in accordance with their directions. He should relate the customer's reaction and any conclusion. Few things annoy a company's executives more than to receive the results of this kind of meeting with no assurance that the key points, arguments, and topics they suggested were included and supported as instructed.

Sales Example

Twenty years ago, I was working with one of my customers on a big job. All quotations were in and the customer's engineers needed uninterrupted time to analyze the bids. They passed the word to salespeople to avoid calling that week, so I stayed away and obeyed their rules. A competitive salesperson bypassed the receptionist and went upstairs to see the engineers. While there, he was discovered by an executive, who immediately called the salesperson's company and demanded that he be taken off the account. He was removed from the account and transferred. His career with his company never recovered. Needless to say, he did not get the order.

Summary

A salesperson must bc loyal to his company and obey its rules. He must also respect and obey his customer's rules. It will enhance his reputation and enable him to close more orders.

56

Be Available to Customers

After placing an order, many customers feel vulnerable and still expect to have ready access to someone in the vendor's organization. They prefer to deal with the person to whom they gave the order. It is, therefore, very important that a salesperson always be available to his customers. He should neither hide from them nor dodge them. If they placed the order with the salesperson, they may still have lingering doubts about their decision. Thus the salesperson should be readily available to give responsive service and to continue to reassure them that they made the right decision.

While it is acceptable for a salesperson to refuse telephone calls when he has visitors in his office, he should otherwise either be available to everyone, or he should refuse all calls or visitors. The salesperson's office assistant should promptly tell the caller when the salesperson will return and when he will be able to call back. When one of a salesperson's customers calls him, he must personally return the call. He should not delegate this responsibility, even though he may think he knows why the customer is calling. Even if someone else must provide the information, it is possible that something new may have developed. Furthermore, the customer may not be calling for the purpose the salesperson suspects.

If it is more convenient to both parties for someone else to pass the information directly because of complexity, the salesperson should still call and explain this cordially to his customer. He should ascertain that this procedure is completely satisfactory to the customer. If he detects any hesitancy or annoyance, then he should stay involved and give the information himself. Virtually every customer is disturbed and feels somewhat neglected and let down if someone else, especially a stranger in the vendor's company, returns his call to the salesperson. Good communication with customers is of paramount importance to the salesperson, so he should always stay directly involved in one way or another. He should not shirk his duty by treating these calls too casually. He must maintain and cultivate such a vital link. It will take time for him to do this, but it will be time well spent.

If the salesperson is out of town, he should not allow the customer to chase him down. He should have his assistant tell the customer that he is out of the city but will return on a certain date. The assistant should add, "If you would like to speak to him before then, I shall be happy to pass the word for him to call you right away. Otherwise, he will call as soon as he returns. Which would you prefer?" That leaves the customer with the satisfaction of an option. If the customer would like to talk to the salesperson before his scheduled return, the assistant should communicate the message to the salesperson so that he can return the call. If the salesperson allows the customer to chase him down, he might interrupt an important meeting with another customer or create unnecessary trouble and expense.

For this procedure to work well, the salesperson must provide his assistant with a list of where he will be each day, along with telephone numbers, if he is going to be out of his office. The assistant can then call the salesperson on his cellular telephone or call the office he is visiting and leave word for the salesperson to call when his meeting is finished. When returning calls, a salesperson should avoid calling from the customer's office. He should instead go to a public phone or use his cell phone to place his call. This not only avoids inconvenience to a salesperson's customers, but it will also keep his calls private. He may need to discuss something his customer should not be involved in or know about. Also, if the salesperson learns that his customer is requesting information that must be developed or worked up by others in his organization, he can get this started while he is still out of town. It will then be ready sooner than if he waits until he is back in his office to return his customer's call.

When a salesperson gets back to his office, he should return all customer calls immediately, with or without all of the information the customer is seeking. He should return their calls to give them reports and to tell them that he is expediting the answers. Their situations or requirements may have changed, so he should not delay in calling them back.

If a customer calls urgently requesting information, the salesperson should keep him informed of his progress in obtaining it. He probably has someone, perhaps his boss, bugging him for answers. It is, therefore, necessary for the salesperson to not only follow this closely with his factory or home office people, but also to keep the customer informed so he in turn can keep his associates happy. A call simply reporting a salesperson's expediting efforts will always be appreciated. Even if a salesperson has no answers, he should call the customer and apprise him of what is being done. He will not know unless the salesperson tells him. Only if he receives progress reports will he know his request is being taken seriously. I have always had trouble convincing other salespeople to call a customer when they felt they had nothing new to report. It is still a valuable use of time for a salesperson to call and tell his customer that although he has nothing new to report, he is following the situation closely.

A call simply reporting a salesperson's expediting efforts will always be appreciated.

Following the receipt of an urgent request, the salesperson should, after passing it along to the people who must generate the information, call the customer to tell him what has been done with his request. He will be grateful to be able to tell his associates that the salesperson is working on his request.

Many customers prefer to deal with only the salesperson throughout all stages of the job. They will deal with him from the inquiry through the order, the engineering, the manufacture, the testing, the commissioning, and plant operation. This is contrary to the manner in which many large companies now move orders through their organizations. After an order is received by a large organization, it is usually turned over to marketing, which hands it to engineering, which passes it to manufacturing and testing, and so on. In most organizations, a different person is in charge each step of the way. If this is the way a salesperson's firm is organized, he probably is stuck with it.

If the customer is the least bit anxious about the arrangements in the salesperson's company, the salesperson should assure him that he will monitor the order every step of the way. He should reassure his customer that he will receive and read copies of every relevant piece of internal and external correspondence on the job and intercede immediately if a problem develops. He should explain that he will be available to attend every follow-up meeting the customer has with the salesperson's company. Finally, he should tell the customer that he will get his top management quickly involved in case of internal delays or problems. These assurances should put his customer at ease.

The salesperson must make these commitments in good faith. He should follow them up and do as he promised. If the salesperson has any problem internally with this arrangement and is otherwise unable to convince his own people, he should ask the customer to write a letter requesting this procedure. Hopefully, this last step will be unnecessary. It will not be necessary in a truly sales-oriented company.

Sales Example

Several years ago I was working on a job overseas involving a substantial amount of products. The project manager was based in the city in which I lived. I spent several days promoting our units, and before returning home, I wrote a letter to the project manager pledging my continual involvement in the project. I wrote this letter by hand on my personal stationery and left it at his hotel.

I promised to attend every meeting, follow the job closely throughout the manufacturing cycle, and monitor all correspondence. We received the order, and this commitment was the clincher.

Summary

The salesperson can have his accounts in much better shape and sell more products if he is always available to his customers.

57

Do Not Shirk Responsibility

Many salespeople seem to think that they can convey bad news or unfavorable decisions to a customer through a low-level person and avoid some of the consequences. This is not the case. Unfavorable news or decisions usually must be passed to the customer through normal working channels, which may mean a relatively junior person. This often is unavoidable. Nevertheless, after the salesperson gives this information to the lower level people, it is almost always a good idea for him to call their superiors or senior people and personally explain his firm's position. This will have many advantages for the salesperson. The senior person usually is then better able to understand the salesperson's position, because the salesperson can deliver a more complete story when speaking to him directly.

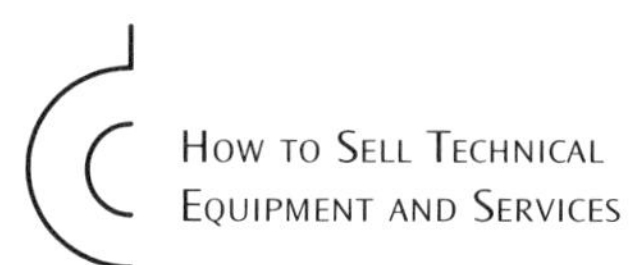

Invariably, much important information is omitted or distorted as a story is passed upward or downward in an organization, especially under adverse circumstances. The salesperson's call to an involved customer executive affords the executive an opportunity to ask additional questions. It also allows him to express directly what is on his mind, what his reactions are, and the full impact of the problem. Sometimes his comments will shed a new light on some aspect of the problem and enable the salesperson to return to his own management for a faster response. The salesperson's management might authorize a better warranty settlement, a shorter delivery, or relief of some other sort. Even the venting of the executive's anger directly on the salesperson will make the customer feel better.

Obviously the salesperson should use good judgment concerning others to call within the customer's organization. He certainly would not want to spread word of the troubles or to involve anyone needlessly. If he knows the accounts well and is fairly certain that others will otherwise hear about the trouble, it is usually best if he eventually talks directly to the key people. This will allow the salesperson to explain his position and answer any questions. However, he must keep the lower level people he is dealing with fully informed as to which people he will be calling. He does not want to give them the impression that he is going over their heads. It is usually best for the salesperson to wait until the senior people learn about the problem from their own people. By closely monitoring the situation, the salesperson can determine which people have been told, and then he can decide when and if he should talk to others.

Perhaps the junior person to whom the salesperson relayed the bad news was not too upset and said very little. If he were the only one to whom the salesperson talked, the salesperson could easily obtain and report to his management a false impression of the customer's reaction. On the other hand, if the salesperson eventually discusses this with the senior people, he will have a much more accurate interpretation of their reaction. Sometimes the reaction is extremely unfavorable. In this event, the additional information the salesperson receives will help him realize that he must do more than originally planned, or do it faster, to sort out this problem to the customer's satisfaction.

Speaking directly to the people higher up also proves that the salesperson is not shirking his duty and is willing to face unpleasant issues. Situations like this also enable the salesperson to meet upper management and executives he would ordinarily not contact.

Problems promptly and expeditiously sorted out can enhance and improve a vendor's image. By talking to someone in authority or in upper management at times like this, the salesperson can be sure he is covering all bases.

Problems promptly and expeditiously sorted out can enhance and improve a vendor's image.

The best approach is for the salesperson to check with his customer's normal contact person for approval to call higher level people in the customer's organization. The salesperson could offer to call the supervisors and explain directly what happened and what the salesperson's company is doing about it. This offer will usually be welcomed and accepted. Again, the salesperson should avoid spreading bad news to people who will not otherwise become involved. He should make these calls only to get his complete story across in the most favorable light and to accurately gauge the impact.

Suppose, for example, the salesperson proposes to correct the problem by replacing a part. The lower level person may tell him that two months delivery is acceptable, since they cannot afford to stop production before then to install the replacement. However, the upper management people may tell him that they will shut the plant down as soon as the replacement part is available, and the sooner the better. This direct discussion can often enable the salesperson to rectify the problem with the minimum amount of damage to his company's image and his reputation with this customer. In any case, if the salesperson has these direct discussions, he will then know that he has done his utmost to be responsive and to smooth over any problems.

Too often salespeople will step aside and avoid the issue when a problem develops or products have failed. They will leave the solution and the passing of bad news to the service or engineering people. The customer will by then be fuming.

This reasoning also applies to leaving word with a customer's office assistant or an intermediary. It is very difficult to leave clear messages in a situation like this. It is much better for a salesperson to only leave word that he called and will call back right away. If he leaves any kind of negative message, the customer will be unhappier than if he had heard it directly from the salesperson. Then he could have asked clarifying questions immediately.

Also, if the information is left with an office assistant or any other intermediary, someone else may learn of this bad news before it has been revealed to the salesperson's customer. The customer may not have wanted this person to know about it until he had an opportunity to discuss it with the salesperson and to obtain a full explanation. The salesperson should remember that rivalries exist inside his customers' organizations. The salesperson should never embarrass his contact by inadvertently allowing information to leak out to his chief rival and do him harm.

When something goes wrong, virtually all customers want the salesperson involved. They feel they have the most leverage with him, since he is the person who must come in later soliciting orders. From this, it follows that if a salesperson receives a call from his customer reporting a difficulty with his purchased product, the salesperson should be the one to call him back with the information.

The salesperson should be careful how he delegates this to someone else, or he could easily alienate his customer. The customer will feel that he has been shuffled off to someone who does not have the salesperson's obligation to be responsive. The salesperson is the one who must maintain good rapport with his customers. He has more at stake and more to lose than anyone else, and thus the customer wants to keep him involved. Furthermore, the salesperson should want to stay involved in order to do his job well and to reassure his customers that they still have his help and influence.

Following the same line of reasoning, if the salesperson's president or a senior executive is the first to receive a complaint call, then that person should be the one to call the customer back. Others may work up the details for the response, but whoever received the first call should respond to the customer with the results and the corrective plans. The president may then turn the implementation over to the salesperson or others, but it is very important that he give the initial reply if he received the complaining call. To do otherwise will give the customer the feeling that he has been let down, that his complaint has been downgraded, and that the salesperson's firm is not responsive. Even if the answers are the same, they will be better received if the salesperson's president gives them directly to the person who initially called him. When he follows these approaches, the salesperson's customers learn that he really cares about the relations his firm has with them.

Such sensitivity also applies internally within a salesperson's company. Although the preceding discussion concerned a salesperson and his customer, this same logic applies internally. This is true when a salesperson is making a special request of another department or when bad news must be passed along to them. The salesperson should not expect someone else to speak for him. He will need to have a full explanation when requesting something special from the manufacturing, engineering, or other departments. For this reason, he should not delegate such requests. He must make them personally so he can defend the reason behind the requests and also explain why the customer requires this information or why supplying it is necessary.

People in authority in other departments invariably feel that someone is pulling a fast one on them or trying to sneak something by when these special requests are delegated to a subordinate. A successful salesperson should not delegate this task but should make the requests personally.

The salesperson should never be too busy to take the time to explain a request or problem to other departments in his organization that must execute and implement his requests. If the person the salesperson should talk to is out or temporarily away from the telephone, he should not use that as an excuse. The salesperson must call the person again and leave messages so he will know that the salesperson is trying to reach him.

If a salesperson must leave his office before he can make these vital contacts, he should not hesitate to call on his cellular telephone or stop at a pay phone and call. Too many salespeople hide behind weak excuses to avoid facing the music. They should not avoid explaining directly to the person involved the reasons for making special requests. A salesperson who does this often will develop a reputation for sidestepping responsibility.

The salesperson should avoid those difficulties by explaining his side of the story directly to his own management and to his customer's senior people. He is then able to answer their questions directly and explain in detail any area that concerns them. He will thereby develop a solid reputation as a salesperson who does not shirk his duty in unpleasant situations.

Sometimes a salesperson must convey bad news internally or wants something exceptional done for his customer. He should not be afraid to discuss it with those who are in charge or in superior positions who will be involved. The salesperson can always explain his reasoning and his customer's thinking or requirements better than someone else who merely passes along the information. By the time that it goes through several hands, too much is lost. Sometimes people unintentionally reflect their own views and impressions when they are verbally repeating information. This is particularly true when a large order is lost. The salesperson should not feel that he can tell a low-level person the information, leave the office, and thereby minimize the impact. Working through channels, he should convey this information directly to senior people together with explanatory comments.

Sales Examples

There are four serious and one frivolous example that support this point. The serious examples are offered first.

Example 1

We had a dispute on one of our contracts involving an extra charge on custom-made products, and despite long discussions, had been unable to resolve it satisfactorily. It is common to have additions on products like this, some of which run into a lot of money, and some of which cause disputes. It came time to ship the units and to force a solution. Our general manager sent a telex saying if the customer did not agree to the extra amount, we would not ship the products. Since this was custom-made machinery requiring almost 12 months to complete, the customer could not easily make a substitution. He therefore felt we had him in a corner and that we were taking advantage of the situation.

Sending a stern wire was the worst possible thing to do. A meeting should have been requested. The general manager should not have shirked his duty. He should have met with the customer in person and explained our position, asking what else we could do to resolve the problem. To make matters even worse, the wire had originally been sent to an intermediary company that was assembling the package. The intermediary customer's people forwarded the nasty wire exactly as received to the ultimate customer. We destroyed a very fine relationship and never again sold this customer any more products. Even when the stations were expanded, they did not buy our units largely because of this insulting treatment.

Example 2

We were asked through an engineering contractor to bid products for a major European oil company. The specifications asked us to also include a competitor's component rather than one that we manufactured. This was against our company policy, and the salesperson told the contractor that in no uncertain words. However, he shirked his duty. He should have met with the ultimate user and the oil company engineers and courteously explained our dilemma. If this had been done, the specifications would have been changed. Even if they had not been, the customer would have understood our position, and our image would not have suffered. Instead, the oil company knew only that we declined to bid but did not know why. I later heard about this situation from the oil company's mechanical expert, who was directly involved. I know that if the salesperson had done his duty, this could have been worked out.

Example 3

We received a large order from a U.S. engineering contractor for a project in the Soviet Union. Shortly thereafter we learned that we could not at that time build and ship the product to the Soviets, because we would be unable to obtain an export permit from the Commerce Department. Rather than pass the word to a low-level engineer, I traveled a great distance to meet in person with the president of this engineering company. I wanted to fully explain what inquiries we had made with our government and exactly why we could not perform on this order. Later, we also met in London with a high-level Soviet delegation to explain to them our predicament. We did not leave it to the engineering company to get our story across to the Soviets. We explained that we had government rules and regulations much the same as they did, and that we were compelled to obey these rules. We explained that we had at all times acted in good faith and initially felt there was no problem with the export permit.

Our explanations, while disappointing, were appreciated by the engineering company and by the Soviets. As a result of our handling of the situation, when the political situation later improved, we did a lot of business with not only the Soviets, but also with the engineering contractor.

Example 4

We were given an order by an American petrochemical company for seven large reciprocating engines, mainly because we offered nonturbocharged units, whereas our major competitor quoted turbocharged machines. Two weeks after we entered the order with our factory, we were informed that because of the unusually high friction load, the nonturbocharged engines could not meet the guaranteed capacities. Thus we would be forced to also supply turbocharged units.

We certainly did not pass this devastating news to a low-level person. Instead, we got our story together, requested a high-level meeting, and presented a proposition to the customer that offered substantial advantages. We not only retained the order, but also kept the customer happy. We could not have accomplished this if this discouraging news had been passed to a low-level person. If we had done that, in all likelihood the order would have been summarily canceled before we could have done anything about it.

Example 5

During a recent baseball game, the losing team accused the opposing pitcher of scuffing the ball, and accumulated a quantity of balls to be examined. The umpire who worked home plate during the game was critical of the allegations. He said, "I don't appreciate the losing manager sending over a ball boy with a box of balls. If he was serious about his protest and wanted us to have the balls, he should have brought them himself." The manager shirked his duty. If he wanted the balls examined, he should have handed them directly to the senior umpire. It would only have taken a couple of minutes.

Summary

The salesperson should not shirk his duty when bad news must be relayed to the customer.

58

Keep in Touch

A frequent complaint heard from customers is that many salespeople come around only when a large order is up for purchase.

As salespeople go about their work, it is very easy for them to lose touch with people they are not currently calling on to sell products. It is always a good idea for a salesperson to keep in touch with potential customers who are not now buying, because sooner or later they will reappear in the marketplace. Keeping in touch can be done in many ways.

One way that a salesperson can stay in touch when his time is short is to have telephone conversations with his customers. Another is for him to have lunch with them, even though there are no jobs anticipated and he has no current business with them. Almost everyone goes out for lunch, and the salesperson can take advantage of that for a brief exchange of thoughts without absorbing much of anyone's time. For customers in other cities, the salesperson can call to see what is going on and to tell them anything new that has happened in his organization. This might be the design or sale of a new model of his products or a large order recently received. A salesperson should have a list of customers whom he has not seen or called recently, and he should check through it regularly. Otherwise, as he gets busy, months will pass without him realizing that he has not been in contact with important buyers or potential buyers of his products.

It is also important for a salesperson to keep in touch with people he knows well who have moved out of his area of responsibility. When a customer moves, the salesperson should notify his sales colleague in the appropriate area. He should include important information such as his likes, dislikes, and the degree of his past involvement with their firm. After a customer moves, a salesperson may not call him as regularly or write as often. However, the salesperson can send his customer postcards when he is on trips or write a note at Christmas time. These are good ways to remind the customer that the salesperson still exists and still remembers him.

The salesperson can also write notes when he learns his customer has been promoted or has had new additions to his family. Handwritten notes kept on a personal basis are more effective. Former business acquaintances will remember a salesperson pleasantly if they move back into his area or if he is promoted or transferred so that he is again responsible for the area in which they live.

Handwritten notes kept on a personal basis are more effective.

The salesperson should cultivate this habit of keeping in touch with individuals while he is young. In later years, he will find that he has a lot of friends in very important and high positions in their organizations. This will enhance the salesperson's prestige, not only within his company, but also with the customers' organizations.

There are other times it can be very rewarding for a salesperson to keep in touch with his customers who are no longer within his area for product sales. Perhaps a key decision maker has moved to work on another project or another aspect of a project, but is still within the same company, perhaps in the same city. Sometimes when that happens, the salesperson will make no further effort to contact him and will eventually forget he existed. A good salesperson, however, will continue to show his customer the same respect. He will call the customer occasionally, and take him to lunch when possible, even though the customer is no longer directly involved in evaluating and purchasing the salesperson's products.

The continued casual contact is important. While these individuals may leave a certain position, they rarely leave the industry and all of their acquaintances. They will continue to see them occasionally. In casual conversations they can say things that will help the salesperson if he has been one of the few who have kept in touch.

The salesperson would probably not continue to regularly entertain this former customer and invite him on trips to job sites or to factory demonstrations. This attention must now be transferred to the customer's successor, but the salesperson should still take time to be cordial to his former customer and to see him occasionally. He should always invite the former customer to general receptions or company functions held in the area.

It would be wise for a salesperson to remember that individuals who move to other areas are often those on their way up within their companies or in their industry. They will frequently return to the salesperson's territory, but in a position of more responsibility. The salesperson is ahead if he has continued to maintain contact. The following two examples indicate the results of my staying in touch with two of my customers.

Sales Examples

Example 1

The main evaluator and purchaser of our products was moved by his firm to another area to work on a special project having nothing to do with my products. Once every month or so I continued to call him, have lunch, and tell him what was going on in my sector. Two years later, he was promoted and moved back into the area where my products were evaluated and purchased. Six months later, he called one day, requesting delivery on our units. I obtained the shipping schedule from our factory and called for an appointment to present this delivery. As I gave it to him, he made notes.

When he finished taking notes, I figured a good salesperson should ask for the order, so I suggested that we go ahead and tie down the delivery and put the units on order. To my amazement, he said, "Okay, I will obtain order numbers for you." While he dialed his purchasing department, I almost passed out with shock. He gave me three purchase orders, since they were destined for three different locations. When I reported these orders, my factory was even more astonished than I was.

We had not even quoted these machines, but the customer then asked me to prepare a bid so that the formal orders could be sent along. That $3.5 million order was placed in the late 1950s—think what this would be worth today. Even though the city was not a large metropolitan center, our competitors did not learn about this purchase until weeks later, because the customer and my company, on request, kept quiet about it.

Years later, this customer told me he decided before I came to his office that he was going to give me the order and had already discussed it with his superior. His superior, expressing amazement, asked, "What are you going to tell the other vendors?" My friend said, "I can take care of that." He clearly wanted to give me the order. Keeping in touch with this gentleman when he was on another assignment was, in my opinion, the deciding factor in our obtaining this extremely valuable order.

Example 2

A senior engineer with a major customer resigned to start his own business. Upon learning this, I called his new office and asked him to have lunch. After our meeting, he sent me a handwritten note saying, "I enjoyed our luncheon meeting today as I've enjoyed all of our previous meetings/associations. I appreciate your thinking of me in my new venture. It was very thoughtful of you—particularly in light of the fact that I'm no longer in a position with one of your customers to have influence on their purchasing decisions. I do hope though that our business paths will cross in the future. If I can ever do you a favor, I hope you will not hesitate to call me."

Unfortunately, his business was not successful, but he went back to work for his old employer, who was one of our best customers. Later he told me I was the only salesperson who called him or showed him any attention when he was no longer in position to buy from them. I had only taken two hours to have lunch with this individual and to show genuine interest in his new undertaking. However, this effort placed my company in an even better position to obtain new business from the company to which he returned.

Summary

Specialized equipment or products may be sold over wide areas, but they are actually very small industries in terms of the salespeople and customers involved. Individuals get transferred and move around, but usually they stay in the industry. It will pay big dividends to a salesperson if he stays in touch with his customers.

59

Get the Next Order

Virtually all of a salesperson's selling should already be done when a major new inquiry is received. He should not wait to call on a customer until they are in immediate need of products. Everyone targets them when active jobs come up. One of the criticisms heard from decision makers is that some salespeople only show up when they hear about a new project or new business. Customers are usually sensitive about this, and they realize when a salesperson is paying attention to them only because he expects them to make expensive purchases. It is better if the salesperson makes an effort to contact his customers regularly between major purchases. He will be way ahead if on a continuing basis he helps them with estimates, keeps them posted on new developments, and sees that there are no problems with his products.

The salesperson should be going in to see his customers on a routine basis, even when he does not expect them to have a major inquiry coming out. He should tell them what is new in the industry and what improvements have been made in his products. He also should tell them about new orders he has recently received. Even if he has not personally had any new orders lately, someone in his organization has, and his customer will be glad to hear about them. He should show photographs of new, larger, more efficient, quieter, or stronger products.

The salesperson should also ask them about their expansion plans. This will help in his forecasting, and he will often learn very early in the game about new projects. He should check to see if the product they have purchased from the salesperson's company is working well. If it is not, he then has time to do something about it before a new project is underway. On a continuing basis, the salesperson should show a sincere interest in the customer, his requirements, and his industry.

If things are slow with the customers, they probably have not seen many salespeople. They may be interested to know what is happening in the industry, and they will be more available. The salesperson can provide useful information to them and perhaps help their reputations with their supervisors by keeping the contact people informed at a slack time in their activities.

When they are deciding on major capital expenditures, most professional people make up their minds slowly over a long period of time. By the time the inquiry is out, the decision makers have either basically made their decisions or they are leaning in a certain direction. It may be too late at that point for a salesperson to do very much influencing except with a dramatically low price or extremely short deliveries. He should not rely on either of these. These occasions make it obvious how important it is for a salesperson to work all the time toward obtaining the next order.

By the time the inquiry is out, the decision makers have either basically made their decisions or they are leaning in a certain direction.

When there is no major project currently in the works for a customer, the salesperson should be alert as to how he can help his customer's people in other ways. He could improve his rapport by sending technical papers or technical information that the customer's people do not already have. This is also the best time for a salesperson to provide tickets to sporting or musical events. Customers will welcome them more during this slack period in between big jobs. They are usually nervous if the salesperson offers these things when they are in the middle of making a decision on which products to purchase.

The salesperson should work constantly on getting the next order. While thinking about and working on the next order, a salesperson should continually be looking for ways to increase his sales. He should also be looking for new customers. There are many reasons a salesperson must keep up his efforts in more than one direction. These include the following:

1. A good salesperson will want his income to grow each year.
2. Existing customer bases in virtually all industries tend to shrink.
3. The salesperson's served market can get smaller due to products being shut down, becoming obsolete, or being replaced.
4. The decision makers with whom the salesperson is well established will move on to other jobs, get promoted, retire, or otherwise leave their positions, thus diluting his influence.
5. As technology changes, the demand for what the salesperson can provide decreases.

How does a salesperson locate new customers? Here are some suggestions:

1. He can ask his existing customers about any other potential customers who might buy his type of products.
2. He can talk to other salespeople in his industry (not competitors) and ask for leads.
3. He can read the business sections of newspapers in his territory for new plant announcements. He can identify and contact the decision makers who might purchase his product.
4. He can join and attend trade associations in his line of business. He can fraternize with customers who attend and also with noncompetitive salespeople. He should be alert for leads.

5. As he travels in his sales territory, he should look around for new or old installations that he did not know about. He should locate the operators and go see the buyers.
6. He can subscribe to and read industry trade journals to learn about new developments that could use his products. He might also read announcements about new plants or installations.
7. He should make absolutely certain he is calling on all known prospects in his area.
8. He should ask his existing customers to suggest other items he could provide beyond what he now offers.
9. He should make a lot of friends, because a salesperson never has enough friends. If he makes a lot of friends and has a good reputation, he will receive a lot of referrals.

Summary

The salesperson should not neglect his customers between large projects. He should visit them regularly and demonstrate that he is interested in them. He can bring news concerning the industry and any new products his company is offering. In order to increase his sales, he should always be prospecting as well as thinking about how he can obtain the next order.

Utilize Time Effectively

Dost thou love life? Then do not squander time, for that is the stuff life is made of.

—Benjamin Franklin

No problem is more universal than poor management of time. Everyone can do a better job in this area, and if they do, they can accomplish much more.

The paradox of time is that there is never enough, but we have all there is. A recent poll of managers revealed that 99% said they never had enough time to get their jobs done. This is equally true for salespeople. Unfortunately, the clock cannot be jiggled to squeeze out an extra hour. All that can be changed is what we do with the time we have. Many people waste up to one-half of every workday, starting with the first hour on the job. They participate in an opening exercise, such as having coffee, visiting, and socializing about the previous night's activities. On Monday, they discuss the weekend's activities.

There is an old adage that says, "As the first hour goes, so goes the day." Proper time management can make the entire day much more productive. A salesperson will produce better results and is likely to be rewarded with an increase in pay or a promotion.

A good place for a salesperson to start improving his time management is to accurately determine where he now spends his time. He can do this by logging his time usage in 15-minute intervals, noting his chief activity for each quarter hour. He should record this information hourly, not at the end of the day, because a person's memory can be deceptive. Making this record may be unpleasant, but the more serious the salesperson is about managing his time, the more important it is for him to keep this log. After he has logged his time usage for a week or so, or at least until he has a representative sample, he should evaluate the results. From this the salesperson should try to determine if some activities can perhaps be discontinued or shortened. He should not be too hasty in dropping activities. He should merely review this log and start planning better.

To all of us, time is precious, but to salesperson, it is so important as to actually represent money. A salesperson should continually think about what he can do to stretch himself further, because the really effective and successful salesperson never has enough time. Many good books have been written on this subject. An ambitious salesperson will read several of them, but reading about saving time is not enough. He must always be alert about conserving time and utilizing it well.

To all of us, time is precious, but to salesperson, it is so important as to actually represent money.

To grasp the idea of how important it is to save time, one should consider the following fact. If a person saves 10 minutes each work day, he will net more than one full week of productivity each year based on a 40-hour work week.

When the salesperson arrives in his office in the morning, he should already have in mind the first two or three most important things that he has to do that day. He should start on the most important one first. Occasionally, the salesperson might work on just one item all day, but at least he has the satisfaction of knowing that he was working on the most important thing. He should never walk into his office and then decide what ought to be done. All too often if a salesperson does that, he will allow events to control his time rather than making sure he is controlling his time.

Sometimes shortly after his arrival in his office, someone walks in to chat with the salesperson. In this situation he can sometimes become so involved that he does not start the most important thing until after he has allowed substantial time to pass. On the other hand, if a salesperson knows precisely which person to call or what he has to do when he walks into his office, he can start these things right away. He not only will be getting his work done, but he will deter people who want to casually visit with him. If they see he is intent on doing something, they will usually not interrupt. The salesperson will have to stick with this stringently to make this work. Even if someone is waiting to see him, he should excuse himself until he gets his priority items started. Often it will involve getting in touch with a customer in a different time zone. The sooner he gets started, the quicker he will accomplish his task.

The salesperson should remember that the early morning time is the most productive. The salesperson should not waste this time when he is fresher and can accomplish more. His customers are also fresher early in the day. It is wise for a salesperson to remember that more people seem to be in their offices early in the day, and they may well be in meetings or out of the office later in the day. Many times by starting early on his primary task, the salesperson can save an entire day. A delay in starting will inevitably cause him to miss the people he needs to contact, since later they will be unavailable. For example, if a salesperson knows that a certain customer goes to his office unusually early, he can capitalize on this by calling or arranging to see him at this time of day. Getting started early also will help the salesperson get more done within his own company.

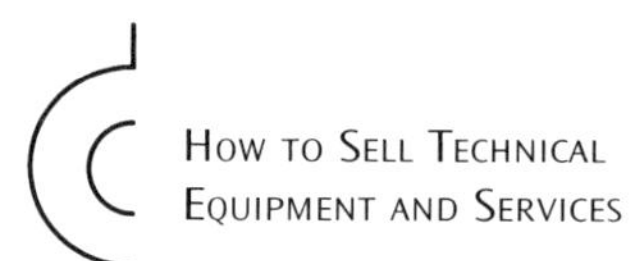

When the salesperson is in a customer's waiting room, on an airplane, in an airport, or other places where he has to wait, he should always have something he can read, work on, or study. Generally, this should be done unobtrusively, because he should not spread his files all over. These are excellent times to refresh his memory on his products, to make plans for the days ahead, or to read his accumulated low-priority mail. There might be people he should call, or this time might allow him to think about things that he needs to consider carefully. These periods can be well utilized by the salesperson if he makes notes of what he needs to do later. It is particularly important to make notes when he thinks of items to accomplish.

The salesperson should never wait to take notes until details are forgotten long after he has had a meeting. He should make notes as soon as he leaves an office. The sooner he makes the notes, the less time it takes and the more complete and accurate they will be. If he waits until later, he often must spend valuable time reconstructing events in order to recall and put in writing the salient points.

When the salesperson is returning by plane from a trip, he will find that the first two or three hours offer the best time to work. The longer his flight is, the duller his mind becomes and the less inclined he will be to work. He should sit down the first thing and make notes, write reports, work on expense books, and make lists of what he will do the first morning back in his office.

If the salesperson plans to see a customer in another city or a long way from his home or office, he should travel the night before or leave early enough to be in his office at 8:00 AM. He should never schedule a meeting for 10:00 AM or 11:00 AM and thus spend the prime early morning hours traveling. If the distance is great, it is smarter for the salesperson to go the night before so that he is where he needs to be before he goes to bed. Taking a very early flight is risky, because if it is delayed for any reason, his entire day can be lost, and his trip might have to be rescheduled.

Here are some other ways that a salesperson could utilize his time more effectively and get more done:

1. The salesperson can increase his alertness. He can do several things to help his alertness:
    - He can focus on his job.
    - He can shut out all unrelated thoughts.
    - He can concentrate on being more alert.

- He can concentrate only on what he is doing. Generally a person does so many things by rote that too often he does not concentrate enough when working on problems that require serious thought.
- He can change his routine. This forces him to be more alert as he follows his new method.

2. The salesperson should avoid the following negative factors that can sap his energy:
    - resentment
    - suspicion
    - fear
    - worry
    - dwelling on mistakes
    - criticism of others
    - self-criticism

3. The salesperson should protect his energy.
    - He should avoid thinking critically of people or events.
    - He should avoid being defensive. If he is asked if he finished an assigned task or mailed out a quotation, and he did not do so yet, he should say so and should not make excuses.
    - He should be sincere and be himself at all times.

4. The salesperson should maintain a businesslike approach. He should always give the impression that he is in a hurry and is working diligently to get his tasks done. If he is obviously working and not merely killing time, others are less likely to engage him in idle conversation and thus slow him down. He should aim sincerely at being productively busy and not just put on a show.

5. The salesperson should keep good records and keep them with him, especially addresses and phone numbers. He should not waste valuable time looking up phone numbers. Sometimes they are difficult to find, and then he will have to make several calls to obtain the number he needs.

6. The salesperson should not waste valuable time visiting with his colleagues. He should take time to be friendly but should not stretch out these encounters.

7. In a customer's office, the salesperson should proceed to business discussion with a minimum of small talk. The customer's time is important also, and the salesperson will find that more customers' doors are open to him if he has a professional reputation of promptly getting down to business. This also is important for a salesperson to practice with his colleagues. He should not drag out his departure from a meeting with a customer or with his colleagues. When his mission is completed, he should leave.

8. The salesperson should not spend too much time reminiscing, since valuable time can be wasted. It also can be boring to those who cannot easily relate to the events. A lot of customers put this at the top of their list of what salespeople do that bothers them.

9. The salesperson should not argue unnecessarily to prove his point on minor issues. Often it really does not make much difference.

10. Before beginning, the salesperson should think through his problems or tasks and plan how he will approach them. If he needs to make a telephone call or to write a letter, he should decide what he wants to accomplish and make notes before starting. The same thing is true if he must go to another department for answers. He should organize his thoughts before the meeting and go over his questions to make certain they are clear. If he plans his approach, he will have with him any necessary documents, memos, or files. He should also take notes on full-size paper and properly file them later. Doing these things will not only present a well-organized, professional approach, but it will shorten the meeting, saving time for everyone.

11. The salesperson must know when to stop working on something. If he has spent considerable time searching for a solution to a problem and seems to be getting nowhere, he should stop for a while He could work on something else or go for a short walk before continuing. Sometimes it might help the salesperson to restate his problem and see if a new angle or a solution occurs to him.

12. The salesperson should make sure he is well organized. He should cultivate the ability to handle details and develop the capacity to keep many things in mind simultaneously.

13. The salesperson should evaluate how to spend his time wisely. An effective salesperson must be constantly studying, evaluating, and making decisions on how to spend his time most profitably. For example, a salesperson should sit down, set goals, and assign himself quotas concerning the numbers of

    - calls he will make on existing customers;
    - calls he will make on new customers;
    - attempts he will make to sell new products;
    - sales letters to be written to new and existing customers.

The salesperson can also set goals on how often he will visit a certain area of his territory. He should set daily, weekly, monthly, and yearly goals. In fact, he should have lifetime goals. He should regularly take inventory to see how he is doing, and he should be honest in his evaluation.

There are several things that might help a salesperson better manage his time. The salesperson should remember to:

1. **Compartmentalize his time.** When he has a difficult task or a project that requires a lot of thought, he should set aside some time exclusively to accomplish this. He could find a secluded area or go to the library so that he can shut out everything else and avoid distractions and interruptions until he finishes. If he follows these guidelines, he will not only accomplish his tasks more quickly, but he will also reduce the possibility of making mistakes.

2. **Learn to concentrate.** The ability to concentrate is the ability to persevere on a course of thinking without distraction or diversion. The salesperson should keep in mind that this ability is a characteristic that enables people of only moderate capabilities to reach heights of attainment that have eluded geniuses.

3. **Avoid procrastination.** The salesperson should not postpone tasks just because they are distasteful. He certainly should have a priority list as mentioned earlier, but if something he must do is high on his list, he should not put it off just because it is troublesome. What usually happens is that he starts working on it and then puts it aside, which is a waste of time.

4. **Avoid personal chores during working hours.** The salesperson should avoid personal tasks during work hours unless absolutely unavoidable. Most people realize how much time can be lost while shopping, paying bills, making out expense records, or making personal telephone calls. The salesperson should keep these to an absolute minimum during working hours.

5. **Have a sincere desire to utilize his time wisely.** The key to success in anything is desire. To manage his time better, the salesperson must have a passionate desire or obsession to do so. Everything he does must be a servant of this desire. No matter the level of his ability, he has more potential than he can ever fully develop in a lifetime if he is truly focused on this.

6. **Work in an inspired manner.** The salesperson should plunge into his tasks with gusto as if he just cannot wait to get them finished.

The salesperson should not look for gimmicks in order to save time. The answer to the salesperson's shortage of time can only be found by carefully examining his basic work habits. To overcome time pressure, he should bear in mind that time is related to output. If he increases his output, he will have more time. Furthermore, output is related to his technique. If he improves his techniques, he will increase his output.

Regardless of a salesperson's education, experience, position, or age, it is never too late for him to start managing his time better.

Another reason for a salesperson to work diligently toward getting more done in less time has to do with his health. When a person suffers a health problem as a result of his job, it is invariably a time-centered problem that causes the stress. The individual complains that he just never has enough time to do all the things expected of him.

Summary

It is no longer enough for a salesperson to have a good education, to be conscientious on the job, and to work hard. To really be successful in his chosen field, the salesperson must spend part of each day or each week in improving his efforts and techniques. There is no better place for a salesperson to start than by learning to manage his time better. There are only 24 hours in a day, and this will never increase in spite of inflation, atomic energy, computers, or any other change that takes place in the world. The race belongs to the swift and to the salesperson who utilizes his time wisely.

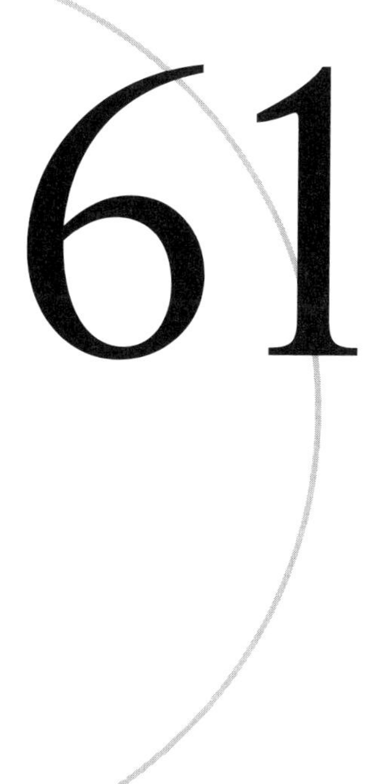

KEEP UP WITH PAPERWORK

A salesperson's duties, as in most jobs, involve a lot of paperwork. This paperwork usually falls into two categories:

1. **Timely paperwork.** This is paperwork that has a specific deadline, such as a quotation, forecast, weekly report, call sheet, or reports on problems or with active jobs. This also includes letters from customers and internal memos.

2. **General paperwork.** The remainder of the paperwork contains general information and will not always have deadlines.

The salesperson cannot do all of his paperwork every day. However, he must keep up with and expeditiously handle the timely and important paperwork, which if delayed will cause problems. The most successful salespeople are the ones who get the most things done, including the expeditious handling of paperwork.

The salesperson must make a commitment to excellence if he wants to succeed in the competitive world of sales. This means that he will have to work harder and strive to be faster, sharper, and smarter than his competition. It means that he will have to push himself and demand more from himself, even though others might settle for less.

To be successful in selling, a salesperson must get things done on time and should never procrastinate. Postponing a task rarely accomplishes anything. Sadly, many salespeople procrastinate anyway, and they are always late and trying to catch up on their paperwork.

Postponing a task rarely accomplishes anything.

In technical selling, there is always a vast amount of paperwork to take care of, either from a salesperson's customers or from within his company. It is important for a salesperson to stay on top of this work so that it does not become unmanageable. He should jump on his paperwork and take care of it quickly. It will be necessary for him to handle some of it during working hours. However, the routine paperwork or low priority items should be saved for outside working hours or at a time when the salesperson cannot call his customers.

One important piece of paperwork for a salesperson is his weekly plan. At least once a week, he should go through his notes, think seriously about what he needs to accomplish, and make a list. Then he should arrange it in order of priority and do the most important thing first. As he takes care of items on the list, he can check them off. If he begins with the most important item, then he can be assured he is making the best use of his time.

The salesperson should make notes as soon as possible after leaving a customer's office or returning from a meeting in which it would have been inappropriate to take notes. As pointed out earlier, many customers clam up and will not say much if the salesperson makes them feel like they are talking to a reporter. The exception would be if there are specific details that the customer would expect the salesperson to record. The salesperson should use memos to record the important points of his meeting as soon as he can conveniently do so, and the sooner the better. Also, he should always make notes of anything he learned, agreed to do, or wants to remember.

It is surprising how little a person retains if he waits two or three days to make these notes. This is particularly true if his area is big or he is very busy. There is something about a shift in scenery that causes details to be forgotten. The salesperson should jot down these details in the lobby or in his car as soon as he leaves the customer's office or plant. If he includes any facts and key phrases regarding what he has observed, he will find those notations most helpful in writing a report or memo later. The more notes he writes, the better his report will be. It is mandatory for a salesperson to make these notes right away if he promised the customer he would do something. He should never trust these promises to memory alone. He must write them down. Even when it is not necessary to convey certain facts to others, he should write a memo for his file to document valuable or reusable information. He should file some of these notes in the appropriate sales kits for use on future jobs or projects.

If the salesperson has letters to write as a result of meetings he attended while traveling, he should write them as soon as possible. If he is flying home, he can write or record these while he is traveling rather than waiting until he returns to his office. The quicker he puts these in writing, the less he will have forgotten, and the more accurate his notes will be. Usually after being absent for a few days, the salesperson will find people waiting to see him in his office. He will also face a number of other things that he must do right away.

The salesperson should not procrastinate regarding suggestions he has concerning improving his company's service to his customers. He should put them in a memo to his supervisor. It is also important for him to promptly report to management any difficulties he has with an order going through the plant. The earlier he writes about these problems, the earlier something will be done. Often it will lose its impact or importance if it is delayed. Furthermore, the same mistake or error may continue to be made if a salesperson does not report it immediately to the people who should correct the situation.

If the salesperson gives a customer technical information by telephone, he should confirm this information with the customer immediately, not days later when it may no longer have any significance. This is also true if the salesperson gives the customer additional details on his quotations or answers questions about a bid. A quick written response shows the customer that the salesperson is

well organized and indicates how he will also take care of the customer's orders. He should quickly confirm these additional details and take advantage of the opportunity to get across in print any additional selling points.

Sometimes a prompt report is necessary to keep a salesperson's supervisor properly informed concerning a problem or the status of an active job. This will keep the supervisor from being embarrassed if he is asked the status by his superiors. A successful salesperson should never do anything to make his boss look bad. In fact, he should do everything he can to make him look good. It will help the salesperson get raises and promotions and will otherwise help him be more successful, since his supervisor will be more likely to assist him when he needs help.

A salesperson should follow these same overall guidelines with his expense books. He should make notes each day on his expense forms. These books should then be completed as soon as the week ends. The longer he postpones making out these reports, the longer it will take to do them. If he allows several weeks' worth of forms to accumulate, it announces throughout the company that he is sloppy with paperwork. In my opinion, the final form of the expense books should always be completed outside of normal working hours. The time during the day should be spent in selling. This time is too precious and too important to be spent on routine paperwork.

If a report requires a lot of thought, the salesperson should work on it outside of the office. He will have fewer interruptions and can complete the work in a fraction of the time it would take during his office hours. He can then use his sales time to its maximum effect.

These same suggestions about promptness in paperwork also apply to a salesperson's weekly plans and his call reports. The salesperson should realize that his supervisors expect these reports punctually each week. Postponing or delaying them will not make them any easier for him to do, nor will they require any less time. He should keep in mind that this is a weekly requirement and should get on with it. Delays and carelessness in completing these reports are noted by management and taken into consideration when merit increases and promotions are discussed. Some salespeople spend more time complaining about how much time these reports require than it would take them to complete their paperwork.

Some salespeople delay reports or memos concerning problems because they hesitate to put things in writing. If a salesperson falls into this habit, he will create a bad impression of his work habits. It usually indicates that the salesperson is also poorly organized in his sales efforts and in taking good care of his accounts. Sometimes these delays on problems come about because the salesperson is afraid of offending someone. He should not be fearful about this if he is absolutely factual. He must act in good faith, be objective, use temperate language, strive to solve the problem, and avoid crucifying anyone. He should always be diplomatic and positive in verbal or written comments regarding in-house problems. If he follows these guidelines, he should have no hesitation about submitting his suggestions and remarks in writing. If he aims to do this constructively and sincerely, he will benefit himself, his company, and the other employees.

The amount of paperwork increases every year. To be a good salesperson and to progress in his organization, he should develop a reputation for keeping up with his paperwork, including forecasts. He should quickly answer requests from his customers or his own people. This will soon earn him a reputation for being prompt and conscientious. No one needs a reputation of being a procrastinator with his paperwork.

The salesperson's administrative assistant can be a great asset in handling the paperwork if there is a lot to do. This person can be trained to sort the originals and faxes in one box and copies in another. This is not to say that copies are not important. They are vital records, but originals certainly have priority. For a large territory, an assistant can simplify the salesperson's handling of correspondence by separating the mail according to geographical areas, districts, or regions. Messages requiring immediate attention can also be marked in red.

Sales Examples

Example 1

One of my overseas salespeople attended a meeting along with experts from our factory. The meeting took place on Thursday. The factory people flew back home, and the salesperson returned to his base. That weekend, the salesperson left for a previously scheduled three-day technical meeting and then went on holiday for a few days.

The factory people called me as soon as they returned to their offices to obtain my reaction to the meeting, so we could make a decision on our next step. I was completely in the dark, having not yet heard from my representative. When I finally tracked him down, he attempted to rationalize not writing a report. He reminded me that he had had to leave soon after his arrival home for the technical meeting and then had left on a previously scheduled holiday. I pointed out to him that he should have written the report on the eight-hour plane ride home from the customer meeting. By doing this, he would have remembered more of the facts and would have been able to leave it at his office to be typed and sent out before departing for his technical meeting.

Example 2

At another time, one of my salespeople left his domestic territory to spend 10 days working on an overseas order because an engineering contractor from his area was deeply involved in the project and had representatives on the overseas scene.

A few days after his return, the salesperson called to give me a long oral report, including the details of the many meetings that took place over several days. Since it was getting difficult for me to follow all of the new names and players, I interrupted to ask if all these details would not soon be coming to me in written form. His reply was that he had not found the time and that he had been very busy since arriving back in his office after being gone for so long. I told him that he should have written a daily account of the developments on the spot. He could have completed and polished up his report on the long flight home so it could have been sent to the various parties while he resumed his sales activities back in his home territory.

Summary

A salesperson must develop good work habits concerning paperwork. It is not going to go away. In fact with most companies, it increases every year. If a salesperson will come to grips with paperwork and get it done, he will be free to devote even more time to selling. He will receive more orders, because customers will quickly recognize that they are dealing with a well-organized salesperson.

VI

Troubleshooting Difficult Situations

62

Tough or Unpleasant Customers

Most salespeople tend to call only on the customers who treat them best, or the customers they like and know well. However, this is a mistake. While a salesperson certainly should pay attention to these customers, as well as those who historically buy from him, he should not avoid the unpleasant ones. Almost everyone will get along with customers who are easygoing. Most salespeople, on the other hand, will avoid tough and unpleasant customers. The salesperson should focus on this group, because the ground is fertile and the selling crowd will be smaller. He likely will discover after he gets to know them that many of these customers are fine people.

The initial demeanor of these customers can dissuade salespeople from follow-up calls. Many of these customers dislike all salespeople, so a salesperson should not take their rejections personally. Such customers often give the initial impression that they are extremely tough and unreasonable, but they rarely maintain that image if approached repeatedly with understanding.

With unpleasant or unfriendly initial demeanors, these customers will indeed scare most salespeople away. Many salespeople will say life is too short to bother trying to get along with them and will avoid them, but this is the wrong attitude. The proper approach is for a salesperson to listen carefully, be sympathetic to their views, ask questions, and encourage them to talk. By doing all of these things, he will usually win them over.

Some individuals do not talk much in meetings and do not respond immediately to comments or even questions. However, the salesperson must give them time to respond. Salespeople generally abhor silence like nature abhors a vacuum, but they must be patient and give the customer time to answer. With a tough customer, it is even more important that the salesperson get right down to business when he enters the customer's office, almost before he reaches his chair.

Before going to see these individuals, a salesperson must plan his strategy well and should outline exactly what he wants to accomplish. He should make notes and review his proposed comments to be sure they are solid and difficult to dispute. These individuals generally pounce on any misstep, particularly any statement they perceive as being too boastful or self-serving.

If a salesperson is challenged on any of his comments, he should ask questions and listen. He should never try to match wits and get into arguments with this type of individual. It is not necessary to roll over and play dead, but by asking questions, the salesperson gives the tough customer a chance to expound on his theories and his knowledge. This will allow him to vent his frustration, and he will usually then feel better toward the salesperson. The salesperson thus will learn more about the customer.

This type of customer is usually upset at things in general—his company, all salespeople, and even society. The salesperson could ask him if he is a native of the area, ask him about his family, or ask him questions about his job. He can ask the customer where else he has worked and if he has had experience on the salesperson's products or the competitor's products. He could ask what professional achievement gave the customer the most satisfaction.

The salesperson should listen carefully to the customer. When it is appropriate, he should tell the customer that he does not blame him for being upset at what goes on in the industry. The salesperson should explain that he is also a professional and an expert who can be of valuable service to the customer's company. The salesperson should mention that he could provide technical information, help the customer and his company make better decisions, and help them save money.

The salesperson should welcome these encounters and prepare for them. These experiences will teach him how to get along with the many different types of individuals he will meet in sales.

Another way for a salesperson to get along with people like these is to be oblivious to their idiosyncrasies. He can ignore their unusual traits and avoid harsh judgments. The salesperson's primary objective is to sell, not to analyze or criticize people. Many times if the salesperson makes harsh judgments or reads a lot into what someone says or does not say, he will be off base. The salesperson should give the customer the benefit of the doubt. He should not leave the customer's office mumbling about him or telling others how odd or unusual he is. These bad thoughts will stick in a salesperson's memory and will without doubt later subconsciously influence his relations with that customer.

The salesperson should give the customer the benefit of the doubt.

The salesperson should accept the customer at face value, treat him as a normal person, continue to call on him, and summon all his resources to know him better and to take care of his requirements. The experience gained will make it easier the next time the salesperson encounters this situation. Most assuredly, the salesperson will later run into many other people who are not easy to communicate with or who are unpleasant.

This does not mean that a salesperson should not try to evaluate and size up people, because that is an important part of his job as a salesperson. However, he should avoid trying to be too clever in this area. He can do this by remembering that his objectives are to get to know the customer and to convince him to buy

from the salesperson's company. He primarily wants to get the orders, not to analyze or find fault. Once converted or won over, these individuals will usually be the salesperson's most loyal customers.

The salesperson should not be dismayed or discouraged at what might seem to be unreasonable approaches and demands made by a few of his customers. This requires a supreme effort on the part of the salesperson to accommodate them the best he can. He must do this in a manner that is consistent with the economics involved and his company's policies. A salesperson certainly cannot give away major financial concessions, but he should at least try to understand the request by asking many questions.

When a request is made or information is asked for, the salesperson should not quickly jump to conclusions. He should try to learn what the customer wants to accomplish and then do his best to accommodate the customer within company guidelines. Perhaps what he is asking for is not what he really needs in order to achieve his objective. Only by accurately determining his aims can the salesperson evaluate his true needs. For example, the customer may ask for a manufacturing drawing which, because of company policy, the salesperson cannot provide. By asking why he wants the drawing, the salesperson can determine how to solve his problem and give the customer what he needs without providing a manufacturing drawing.

Usually if a salesperson fully understands what the customer wants, and he explains the internal problems he faces, an acceptable compromise can be worked out. This may require several meetings, but the salesperson should do his best to reach a solution acceptable to both sides. Usually by thoroughly analyzing the situation, he can accommodate the customer by furnishing much less information than was originally requested.

It is easy for a salesperson to say that a customer is unreasonable, but anyone can do that. If a salesperson is truly interested in selling the maximum amount of products, he will make every reasonable effort to accommodate difficult customers. Learning how to sell to tough customers will make the salesperson's job easier with all of his other customers, with dramatic overall results.

Sales Examples

Example 1

Early in my career, I called on a young engineer who occupied a very strategic position within his company. All inquiries and quotations had to go through him. He was very bright and obviously on his way up. He really did not like salespeople and often made that known verbally and by the way he treated sales representatives.

Realizing this, I was extremely careful with this individual. I made certain I was well prepared before I went to see him. I did not ask for appointments with him very often, and then only if I had something important to convey. I got down to business immediately, and there was almost no small talk, even at the end of our meetings. I handled all of his requests for information expeditiously and presented a professional approach. I ignored his idiosyncrasies and asked a lot of questions when I was with him. I got him to talk, and then let him talk about himself.

After a while, our meetings in his office became much more productive, and he often asked only my company for early estimates on new projects. Before too long, he started dropping by my apartment late at night if he was driving by and saw the lights on. He would show up at my door, and we would chat for hours.

We became very good friends, and my company received more than our share of the business from this customer. This was largely because of my persistence and patience in genuinely trying to get along with this unusually bright and talented individual.

Example 2

The key decision maker with a large company was always easy to get in to see, but he would not say anything. He never refused a request for an appointment, but he just would not talk. He would merely sit at his desk and look at me. After several calls stretching over several months, I became very frustrated. I decided I was going to get him to talk and would win him over to our side. I planned my next meeting carefully. I rehearsed what I was going to say and do in his office, and then I made an appointment.

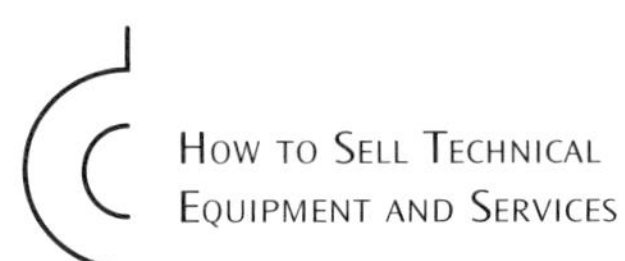

I took with me a lot of photographs of the products I was trying to sell. I spread out several pictures in front of him and made short identifying comments about each. Then I asked him what he thought about these. As expected, he said nothing, but this time I was prepared. I just waited and kept on waiting. Of course, to a salesperson in a customer's office, it seemed like an eternity, but actually it was only a few seconds. Eventually, he began to talk and to answer my questions. He commented on each photograph, explaining how they had similar products or had done things differently in their installations.

I discovered that previously in similar circumstances, I had been too impatient and did not give him enough time to respond. I did not wait long enough for him to reply and started talking again myself, and thus ended up doing all of the talking. After that, I always had good meetings with this gentleman, because I gave him time to answer and to talk.

This taught me a valuable lesson about dealing with customers: When a salesperson asks a customer a question or requests his opinion, he should stop talking and give the customer time to answer. Too many salespeople simply cannot stand silence and start talking again too soon.

Summary

A salesperson should never avoid tough or unpleasant customers. Instead, he should view them as opportunities to sharpen his sales skills and to win them over.

Resurrecting an Account

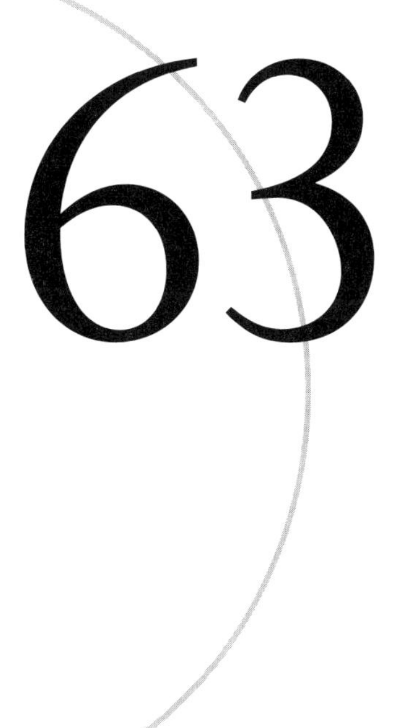

All sales companies at one time or another will have major accounts that are in bad shape—accounts with which they are receiving little or no business, even though they once did. A successful salesperson will not allow this situation to continue. All problem, or *blocked*, accounts under his jurisdiction should be identified, and he should initiate a plan of action for each. The salesperson's competition is selling to the customers, and so should he. The salesperson's goal in recapturing these accounts should be to develop a new image for his firm and a new perception of how the customer views his company. He needs to understand how the customer views his company.

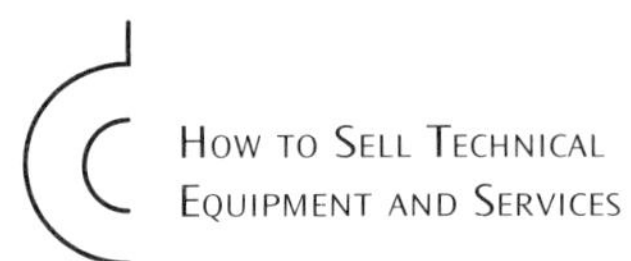

Before undertaking this task, he should thoroughly analyze the problem. He must determine how and why the situation reached this stage. To do this, he should first obtain all the recent files and read them. Next he should make a list of his company's people and the customer's personnel whose names appear in the internal and external correspondence. The salesperson must learn as much as he can about the problems by reading these materials, and then he should objectively summarize them. He should not jump to conclusions and should not try to decide at this stage who is at fault from what he has read.

When all is said and done, the responsibility for correcting the problems and restoring the account rests with the salesperson and his company. Regardless of anything the customer may have done wrong or to what degree the customer was at fault, the salesperson is responsible for discovering and implementing the solution. He can only do this through his own efforts and with the help and support of his company. As he approaches this task, he should bear in mind that companies are composed of individuals, so it is individuals who will have to be won over.

After reading all the files and available correspondence and using the lists made, he should talk to all of the people in his company who have been involved with this account to see what he can learn. He should then ask for information about why the customer is unhappy with their firm, what they know about the customer's personnel involved, and what they feel needs to be done to correct the situation. He should also ask what input they can give regarding why the customer does not buy from them and the reasons the customer feels the way he does about their company.

If possible, the salesperson should identify other salespeople who do not sell competitive products and are familiar with this account. He should ask them why they think this customer buys from their current suppliers and not the salesperson. Perhaps some other employees of the customer, if a salesperson knows them well enough, can be asked this same question.

Information gained from these sources can be very instructive and valuable. There may be many possible reasons that a customer is not currently buying from the salesperson. These include the following:

1. A previous salesperson may have gone over the head of the customer's contact person when a job decision was going against him.
2. A salesperson or an engineer may have failed to keep promises.

3. The customer may have experienced costly, chronic, or unresolved operating problems with the salesperson's products.
4. The customer may have received inadequate service.
5. The customer may have received poor-quality spare parts or poor delivery.
6. The salesperson's company may have failed to make committed deliveries on new products.
7. The customer may have experienced efficiency or reliability problems with the machinery or products.
8. The customer may feel the salesperson's products are just not competitive.
9. The customer may feel the products are more expensive to install, operate, or maintain.
10. The customer may have the impression that the salesperson's product takes longer to assemble or commission.
11. The customer may think the design of the salesperson's engineered products is poor or noncompetitive.
12. The customer may have key people who have had excellent service from competitive products but do not know the salesperson's products very well.

A salesperson should use this list and take into consideration the knowledge gained from studying the files and talking to the people who have been involved. He then should be able to make a list of the major reasons for the customer's dissatisfaction. Once a salesperson has a list of what caused the customer's unhappiness and which of the customer's people were involved, he should have some idea of what to sort out and with whom.

The salesperson should not underestimate the task of sorting out these problems. It will be difficult, and he cannot do it alone. It will take a lot of time and effort. The salesperson will need extensive help, especially from his top management, in order to give a high priority to this customer's current problems and future requirements. To gain maximum support, the salesperson should give his management an estimate of how much business is now being lost and the potential sales this customer represents. This should enhance his chances of getting help when he needs it to give this customer special consideration and service.

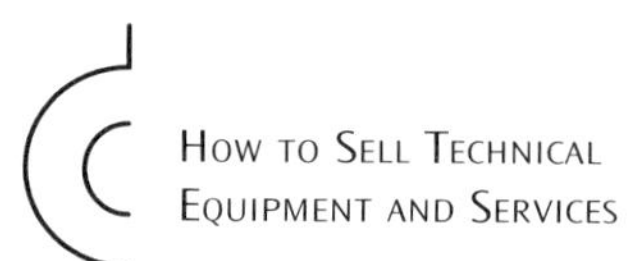

The salesperson's approach to his customer depends on what the problems are. In some cases, the salesperson can only apologize for past mistakes by his people and assure the customer that he will make every effort to prevent future problems. He should bear in mind that the customer will probably be skeptical. If the salesperson is new on the account, his chances may be a bit better, because he will bring a different face and a fresh perspective to the problem.

The customer in any case will be doubtful and will remember that he has had trouble and unsatisfactory service from the salesperson's company in the past. Several questions will concern him, such as:

- Why should I listen to them?
- Why should I waste my time meeting with this company's representative?
- What's in it for my company?

In deciding what approach to take, the salesperson should put himself in the customer's shoes and look at the situation as he would. What does the customer now expect in order to be able to again look favorably on the salesperson's company? From the viewpoint of the customer, the salesperson should decide how to appeal to the customer's interest in benefiting his company.

After considering the customer's viewpoint, the salesperson should make a preliminary plan and review it with his management. After obtaining their input, he should try to predict what the customer's reaction to the plan might be and what questions he might ask. The salesperson should analyze these reactions and questions and decide on the proper response with his management. This level of preparation will go a long way toward avoiding surprises. By discussing the plan with his management, the salesperson will be taking a planned approach and can present a united front and offer replies that will do the most to improve his company's tarnished image.

The salesperson should then request a meeting with any decision makers involved. By meeting with the people directly and influentially involved in potential purchase orders, he can obtain their input so he can finalize his plan. He should tell the customer that he is aware that a problem exists and that he is taking steps to correct his company's past shortcomings, without necessarily mentioning all of them. He should ask for guidance.

During this meeting, the salesperson should try to determine who the customer's current supplier is and what the customer particularly likes about them. He should find out what the customer expects from his vendors. It is important that the salesperson not assume that he knows all of the customer's expectations. He will know many of them, but by asking, he may flush out additional subtle or unique requirements that will really help with his task. He might learn something not generally known, even to his competitors.

The salesperson also should ask the customer what he buys the most of and in what areas his purchases are increasing or decreasing. During all of this, the salesperson should try to zero in on items the customer needs and that the salesperson's company excels at producing. He should show how his company can help the customer by offering better quality, better prices, or better deliveries. He should demonstrate to the customer the benefits of resuming business with the salesperson's firm.

If the salesperson is successful in determining answers to several of these questions, he will know much more about where to concentrate his efforts. This will also allow him to supplement his preliminary plan of action.

During the meeting with the customer, the salesperson may learn that the customer starts to work very early. With this information, he may be able to call on the telephone or meet with the customer more often by arranging early appointments. The salesperson may learn that the customer likes football, baseball, basketball, or even the opera. He may learn that the customer has a special interest, either business related or outside of work. This would enable the salesperson to give him a new book on the subject or to send him newspaper or magazine clippings that he may have missed. Virtually all buyers have a special interest that, when discovered, will enable a salesperson to more successfully sell to him.

Virtually all buyers have a special interest that, when discovered, will enable a salesperson to more successfully sell to him.

The salesperson should take his cues from the responses he gets. Hopefully, he will be given some directions and encouragement concerning how to proceed. Even if the customer does not tell the salesperson what he must do to get back in good graces, the salesperson should gauge his reactions. This should give him some idea of what he must do next, especially if he listens carefully to what the customer has to say. Of course, the salesperson should ask a lot of questions about the past problems so he can do what is necessary to sort them out and to prevent a reoccurrence.

If the problem was poor field service, the salesperson should be sure that the next time the customer requests assistance, the best person in the plant is immediately dispatched to help. The salesperson should suggest that the customer alert the salesperson directly when next he requires help, so he can personally make certain his firm responds quickly. The salesperson must be sure to follow up on this request. If the problem was poor delivery, the salesperson should tell the customer what he has done internally to monitor production and to avoid late shipments. He should insist that future orders from this customer receive special priority handling throughout engineering, manufacturing, and shipping. The salesperson must monitor the order regularly himself to make certain there are no problems.

If the trouble was due to chronic operating problems, the salesperson should make sure the problems are now sorted out. If not, he should get busy on them, regardless of the product's age. This will require special authorization if the product is out of warranty, but if the customer is not now buying from the salesperson's company because of this chronic problem, something must be done. The salesperson should obtain details of these problems and present the situation to his top management. Again, he should remind his management how much business is now going to their competitors. He should point out that if they are to participate in this business, he must solve their past product problems, regardless of the age of the equipment.

The salesperson should not give up until his customer is satisfied. This may require a lot of persuasion on his part. At this time he should employ his sales skills with his management. Then he will be able to tell the customer how his company has corrected these problems on its new products. The salesperson will thus remove the stumbling block when the customer is considering new purchases.

The salesperson should then begin at the lowest level in the customer's organization to give good service and to correct any outstanding problems. He should be sure even the smallest request is handled promptly. He must closely monitor everything that is going on between this customer and his company so he can prove by his deeds that he intends to create a new perception of his firm.

He must always act in good faith. The salesperson should create a new image for his company and prove that his product is both reliable and competitive. He must show that his company will support it responsively.

There are several ways a salesperson can improve his company's image. He can show a list of well-known firms regularly buying his products. He could demonstrate that he can quote competitive prices. Depending on the problem, he could offer to take this customer on plant visits to see satisfied product users. Customer visits to the salesperson's factory to see the facilities may improve the situation. The customer might also appreciate product presentations or discussions with the salesperson's executives, design engineers, and manufacturing people. The salesperson should invite the customer's decision makers and top-level people to his headquarters and if far away, offer to pay their travel expenses. If they cannot travel to the salesperson's facilities, the salesperson could take key people from his firm to visit the customer. He should keep emphasizing how his products and service can benefit the customer.

The salesperson should identify and concentrate on the people in areas of greatest resentment. He should tell them what he is attempting to do and ask for their guidance. Most will offer suggestions. When appropriate, he should move progressively up through the organization. By the time the salesperson reaches the upper management, the climate will already be different. He can review with them what he has done so far. He should also ask for their guidance and suggestions and follow them as closely as possible.

A salesperson who has thoroughly identified any problems will make great strides in solving them. Such is the case with a problem account. When a salesperson puts down on paper the details of the difficulties, most of the solutions will be readily apparent. A salesperson can resurrect problem accounts with perseverance and a sincere, earnest effort by himself and his firm. He must demonstrate through his actions that he represents a serious, honest, and reliable supplier.

This will require a sustained effort of providing extraordinary treatment for customers who are unhappy with the salesperson's firm. It cannot be done overnight. It can be accomplished if the salesperson demonstrates over a long period of time that he and his company are taking a sincere approach to correcting the past problems. The salesperson should demonstrate through his actions that the customer's orders will receive the best care if placed with the salesperson's firm. He must convince those who are dissatisfied that he will make the difference, working diligently to give outstanding service.

As the salesperson attempts to resurrect an account, he should be alert to any progress that is being made. If he feels he has made substantial headway, he may be near the opportunity point. If so, he should increase his efforts and concentrate on obtaining an order of some kind.

The salesperson should ask to be given a chance to show what he can do. One approach is to ask for a small order or one that is not too crucial. If he does receive one, he must bend over backwards to do an outstanding job. He should make sure that it is followed daily to avoid delays. He also should insure that it ships in entirety and on time, following through until the product is placed in service.

Sales Examples

Example 1

Many years ago, upon being transferred to a new territory, I was assigned a major account whose main office was in my area. The previous salesperson on this account was transferred out of town before I arrived. Prior to going to see this customer, I called the previous salesperson to ask if he had any suggestions or guidance. He replied, "When you mention our company's name in their presence, they say a bad word."

With this background information, I decided that I would not take even my supervisor with me when I made my original contact. I knew a few people in this company. With some research, I learned that this customer was unhappy because he had received poor service on quotations and on spare parts deliveries.

I started at the very bottom of their engineering organization. I called someone I had known earlier and made an appointment. I took with me photographs of our new products. After showing these photographs and making my pitch on our various models, I asked to be introduced to his colleagues or office mates. Within a week or so, one of them called for information to make an estimate on a new project.

I next moved up a layer and repeated this procedure. I then went to the operating department and did the same thing. I learned they also had problems in the field with some of our units. Using my telephone credit card in their offices, I called the factory service manager to get the solution started. I closely monitored the situation until the problems were solved.

They also had difficulties with spare parts. I took careful notes and sorted out their problems, often appealing to the top officials in my firm. If urgent, I would call from their offices to initiate solutions. That way, if our factory people had questions, I could answer them on the phone by consulting with the customer on the spot.

I demonstrated by deeds that I cared about their problems, and I got results from within my own firm. If I did not succeed at first, I tried again, going higher in my own organization until I obtained what the customer wanted and was entitled to. I found that all his requests were reasonable and appropriate, but in the past, they had just been ignored. Any time their engineering department or the operating department called, I jumped on top of the problems and got them solved. If I promised an answer by a certain time, I delivered. If occasionally I could not, I called and explained and kept them fully informed on our progress.

After a few months I was ready to call on the vice presidents. By the time I did this, they were already hearing good reports on my efforts, so I received friendly receptions.

Following these efforts, my company received more than its share of new products and spare parts business from this customer during the three years I handled this account. I did not give the store away. I just made certain the customer received good service and that all problems were expeditiously handled. I made sure that any back charges were settled fairly and equitably. I practiced the Golden Rule.

The main thing I did was to show this customer that I cared about his business, and I responded when he needed help. I convinced him that his orders were in better hands if given to us. I showed the customer what was in it for him. When a salesperson demonstrates to his customer that he is really trying to solve his problems, he will respond favorably.

Example 2

A major oil company in Southeast Asia had a serious problem on one of our models. Since it was in a critical duty, the customer asked our service people to treat the problem confidentially. For this reason I did not learn about it for several months, even though it was in an area over which I had sales responsibility. When I learned of the trouble through an interested third party, I requested a meeting through this source. The customer replied by saying that he saw no reason for discussions, since my company in the past had shown no interest in solving his problem. He turned the request down flat.

I sent word back that if they would agree to a meeting, I would do my very best to find a solution. I made no other commitment. With this assurance, they agreed to let us come to their main office for discussions.

I located all of the files on this problem and read every page. I made a list of all of the people from my company whose names appeared in the files and had been involved with these difficulties. I then called every person on the list and found out what they knew about this difficulty. From all of this I learned that the customer wanted us to repair his recently failed parts at no financial gain to us.

Before leaving on the trip, I discussed the settlement possibilities with management, since I knew telephone communications from our destination were impossible. I was given full authority to settle the claim and to do whatever was necessary.

When we arrived in the customer's office for the meeting, there were seven or eight people on their side, including a lawyer. After reviewing the current status of the situation, the customer asked for our offer on this repair. I responded by showing a copy of our company's most recent annual report and said that as a corporation, we had earned 12% the previous fiscal year and expected to earn 15% this year. Therefore, I felt a 15% discount would satisfy their request that we do this repair "at no financial gain." Their lawyer immediately responded by saying, "Oh, no—we mean no financial gain on this specific transaction."

I had anticipated this question and had carefully thought out my reply before leaving on this trip and had committed it to memory. I answered by saying I did not believe his company could calculate the exact cost of a quart of their oil or a gallon of their gasoline that I purchased back in my home town. I also did not believe they could accurately know the cost of a shipload of refined products at their dock out our window. I said that we must deal in average numbers. The managing director had been carefully listening to these exchanges and replied that I was exactly correct and that they would happily accept my offer.

This satisfied the customer completely, and when our management learned of this settlement, they were ecstatic. It came about by thoroughly researching the problem and by listening to and giving the customer what he wanted. This was easy, since it was a reasonable request. I showed what the customer what was in it for him.

A salesperson must work diligently at resurrecting any problem accounts. He will never have enough customers, so he cannot afford to have large purchasers mad at his firm. He must determine what it will take to bring back the customer's business, and then he must do it.

Summary

1. Virtually all companies have major accounts that are in bad shape.
2. All problem accounts should be identified, and a plan of action should be initiated for each.
3. To resurrect an account, the salesperson must analyze carefully and objectively what caused the customer to stop buying from his firm.
4. To accomplish this, he should review the files and talk to everyone who was previously involved.
5. The salesperson should not jump to early conclusions but should be strictly objective.
6. The salesperson's company must be the one to initiate solutions to the problems and to get its own house in order.
7. The salesperson should question the customer's people and any salespeople who are not competitors.
8. From this investigation, the salesperson should write down his opinion of what went wrong and what caused this customer to stop buying from his company. He should show what is in it for the customer if he again buys from the salesperson's firm.
9. In consultation with management, the salesperson should formulate a tentative plan to implement the necessary corrective actions. He should take into consideration what he feels the customer expects and what will satisfy him.
10. In arriving at an action list, the salesperson should put himself in his customer's shoes and look at the situation as he would.
11. The salesperson should schedule a meeting with the customer's personnel.

12. The salesperson should find out what the customer's people have to say about why they have not been buying from the salesperson's firm. They may not reveal much, but usually most of what they say will already be on the salesperson's list if his investigation was thorough.
13. The salesperson must find out who the customer is now buying from and why.
14. The salesperson must determine what the customer purchases most and then evaluate his company's future sales potential with the customer.
15. The salesperson should identify any unusual interests and work habits.
16. From these customer meetings and his internal investigation, the salesperson should finalize his list of complaints that must be addressed.
17. The salesperson must implement his plan, ranking the items in order of importance so he addresses the most serious first and then works down the list.
18. The salesperson should concentrate on the individuals who appear to have the greatest resentment. He should start at a low level in the organization and work up to the top-level executives. He should not start at the top.
19. The salesperson should give all future orders special treatment so as to avoid past mistakes.
20. The salesperson should concentrate on all large accounts that are not now buying from his company.
21. The salesperson should make himself the difference. He must convince the customer that the orders will be in better hands if placed with the salesperson's company.
22. The salesperson should work hard at resurrecting any problem accounts.
23. Correcting any of his firm's past mistakes will pay the salesperson big dividends in the form of new business.

Resolve Equipment Problems

Every manufacturer who builds products will have operating problems sooner or later. The salesperson should never minimize these difficulties, because they are expensive, time-consuming, and have the potential to severely damage his relations with his customers. They could cost him future orders. On the other hand, troubles or problems can present opportunities to show the customer how the salesperson and his company perform when adversity strikes. If a salesperson promptly sorts out the difficulties, he may be more respected and his sales position with the customer may be stronger than when he started.

While no salesperson likes to hear complaints from his customers, he should be highly suspicious if a customer never complains. One of the surest signs of a poor or deteriorating relationship is the absence of complaints. No customer is ever that happy and that satisfied. The customer is either not telling the salesperson about his complaints, or he has not had the opportunity because the salesperson is not calling on him often enough. Sometimes the problems are simmering at a lower level within the customer's organization than the salesperson contacts.

The salesperson should welcome complaints, because they are actually a wake-up call, providing him with an opportunity to work with the customer to sort out problems. Statistics vary, but the experts say that for every complaint a salesperson receives, there are 15–20 dissatisfied customers who do not complain and do not let him know they are unhappy. They just take their business elsewhere.

The salesperson should welcome complaints, because they are actually a wake-up call, providing him with an opportunity to work with the customer to sort out problems.

When a salesperson receives a complaint of any kind, he should bear in mind the following:

- If he listens to the customer and pays attention to the problem, he will stay in business.
- The customer's expectations have not been met.
- The problem provides an opportunity for the salesperson to satisfy a dissatisfied customer by fixing a service or product breakdown.
- The salesperson and his company will benefit by welcoming this opportunity rather than getting upset and lashing out at the customer.
- The customer is giving the salesperson and his company an opportunity to respond so that he will keep buying from them.

- Too often the salesperson will address the surface complaint and will miss the deeper concern. This might cause the customer to look elsewhere next time if the salesperson does not take care of the real problem.
- To better understand a complaint, the salesperson must see it through the eyes of the customer.
- The salesperson should try to imagine that whatever just happened to the customer has just happened to himself. He should practice empathy and consider what his customer would be thinking and feeling. He should consider how the customer might react, what he would expect, and what it would take to make him happy. What response would be necessary for the customer to walk away from this encounter and feel good about the salesperson's company?
- Someone has said that problems or complaints are opportunities in work clothes.
- It is true that there are some customers who will try to cheat the salesperson, but they represent only 1–2% of the total. The salesperson cannot treat all customers as if they are thieves in order to protect himself from this small percentage.
- Sometimes a salesperson gets upset at the way the complaint is delivered. The individual voicing the complaint may lack social skills and come across very harsh, angry, or even stupid. The salesperson must learn to focus on the content of the complaint and not on the way it is delivered.
- If a complaint is handled properly, the salesperson's relations with the customer can be even stronger and better than they were before the problem.

When a casualty or mishap occurs with a salesperson's machinery or parts, time is very important. He must report promptly to his service department if he is the one first notified by the customer. His first impulse may be to pick up the phone, but this is not the best approach, especially if the service department is in another city. When the customer calls to report a serious difficulty, the salesperson should ask as many questions as he can think of and make complete notes. Next, he should send an urgent written report, informing the recipient that he will call as soon as he knows that the message has been received.

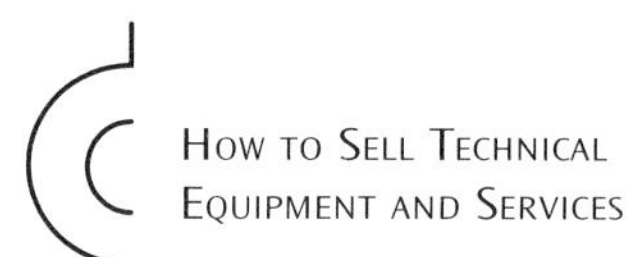

It is important for the salesperson to put this information into writing. Otherwise, his contact must make notes from their telephone conversation, and too many facts are likely to be lost. The salesperson's contact probably must pass this information to others for handling. It is much better to have the details in writing directly from the salesperson. It is best to send a written report even if the service department is just down the hall from the salesperson's office. After his message has had time to arrive, the salesperson should call and start exerting pressure for a prompt response. By then, the service manager or the person who will handle the problem will probably have additional questions. The salesperson can answer them or expedite the replies from his customer.

When a product or a part fails within its warranty period, the first thing for a salesperson to do, of course, is to get the necessary replacement parts on the way to the job site. Since the product is still under warranty, the salesperson's company will in all probability be blamed for the failure. Therefore, he should consider sending a service person there to help in the repair but also to investigate. The service specialist can determine and report on the cause of failure. This procedure will provide an excellent source of information when the time comes to establish responsibility. The inconvenience to the customer will be minimized, and the damage to the salesperson's relations with his customer will be reduced.

If a major failure occurs at a plant site within the salesperson's territory, he should, if at all possible, go to the job site. This has many advantages:

1. It shows interest and concern.
2. It will impress the customer. The salesperson should never underestimate the importance of his presence.
3. It will enable him to make sure top priority is given to the problem within his service and spare parts organizations.
4. His presence will assist in getting information necessary for his engineers to determine the cause of failure.
5. He will learn more about his product.
6. He will meet operating people and possibly management people he otherwise would not encounter.

The salesperson should insist that the involved service people daily write complete, thorough, and accurate reports and not rely on verbal reporting. Certainly, phone calls are necessary to get things moving, but reports should be written every day so that nothing is forgotten due to the passage of time. Events will be happening fast, but the serviceperson should make notes. Before retiring for the night, he should put down in a written report all relevant data and events occurring that day. Even if the situation is static, the daily circumstances should be reported and recorded.

When settlement time comes, sometimes months later as it does with especially chronic problems, the salesperson will be grateful to have complete reports. Settlement time is the time when a salesperson will have to conduct his business in the finest fashion. When machinery fails, the factory will almost always say that it was improperly installed, it was operated inappropriately, or that it was overloaded. Rarely, if ever, will there be an immediate admission that there was anything wrong with the company's design, engineering, manufacture, or quality control.

The customer, on the other hand, will usually blame the vendor and insist that the product was too weak, too small, or too sensitive, or that it was poorly designed or manufactured. The case is rarely cut and dry. There is usually some blame or responsibility on both sides, and plenty to spare. Getting the two sides together on a settlement can prove to be a monumental task, but the salesperson must get them together. It is his duty. That is why it is important for him to get involved early and to stay involved until the problems, including the financial obligations, are settled.

Everyone in the salesperson's company should be cautioned against making misleading or damaging comments to customers about the company or its products when a failure occurs. Suppose for instance that when a failure occurs, someone in the salesperson's company says, "Well, it happened again. I told engineering the structure was too thin." Such remarks put the salesperson in real trouble, even if the failure was entirely the customer's fault.

Often when a failure occurs, the customer will ask, "Who is going to pay for this?" or "Whose responsibility is this?" The salesperson should calmly say that his company is primarily concerned with getting the product back in operation again so that it can continue to make money for the customer. He should explain that the failure will be thoroughly investigated with equitable and fair settlements when all the facts are known.

The salesperson must avoid initial comments like, "You operated the product improperly," "You installed it improperly," "You did not maintain it properly," or "You used the wrong lubrication." These comments will be counterproductive. They will put the customer on guard for trouble in getting a fair settlement. He will pass the word to others in his company, and the salesperson will lose in the long run. The customer's maintenance and operation records will exceed the salesperson's records.

When warranty or service problems stretch out over a considerable period of time, it is best to have one spokesperson designated from the salesperson's company. His job will be to communicate with the customer for the following reasons:

1. Control can be maintained on what the customer is told. Then the salesperson will not have several people inside his company making comments that may be misconstrued or misinterpreted to their company's detriment. People hear what they want to hear, and some customers are not above manipulating the vendor's people and playing one off against another. At times like this, only consensus statements or comments should be given to the customer, not an individual's opinions.
2. One person will have immediately available all input and comments from the customer.

When the time comes to settle up financially, the salesperson should make sure he is still involved. His company will usually have service or factory people whose responsibility it is to handle these discussions with the final decision resting with his top management. The claim could be unusually large, and the two sides might be very far from a settlement. In this situation the salesperson must take the lead and join in the meetings until the customer and the salesperson's company are both happy.

Initially the salesperson should never take a hard-nosed posture or speak in strident tones, regardless of how good his company's position is. If the customer has abused the product and has substantial blame or responsibility for the failure, he usually knows it. He will be sensitive to having it pointed out repeatedly. As a supplier the salesperson will, in most cases, be vulnerable to some extent. An initial overbearing position will harden the customer's resolve to make the salesperson and his company pay dearly in any area where they are at fault. The customer also could deny them future orders.

The salesperson should not approach the negotiations with an extremely one-sided settlement offer that is heavily in his company's favor. He should take a reasonable, even-handed approach. He should not throw out a take-it-or-leave-it offer early in the discussions. Clearly he would not want to come in with his best offer initially, because he will invariably have to offer more. He should, however, assume a fairly reasonable posture initially to demonstrate a good-faith approach. He should not expect to conclude an agreement overwhelmingly favorable to his company. If he does, it will usually come back to haunt him.

If the salesperson's initial approach has been reasonable, and if he negotiates in good faith, he will usually reach a solution that is mutually beneficial. Customers are smart and will quickly recognize offers that are fair and equitable without being one-sided. Knowing his customer's negotiating method is very valuable to a salesperson as he approaches these discussions. Most organizations have characteristic negotiating styles that remain fairly constant. A salesperson should learn these and plan his strategy accordingly.

As a salesperson, it is his job to ascertain what the customer expects in the way of a settlement. Not only should he know his expectations and reasons, but he should also know what his people are willing to do, and why.

If the problems are manifold and perhaps spread over more than one plant site, the following is a good approach to begin:

1. The salesperson should ask his service department to prepare a list of all the problems already encountered and fixed or solved.
2. He should have them prepare a list of all unresolved problems or things yet to be changed or modified.
3. He should indicate which items on both lists are clearly his firm's responsibility.
4. He should indicate which items are clearly the customer's accepted responsibility.
5. All remaining items then fall into the disputed or questionable category.
6. For each of these disputed items, the salesperson should ask his service people to tabulate
    - why they feel the customer should be responsible;
    - why the customer thinks the vendor should be responsible.

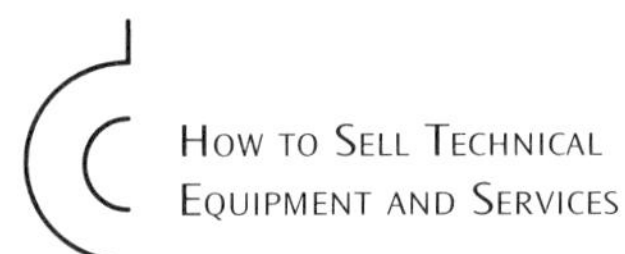

With this information, he can get the two sides together again to discuss the points of disagreement. He should ask both sides many questions until all the facts are on the table. Usually the longer the two sides talk, the closer together they get. If no settlement can be agreed upon at the initial meeting, it is usually a good idea to adjourn while each side studies and considers the new facts, opinions, and positions taken.

The salesperson should never agree nor allow anyone from his company to agree to something during a meeting without knowing his company's financial exposure. If he is in doubt, he must find out, and he should not proceed until he knows. For example, if a salesperson must replace 10 pieces, and each piece costs $5.00, his company's exposure is $50.00. However, if each piece costs $1,000.00, his company's exposure is $10,000.00. The salesperson absolutely must not agree to do something and then try to renege when he determines the actual cost. He should realistically determine his company's exposure but should not inflate the numbers.

The salesperson should also place a time limit or a number cutoff on all agreements. He should never leave a settlement open-ended. If he agrees to replace parts that fail in the future on a reduced or no-charge basis, he must always establish an ending date. He should make sure his agreement is clearly spelled out in writing. It is best to obtain the customer's written acknowledgment and agreement. One way to accomplish this is for the salesperson to include a place on his correspondence for the customer to sign. If he is not agreeable to this, the salesperson should include a closing sentence saying this document represents the salesperson's understanding of the agreement, and unless notified otherwise, he is proceeding on this basis.

It is very important that negotiations and discussions from the salesperson's side be undertaken in good faith, truthfully, and aboveboard. Customers are usually very intelligent and experienced. They will spot and react unfavorably to sharp practices, inflexible attitudes, insupportable positions, game playing, and deceit. While the salesperson cannot control the attitudes and morality of his customers, he will find virtually all of them honest and honorable. They will usually respond favorably to a salesperson's good-faith approach.

Sometimes a salesperson's company has a serious or chronic problem involving products that his customers are operating or that he normally quotes or is quoting to his customers. He should insist on periodic status reports and an official position paper that outlines the problem and what is being done to remedy the defect. The salesperson should not settle for less, even if the product giving trouble is outside of his territory. If the salesperson is expected to sell it, he should be informed and prepared to respond if his customers ask about these difficulties. If the problem is acute, chronic, or serious, his customers will eventually hear and inquire about it.

Whether or not the salesperson voluntarily advises his customers before they hear about it involves a lot of factors that should be carefully weighed. These include, but are not limited to, the following:

1. How serious is the problem?
2. Does failure cause minor or extensive outage?
3. How long has it been going on?
4. How close is the salesperson's company to a solution?
5. Is the customer operating, or does he have on order, any of these products?
6. Is he thinking of purchasing products like this?

With answers to these questions, a decision about a salesperson involving his customers should be obvious. In general, it is best for a salesperson not to voluntarily spread the word about his product problems. If a salesperson's customers are otherwise likely to learn about the difficulties (and they probably will), it is best if he tells them himself. This is especially important if they are considering purchasing, are now operating, or are about to start up similar models. The salesperson must, of course, also explain his company's proposed corrective measures.

The salesperson should strongly insist that the factory service department correct problems in his area. They expect the salesperson to sell their products; therefore, they should clean up their operating problems. The salesperson should not let them off the hook. He must work through channels initially but should not hesitate to appeal to the very highest level if it is necessary to get action. To do anything less leaves him wide open to criticism. He should not wait until he loses an order to make a fuss about problems. He should speak firmly ahead of time and should put his concerns in writing when appropriate.

The salesperson should never let problems simmer and continue uncorrected just because the customer is not grumbling. Some outspoken customers will complain. Others may not be so well organized and will not say too much until long after the problem has become extremely serious. Then they often overreact, and the salesperson is in big trouble. Occasionally, the

dissatisfaction is developing but no one has yet expressed a complaint to the salesperson. Sometimes problems show up in high operating costs or low operating availability. These or other records and reports may not be noticed until revealed by someone or discovered when they start to buy additional products. By then it may be too late for the salesperson to correct the problem and still get the new order. He should stay in touch with his customer so he learns early about any dissatisfaction with what he sells.

When the salesperson learns of a problem with new products just introduced, even if it is minor, he should report it. That is especially true if it is his firm's responsibility to sort out the problem. Even if it is a customer operating problem, it can give a bad impression of the product. The salesperson should consider helping the customer solve it, or at least helping the customer to clearly and correctly define it so the product is not blamed. Operating problems are blamed quite often on the product. The salesperson should not let this happen to what he sells. If he visits newly installed machinery, he will easily be able to spot these problems early.

Generally, people in the salesperson's organization have good intentions and mean to correct all problems quickly. Unfortunately, it does not always happen this way. They are very busy, usually are overworked, and invariably need nudging. Since the salesperson cannot regularly visit all job sites, he should insist on receiving copies of all service or trouble calls and reports involving products in his territory. If the salesperson cannot read all of them, he should have his assistant read them and highlight any problems reported. The salesperson can then get involved, monitor the situation, and see that the problems are cleared up promptly.

Sales Example

I was once assigned to an account with which we had done very little business, even though they purchased a great deal of products that we were capable of supplying. I questioned the most influential decision maker about our low market share. He told me that many years earlier, they had broken a crankshaft in a competitive unit during the dead of winter when the unit was needed most. The competitor turned things upside down and got the product back into service in a very short time. This influential decision maker said his president later told him, "Those are the kind of people to keep in mind when you buy additional equipment." This competitor received the lion's share of this customer's business for many years thereafter because he took care of their very serious problems.

Appendix A

Sales Do's and Don'ts

Do. . .

1. Be a good listener.
2. Keep all of your promises.
3. Be the same person at all times to everyone.
4. Maintain the highest moral posture at all times.
5. Approach all endeavors in a serious, sincere fashion.
6. Show gratitude for assistance from any source and to customers when they place orders.

7. Be a balanced person. To be successful, you must look and appear successful.
8. Be an upstanding citizen.
9. Find time for your family.
10. Be sympathetic to the misfortunes of others, not joking about them or making light of them.
11. Get involved and stay involved. Your physical presence can exert a profound influence and can make a difference.
12. Act as a catalyst to promote harmony and get things moving. Promote amity and not discord.
13. Maintain a pleasant, confident, unobtrusive attitude.
14. Think and act positively and demonstrate sincere, controlled enthusiasm.
15. Be a clear communicator so that you are never misunderstood.
16. Make certain that all lunch, dinner, or social invitations to customers are clear. Extend these invitations personally and not through someone else. If spouses are included, make that clear.
17. Drink sparingly or not at all.
18. Respond to all invitations, both inside and outside the company.
19. Decline unwanted invitations graciously, so as not to insult the person who extended the invitation.
20. Return all phone calls, even from people you never expect to do business with.
21. Keep your teeth in excellent condition and attend to any dental work that is needed.
22. Be a bridge to keep conversation and discourse going between your firm and your customer's during a dispute.
23. Always reveal your own true nature rather than cover up who or what you really are.
24. Keep in touch with people who change jobs or responsibilities. They always seem to end up in the same business, but often with more important jobs.

Don't . . .

1. Make enemies. The industry is too small.
2. Leave problems with customers unsolved. Work hard to reach equitable solutions and follow up to make certain the customer is satisfied.
3. Barge in and interrupt people engaged in conversation. Join unobtrusively by listening a little while and then easing into the conversation.
4. Give Christmas presents.
5. Give liquor as a present at any time. Give something that lasts, such as technical books or magazine subscriptions.
6. Interrupt a customer when he is talking.
7. Raise your voice in conversations.
8. Tell long, drawn-out stories and monopolize the conversation. Let others talk and listen when they speak.
9. Have bad or unpleasant thoughts about customers.
10. Look for shortcuts to selling. There are none.
11. Accept anything less than the best. Don't be mediocre.
12. Talk religion or politics with customers.
13. Give false or unreliable information.
14. Arrange inappropriate entertainment for customers.
15. Reveal your company's internal disagreements to customers or to anyone outside the company.
16. Fumble through product bulletins in a customer's office.
17. Use inflammatory words.
18. Argue with customers.
19. Try to ask overly familiar questions to someone you have just met.
20. Burden others, especially customers, with personal troubles. Most people have all the troubles they can handle or care about.
21. Criticize the customer's methods.

22. Repeat a person's name too often in a conversation with him. It becomes monotonous.
23. Pressure the customer too much for an answer or a decision. Give room to wiggle and time to think. Most people do not like to be backed into a corner or pressured.
24. Be too boastful of possessions or achievements. A successful salesperson probably earns more money than most of his customers. Don't play this up and certainly do not brag about what you have.
25. Be afraid to ask for help.
26. Agree to provide something no charge unless you know your company's financial exposure.
27. Call on the same person every time if it is late in the day or late on Friday.
28. Try to pay the check when invited as a guest to dinner or cocktails with customers or friends.
29. Assume that just because you met or called on someone once that the individual will automatically remember you. When calling on the telephone, don't leave the other person guessing—state your name and company to prevent embarrassment and confusion.
30. Mention reciprocity. If you do, you will almost always come out on the short end of the stick.
31. Give abrupt answers. As far as customers are concerned, there are no dumb questions.
32. Criticize the competitors. Customers resent this.
33. Say, "You told me that before." Even though hearing something several times, don't insult the speaker.
34. Make threats.
35. Promise more than you can deliver.
36. Take advantage of others' misfortunes.
37. Repeat unpleasant or negative things you hear but should focus on the positive things.
38. Acquire the reputation of making a bad situation worse.
39. Take other people's misfortunes lightly. Dwell on them, but take time to be sympathetic.

40. Criticize or disparage your company to customers or to other colleagues in your company. The salesperson may not work for his company his whole career, and the salesperson could end up with a negative reputation throughout the industry.
41. Start answering a question until the questioner has finished stating the question. You may think you know what the other person is going to ask, but extend that person the courtesy of hearing him out.
42. Insist that a customer have a drink or extra drinks against his will. If someone prefers to abstain or to have just one drink, the salesperson should respect the decision and not make any comments or jokes about it.
43. Reminisce about things that many in the group know nothing about.
44. Ask a question and then keeping talking. Ask the question, then stop so that the other person can respond.
45. Change the subject abruptly, or jump from subject to subject, when talking to a customer.
46. Ask extraneous questions that disrupt the customer's train of thought.
47. Toss literature or bulletins across the desk for the customer to view. Place them down gently in front of the customer.